GEORGE WASHINGTON
AND FREDERICK THE GREAT

George Washington and Frederick the Great

PARALLEL LIVES

JÜRGEN OVERHOFF

TRANSLATED BY
PATRICK BAKER

PRINCETON UNIVERSITY PRESS
PRINCETON & OXFORD

Originally published in German as *Friedrich der Große und George Washington* © 2011
Klett-Cotta J.G. Cotta'sche Buchhandlung Nachfolger GmbH, Stuttgart

English translation copyright © 2026 by Princeton University Press

Published by Princeton University Press
41 William Street, Princeton, New Jersey 08540
99 Banbury Road, Oxford OX2 6JX

press.princeton.edu

GPSR Authorized Representative: Easy Access System Europe - Mustamäe tee 50,
10621 Tallinn, Estonia, gpsr.requests@easproject.com

All Rights Reserved
ISBN 9780691226712
ISBN (PDF) 9780691230290
ISBN (epub) 9780691287690

British Library Cataloging-in-Publication Data is available

Editorial: Ben Tate and Josh Drake
Production Editorial: Terri O'Prey
Jacket/Cover Design: Emily Bluedorn
Production: Danielle Amatucci
Publicity: James Schneider and Carmen Jimenez
Copyeditor: Ashley Moore

Jacket images: (*left*): Gilbert Stuart, *George Washington*, ca. 1803, oil on canvas,
74.3 × 61 cm (29¼ × 24 in.). Corcoran Collection (Bequest of Mrs. Benjamin Ogle
Tayloe); acquired by the National Gallery of Art, Washington, D.C., 2014 (Acc. no.
2014.136.4). (*right*): Anton Graff, *Friedrich II of Prussia* (1781 or 1786), oil on canvas.
Collection of Stiftung Preußische Schlösser und Gärten Berlin-Brandenburg,
Potsdam / Berlin.

This book has been composed in Arno

Printed in the United States of America

10 9 8 7 6 5 4 3 2 1

This book is dedicated with heartfelt gratitude to
QUENTIN SKINNER,
in recognition of its profound debt
to his pioneering work on historical discourses.

As always, I reserve my most heartfelt thanks for my wife, Kerstin.

The value of her support remains beyond words.

—J. O.

For Tay, who loves history and politics,
and who may find answers in the Enlightenment.

—P. B.

How to explain what's in people's heads, what they think? It's like with love: impossible to explain. But who would we be if we did not try?

—PER OLOV ENQUIST (2001)

CONTENTS

FIGURES

TRANSLATOR'S NOTE

TRANSLATING THIS book has been both a distinct pleasure and a distinguished challenge. Jürgen Overhoff's German is brilliantly ornate, a baroque performance worthy of the Enlightenment that is his ultimate subject. His style is classic but not archaic, antique but not antiquated, its extended periods artfully arranged into a fugue of complex clauses and florid detail in which all is balanced, nothing is superfluous, and everything is in its right place. I have tried, to the best of my ability, to channel this Ciceronian *concinnitas* within the limits of comprehensible modern English prose. The idea is not only to capture the author's voice but also to convey something of the sense of the eighteenth century that his own writing embodies.

Rendering Frederick the Great in English has also presented special challenges, as his preferred idiom was French, whereas his German has the scent of a second language. He and other figures populating this book availed themselves of both tongues at will. Complicating the situation further, many quotable sentiments were captured by others and thus have come down to us in the form of stylized hearsay. Wherever possible, I have relied on existing translations of primary sources. When I have translated them myself, the original German or French is always included in the notes.

When reporting premodern English-language primary sources, from the philosophy of Thomas Hobbes to the works of George Washington and his contemporaries, I have generally modernized the spelling, capitalization, and punctuation in order to make them more intelligible to the modern reader. Modifications are especially heavy in Washington's earlier diary entries.

My object has been to provide a faithful rendering of both the content and the style of the original German monograph, conveying its scholarly excellence, masterful storytelling, and literary merit to a new and broader audience. If I have succeeded, it will be in no small part because of the generous contributions of others. Of the many debts I have to redeem, I am pleased to recognize Jürgen Overhoff for his steady guidance, conscientious collaboration, and many invigorating breakfast conversations. My wife, Katrin, also provided invaluable support, especially in the project's final phases. Finally, I would like to thank Tay Baker for assistance in tracking down numerous quotations and correcting the proofs.

Patrick Baker

GEORGE WASHINGTON, the pathbreaking first American president, has notably been called "the indispensable man." There are good reasons for this high esteem. Without Washington, the Continental Army would not have been able to defeat the mighty British forces in the Revolutionary War. And in the volatile early days of the republic, no other political leader of the newly founded United States would have been able to hold the highest office as firmly and resolutely as he did. On the other hand, indispensability is not the same as incomparability. Indeed, outstanding individuals ought to be compared with other remarkable and great figures, as this undertaking promises new and interesting insights. Accordingly, the "indispensable" Washington has been aptly studied in the light of several of his "founding brothers," such as Thomas Jefferson, Benjamin Franklin, and John Adams, who also played a unique part in the creation of the United States. But has the great American general and statesman ever been compared in a similar fashion to a *European* military and political leader of his day and age? Until very recently, not at all; only in 2025, with the appearance of an exhibition companion volume entitled *The Two Georges* (edited by Susan Reyburn and Zach Klitzman)—a collection of essays dedicated to Washington and King George III of England—did the situation somewhat change. Still, no monographic treatment has appeared. Yet one of Washington's European contemporaries stands out as an ideal candidate for a full comparative biography: the Prussian monarch Frederick II.

For his part, Frederick II (legendarily called Frederick "the Great"), king of Prussia and elector of Brandenburg, has been repeatedly styled by his most important biographers and interpreters as one of the most interesting, challenging, controversial, and eminent characters of European history. Cambridge historians such as Tim Blanning and Christopher Clark, French authorities like Pierre Gaxotte and Jean-Paul Bled, and German scholars of the rank of Johannes Kunisch and Jürgen Luh have all emphasized the enormous impact the Prussian monarch exerted on the fate of European politics—as a strong-willed statesman, as a skilled politician, and as a warrior (if not to say a warmonger). What is more, they argue, Frederick was a philosopher of European eminence. He was an *homme de lettres* who wrote his treatises and poems in French, a language he adored. He was an inquisitive adventurer who traveled incognito through the Dutch Republic, an economically powerful state he respected. He was a gifted musician and composer who played the flute and loved the opera, particularly in the Italian style.

Frederick, it seems, was a powerful ruler and an ingenious, quick-witted thinker whose intellectual horizon was shaped and defined by *European* civilizational standards—and that is why he has been studied almost exclusively from a *European* perspective. But to focus solely on the European context of Frederick's life and writings is to miss the bigger picture. As a political agent, as a philosopher, and as a protagonist of the Enlightenment, the Prussian king belonged to a sphere of cultural exchange, a nexus of manifold interconnections between regions and civilizations on both sides of the Atlantic. Intellectually and strategically, Frederick moved in the geopolitical space of a *transatlantic* community. He was indeed one of the leading figures and key players in what Bernard Bailyn and others have come to describe as "Atlantic history." His thoughts and actions affected and influenced the course of events in Europe and North America in particular, and Frederick himself as well as many of his coevals were aware of it. Yet during the past two centuries only a handful of authors have devoted attention to the transatlantic context of Frederick's intellectual and political world—or to the importance that North America, especially the United States, had in his thought.

Frederick's contemporaries' well-informed knowledge of his role as a key historic figure of transatlantic importance started to wane in the nineteenth century. Frederick's greatest biographer of the Victorian era, the British historian Thomas Carlyle, dedicated the astonishing number of eight masterly volumes—written between 1858 and 1865 in a graceful style and garnished with trenchant observations—to the meticulous description of the Prussian king's life and times. Yet this monumental study focused almost exclusively on the European battles of the Silesian Wars and the Seven Years' War. Only in the concluding volume, entitled *Afternoon and Evening of Friedrich's Life (1763–1786)*, in which Carlyle almost randomly summarized the events of this quarter century, did he mention American affairs—and then rather incidentally, referring to General François-Claude-Amour de Bouillé's West Indian exploits and his visit to Frederick in August 1784. The emergence of the United States of

America on the world stage of politics in 1776 was, for Carlyle, not even worth a subheading in his otherwise detailed and elaborate analysis.

The nineteenth century did, however, produce one truly pioneering study: *Friedrich der Große und die Vereinigten Staaten von Amerika* (Frederick the Great and the United States of America) by the German-American lawyer, writer, and politician Friedrich Kapp. This book, written and published in 1871, described the sudden and unexpected beginnings of diplomatic negotiations between the Kingdom of Prussia and the newly formed American democratic republic in the immediate aftermath of the War of Independence. In his intro-duction, Kapp stated that "the stance Frederick the Great adopted with regard to the United States has been discussed in the relevant literature on the king— swollen to a veritable library—only very rarely, if at all." For the first time, Kapp provided readers with solid knowledge of Prussian-American relations in the 1780s. Yet his erudite examination lacked an interpretation of Frederick's transatlantic commitment during the Seven Years' War. It also omitted any account of the American colonists' enthusiastic support of the Prussian king in this global military conflict. Kapp also failed to reflect upon George Wash-ington's attitude toward Frederick the Great.

The first to show the potential inherent in a comparison between these two leading statesmen for illuminating important aspects of eighteenth-century politics, diplomacy, and Enlightenment principles was the Expressionist dra-matist, poet, novelist—and Prussian aristocrat—Fritz von Unruh. In 1954, only a few years after the Second World War, he wrote a play called *Duell an der Havel* (Duel at the Havel River), about Frederick II and his views on stern Prussian duties as opposed to the American promise of the pursuit of happi-ness. Von Unruh drew a deft, pinpoint portrayal of the Prussian monarch, including explicit references to the transatlantic, North American context. The playwright von Unruh, an extremely interesting and almost forgotten author, spent his adolescence with Emperor Wilhelm II's sons Prince Oskar and Prince August Wilhelm, and he emigrated during the Nazi period to the United States. Frederick the Great, Prussia, and America were lifelong objects of interest for him. In his play he orchestrated a fictional meeting between Frederick the Great and George Washington in Germany, and it is clear that his own sympathies belonged to the first American president—as an unerring defender of democratic principles.

In 1963 the German historian and journalist Paul Sethe, editor of the pres-tigious daily *Frankfurter Allgemeine Zeitung*, soon followed up on this compari-son when he published a popular book on the history of the eighteenth century called *Morgenröte der Gegenwart* (The Dawn of Modernity). He chose as its subtitle the telling phrase *Von Friedrich dem Großen bis Washington* (From Frederick the Great to Washington). In the final chapter of his book, Sethe compared and described Frederick's Prussia and Washington's America as the most advanced nations of their day. He did this, however, in the form and style of an all-too-brief essay, leaving it to later historians to elaborate on this subject at length. This task has now been carried out for the first time in the present volume.

It is striking to realize how many interesting comparisons and parallels can be found if one traces the intertwined history of Frederick II of Prussia and the first American president, George Washington. For the Prussian king had a far greater impact on the early history of the United States than most of us realize today. First of all, Frederick was an indispensable and loyal ally of British North America during the Seven Years' War (or, in American parlance, the French and Indian War). Without his surprising military movements on the battlefields of Germany against the French, the American colonists would not have gained the upper hand over France on the North American continent—hence the British Prime Minister William Pitt's poignant aperçu: "America was conquered in Germany."

In the course of the Seven Years' War, Frederick came to enjoy the status of an all-American hero. Souvenir cups with the likeness of the Prussian king were sold in the American colonies. When the news of Frederick's victories reached American shores, the church bells of Philadelphia were rung. Around 1760, many Americans wanted to find out as much as possible about their important European ally Frederick. Even the radical pacifist Christoph Saur (sometimes spelled Sower), a Pennsylvania printer of German origin, issued a popular biography of the Prussian king. Printed in Germantown, Pennsylvania in 1761, it was written in German but designed for the American market. English-language biographies of Frederick were sold in America too. George Washington was the proud owner of a book on Frederick the Great's life.

During the American Revolution, Frederick did not side with the British, thereby lending tacit support to the American cause. Shortly after the outbreak of the War of Independence, large numbers of soldiers from German principalities, such as Hesse-Kassel, were hired by the British and transported to America. These Hessians soon became detested military opponents of the Americans. They were also a striking symbol of the despotism of all those European princes who sold their subjects only to increase their own personal fortune, which they then used to finance a luxurious lifestyle. Frederick condemned the trade in Hessian soldiers. On the other hand, a former officer from Frederick's army, Friedrich Wilhelm von Steuben, became Washington's trusty aide as inspector general of the Continental Army. Frederick became so popular that a public house in Pennsylvania was named after him in the late 1770s, and a wooden signboard for the inn depicted the great king of Prussia on horseback. This tavern still exists today; it is the nucleus of the modern community of King of Prussia in Montgomery County, Pennsylvania.

At the end of the War of Independence, the Prussian king actively sought to sign a treaty of amity and commerce with the newly founded and victorious American federation—a federation that was, in essence, a union of republics. For the Americans, such a treaty with the Prussian king was an important step toward achieving general international recognition of their status. Benjamin Franklin, serving as ambassador to France, was given orders by the American Congress in Philadelphia to negotiate details of an agreement with Prussia. Franklin sought to shape a model for all future international treaties, and Frederick wanted to participate in this ambitious project. The treaty not only stipulated the terms of flourishing mutual trade but also guaranteed the mild and humane treatment of civilians and prisoners in times of war. The American-Prussian treaty was signed and ratified by Frederick on September 24, 1785. It anticipated in many respects the later Conventions of Geneva and The Hague. George Washington lavished superlative praise on this innovative and path-breaking deal with Frederick the Great in July 1786, calling it "the most liberal treaty which has ever been entered into between independent powers."

Comparing the life and times of Frederick the Great with those of George Washington will give us a better understanding of the two men's achievements, helping us as well to see both the rise of the Kingdom of Prussia and the emergence of the United States in a surprisingly new light. The original German edition of the present book found many enthusiastic readers who particularly cherished the transatlantic dimension of the story told. For the English edition, the latest scholarship on Frederick the Great, George Washington, and the eighteenth-century history of Prussia and the United States has been consulted and is aptly represented in the notes and the bibliography. The brilliant translation was provided to my great joy and satisfaction by Patrick Baker, whom I would like to thank most sincerely for his steadfast and inspiring collaboration.

Jürgen Overhoff

GEORGE WASHINGTON
AND FREDERICK THE GREAT

1

Parallel Lives

GEORGE WASHINGTON had many good things to say about Frederick the Great when, in the summer of 1786, he felt moved to honor the achievements of the world-famous king of Prussia in a few pointed words. His European friends had informed him about the pitiable state of health of the once so vigorous monarch, the man who had shaped the destinies of Prussia and Europe for nearly half a century. The resulting letter Washington sent to the Marquis de Lafayette twelve weeks before Frederick's death resembles a premature obituary.

Lafayette, Washington's companion from the days of the American Revolution, had himself sought out the infirm Prussian monarch only a few months earlier in Germany. Now Washington wrote to him that no one in the world was Frederick the Great's equal as a soldier. Likewise, having given his efficiently run Prussian state a rational imprint, he could "yield the palm to none" as a "politician." As a military leader and head of state, the king remained an unrivaled model for many generals and chief executives. Washington was one of them. And now, as he wrote, the "discernment" that the Prussian ruler had shown in receiving Lafayette so honorably would only "increase my opinion" of him.

But Washington did not leave it at this lavish praise. Surprisingly, his remarks culminated in a radical criticism. It was "to be lamented" that, like most "great characters," Frederick's was "not without a blot." Since the American Revolution of 1776, the people of Europe had also increasingly demanded a say in government as full citizens endowed with rights. Throughout his whole life, however, Frederick had opposed every form of popular participation in affairs of state. Even now, as a sick old man, he continued to rule his Prussia as an unfettered autocrat, handing down commands, edicts, orders, and decrees. The single touchstone of his political action was his own will. Yet in

Washington's view, it was disgraceful for "one man" all alone to rule over the inhabitants of a large empire according to his own whim, and thus to "tyrannize over millions." It cast "a shade" on his character that would "always" darken his achievement in the eyes of posterity.

Washington was very well acquainted with Frederick. As a young man, he had assiduously kept up with the Prussian king's career. When he himself first commanded an American regiment in Pennsylvania against the French in the Seven Years' War, he devoured reports of the bold victory that Frederick, as general of the Prussian army, had won over the same enemy at the Battle of Rossbach in Saxony. He earnestly admired the audacity with which the daring Frederick—although often outnumbered—subdued his opponents. And he owed him a debt of gratitude: By entangling the French troops in Europe in a long, debilitating war, Frederick contributed decisively to breaking French dominion over large parts of North America.

It is therefore no wonder that in 1759 Washington ordered a large bust of the Prussian king from a London merchant—a costly purchase intended to adorn the entrance hall to his Virginia estate of Mount Vernon. A few years later, he bought his stepson Jacky a figurine of a Prussian dragoon. This artful miniature of one of Frederick the Great's elite soldiers saw action on the wooden floors of the nursery at Mount Vernon.

As Frederick's luck in the Seven Years' War took a dramatic turn for the worse in 1760, and the Prussian king thought himself close to destruction, Washington felt his suffering. In letters to European informants, he inquired into the fate of the Americans' crucial ally. When the tide then unexpectedly turned and, after the Treaty of Hubertusburg in 1763, Frederick once again energetically ruled his country, Washington rejoiced for him. But then his enthusiasm for the heroic Prussian ruler waned—gradually at first, but irreversibly.

The deeper reason for this shift was that Washington's stance toward kingship in general radically changed. For, only a few years after the end of the Seven Years' War, the British king had declared war on his American subjects for steadfastly refusing to pay taxes to the Crown that they had not approved in their own colonial legislatures. Washington became a bitter foe of all forms of monarchy. From 1775 on, he led the War of Independence against the former mother country with feisty courage and fierce resolution as a republican general. Chosen by the democratically elected Continental Congress as supreme commander of the freshly founded United States of America, he developed into an uncompromising defender of the principle of popular sovereignty.

Upon his first great military triumphs, which launched the commander in chief to worldwide fame, Washington in turn drew the attention of Frederick the Great. In 1777, the Prussian king ordered his brother Prince Henry to follow every movement of the American general by assiduously reading reports of the war in newspapers and gazettes. Frederick quickly grasped that there were extremely few military commanders of the day who acted with as much bravery and strategic savvy as Washington. Yet the king's praise remained restricted to Washington's martial prowess. He had no taste for the new democratic-republican order of the United States. Although only two years after the American victory, in 1785, Frederick the Great signed a thorough Prussian-American trade agreement that met with Washington's approval, the monarch nevertheless regarded the political future of the United States with skepticism.

That is the spirit in which he expressed himself to Lafayette during their aforementioned meeting, which took place shortly after the agreement was concluded. In his view, democratic republics must sooner or later end in chaos. Not even the United States of America would manage to escape this fate. Only enlightened absolutism of the kind he himself had practiced with such conviction since ascending the throne in 1740 could vouchsafe to people—at least in his own country—enduring tranquility and order, peace and happiness. Lafayette immediately communicated these words to Washington, to whom they were doubtless addressed in spirit. In response, the American general—whom his countrymen would soon elect as their first president—penned the obituary-like letter in summer 1786 in which he enshrined his summary judgment of Frederick the Great.

The fact that Washington and Frederick constantly had their eye on one another, and that they time and again expressed fondness for each other despite all their differences, may have resulted from an intuitive sense of just how similar their lives were regardless of the many superficial contrasts between them. Indeed, the list of their common proclivities, desires, disappointments, and victories is as surprising as it is long.

As young men, both of them suffered terrible emotional distress when forced to forsake the love of women whom they would have married if only the latter had been available. Frederick and Washington could not indulge with the women of their first choice in the sensual passion and stormy sexual delight that they unabashedly endorsed. Both had to marry other women for reasons of expediency. In Frederick's case, political calculation was decisive. For Washington, it was a handsome dowry. Neither man sired children with his wife. Instead, they assumed the guise of adoptive parents to the people whom, as heads of state, it was their duty to lead, nurturing them with a strict attentiveness that was very deliberately denoted as "fatherly." The nations they took into their patriarchal charge became like adopted children.

This special sense of devotion extended as well to the animals they lived with. Thoroughbred horses and fleet-footed dogs received extremely lavish care. Washington and Frederick were practically besotted with their silvery greyhounds, whose aesthetic beauty, frisky playfulness, and lightning speed amazed them. Whenever one of their dogs died, they provided the animal with a dignified burial in a specially constructed vault. Frederick had the names of his greyhounds carved on a tombstone. Washington buried his favorite greyhound, Cornwallis, in a brick tomb furnished with a marble slab.

Both men also picked out their own burial places early on. They desired no monumental state funeral, no obsequies celebrated in stone cathedrals or palaces, but rather a simple service under an open sky. Their bodies, so they ordered, should be returned to the bosom of God-begotten nature whence they had sprung. Thus, they chose gravesites for themselves in the secluded areas where they most enjoyed spending time while alive: Frederick on the terraced hill of his pleasure palace Sanssouci, all framed in green; Washington on the verdant hill of his Mount Vernon estate, set in enchantingly beautiful surroundings.

The manicured scenery in which Frederick and Washington, both capable landscape architects, desired to find their eternal peace was largely the product of their own design. They planted borders and tended orchards with their own hands, and kept detailed records about their trees and the fruits they produced. The plants most highly valued by both men were the vine and the fig tree, in whose shade they built homes where they could find peace and quiet— just as the Bible describes life in the house of the Lord in the last days (Micah 4:4). These elaborate, architecturally sophisticated residences—Sanssouci and Mount Vernon—were likewise the fruit of Frederick's and Washington's own sketches and imaginations.

Not only Washington, the country gentleman from the American South, but also Frederick, the king of Prussia, were aided in their daily tasks from a tender age by slaves and valets imported from West Africa, without ever grappling very directly with the dubiousness of this form of servitude. On the other hand, they were both astonishingly generous, liberal, and open-minded when it came to paving the way for members of the most disparate confessions to practice their religion freely and peacefully.

FIGURE 1.1. Washington's peaceful estate: Mount Vernon (akg-images).

Tolerance, acknowledgment of the right of differently minded people to think and act as they see fit, was a divine commandment that they respected absolutely, at least in the realm of religion. The Protestant Frederick, scion of a Calvinist dynasty, allowed a Roman Catholic cathedral to be built in the heart of his capital of Berlin. It was one of the most magnificent houses of worship of its day. Washington, an Anglican Protestant, not only showed support to Catholics but was also a perennial friend to American Jewish congregations. He regularly visited synagogues in a spirit of heartfelt sodality with those fellow citizens who gathered to worship there.

The equanimity with which Frederick and Washington observed and promoted the activities of all manner of religions in the states they governed was to a large extent rooted in their steady, profound faith in divine predestination, which both men had regarded since their youth as the ultimate cause of the world's events. Which prayer or which virtuous behavior pleased the will of the prime mover of all things was, in their estimation, the exclusive purview of this unfathomable, highest being that guided human affairs according to an inscrutable plan, dispensing grace and wrath at its pleasure. This unmistakably deist

FIGURE 1.2. Frederick's carefree country idyll: Sanssouci Palace.
Painting by Carl Blechen, 1830 (akg-images).

conception of God, which Frederick and Washington shared their whole lives, also enabled them to exercise patience on days that were not as bright. For as willful as they were, they were also cognizant of how thoroughly their actions depended on favorable conditions, lucky coincidences, and everyday circumstances beyond their control. Both men were humble and composed enough to recognize the boundaries providence prescribed to their scope of action.

Yet faith in the power of providence also gave them the strength to persevere, even in seemingly hopeless situations, especially in war. Never giving in prematurely, they took risks and sought out bold solutions no matter the odds. This determination, born of unswerving faith, ultimately made them indomitable combatants in the Seven Years' War and the American Revolution. Given the astonishing victories they managed to win thanks to their staunch character and faith, they were not entirely free of the sense that they had been specially chosen by providence to perform extraordinary deeds.

Being so suffused with this sense of destiny, when it came to increasing the happiness of the states that they dutifully defended and conscientiously governed, they did not hesitate to co-opt regions and territories that had been inhabited and ruled by other peoples for centuries. Frederick steadily expanded his Kingdom of Prussia at the expense of eastern regions of the Holy Roman Empire and western Poland. He forcibly jammed his state between two age-old European realms, one ruled by an elected emperor and the other by an elected king. Having no use for the Kingdom of Prussia, which at the turn of the eighteenth century had not even existed, its neighbors were long standoffish and even hostile to it.

Similarly, Washington was the president of a gigantic federal state that, despite only coming into being in the eighteenth century, had since expanded ever more quickly and voraciously over the hunting grounds of the Iroquois Confederacy. The Indians, whose smoothly functioning alliance had been formed back in 1575, had gotten along just fine without white settlers for a very long time. Thus, both Prussia and the United States of America were brand-new, artificially created states that did not emerge organically but rather were constructed according to the rules of coolly calculating reason. There was no necessity for either of them to exist on the world map. Rather, they imposed themselves there, and consequently they were established largely on conquered and colonized country. Frederick and Washington had very clear ideas about how to shape and cultivate this newly acquired territory.

The model of civilization to which both men adhered was an ideal of light and progress that called for the comprehensive education of all social strata—a concept that had been proposed by Enlightenment philosophers at the turn of the eighteenth century and developed and refined in the following decades. Frederick and Washington gravitated toward different authors within this tradition. The former was an enthusiastic admirer of the Frenchman Voltaire, the latter of the Englishman Joseph Addison. Like his model Voltaire—and under his tutelage—the Prussian king himself wrote philosophical poems. Washington, inspired and animated by the art of argumentation brought to rhetorical perfection by Addison, composed speeches, articles, and letters to convince Americans of the value of his political goals. Despite this difference in personal taste, both men were united in the view that without the writings of the English philosopher John Locke, whom they admired and on whose work both Addison and Voltaire had built, the Age of Enlightenment never would have been born.

Frederick the Great and Washington lived proper Enlightenment lifestyles. They were abiding readers of belles lettres, scientific treatises, political essays, letters, and sentimental poetry. They both also authored texts of their own. Frederick devoted himself to poetry, philosophical and political essays, and political historiography. Washington composed speeches and political appeals that often took the form of public letters. The Prussian king and the American president collected books with bibliophilic passion. When they died, the shelves of their libraries were bursting with volumes of every format. Yet it was not only themselves whom they wished to educate through lifelong reading and learning. In line with the tenets of Enlightenment philosophy, which could not imagine the permanent increase in individual understanding without a steady advancement of knowledge on the societal level, they fervently championed the improvement of school and university education in the states they governed.

Pleasure and learning were by no means mutually exclusive for them. Both men regularly took in dramatic performances. Visits to the theater were welcome, valued pastimes in their hours of leisure. They often found enjoyment in parlor games, music, and dancing as well. They were similarly fashion conscious and loved good food and drink. Although as soldiers they could display extreme toughness and severity, they were also capable of big emotions, radiating quasi-romantic tenderness in their most intimate moments.

The parallels between Frederick the Great's and George Washington's lives can therefore not be overlooked. They are numerous and significant. Indeed, one can justifiably claim that these two men are unique in this respect, as there is practically no other historically significant and politically relevant figure across the entire eighteenth century whose life story even remotely approximates those of this king and this president. Neither the Habsburg ruler Maria Theresa (Prussia's faithful arch-antagonist) nor the enlightened absolutist Empress Catherine II (herself celebrated as "great") nor any male head of state of the Age of Enlightenment had as much in common with Frederick and Washington as they had with one another.

It is therefore all the more astounding that no comprehensive assessment of Frederick's and Washington's parallel lives has as yet been undertaken, despite the fact that a comparative approach to their biographies promises to be especially informative. For despite their many arresting similarities, Frederick and Washington understood themselves to be the leading representatives of two highly disparate forms of rational political enlightenment: the "top-down," absolutist, monarchical type in Prussia and the "bottom-up," democratic, parliamentary version in America. What is more, they understood one another in this way, and they grasped each other's manifest political significance as the nonpareil personification of Prussia and the United States, the most modern nations of the day. Indeed, this distinction was the reason that, despite their mutual admiration, they ultimately vilified one another. While Washington disparaged the Prussian king as a tyrant, Frederick condemned the American political system that Washington helped found as a descent into anarchy.

The cleft between Frederick and Washington was such a great source of provocation because it highlighted the glaring contradiction between the two paths of political enlightenment from which progressive minds in the eighteenth century had to choose. Both men had fervent supporters, even in Germany. The writer Karl Philipp Moritz celebrated the elderly King Frederick as the "morning sun" of the Enlightenment, while Immanuel Kant referred to the entire eighteenth century as the "century of Frederick." In contrast, Johann Wolfgang von Goethe described Washington as a shining star in the Enlightenment's "firmament of politics and war." This shows that the Prussian king's enlightened absolutism had ceased to be regarded as the sole possible form of political enlightenment long before his death. Even Frederick's brother Henry praised the liberal aspirations across the Atlantic that, now in Europe as well, provided a model for a different understanding of enlightened government.

Even though it was not yet clear in the eighteenth century which path of political enlightenment the future would belong to, contemporaries were at least well informed about the alternatives and what they entailed. They certainly had a choice. Frederick and Washington, too, made a deliberate decision to adopt one specific political system over another. Once, when one of

Washington's officers suggested to him that he set himself up as king, the latter angrily rebuffed the proposal as outrageous intrigue—very different from the path taken a short time later by the republican general Napoleon Bonaparte in France. As for Frederick, he had no shortage of opportunities to introduce forms of parliamentary participation in Prussia. Yet he did not act on them. Indeed, whenever possible he ignored even long-established representative assemblies in the territories he ruled and conquered.

Considered objectively, then, Frederick and Washington were able to choose which path of enlightenment they wished to take. On the other hand, both were born—in 1712 and 1732, respectively—into highly circumscribed patterns of life, very traditional families, and entrenched political frameworks. These circumstances shaped them so profoundly that it is worth considering what options they subjectively believed were available to them. Their individual lives were so tightly intertwined with the history and likewise parallel development of the Kingdom of Prussia and the United States of America that they cannot be interpreted distinctly from them.

The model for writing parallel lives was created nearly 2,000 years ago by the Greek author Plutarch. His comparative biographies of great Greeks and Romans, which he called *Bioi paralleloi* (*Parallel Lives*), inspired countless biographers in subsequent centuries to review the personal characters of two like individuals who had been in similar historical situations, culminating in a fair and balanced judgment of their individual achievements. Plutarch's diptychs continue to instruct us today, as they are still exemplary models for how great figures from the past can be deftly and meaningfully compared to one another so as to draw lessons for the present.

Plutarch teaches us that anecdotes—"a slight thing like a phrase or a jest"—tell us more about the character of an individual than "battles when thousands fall, or the greatest armaments, or sieges of cities." It is therefore unnecessary to narrate the glorious deeds of the compared figures "exhaustively . . . in each particular case." Furthermore, although biographers are always required to render their historical judgment, they may not point the finger of the holier-than-thou moralist at the mistakes and weaknesses of their subjects. Rather, their accounts must convey a sense of regret that human nature, weak as it is, can never produce an entirely spotless moral character.

Plutarch's guidance is indispensable. Yet when comparing the lives of Frederick the Great and George Washington, the historian must go beyond Plutarch, as the latter described and compared lives that were similar but sometimes separated by a vast temporal distance. He focused first on the life further in the past, then separately on the one closer to his own day. Only in a final assessment of the personalities and achievements of the two men did he then undertake to compare them and render his distilled judgment in a way that he considered emblematic and instructive for contemporary readers.

In the case of Frederick and Washington, a comparative portrait can only be meaningful and illuminating if their parallel lives are sketched within the frame of, and as an integral part of, a much larger historical context that is common to both of them. This context includes the origin stories of Prussia and the independent United States, but it is broader still, encompassing the main features of the intellectual history of the Age of Enlightenment. For only within such a comprehensive historical framework can the significance of their constitutional legacy be adequately assessed. And we must constantly grapple with this legacy if we are to gain insight into which path of enlightenment we want to continue on today—a journey that began in the year 1701 with a dazzling political sunrise.

2

A Rising Sun (1701)

THE EIGHTEENTH century was still in its infancy when the English philosopher and member of Parliament Anthony Ashley Cooper, third Earl of Shaftesbury, claimed that it heralded the beginning of a new, unprecedented age. In 1706, in a visionary, poetic letter to Jean Le Clerc, an erudite Genevan theologian and editor of several encyclopedias, he wrote, "There is a mighty light which spreads itself over the world," promising progress to humankind in all realms of life and "in greater proportion than ever." This sentiment, confided in the hushed tones of an almost esoteric missive, would eventually become a universal truth in the eyes of the American self-made man and newspaper editor Benjamin Franklin. By the sheer strength of autodidacticism, this ambitious entrepreneur had "emerged" from "poverty and obscurity" and risen "to a state of affluence and some degree of reputation in the world." In 1743, he spoke of an ever-brighter "light" illuminating "the nature of things"—a light that had not only enabled his own elevation but that had also been continually expanding "the conveniences or pleasures of life" for all people for over four decades.

In the second half of the century, people continued to see the world in an increasingly cheerful hue. One was Gottfried van Swieten, a diplomat who figured among the staunchest supporters of Joseph Haydn and Wolfgang Amadeus Mozart. In 1774, he wrote from his post in Berlin that he and many of his contemporaries admired the "new luster" that, after several eras of being covered "by dark clouds," was now ever more radiantly enriching and beautifying the life of all the inhabitants of the earth. This sentiment was echoed by the English writer and women's rights advocate Mary Wollstonecraft, who had begun her working life in relative poverty as an unskilled seamstress. In 1790, she rhapsodized about the brilliant "ray of light" that, growing ever "more luminous" since the turn of "this very century," had substantially brightened the "dark days" of humankind.

Throughout the entire eighteenth century, this bold metaphor of light was used by men and women, by young and old, by Europeans and Americans, and by members of the most disparate nationalities, confessions, social classes, and occupations to describe the special, increasingly incandescent sheen of their age. We encounter it so often in orations, letters, pamphlets, and books of the day that it could be considered the signature of the era. People living at the time had an inexhaustible palette of words and phrases to illustrate the brilliant luminosity that encompassed and infused their world.

But what exactly were they referring to? What glowing progress had been made? What lustrous, widespread improvement in living conditions had been achieved? Indeed, what radiant and rapid expansion of creature comforts could they boast of? First and foremost, the "mighty light" praised by so many writers referred to the novel state of knowledge provided by science. Modern science, of course, began in the seventeenth century, but it was now advancing quickly, and its fruits were available to more and more people. Not only in the realms of physics, anatomy, and medicine but also in the nascent fields of chemistry and biology, groundbreaking discoveries were made that improved life in previously unimaginable ways, easing the harshness of human existence. The lightning rod, which Franklin invented in his spare time in Philadelphia at the century's midway point, was viewed by contemporaries as an especially spectacular and impressive example of useful science; after terrorizing humanity for millennia, one of the most catastrophic forces of nature had finally been tamed. Likewise for the smallpox vaccine. Initially experimented with in England and then used with increasing success elsewhere in Europe and in America, it provided more and more people with artificial immunization against one of the most dread diseases of all time.

These astounding discoveries and inventions resulted from the determined application of reason, logical thinking, and common sense. Indeed, even amateur scientists and nonspecialists could be involved in the advancement of learning. All this nurtured the hope that a permanent increase in knowledge could, in principle, be contributed to and brought about by all members of society in the future. This belief was the impetus for an overhaul of schooling and education. In the early eighteenth century, a steadily increasing number of princes and patricians, theologians, scientists, and business magnates already considered it their duty to found schools in which as many people as possible—including more and more girls and women—could receive a good education, thereby increasing the number of individuals capable of contributing to the good of the state and society. Accordingly, literacy and the desire for learning expanded appreciably, in part because teachers received better training at institutions created expressly for that purpose. Classroom practice often integrated new, playful forms of pedagogy that encouraged students to continue learning and improving on their own.

It was these concerted efforts toward the comprehensive accumulation and effective communication of knowledge that enabled many swiftly emerging social developments and technological innovations. They brought about a radical transformation of living conditions in Europe and North America in the eighteenth century—a change that could be keenly seen and felt. Forests literally became brighter as they were cleared to create new farmland. For the same purpose, swamps were drained and coastal dikes built. Improved methods of agriculture enhanced yields from fields old and new, providing increased sustenance. As a result, average life expectancy rose and the population steadily swelled. New roads and canals in the interior and newly discovered sea passages made it possible for coaches, barges, and ships to transport people and essential goods faster and more safely around the globe. If the harvest was bad in one place, grain could easily be imported from another. Thanks to the invention of the hot-air balloon in 1783, it even became possible to ascend to the skies and cruise on currents of air.

It became fashionable for agricultural goods from the farthest corners of the globe to be consumed for sheer enjoyment, such as the drinking of tea and coffee and the smoking of tobacco; pleasure became a pastime. More and more people visited theaters, museums, and cabinets of curiosity, and it became clear that this type of simultaneously educational and entertaining contemplation of people, of newly discovered exotic places, of glittering artifacts and previously unknown wonders of nature could improve society in unimagined, powerful ways. Numerous newspapers and magazines sprang up to report about all these incredible novelties, as well as about political events. In the public libraries then being opened, these publications could be read by all comers free of charge or for a trifling fee, thus promoting a discourse, shared in by large swaths of society, in which freedom of thought and tolerance became paramount. New streetlamps turned night to day—at least on the boulevards of large cities—thus allowing people to engage in illuminating conversation in public at nearly any hour.

Since so many people were now determined to banish darkness and shed ever more light on the world, the need was felt for a clear word to denote this general striving for illumination in personal life, politics, and society. The term that emerged was *enlightenment*. By the late eighteenth century, this felicitous coinage had become so common that the philosopher Immanuel Kant of Königsberg (now Kaliningrad) announced flatly in 1784 that he lived "in an age of enlightenment." The term was adopted everywhere in Europe and North America that had been animated by this spirit. The German word used by Kant was *Aufklärung*. The Dutch prided themselves on their *voorlichting*. The Danish sought to expand the realm of *oplysning*. The French praised the *siècle des lumières*. And the Italians had *illuminismo*.

Artists of the eighteenth century developed a simple and intuitive (and therefore powerful) image to encapsulate the emanating light of knowledge, an image that would become an especially popular, universally understood symbol of the age. In countless paintings, engravings, watercolors, and sketches, they portrayed their day, the shining aura of their century, as a marvelous sunrise. An especially evocative depiction of the rising sun can be found on the frontispiece of a book first published in 1720 by Christian Wolff, a philosopher from Halle, entitled *Vernünfftige Gedancken von Gott, der Welt und der Seele des Menschen, auch allen Dingen überhaupt* (Rational Considerations on God, the World, the Human Soul, and Everything Else). It shows a sun rising over hills, forests, cities, and farms, emerging radiantly from amid dark clouds. At the center of its corona, a benevolently smiling human face seems to take endless pleasure in the swiftly retreating shadows. In 1791—more than seventy years later—Daniel Nikolaus Chodowiecki, an engraver in Berlin, was commissioned to portray the Enlightenment as one of the "decisive events" of the closing century. The resulting scene shows the morning sun rising over a town set in a mountain valley. One year later, Georg Christoph Lichtenberg wrote in his *Goettinger Taschen Calender* (Göttingen Pocket Calendar) that the Enlightenment had "no more generally intelligible, allegorical symbol" than the rising sun. It was so suggestive and forceful that it was of all the "most fitting."

Upon closer inspection, however, the widely held and accepted belief that the eighteenth century was an age of enlightenment, a brilliant sunrise lasting 100 years, is not as straightforward as it might at first seem. For alongside all the amazing achievements, inventions, and discoveries that distinguished the time, there was no shortage of negative developments and outright catastrophes that could have caused contemporaries to take a different view of their day. The middle of the century was marked by a seven-year war fought by several European nations on all the continents then known on earth. Indeed, it can be considered the first global conflict of its kind, the first true world war. Shortly before its first bloody battles were fought, there was a cataclysmic earthquake in Lisbon whose extraordinary magnitude exploded the

FIGURE 2.1. The sunrise was a generally intelligible, allegorical symbol of the Enlightenment. Engraving by Daniel Nikolaus Chodowiecki, 1791 (akg-images).

boundaries of human imagination. In a single stroke, this one act of God extinguished 30,000 lives and left the once majestic capital in ruins. And although a vaccine for smallpox had been found, there was still no shortage of pain and suffering from other diseases like cholera, dysentery, tuberculosis, typhus, diphtheria, and syphilis.

War and violence, starvation and natural disasters, illness and the prospect of a painful death still made up an unmistakably large and undeniable part of life in the eighteenth century. There was no more harrowing depiction of this state of affairs than Voltaire's 1759 novel *Candide*, a widely read and amply discussed admonition against an all-too-naïve optimism and faith in progress. And yet the same Voltaire held fast to the notion—at least in principle—that he lived in an age of enlightenment, an epoch of expanding illumination. Did an inexplicably stubborn focus on the rising sun ultimately lead to a kind of blindness, a delusion that demoted even the most obvious horrors of the age to insignificant incidents incapable of impeding the triumph of the light?

In order to understand why the image of the sunrise—regardless of any and all objections to its aptness—nevertheless managed to become the symbol of the eighteenth century as a whole, of the Age of Enlightenment, one must consider certain decisive events of the seventeenth century, the period when the major philosophical foundations of modernity were laid. Sometime between 1610 and 1611, the ingenious Italian mathematician and natural philosopher Galileo Galilei gazed at the sun through a telescope, invented only one year earlier in the Netherlands, thus seeing the radiant heavenly body like no human being had ever seen it before. Undertaking his observations with unprecedented precision, he descried dark spots on the sun. He drew them between February and April 1612, and in 1613 he made those drawings available to interested readers in his *Letters on Sunspots*, published in Rome. He interpreted the spots as cloudlike formations, as gases of irregular shape, that were linked to the sun and that seemed to be located on its surface. Their motion followed the rotation of the sun, one cycle of which lasted about one lunar month. While the sun rotated, the spots gathered together as dark shadows and then broke apart again into fragments, thereby changing the intensity of solar radiation. Galileo concluded that sunspots recurred in regular phases and therefore that the light of the sun, which natural philosophers and theologians had always described as absolutely unchangeable and perfectly pure, was actually in permanent flux.

In subsequent years, these insights led Galileo to hypothesize that the earth revolved around the sun and not vice versa. On the one hand, his discoveries earned him the enmity of the Catholic Church, which resented how radically he had cast doubt on the traditional order and purity of the firmament. On the other hand, the more liberally minded natural scientists of Galileo's day were enthusiastic beyond measure about his spectacular observations. Like him, they were in no way alarmed that there were dark spots on the sun even though it shone brightly. Instead of debasing the value of the sun's light, Galileo's discovery could be seen as promising evidence that one could trust in the power of the sun not only when it shone brightly but even when its radiation seemed hidden behind shadows, clouds, fog, and dark spots. Indeed, the latter might even contain that very power. Nothing could diminish the light and warmth it provided. As the physicist Lichtenberg wrote toward the end of the eighteenth century, "So long as the sun rises, no fog can detract from it."

Initially, however, until the middle of the seventeenth century, this view remained the province of leading scholars. Indeed, most Europeans experienced the age of the scientific revolution instigated by Galileo primarily as a period of extreme anxiety and affliction. With the Thirty Years' War in Germany, the English Civil War, and the Fronde in France, an inexorable series of religious and civil wars ruled the day, in some places unleashing an unimaginable level of brutality and devastation on civilians. When marauding horsemen shoved muck down the throats of helpless peasants, raped their daughters, ransacked defenseless farms for food, and defiled the bodies of the dead by cutting off their noses and ears, not many poets were inclined to extol the exalted, inventive, indomitable spirit of man. Instead, they composed dirges lamenting the lot of their fellow human beings. At the end of a life dominated by war, the Silesian poet Andreas Gryphius sighed,

> What indeed are men! A dwelling place for grim pains,
> A ball of false fortune, a will-o'-the-wisp of their times,
> A stage of bitter fear, set with a sharp pain.

Nevertheless, during those long years of war, there were also philosophers who praised Galileo's intellectual acumen, his unprecedented description of the sun, and the subsequent development of wholly novel technologies as an encouraging sign that the world would soon become a better, brighter, and more benevolent place. One of them was the English political theorist Thomas Hobbes, who, having visited Galileo in Florence in 1636, considered him the "greatest philosopher not merely of our own but of any age." In Hobbes's view, the same mathematical precision and degree of rationality with which Galileo observed the motion of the planets must be applied to studying and

FIGURE 2.2. Pioneer of the Enlightenment: Thomas Hobbes (1588–1679).
Anonymous color engraving, after a painting by Jan Baptist Jaspers, 1661
(akg/North Wind Picture Archives).

interpreting political developments on earth. Then one could discover what
political system would be most likely to secure peace and a general flourishing
of the sciences, and in this way usher in an age of universal tranquility and
happiness.

In 1642, Hobbes proposed a solution to the grand problem of politics that
would soon be discussed all over Europe. In his treatise *De Cive* (*On the Citizen*), he emphasized in the immortal phrase *homo homini lupus* that human
beings all too often treat each other like wolves treat sheep. With his own eyes,
he had witnessed the "dominion of passions, war, fear, poverty, slovenliness,
solitude, barbarism, ignorance, cruelty." Nevertheless, he believed human beings were not "evil by nature" but rather were capable of creating a "dominion
of reason, peace, security, riches, decency, society, elegancy, sciences, and

benevolence." In order for that to happen, political philosophers had to "discharge their duty" with the same method the great mathematicians applied to "the observation of the heavens." Only then could one contribute to "the completion of that happiness which is consistent with human life" and bring everything *in lucem clarissimam*, "into the clearest light."

Hobbes conceded that armed conflict between states can never be completely eliminated, since good people will need to cultivate warlike virtues to protect themselves from the corruption of the wicked. Nevertheless, he argued that it is possible to create states that neutralize the inner turmoil and bloody civil wars that had constituted some of the most disastrous armed conflicts of his own day and of all world history. At least within the borders of such a pacified, stable body politic, the arts and sciences could increase steadily and undisturbed, as could general prosperity. The larger the number of well-ordered states, the more peaceful the world would be. In order to reach this worthwhile goal, it sufficed to establish in as many states as possible a new social contract, one based on an enduring and very special kind of *consensio*, or consensus: a fundamental harmony in the political will of the ruler and the ruled, effected by the creation of a constitution with this express purpose.

As Hobbes explained, this kind of consensus between governor and governed could be created in two very different ways, on account of which there were generally two kinds of state. In one, "the lord acquires to himself such citizens as he will." In the other, "the citizens by their own will appoint a lord over themselves." The first kind of government is usually called "monarchy." In the form of a hereditary monarchy, it exercises a judicious and just "absolute" or "supreme power" over a populace that, for its part, abides in conscious and thankful subservience to it, silently acknowledging its authority. In the second kind of government, called "democracy," free citizens "met together" and, "in the very act of meeting, [formed] a democracy" in which everyone is "obliged to the observation of what shall be determined by the major part." In Hobbes's view, knowledge of these two kinds of state formation—both of which, monarchical and democratic, aim at the consensus of all in the state of a united people—must be spread not through fear or punishment but rather through plausible reasoning. Anyone who works toward this end makes an outstanding contribution to peace and the expansion of light in the world.

Hobbes's theory of a social contract based on consensus, which formed the basis for a whole new understanding of the state, met quickly with widespread approval. Especially in the second half of the seventeenth century, more and more philosophers and political theorists became interested in his ideas and

FIGURE 2.3. Advocate of the people: John Locke (1632–1704).
Painting by Herman Verelst, 1689 (IAM/akg).

even sought to apply them in practice—some of them drawn to the monarchical model, others preferring the democratic approach. Two especially ambitious thinkers who took Hobbes's suggestions in very different directions were
the German polymath and constitutional theorist Gottfried Wilhelm Leibniz
and the English physician and philosopher John Locke. Leibniz was in the
service of the Electorate of Mainz when, in 1670, he wrote a letter to Hobbes
praising *De Cive* as an unparalleled masterpiece of political theory, one that
had finally "kindled a great light" on the otherwise dark path toward the establishment of universal peace. That same year, in a treatise devoted to the
security of his homeland, he wondered whether it might not be possible "for
the Emperor to become a perpetual dictator or absolute monarch," or at least
for the quasi-sovereign electoral territories composing the federally constructed Holy Roman Empire to be given strong governments that cooperated
with one another. For his part, Locke had read *De Cive* in the mid-1660s and,

FIGURE 2.4. Advocate of princely rule: Gottfried Wilhelm Leibniz (1646–1716). Painting by Christoph Bernhard Francke, 1700.

in 1673, acted as an adviser to the British government along with Hobbes. In his *Two Treatises of Government*, written between 1679 and 1681, he argued that sovereignty in England—as well as in the English colonies in North America—always resided "in the people." For when government failed in its purpose, citizens always had the right to create a new one in order to preserve their safety.

Leibnitz initially sought to make his political ideas a reality in the Electorates of Mainz and Hanover. In 1697, he was then invited to the court of the Electorate of Brandenburg in Berlin, where he functioned as a significant source of philosophical inspiration. During that time, he witnessed at close range how Elector Frederick III, all on his own and (as Hobbes would say) "as he willed," founded a state that he ruled as an absolute sovereign. Locke, on the other hand, became an adviser to William Penn in 1686. The wealthy

English Quaker allowed colonists from all over Europe to settle his massive landholdings around the city he had founded, Philadelphia, where they (to again borrow a phrase from Hobbes) "met together" in order to establish a democratically structured commonwealth.

In a strange twist of fate, two unlikely cities, Berlin and Philadelphia, became the capitals of states that, at exactly the same moment—the year 1701, right at the outset of the eighteenth century—received radically novel constitutions, thanks to which they were set on wildly disparate paths to becoming model polities of the Age of Enlightenment. We must wonder what historical factors led to the formation of these two so momentous, artificially created states: Prussia, a kingdom entirely subject to the will of its monarch, and Pennsylvania, a commonwealth governed by citizens and destined to be the nucleus and keystone of a massive American confederation of states.

When Leibniz was invited to Berlin by Frederick III, the head of the House of Hohenzollern, the elector's ancestors had governed affairs in Brandenburg for nearly 300 years. Originally from southern Germany, the Hohenzollerns were enfeoffed with the Margraviate of Brandenburg in 1417. According to the Golden Bull of 1356, the basic law of the Holy Roman Empire of the German Nation, the margrave of Brandenburg was one of the prince-electors endowed with the privilege of choosing the Roman-German king. The man designated king in this way also became the emperor-elect of the Holy Roman Empire. The electors of Brandenburg were therefore, according to the stipulations of the Golden Bull, seen as "pillars" of the Empire. As such, it was their duty to steadfastly maintain the integrity of their territories and to expand them if possible. In 1473, Elector Albert Achilles issued the *Dispositio Achillea*, legally establishing the Hohenzollern family's hereditary claim to Brandenburg and stipulating that the margraviate could not be split up by subsequent generations. His successors then consolidated and sought to increase its territory.

It was Elector Joachim II Hector who, over the course of the sixteenth century, laid the foundation for the acquisition of Prussia, a duchy located on the southeastern coast of the Baltic Sea. Prussia was not part of the Holy Roman Empire. In the Middle Ages, it had been ruled by the knights of the Teutonic Order. In 1523, after the Reformation of Martin Luther, it became a Protestant duchy under Polish suzerainty. Thenceforth it was ruled by Albert of Hohenzollern-Ansbach. Duke Albert of Prussia was a cousin of Joachim II Hector, who, as elector of Brandenburg, had introduced the Reformation to the margraviate. Given the family relationship, Joachim succeeded in having the male issue of his own line recognized in 1568 as co-heirs to the Duchy of Prussia. Accordingly, when Albert's son died in 1618 without being survived by any sons of his own, Elector John Sigismund of Brandenburg, a great-grandson of Joachim, inherited the title to Prussia. From then on, the electors of Brandenburg—who converted to Calvinism in 1613, albeit allowing their Lutheran subjects to retain their faith—were also dukes of Prussia.

On account of the Thirty Years' War, however, John Sigismund could not immediately do anything with the newly won territory. Only in 1640, when Frederick William became elector, did opportunities open up. By the terms of the 1648 Peace of Westphalia, he was given Farther Pomerania, the Principality of Halberstadt, and a claim to the bishopric of Magdeburg, including the city of Halle. When King Charles X Gustav of Sweden invaded Poland in 1655 in a move to reassert Swedish hegemony in the Baltic region, Frederick William lost no time in allying himself with the Swedish army, using its help to throw off the yoke of Polish suzerainty in Prussia.

The Polish troops were conquered by the united armies of Sweden and Brandenburg in the summer of 1656. Unexpectedly, the Swedish king did not give Prussia to Frederick William, causing the latter immediately to change sides. This strategic volte-face was a boon to the elector. The terms of the Treaty of Wehlau and Bromberg, signed in the fall of 1657, released Frederick William from his vassalage to the Polish king, making him sole sovereign over Prussia "with absolute power and without the previous limitations." Leopold I, who was chosen Holy Roman Emperor in 1658 in part thanks to the elector of Brandenburg's support, confirmed this arrangement on May 3, 1660, in the Treaty of Oliva.

In *De jure suprematus ac legationis Principum Germaniae*, a legal opinion published in 1677, Leibniz placed the Duke of Prussia on the same level as the crowned heads of Europe. Eager to enhance his international status, Frederick William sent a trade expedition to the Gold Coast of West Africa in 1683, composed of several ships built in Prussia's Baltic port of Pillau and commanded by experienced Dutch captains. There he founded a settlement under the flag of Brandenburg, naming it after himself: Groß Friedrichsbug. It fell to his son and successor, Elector Frederick III, however, to acquire a royal title for the House of Hohenzollern. This was a consequential event, more than a mere seal of recognition for the rise of the dynasty that had achieved absolute rule in Prussia.

Soon after inheriting the title of Margrave and Prince-Elector of Brandenburg in 1688, the new ruler posed the following question with regard to his sovereignty in Prussia: "Since I possess everything pertaining to royal dignity, and indeed to a much greater degree than other kings, why should I not also seek to attain the name of king?" The desire for resplendent royal majesty in Prussia was about more than increasing the intensity of Frederick's aura. Obtaining the title of king also meant achieving a higher princely rank, which entailed a concrete increase in power both in Europe and in the Holy Roman Empire. As Hobbes had taught in 1651, "Reputation of power is power." This also explains why other German prince-electors besides Frederick III were on the hunt for a royal title. Frederick Augustus I of Saxony, of the House of Wettin, even voluntarily converted to Catholicism in order to have himself crowned by the Polish nobility as King Augustus II of Poland, which then occurred in 1697. Four years later, in the Act of Settlement, the English Parliament pledged the right to the throne of England to the Welf House of Hanover.

Frederick III, however, had no desire to have the crown of one of Europe's venerable kingdoms of ancient ancestry bestowed upon him by the grace and favor of local magnates. Rather, his mind was set on inventing an entirely new kingdom by his own power, which he could then govern as an absolute ruler without respect for any local customs or traditions. The only way to achieve this desire was to convert the Duchy of Prussia into a new and novel kingdom—a process that resembled less a metamorphosis than a creation ex nihilo.

He took the first step in the desired direction in 1692, when he related his bold plan to become king in Prussia to his privy councilor Paul von Fuchs. Initially Fuchs dissuaded Frederick, as he believed that it would only earn envy and enmity for Brandenburg without appreciably increasing its influence on European politics. Nor could he see any reason why the Habsburg Emperor Leopold I in Vienna or the other European kings might approve of the plan. Yet the cunning and patient elector knew how to bide his time. It paid off when Joseph Ferdinand of Bavaria, the designated heir to the Spanish Empire, died in 1699, and the childless Charles II of Spain seemed likely to give up the ghost as well. With Leopold I fearing that a renewed dispute over the Spanish succession would lead to a grand European war, Frederick III made him an offer he could not refuse.

He committed to providing the emperor with 8,000 troops and pledged his unwavering support in the future to the House of Habsburg. In return, all the emperor had to do was recognize Frederick's title as king, which the latter naturally would not use in Brandenburg but only with regard to Prussia, and encourage the other European powers to recognize it as well. It was extremely important for Frederick that the emperor not create the new royal title but rather simply recognize it. For instead of a vassal king, Frederick wanted to be an "independent king," entirely free of the court in Vienna. Leopold I acquiesced and, on November 16, 1700, guaranteed the elector of Brandenburg in a corresponding "Crown Treaty" that he would "immediately honor, esteem, and recognize [him] both in and outside the Empire as King in Prussia."

Frederick III was certain of becoming king even before the emperor gave his official placet. As if to illustrate the fact, in the mid-1690s he was already building magnificent palaces worthy of a king in and around Berlin. In 1696, a palace was built for Frederick's wife, Sophia Charlotte of Hanover, in the town of Lietzow, west of Berlin; the palace was later named for her, as was the town eventually: Charlottenburg. In 1699, the architect Andreas Schlüter began renovations on the old Berlin City Palace, transforming it into an astoundingly sumptuous royal residence. But Frederick III desired to do more than represent his power in Baroque splendor. He wanted to use that power to make his state a home of the arts and sciences, and in this way to improve the welfare of its residents and to bring stability and domestic tranquility to Brandenburg-Prussia.

Accordingly, he founded a new university in Halle in 1694, and in 1696 he established an academy of arts in Berlin on the model of those in Paris and Rome. And since all these efforts were undertaken with the aim of developing the very kind of state Leibniz had been dreaming of since the 1660s, the jurist and philosopher encouraged the court in Berlin to found an academy of sciences as well. In March 1700, after three years of rather intimate acquaintance, Leibniz elaborated his ideas for the elector. Very soon thereafter, on July 11, the Churfürstlich-Brandenburgische Societät der Wissenschaften (Society of Sciences of Electoral Brandenburg) was established. Frederick III named Leibniz its first president. Leibniz himself designed the academy's seal, thus providing a very clear illustration of his political hopes. It featured an eagle soaring to the stars, the symbol of a fledgling but powerful state with its sights set on the light of science.

Honored by Leibniz and legitimized by the emperor, Frederick III journeyed through the bone-chilling cold of December 1700 to the Prussian capital of Königsberg. For only there, outside the borders of the Holy Roman Empire, was he allowed to ascend the royal throne. After a long and onerous journey, he placed the crown on his own head on January 18, 1701. Leibniz celebrated the coronation as one of the most significant episodes in human history. Kings had crowned themselves before, in Sweden and Denmark, but the new

Prussian king staked his claim to absolute power in a very special way. He refused to take a coronation oath to the realm of Prussia, its nobility, and its estates. In this way, he blatantly disregarded the practice customary in other European nations of integrating the estates into the activities of government, and he did so with absolutely no compunction.

It had snowed and even hailed in Königsberg the night before the self-coronation, but shortly before the ceremony a radiant sun rose over the city. In this heavenly ball of fire, King Frederick I of Prussia saw a symbol of the light that his realm was destined to shed over the peoples of Europe like a new political dawn. During those dramatic days, the poet, teacher, and pastor Johann Kayser of Lippstadt was in Berlin, the future capital of the freshly minted king. Wandering the streets starstruck, he predicted that this metropolis of the new royal-electoral union of Brandenburg-Prussia would illuminate the whole world with blazing light. It was in that spirit that he contrived the anagram *Berolinum—orbi lumen*: "Berlin, light of the world."

Indeed, it was not long before the rest of the world would hear and read about the illustrious and miraculous birth of the Kingdom of Prussia and its recognition by the Holy Roman Emperor, the latter an event of great significance for international law. These tidings would even make their way to America. Ships transported bundles of newspapers with the latest news from Europe across the Atlantic Ocean, bringing them into port at Boston and New York. One of the favorites was *The London Gazette*. These periodicals then quickly found their way to the coffeehouses, inns, and taverns of the North American continent, where English colonists gathered round to inform themselves about the strangest and most striking events in the Old World.

Of course, in the spring of 1701 no one could have accurately predicted the impact that the new state of Prussia would eventually have on the Atlantic World. In any case, colonists in British North America at the time were more keenly focused on the final phase of a very different process of state formation: The citizens of Pennsylvania, then the newest colony in North America, had set themselves the task of drafting the founding document for a totally new kind of civil society. After intense deliberations, Pennsylvanians adopted the Charter of Privileges on October 28, 1701, a very sophisticated constitution that made their commonwealth the most exemplary colony in all of British North America. At the same time, it represented the preliminary culmination of a fascinating political development that had begun 200 years before, with the first European settlements on the American coast.

Between 1492 and 1497, the three Italian seafarers Cristoforo Colombo (Christopher Columbus), Giovanni Caboto (John Cabot), and Amerigo Vespucci undertook voyages of discovery that explored large sections of the coastline on the far side of the Atlantic. Over the course of the sixteenth century, the European powers Portugal, Spain, England, and France went about bringing these territories, described as paradisical lands, under their control. The newly discovered continent was quickly dubbed the New World by the competing European powers. Some honored Vespucci by calling it America, after the Latinization of his first name.

While the Portuguese and Spanish concentrated their colonization efforts on South and Central America, the French and the English were interested almost exclusively in the northern chunk of the New World. Exploration was chiefly in the hands of France until the late sixteenth century. The French navigator Jacques Cartier charted large portions of the land that he named Canada, after an Iroquois word for "settlement." The territory stretched from the hill he dubbed Mont Royal (Montreal) to the lower course of the Saint Lawrence Seaway.

Only in the 1580s did the English begin their own efforts to fully explore and permanently settle the newly discovered continent. Between 1585 and 1587, they established the colony of Roanoke on the southeastern coast of North America. Over 100 settlers, inspired by the Anglican clergyman Richard Hakluyt's 1584 brochure *A Discourse Concerning Western Planting*, worked enthusiastically to lay its foundations. Yet they failed in their design. Ships arriving in Roanoke with fresh supplies in 1590 found the small colony destroyed and abandoned.

The first permanent English colony was founded in 1607, named Jamestown in honor of King James I. It was constructed on a well-protected river island covered with fruit trees, not far from Chesapeake Bay. Jamestown was located only eighty miles north of Roanoke in an area that Walter Raleigh had claimed for England in 1584, naming it Virginia in honor of England's "Virgin Queen," Elizabeth I. Tobacco farming quickly became the colonists' most urgent enterprise, as only the sale of this agricultural product was able to secure the survival of the colony of Virginia in its early years. In addition to earning their daily bread, from the outset the English colonists also devoted significant efforts to self-government. Virginia's first representative assembly gathered in Jamestown Church on July 30, 1619. Following the model of England's Parliament in Westminster, their object was to create their own laws to govern their common life in America. This General Assembly was composed of the governor, his six advisers, and twenty "burgesses" (i.e., elected representatives of the people). When Virginia was declared a royal colony six years later, this body jealously guarded its right to enact its own American laws.

In contrast to the French, whose settlement efforts were for decades aimed exclusively at Canada, the success at Jamestown caused the English to cast their eye on other, equally suitable (and perhaps better) parts of America to colonize. The Virginia Colony was still in its infancy when ships full of English settlers began sailing toward various sections of the North American coast. Between 1620 and 1636, the independent colonies of New Plymouth, Massachusetts, New Hampshire, Rhode Island, Connecticut, and Maryland were founded. These new colonies stretched from Massachusetts Bay, which abutted French territory, down to the northernmost cove of the Chesapeake Bay on the Virginia border.

Unlike the Virginians, the new generation of settlers was not primarily focused on fertilizing the virgin soil of the New World, laying out fields, and tilling them in order to sell their produce for profit. It was not economic but rather religious motives that now sent droves of English immigrants to American shores. The Anglican Church, the official state church of England, strictly circumscribed the religious lives of English Catholics. In addition, it increasingly forbade radical Protestant groups like the Puritans from pressing further ahead with the Reformation. As a result, the most pious members of these dissenting religious groups saw the voyage to America as the only opportunity to live a life that was truly pleasing to God. Arriving in what to them seemed the pristine wilderness of the New World, the Puritans established themselves in New Plymouth, Massachusetts, New Hampshire, Connecticut, and Rhode Island, while the Catholics settled in Maryland.

Three more English colonies were created in close succession after the middle of the century. Deeply impressed by Virginia's economic flourishing, as well as by the improving prospects of the more northern Catholic and Puritan colonies, King Charles II of England decided in May 1660 to intensify the Crown's engagement in America. In 1663, the colony of Carolina was founded on his initiative and named for him (the Latin form of Charles being Carolus). It was intended to act as a buffer zone between Virginia and the Spanish in the south. The following year, the king's brother, the Duke of York, sent a large contingent of English soldiers to a region between Connecticut and Maryland. Dutch colonists had been settling there since the 1620s, and now, in the mid-seventeenth century, they had become serious competition for the English. Upon the Duke of York's successful conquest of the Dutch colonies, the area previously known as Nieuw Nederland, or New Netherlands, was annexed by the English Crown and divided in two. The smaller part was called New Jersey, the larger New York in honor of the duke whose troops had won the victory.

As a result, as of 1664 the North American Atlantic coast between Canada and Florida was a seamless row of English colonies, all of which had very different histories of development. All of them flourished—not only Virginia and Carolina, which received substantial support from the Crown, but also Catholic Maryland, the Puritan settlements of the north, and the former Dutch territories of New Jersey and New York. England's leading political philosophers took note. The variety of forms assumed by the colonies stoked their imaginations and spurred them on to deeper thoughts.

For Locke, the New World settled by the English evoked an image of a largely pristine earth as it must have been shortly after the Creation—an environment conducive to a radically new political beginning in a way Old Europe could not be. He was given to voicing this view in nearly paradoxical words. For example, in a prominent passage of his *Two Treatises of Government*, he wrote, "Thus, in the beginning, all the world was America." On account of his intellectual acumen and the interest he had shown in America since the 1660s, Locke was asked by his closest confidants for advice when they set about framing constitutions for two of the fledgling English colonies. (This occurred, incidentally, shortly after Locke's enthusiastic reading of *De Cive*.)

First, Anthony Ashley Cooper, first Earl of Shaftesbury, for whom Locke worked as secretary, requested his assistance in writing a constitution for the colony of Carolina. In 1669, the two men submitted to scrutiny the fruit of their common labor: the Fundamental Constitutions of Carolina. In one section of this draft document, Locke stipulated that the less wealthy settlers should have a say in Carolina's affairs via elected representatives in a general assembly. Shaftesbury, however, who possessed a massive tract of land in Carolina, argued in another part that the colony's government should chiefly be in the hands of its large landholders. This stark inconsistency was likely the main reason that the Fundamental Constitutions of Carolina were never ratified.

Only a few years after the publication of the failed constitutional proposal for Carolina, Locke was asked by a different friend to carefully study the draft framework of government of another American colony and, if necessary, to make suggestions for improvement. The colony had been founded under unusual circumstances by this friend, William Penn, a son of the homonymous Admiral Sir William Penn. Defying his father's expectations, the younger Penn had developed a profound distaste for military service in his youth and, in the

FIGURE 2.5. Founder of Philadelphia: William Penn (1644–1718).
Anonymous steel engraving (colored later), ca. 1840,
after a contemporary painting (akg-images).

late 1660s, had joined the Quakers, a sect of radical English Protestants that was mercilessly persecuted on account of its commitment to pacifism. When his wealthy father died in 1670, the son inherited his claim to 16,000 pounds that King Charles II had borrowed from the family in past decades. With great clarity of purpose, William Penn decided to use this inheritance to create an asylum in America for his religious comrades.

Penn proposed to the king that the entire debt could be canceled if the monarch transferred to him a certain amount of land from the Crown's American possessions. Penn intended to turn this land into a safe haven for all those who were tormented and persecuted on account of their religious convictions. Charles II agreed to the proposal, signing over to his dissenting subject a thickly wooded tract of land west of New Jersey, bordered in the east by the Delaware River. On account of its mass of forested land, Penn named his newly acquired property Sylvania (i.e., "woods"), prefixing it with "Penn" in respectful memory of his father. As owner of this new colony of "Penn's Woods," or Pennsylvania, he decided that its future capital should be called Philadelphia, the city of "brotherly love." The name indicated how important it was to him that its future inhabitants coexist peacefully.

In order to win as many colonists as possible for his project of brotherly love, he had countless copies of a promotional pamphlet entitled *Some Account of the Province of Pennsylvania* distributed all over Europe, especially in England and in German lands. The publication vibrantly described all the advantages of the new commonwealth-in-the-making. According to Penn, enlightened government would soon take hold in Pennsylvania as in no other place on earth, for the Pennsylvanians would "settle a free, just, and industrious colony," governing themselves by their own self-made laws and on the basis of "the people's consent." Only that form of life could provide the colony with "good prosperity and security."

When Penn crossed the Atlantic for the first time to view his new territory and oversee the construction of the capital, he joyfully observed that several hundred settlers not only from England and Germany but also from Holland and Sweden had made their way there to build the city of Philadelphia with him. He laid out the streets, divided the properties, sold the best sites for building to the first colonists, and reserved a sufficiency of other lands to lease in the future. Since he planned to enjoy good relations with the neighboring Delaware (or Lenni Lenape) Indians—to whom he gave fair compensation for the lands ceded to him by Charles II—he built no city walls, fortresses, or military garrisons. He intended for Philadelphia to remain a peaceful, tolerant, and open city.

The constitution Penn initially enshrined for the Province of Pennsylvania in his Frame of Government was quite conservative. Taking effect in April 1683, it provided for a Provincial Assembly of up to 200 representatives elected by the settlers. Yet, although it had the power to ratify laws, this body was dependent on the initiative of the governor named by Penn himself. Only the governor and his advisory Provincial Council, analogous to the English House of Lords, had the power to propose legislation. Laws could only go into effect if they were passed by the assembly and then approved by the governor and the council. These limitations obviously contradicted the political promises with which Penn had lured settlers to Pennsylvania. Locke recognized this point when reviewing the Pennsylvania constitution in November 1686. He considered it highly improper that the colonists could not participate in developing the laws they passed. Therefore, he concluded that Pennsylvania was still far from being a well-constructed state.

Locke's argument was adopted by Pennsylvania's colonists themselves. They had taken Penn at his word, and they stubbornly insisted that he improve his Frame of Government. After years of disputes, Penn initially reformed Pennsylvania's constitution in 1696 by giving members of the assembly the right to form their own committees and investigative commissions. Then, five years later, after some very serious conflicts with the assemblymen, Penn gave in. On October 28, 1701, he issued the Charter of Privileges, a constitution that finally gave the colonists all the rights they had demanded.

The assembly was now to be "yearly chosen" and to meet regularly "at Philadelphia." As representatives of the settlers, its members had the same privilege as the governor "to prepare bills in order to pass into laws." The council lost its right to introduce legislation. In addition, the assemblymen were now allowed to adjourn at their own discretion and to choose their own speaker as well as all other Pennsylvania officials. Moreover, the Charter of Privileges stipulated that no resident of Pennsylvania could be "molested or prejudiced" on account of their "religious persuasion." Indeed, Penn the Quaker explicitly invited members of all other Christian confessions "to serve this government in any capacity, both legislatively and executively." In light of these provisions, Penn concluded that the citizens of Pennsylvania could live at least as freely and independently as the residents "in any of the King's plantations in America."

In point of fact, the Charter of Privileges did not simply give to Pennsylvanians the same rights enjoyed by all other English colonists in America. Rather, it guaranteed much more extensive freedoms. The new constitution provided for a unicameral legislature with wide-ranging powers, and it protected religious freedoms. This gave Pennsylvania's citizens much greater democratic control over their own governmental affairs than was available in any other American territory. The newest colony was now the most modern. Pennsylvania had become a pioneering model for all North American settlements. In a sense, it embodied the radiant dawn of the New World. Of a piece was Penn's decision—also dating to 1701—to make it possible for gifted children from poorer families to attend Philadelphia's Public Grammar School, founded in 1689. What is more, the decree applied to children of all religions. For only by providing a good education to as many people as possible, Penn believed, could the arts and sciences flourish in Pennsylvania that were indispensable to the acceptance of his enlightened laws.

At least in the eyes of Pennsylvania's citizens, the enlightened government prophesied by Penn two decades earlier had now come into force. The successful establishment of a new constitution—only two months after the foundation of the Kingdom of Prussia—provided further impressive evidence for the notion that a promising new age was dawning. In Penn's memorable "year of our Lord one thousand seven hundred and one," a brilliant political sunrise began spreading its light on both sides of the Atlantic.

3

War and Peace (1702–1713)

TWO FASCINATING creations of a dynamic new age appeared in quick succession on the stage of world history in the early 1700s: the model kingdom of Prussia and the model colony of Pennsylvania. Yet beyond these two promising polities, there were other states that, while not created out of whole cloth, had radically reformed their constitutions on the threshold of the eighteenth century. In Great Britain, the motherland of the English colonies in North America, a comprehensive reorganization of government was brought about in the wake of the Glorious Revolution, between 1688 and 1701. Step by step, a totally new type of citizen participation emerged, doubtless informed by the freedoms now enjoyed in America.

The official impetus for this constitutional upheaval was the so-called *Invitation to William*, a letter sent in the summer of 1688 to Prince William III of Orange, stadtholder of the Netherlands, by a faction opposed to King James II. In no uncertain terms, the letter asked William to drive the Stuart monarch from the throne he had held since 1685 and thereby save Great Britain from sliding into tyranny. The writers of the letter, all of them members of the English high aristocracy, elaborated their fear that the new king would stop pursuing the general welfare of the state and focus instead on increasing his own personal prestige in the reckless manner of his role model and friend, King Louis XIV of France.

William wasted no time in accepting the audacious invitation. Having fought against Louis XIV in the 1670s as captain general of the Dutch Republic, he knew how aggressively the power-hungry ruler could move against smaller, freedom-loving neighbors. His personal motivation for invading England was to save not only the British Isles but also all of Europe from an ambitious king's repeated abuse of sovereign power. In November 1688, he crossed over into England with an army of more than 21,000 soldiers, quickly capturing key strategic positions without much bloodshed. The hapless James II went into exile in France, and shortly before Christmas the people of London welcomed the victorious Dutch prince with great jubilation.

A Convention Parliament assembled in 1689. It passed a sovereign act declaring itself a regular parliament and transferring the English Crown to William and his wife, Mary Stuart, a daughter of the deposed James II. In return, William, now King William III of England, recognized the Declaration of Right. Issued on February 13, 1689, it guaranteed the freedom of speech, debates, and proceedings in Parliament and stipulated that thenceforth laws could only be executed or suspended by the king and Parliament in common. As a result, the representatives of the king's subjects freshly elected to the House of Commons received a true share in political power, alongside the representatives of the English aristocracy sitting in the House of Lords. From now on, the king was understood to be a mere trustee and guardian of his people's basic rights. Now, for the first time in English history, the monarch's title to rule was based on a contract with Parliament, and the kingdom was subsequently provided with a constitutionally circumscribed foundation.

Once William and Mary were installed on the throne, John Locke emerged as an adviser to the new government. Despite the Lords' maintenance of great authority, Locke was unreservedly pleased with the significant political power conceded to the representatives of the English people in 1689. In his *Two Treatises of Government*, finished in 1681 but only published in early 1690, he had provided a precise, philosophically justified description of the political rights now won by English citizens. In his view, the king's relationship to the people was that of a trustee or guardian charged with protecting society and its fundamental rights. Furthermore, "the people" had the right "to remove or alter" the "sovereign power" if they believed the royal trustee was no longer inclined to perform its duties with the necessary diligence. For if the king lost the trust placed in him, the power he wielded must necessarily "devolve into the hands of those that gave it." They were then free to invest it in whoever else seemed to them "best for their safety and security."

Locke was also pleased with the new government's removal of many legal disadvantages suffered by Puritans and Quakers. In 1689, he had called for broad religious tolerance in England in his *Letter Concerning Toleration*. One of the first laws passed by the new Parliament was the Act of Toleration, which allowed Protestant dissenters to assemble publicly and repealed the vexatious penalties previously imposed on them for not attending Anglican worship. Yet the Church of England remained the official state church, and nonconformists continued to be barred from officeholding. Despite all the progress made, religious freedoms in England were not as broad as in the colony of Pennsylvania, whose citizens—at least after 1701—enjoyed far greater privileges, including in terms of democratic political participation.

Nevertheless, England had taken a giant step toward the kind of civil society desired by Locke and already largely achieved in Pennsylvania. The chief outcomes of the process set in motion in 1688 received official confirmation in the Act of Settlement, passed by Parliament in June 1701. It stipulated that the Crown was now nothing more than a state apparatus, an impersonal office, and was thus no longer tied to the charisma of a dynasty. Accordingly, ascension to the throne thenceforth followed the standard rules for the bestowal of an office, including the taking of a prescribed oath to uphold the law. Moreover, it was Parliament and not the king that determined the rules of succession. Due to the infertility of Queen Mary (who had died in 1694) and the death of all the children of her sister and successor Queen Anne, Parliament declared in the Act of Settlement that, upon Anne's death, the throne would pass to the Lutheran House of Hanover, whose electress Sophia was a granddaughter of James I. After the summer of 1701, whoever was to become king or queen of England knew that their title was now and forevermore based on a contract and the consent of the governed.

At the outset of the eighteenth century, then, England—just like its North American colonies and the Kingdom of Prussia—seemed to be headed for a peaceful future based on the secure foundation of constitutional principles. Four years before the Act of Settlement, William III had even gotten his archrival, Louis XIV, to unqualifiedly accept the outcome of the Glorious Revolution. According to the Treaty of Peace between France and England signed at Ryswick on September 20, 1697, Louis recognized William as the rightful king of England, assuring him he would do absolutely nothing to oppose the new political system.

It was thus a massive shock not only for England but for all of Europe when, in 1701, the same Louis XIV returned to a policy that showed him for what he was: an incorrigible warmonger hellbent on hegemony over the entire continent. It started with a dispute over the succession to the Spanish Empire. The originally designated heir, Elector of Bavaria Joseph Ferdinand, died in February 1699 of a violent stomach illness. On June 11 of the same year, Louis XIV promised William III that he would keep the balance of power in Europe when the childless King Charles II of Spain died, by recognizing the claim of Emperor Leopold I's second son, Archduke Charles. Yet when the Spanish monarch met his maker, Louis reneged on all his promises. In Charles II's final days, Cardinal Archbishop Luis Manuel Fernández de Portocarrero, a partisan of the French cause, convinced the king to issue a will naming Louis XIV's grandson Philip of Anjou as his sole heir. When Charles II died on November 1, 1700, Louis XIV tore up the agreement of June 1699, recognized the dubious will, and had his grandson proclaimed King Philip V of Spain.

Emperor Leopold I considered the will to be invalid. In the face of the French king's abrupt about-face and brash breach of treaty, he immediately announced that he would assert all of his own and the House of Habsburg's hereditary claims. If necessary, he would use arms to force Louis XIV to relent. Leopold's swift reaction was mirrored by the unconditional resolve with which William III opposed the French king. William had more on his mind than the unholy dominance Louis might achieve in Europe. He was also concerned about undue French influence on Spain's overseas territories, fearing an eventual French pincer movement from Canada and Florida against the English colonies in North America. Not unreasonably, William III accused Louis's France of attempting to establish an absolutist universal monarchy that would threaten world peace.

Accordingly, he provided support to Leopold I when the latter sent—still without an official declaration of war—an imperial expeditionary force over the Alps under the command of Prince Eugene of Savoy. The idea was to thwart any French attempt, in the name of succession to the Spanish throne, to take control of the Spanish part of northern Italy. And indeed, in a series of battles and skirmishes, Prince Eugene managed to repel the Franco-Spanish troops and entrench himself in Lombardy. At the urging of the English king, a "Grand Alliance" between England, the Netherlands, and the Holy Roman Emperor was formed in The Hague on September 7, 1701. England was in dire need of this alliance, as emerged only a few days later, on September 16, when James II died in French exile in Saint Germain. Breaking the terms of the Treaty of Ryswick, Louis XIV immediately announced that he was recognizing James's son as king of England and would prosecute the latter's claim.

The French king's boundless arrogance, embodied in his desire to void the principles of succession just outlined in the Act of Settlement and force the English people to accept a king imposed by a foreign power, was perceived by the entire British populace as an unprecedented provocation. The general uproar culminated in William III's request that Parliament provide financial support for war, a proposal it unanimously approved. But just as the king was preparing to officially declare war on France, he died on March 19, 1702, as the result of a riding accident.

The king's unfulfilled plans were brought to a decisive conclusion by his sister-in-law and successor, Anne Stuart. Only a few days after his demise, the woman who had supported the bloodless overthrow of her own father in 1688 now unconditionally promised—as William and her sister Mary had done before her—to the people of the kingdom of England that she would rule according to the provisions, laws, and customs of Parliament. In particular, she invoked her determination to thoroughly respect and uphold the Toleration Act, prompting William Penn to send the queen a heartfelt letter of thanks "on the behalf of" all Quakers. In all subsequent addresses to Parliament, Anne unceasingly underlined the continuity and conformity of her own policies with those of her predecessor. Alluding to William's Dutch origins, she emphasized, "I know mine own heart to be entirely English."

Therefore, she did not hesitate to take up William's fight against Louis XIV with the greatest personal conviction. She chose John Churchill, Earl of Marlborough, as supreme commander, naming him captain general and ordering him to prepare for war. On May 4, 1702, not even two months after William's death, an official declaration of war on France was proclaimed outside the queen's London residence, Saint James's Palace. Eleven days later, on May 15, the other members of the Grand Alliance—the Holy Roman Emperor and the Netherlands—joined England in the incipient, enormous struggle for the future of Europe and the world.

The Grand Alliance's declaration of war against Louis XIV drew other states and political entities into the conflict as well that, although not originally belonging to the Alliance, were to one degree or another bound to the English queen or the emperor. This was especially the case for the American colonies, which were now commanded by London to declare war on France and its ally Spain at the queen's behest. The American declarations of war were read out by the Crown's various governors, with each colony eventually issuing its own proclamation. Thus, on September 19, 1702, William Penn's deputy governor of Pennsylvania, Andrew Hamilton, announced Pennsylvania's participation in the war against France and Spain.

Another important partner of the Grand Alliance was Frederick I of Prussia. He now had to fulfill the terms of the Crown Treaty of November 16, 1700, providing the troops he had promised to Emperor Leopold I in the case of a military conflict over the Spanish succession. This, the inevitable price for obtaining his royal title, he paid one month before the Grand Alliance officially declared war, when the emperor asked him to send a Brandenburg-Prussian army to the Rhine in order to prevent a French attack on the Empire. As a result, by April 1702 nearly 12,000 troops belonging to the Prussian king were stationed in Wesel. Under the supreme command of Captain General Churchill, whom Queen Anne had now named the first Duke of Marlborough, they kept Cologne and the fortresses of Bonn, Geldern, Kaiserswerth, and Rheinberg from falling to the French in the following weeks and months.

Thwarted in Italy in the fall of 1701, Louis XIV now failed to make military progress on the Rhine as well, as his path was unexpectedly blocked by the resolve of imperial, English, and Prussian troops. But the French king was not the kind to be quickly chastened or to prematurely give up his ambitious aims. Nor did his opponents harbor any illusions; faced with a military deadlock, they settled in for a long-lasting war. As a result, only one year after founding his kingdom, Frederick I found himself in a political entanglement that did not suit him one bit. Likewise, the citizens of Pennsylvania had hoped for a much more peaceful future when they adopted their Charter of Privileges.

Thomas Hobbes was right when he prophesied in the mid-seventeenth century that war could never be entirely eliminated. Yet he had also claimed that states like Prussia and Pennsylvania, founded on a broad consensus of the political will of the government and the governed, would at least be able to maintain peace at home in times of war and crisis. How would Prussia and Pennsylvania, the latter locked in confederation with the other American colonies, behave in their first war after their respective foundings—a war in which, at least from a global perspective, they fought side by side as allies? Would they manage to continue spreading light across the world even in times of a war fought on several continents?

The war was an extraordinary challenge for Pennsylvania, considering that the colony's founder and owner, William Penn, was a convinced pacifist who harbored holy contempt for military conflict. His fellow Quakers, who constituted a majority of Pennsylvania's assembly, also had clear scruples about mobilizing for a war that they opposed in their hearts. This was a cause of serious concern and vexation for Deputy Governor Hamilton. He did not plan to attack the French, but he at least wanted to construct a defensive ring around Philadelphia. In September 1702, he wrote to Penn that not many citizens of Pennsylvania had as yet decided to form a militia to protect the capital. And even the few Pennsylvanians who were enlisted in the militia were now being "discourage[d]" and "dissuade[d]" by radical pacifist preachers, who incited "their wives" against them. According to the accusations of these wary women, performing military service was tantamount to improperly "leaving their business"—that is, neglecting their duty to provide for their large families.

However, when news spread in Pennsylvania that several French warships had been spotted at the mouth of the Delaware River and were cruising toward the capital, even the most dovish minds were so daunted and disturbed by the prospect of a bombardment of Philadelphia that they held a serious debate about whether a naked and defenseless city should not at least be protected by a publicly financed fort. A close friend of Penn, the Quaker James Logan, even wondered aloud if guns and powder should not be provided to those whose different interpretation of Christianity allowed them to perform military service in the name of self-defense.

Such considerations quickly became moot, however, when it emerged that Pennsylvania was not a target of French designs. Rather, France's strategy was initially to establish a new settlement zone west of Florida, along the Mississippi River, in order to bar the English colonies from any future westward expansion. In May 1701, Louis informed his royal Canadian officials of the new colonial and military strategy. Accordingly, in 1702 an expeditionary force under the command of the adventurer Jean Baptiste Le Moyne de Bienville established Fort Louis near the mouth of the Mobile River. Named after the French king, this stronghold was to be the starting point for the settlement of a vast territory along both sides of the mighty Mississippi. This still-unexplored region, newly claimed for the French Crown, was naturally named after Louis XIV as well: It was called Louisiana.

Many English colonists were enraged that the French were attempting to keep them from moving west by planning a massive belt of settlements, stretching from Canada in the north, over the Great Lakes, and down the Mississippi all the way to the Gulf of Mexico. At that point, the projected belt of French settlements was just a bold and unwieldy plan that might never be realized. Nevertheless, English settlers in the southern colonies were especially determined to nip the audacious scheme in the bud, hoping to act in time to ward off an unpleasant future.

Consequently, Governor James Moore of Carolina decided in October 1702 to carry out a targeted attack on Spanish Florida, which was allied with France. His plan was to overpower Castillo de San Marcos, an important Spanish fort, occupying it with his own soldiers before it could be reinforced by French troops and thus become impregnable. But the stone fortress surrounded by a deep moat withstood all English attempts to conquer it. After a seven-week siege, Moore marched his militia back to Carolina on December 25.

By the middle of 1703, English colonists a thousand miles to the north were suffering attacks and massive devastation at the hands of the French and their Indian allies. On August 10, five hundred Indians brutally plundered the northern Massachusetts town of Wells. The following fall and winter months witnessed an unbroken series of attacks on the New England colonies bordering Canada. By the end of February 1704, more than twenty English villages and settlements had fallen victim to Franco-Indian attacks.

The New Englanders were proudly conscious of their political rights. In their counterattacks on Canadian settlements and forts, they fought in part to defend the self-government, embodied especially in their colonial legislatures, that distinguished them from French settlers in North America. Unlike their French counterparts, the English colonies had no overall central authority to coordinate their military planning or optimize their collaboration with one another. Instead, each colonial government and assembly—whose form and prerogatives were outlined in the various colonial charters—followed its own strategy for reacting to the state of war with France and Spain that emerged in 1702. For the colony of Pennsylvania, located smack in the middle of the English settlement zone, this consisted primarily in continuing to build the model civil society whose foundation had been laid in 1701. With that in mind, no Pennsylvania politician considered sending the colony's own militiamen to the border areas of Massachusetts or Carolina.

Philadelphia was not immune, however, to a general lament over the consequences of the war. Time and again in his letters to Penn, James Logan complained that the interruption of trade with Florida and the Spanish Caribbean had done heavy economic damage to all the English colonies in North America. "As things are now," he wrote, "we lie under the greatest discouragements." Yet the Pennsylvanians ultimately resigned themselves to these unhappy circumstances. Aware that they were powerless to change things, they lived more sparingly and waited for better times to return. And despite the economic crisis, they never stopped governing their affairs by their own judgment and deliberation in the General Assembly.

In other words, even in wartime, Pennsylvania's assemblymen vigilantly guarded the rights and privileges guaranteed to them by Penn. Whenever the colony's owner threatened to overstep the restricted political boundaries he had voluntarily drawn for himself in 1701, they reacted with jealousy and resentment. They were not about to carelessly risk any of the legislative and civil independence they had wrested from Penn over years of political conflict, some of it quite fierce. At times they struck a haughty tone with Penn, reminiscent of harsh sermons.

For example, on August 25, 1704, the members of the Pennsylvania assembly presented Penn with an assertive letter of complaint, sharply objecting that he had explicitly and solemnly promised to them "by the last Charter of Privileges" that they could "continue and sit upon their own adjournments." Yet "in a direct opposition of the said Charter," during the war he had several times used the flimsy excuse of increased urgency to prompt his deputy governor, John Evans, "not only to call assemblies by his writs but to prorogue and dissolve them as he should see cause." Had Penn forgotten, the assemblymen asked, that Pennsylvania's constitution had not permitted such a procedure since 1701?

In case Penn had indeed forgotten, this letter reminded him of the spirit of the Charter of Privileges he had signed. And indeed, in the sequel he respected the letter and spirit of the charter, working in concert with the assemblymen to help spread the light of the sciences in Pennsylvania even during the troubled times of war. He supported Assemblyman David Lloyd's successful plans to expand the grammar school in Philadelphia, sharing the latter's view that nothing was so urgent in times of social upheaval as the proper, well-regulated education of the young. Incidentally, it was self-evident to the politicians involved in the educational project that the school would continue to promote religious tolerance.

Pennsylvania, then, remained true to the model provisions of its Charter of Privileges even in times of war. The colonists of Carolina and Massachusetts may not have been able to understand the radical pacifist stance of the Pennsylvania Quakers, and some rejected it with contempt. Nevertheless, they continued to admire the expansive political and religious freedoms enjoyed in Penn's colony, which did not exist in similar form in any other part of America or even in the mother country of England. Pennsylvania remained a beacon of civilization for all American settlers.

Only in one respect were the assemblymen of Pennsylvania, the youngest English colony in America, perforce second to the elected representatives of the others. While a representative in Philadelphia like Joseph Growden, who had been a member of the General Assembly since the founding of Pennsylvania, could look back with satisfaction on a twenty-year career, Virginia, the oldest English colony in North America, boasted families that had sent representatives to the House of Burgesses for two generations. Some of them were even watching a third generation of potential representatives come to maturity. One of the young aspirants was Augustine Washington, the son of a planter, whose father and grandfather had governed Virginia's affairs as burgesses without interruption since 1665. He, too, despite the raging war, now ardently hoped he would eventually be elected to Virginia's colonial legislature and then—when the time came—pass on to his own children his enthusiasm for the ideal of popular self-government.

Everyone who lived through the unpredictable years of the War of the Spanish Succession nourished their own individual hopes for a satisfying future. Frederick I, elector of Brandenburg and king of Prussia, while stationed on the Rhine with his troops in the spring of 1702, yearned for nothing more urgently than a swift end to the military conflict in western Europe. Yet this wish was far from fulfillment. For Elector Maximilian II Emanuel of Bavaria suddenly changed sides, threatening the cohesion and even the very existence of the Holy Roman Empire in a manner unknown for centuries.

While the Imperial Diet in Regensburg nearly unanimously endorsed the declaration of war proclaimed by Emperor Leopold I and his English and Dutch allies, Max Emanuel unexpectedly refused to step into line with the German princes and the imperial cities. Instead, in the fall of 1702, he joined forces with the French king. The latter had secretly promised that, were they to be victorious, he would make Bavaria an independent kingdom, enlarging it with the surrounding imperial territories and lands in Austria.

In order to win France's firm support for this outrageous plan and to amply illustrate his loyalty to Louis XIV, Max Emanuel betrayed the Holy Roman Empire. By the spring of 1703, he had invaded and occupied the imperial cities of Ulm, Memmingen, Augsburg, and Regensburg, thereby opening all of southern Germany to French troops. In so doing, the elector of Bavaria not only ended the military stalemate between France and the Grand Alliance, but he also snubbed imperial law as enshrined in the Peace of Westphalia.

His desire to transform Bavaria into a kingdom also contravened the imperial constitution. Admittedly, the electors of Saxony and Brandenburg had recently attained the crowns of Poland and Prussia, and thanks to the Act of Settlement the elector of Hanover was waiting to be crowned in England. Yet all these royal titles lay outside the confines of the imperial confederation. In contrast, Max Emanuel sought to found an expansive Bavarian kingdom within the Holy Roman Empire, even building it out of conquered imperial territories. This feat would have undermined the integrity of the Empire as a whole. For the king of Prussia, who remained faithful to the Empire, this was a depressing prospect.

At the same time, Queen Anne of England was preoccupied with her own concerns. Under no circumstances was she willing to allow the unbound French king to dominate both Spain and the Holy Roman Empire. Therefore, in the spring of 1704, she ordered an Anglo-Dutch expeditionary force of the Grand Alliance to southern Germany, where it was to unite with the imperial army under Margrave Louis William I of Baden-Baden, the Brandenburg-Prussian soldiers commanded by Leopold of Anhalt-Dessau, and Eugene's imperial troops.

When the Anglo-Dutch force joined with the imperial army, Prince Eugene, and 16,000 Brandenburg-Prussian soldiers under Leopold of Anhalt-Dessau in early August, the combined host numbered 52,000. The Franco-Bavarian army, now 56,000 strong, decided to attack. On August 13, 1704, the two sides met near Höchstädt, on the Donau River, on an open field between the placid villages of Blindheim and Lauingen. The gargantuan engagement ended in a triumphant victory for the Grand Alliance.

In a letter written to Frederick I three days after the battle, Prince Eugene noted that, "with his own eyes," he had seen the Prussian infantry "fight against the enemy with undaunted fortitude," causing the latter to "flee the field" and "give us this great and glorious victory." Despite the horrors that attended the Battle of Höchstädt, the engagement was also a cause of great rejoicing, for the continental superpower France had never suffered such a catastrophic defeat. The Empire was saved, Max Emanuel was threatened with imperial ban, and Louis XIV was unequivocally put in his place. The states of Europe could once again devote themselves to their own internal development.

Höchstädt was a devastating loss for Louis XIV, one of the chief enemies of the Glorious Revolution and English representative government. Thus it was also one final, great satisfaction for the philosopher John Locke, who died at his desk on October 28, 1704. If he had lived only three years longer, he would have witnessed a further enhancement of the status of the Parliament in Westminster, the upshot of an even stronger union having been forged between England and Scotland. The two kingdoms had been ruled in personal union since the Stuarts ascended the English throne. Now, in 1707, a unified state known as the Kingdom of Great Britain was formed, as a means to better coordinate the political and economic development of the two realms. From a constitutional standpoint, Scotland was annexed to England. The Scottish parliament was dissolved, and forty-five Scottish parliamentarians were sent to the House of Commons of Great Britain's now expanded Parliament; sixteen Scottish peers joined the House of Lords in Westminster.

A very different path was taken in the years following the Battle of Höchstädt by the still-fledgling state of Brandenburg-Prussia. Instead of strengthening the rights of the Landtage, the traditional representative assemblies of the various parts of the realm, King Frederick I did his utmost to rule without parliamentary oversight. As he wrote in a letter to his wife, Sophia Charlotte, since his coronation he "answered to no one but God" and was not required to "justify his rule" in any way. Accordingly, he called the territorial estates together only when it suited him. And when he did confer with them, his chief expectation was for them to approve taxes for longer periods of time, such that local authorities—that is, the nobility and the cities—had less and less leverage over him.

Frederick also curtailed the power of the highest governing body—the Geheimer Rat (Privy Council)—by meeting with its members only three days a week instead of daily (as had previously been customary), and by steamrolling them with his own independent political views and authority. Real political power at the royal court was transferred to the Staatskonferenz (literally "state cabinet"). This small group of favorites was headed by Johann Kasimir Kolbe von Wartenberg, a longtime confidant of the monarch who had helped him into his majestic, ermine-lined purple cloak for his coronation in Königsberg. The advice given to Frederick I by this group accorded largely with the personal interests of its members. No matter—on principle, the king ultimately made all significant decisions by his own lights.

The Prussian king dealt in like manner with all important matters in his army, deciding on promotions and dismissals, meting out punishments, awarding pensions, and even arming troops on his own and with as little input as possible from his ranking officers. In his view, these military decisions were prerogatives of the ruler and thus not to be delegated. Under his aegis, the army became a mainstay of the state, a monarchical institution under the direct command of the king. In addition, he doubled its size during the War of the Spanish Succession, from about 20,000 men at the time of his coronation to 39,963 at the conflict's end. This was only possible because Frederick I severely punished desertion—which the horrors of the war made commonplace in all the armies of Europe—and paid high bounties for the return of soldiers absent without leave.

Despite such draconian measures, Frederick I always thought of himself as a king steadfastly devoted to the common good of the people he ruled.

Ultimately, he had to wage war against France on the side of the Alliance, as it was the only means to establishing the peace he desired in the Empire. After the victory at Höchstädt, he immediately turned his ever-increasing power to domestic affairs, to further promoting the sciences and improving medical treatment for his people. As a patron of the flourishing University of Halle, in 1706 he created a position for Christian Wolff, an Enlightenment thinker steeped in Hobbes and Leibniz, as professor of philosophy and mathematics. And as a caring monarch concerned with the welfare of his subjects, he issued a cabinet order on November 14, 1709, calling for the building of plague houses and hospitals throughout the realm, so that the sick could be quarantined and given better care.

However, the most glorious virtue of his domestic policy was his upright and tireless promotion of religious tolerance. In 1685, when the Calvinists were driven out of France by Louis XIV, Frederick's father, the "Great Elector," had given his fellow Calvinists a new home in Brandenburg. Since then, these French Reformed immigrants had generally lived in harmony with the local Lutheran population. Jews, too, who had been expelled from Brandenburg in 1571, were allowed to return in the late seventeenth century. Frederick I now not only confirmed his father's generous religious policy, but he even expanded it. Under his rule, Catholics were also allowed to practice their religion unmolested. In a census taken in 1709—in anticipation of the unification of Berlin, to take place on January 1, 1710, with the previously independent suburbs and sister cities of Friedrichswerder, Friedrichsstadt, Dorotheenstadt, and Cölln—it emerged that the now expanded "Royal Capital and Residence of Berlin" counted 800 Catholics among its 55,196 residents.

The Prussian king's policy of religious reconciliation, which found a public supporter in Leibniz, was so successful because Frederick I was the highest secular and religious authority in his lands. He had very deliberately *not* received his crown from the hand of a churchman. On the contrary, only *after* the coronation in Königsberg was he anointed by the Calvinist bishop Benjamin Ursinus, who, along with a new Lutheran bishop, had only just received his ecclesiastical office from the monarch for this very purpose. Frederick felt no obligation to the clergy he himself had created. Still, he was a pious, devout Calvinist, profoundly convinced of the inescapability of predestination, the divine plan for all human endeavors. Throughout his life, as he once wrote to his wife, he had therefore "utterly submitted my will to the will of God." As that life was noticeably nearing its end, all he desired was to feel secure in the knowledge that the crown of his young kingdom—the most astounding creation of his own humble will—would be passed on to subsequent generations.

A secure line of succession was of paramount importance for the ruling dynasties of Europe, as was painfully obvious in the case of the still hotly disputed inheritance to the Spanish Empire. Nor was it an easy feat, even for a queen with the best medical care available. One need look no further than the sad fate of Queen Anne of Great Britain. She bore seventeen children between 1684 and 1700, none of whom survived to adulthood. That was the very reason Parliament authorized new rules for the succession in the Act of Settlement, passing the crown to the House of Hanover.

The Hohenzollerns had their own problems with succession. Ever since the *Dispositio Achillea* of 1473, the oldest male child had been the designated heir. With no Parliament to help decide the issue, a successful succession depended not ony on the ruler's ability to produce children and a well-ordered will and testament but also on the survival of the first-born prince. Frederick I himself was not born to be prince-elector. But with the sudden deaths of his older brothers William Henry and Charles Emil, that was now his destiny. Then, once he became prince-elector, he had to stand by and watch as his first-born son, Frederick August, died at the age of only four months. To his great relief, a second son, Frederick William, reached maturity and, in 1706, as Prussian crown prince, married the daughter of the elector of Hanover and future king of Great Britain. The self-assured Welf Sophia Dorothea then quickly bore him children. But while their daughter Wilhelmine developed into a healthy, lively girl, their sons Frederick Ludwig and Frederick William, born in 1707 and 1710, respectively, each died after only a few months.

The old and decrepit king was therefore moved to tears when, around noon on January 24, 1712, a Sunday, Sophia Dorothea gave birth for the third time to a prince. The boy who entered the world in a room of the Berlin City Palace was very sturdy, had jet-black hair, and seemed the picture of health. Frederick I immediately had himself born aloft on a sedan chair and carried into the room of his daughter-in-law (who, to his satisfaction, seemed to be doing very well) to have a peek at his grandson. "He's a good screamer," the happy king noted later, "and is nice and plump." The Kingdom of Prussia would certainly take much delight in this prince and have good reason to thank God for his existence.

While all the church bells in Berlin rang at his orders and the cannon on the ramparts thundered out a salute, the king tied a ribbon around the boy with the Order of the Black Eagle, the order of chivalry he had created the day

FIGURE 3.1. Gray behemoth: the Berlin City Palace, Frederick the Great's official Brandenburg residence (akg-images).

before his self-coronation. Then he expressed his wish for the child to be named Frederick, like himself. That was the name with which the boy was then christened in the palace chapel on the afternoon of January 31 by the Calvinist court preacher, Bishop Ursinus. His christening gown was covered with brightly colored jewels. As a sign of his future majesty as king of Prussia, a tiny crown richly set with diamonds and pearls was fitted onto his head.

Unlike his deceased older brothers, and in contrast to the French custom followed at many European courts, after the ceremony Frederick was not given away to a governess with a dedicated staff. Instead, he was allowed to stay in the care of Crown Princess Sophia Dorothea, who years before had likewise begged to be allowed to keep her daughter Wilhelmine with her throughout her infancy. Perhaps it was this special motherly devotion that helped the boy to grow so strong and healthy. On August 30, 1712, the proud king recorded "that little Prince Fritz now has six teeth," which had come in without the least difficulty. The child's feverless teething was a certain sign of divine "predestination" and the prince's destiny to become king, since "all his brothers died from it, but he, like his sister, is pulling through just fine."

FIGURE 3.2. Miniature of Frederick's baptism in 1712. Painting in oil on
ivory by an anonymous artist, 1850 (Museum Huis Doorn).

It was as if Frederick I had awaited this very moment, now that he was
conscious of having secured his life's work, to begin slipping away from his earthly
existence in peace and quiet. For the fall of 1712 marked a turning point in history
with profound political consequences, and the enfeebled monarch could no longer keep pace. The month Prince Fritz was born, envoys of the Grand Alliance
had met with French diplomats in Utrecht in the Netherlands, in order to finally
hammer out a workable peace agreement that would end the War of the Spanish
Succession in Europe and America. These negotiations were now reaching
their end.

After the triumph at Höchstädt, the Alliance had enjoyed further victories
in 1708 and 1709 at Oudenaarde and Malplaquet in Flanders. But then, on
July 24, 1712, it suffered a terrible, unexpected defeat at Denain, also in

Flanders. Once again, the hostile powers were at a stalemate that seemed likely to last a very long time. That was the context for the meeting in Utrecht, where the concession was made to allow Philip V to stay on the Spanish throne. The fine print of the treaty, however, made every effort to prevent France and Spain from ever uniting into one state.

In addition, Spain had to give Gibraltar and Menorca to Great Britain. In Europe, France only had to demolish the fortress at Dunkirk, but in North America it was required to cede Newfoundland and Acadia to the British colonists, whose militias had fought valiantly against French troops till the war's end. And while the Electorate of Bavaria was restored to the humiliated Max Emanuel and reduced to its prewar borders, Prussia was rewarded for its efforts with Geldern and Moers in the Lower Rhine region, Lingen in Emsland, and the city of Neuchâtel (an inheritance of the House of Orange) in French-speaking western Switzerland.

Under the terms of the Peace of Utrecht, Brandenburg-Prussia and the American colonies emerged from a war that had threatened their very existence—and in which they had both fought as partners of the Grand Alliance—with increased standing and strength. Even during the war, Pennsylvania had managed to bolster its religious tolerance, educational infrastructure, and lively tradition of legislative self-government. Similarly, Prussia had won great recognition in Europe as an astoundingly tolerant state devoted to promoting the sciences. However, the path it took was different from the political course steered by Great Britain and its American colonies. It was guided not by representative assemblies but rather by the increasingly centralized administration of a thoroughly monarchical government, in which the sovereign ruler retained the last word in nearly all affairs.

When the envoys of the Grand Alliance, France, and Spain formally signed the Peace of Utrecht on April 11, 1713, the founders of the Kingdom of Prussia and the Province of Pennsylvania were no longer able to celebrate the day. Only one and a half months earlier, on February 25, Frederick I had died in the presence of his son Frederick William in the Berlin City Palace. Penn was still alive but, having suffered a severe stroke only a few weeks before the Prussian king's death, was in a deplorable state. He could still speak and walk tolerably well, but his memory was gone, and he had lost the ability to communicate meaningfully. From then on, the management of the colony was provisionally in the hands of his sons and his wife, Hannah.

Despite the loss of their founding fathers William Penn and Frederick I, the citizens of Pennsylvania and the people of Brandenburg-Prussia looked confidently to the future. For their states seemed securely on their way. The citizens of the up-and-coming American colony regularly elected representa-tives from their own ranks to the legislative assembly in Philadelphia. And in Frederick William and his young son Fritz, Berlin now had two successors to the throne who could guide the affairs of Prussia one after the other—and probably for decades into the future.

4

Fathers and Sons (1713–1732)

THE ACCESSION of the new Prussian king, Frederick William I, proceeded with no visible pomp. No sooner had court servants laid out his dead father in a purple-trimmed room of the palace than the town major of Berlin, Alexander Hermann, Count of Wartensleben, directed a simple inquiry to the long-designated heir to the throne: Should the gates to the city be closed immediately to keep the tidings of the king's death from leaving Berlin, to make sure that royal messengers brought this news to the other courts before unofficial riders did? Frederick William I answered in the affirmative, gave the command, and then immediately demanded one simple thing from the privy councilors and courtiers gathered around Wartensleben: "neither counsel nor hollow reasoning, but only obedience."

With that, the succession was complete. There was no elaborate coronation ceremony of the kind staged by Frederick I twelve years earlier in Königsberg, nor was one necessary. Simply by virtue of wearing the High Order of the Black Eagle, it was clear that Frederick William I, as the heir to the Kingdom of Prussia, was from now on the absolute ruler of the royal-electoral realm. He had no need or desire to promise anything to anyone in his domain. On the other hand, he had the knights and citizens of Brandenburg-Prussia take an unreciprocated oath of allegiance, in which they endorsed his firm resolution to decide everything in his lands entirely on his own and to manage his affairs independently. Treating the nobility with open contempt, he informed them that they could continue to spout empty "drivel" in their traditional deliberations at the Landtage. If necessary, he would fill the treasury without their assistance. This financial independence would allow him to "achieve my purpose, firm up my sovereignty," and place the Prussian crown on his head invisibly, as it were, but "as solidly as a block of bronze," even without a formal coronation.

In order to preserve the very broad independence from the estates of Brandenburg-Prussia that his father had established, and to fill the state treasury largely without needing to resort to taxes approved by the Landtage, he ordered his court to adopt a drastic austerity program. Right after taking the reins of government, he reduced the number of courtiers, releasing from service 96 of the 142 men and women employed by his father. The kitchen boy and the master of ceremonies had to pack their bags forthwith, as did the confectioner and the organ maker. Finally, Frederick William I quickly and ruthlessly slashed the wages of the remaining servants by up to 75 percent. These radical measures alone allowed him to reduce the expenses of his court from 276,000 to 55,000 thalers.

Furthermore, he let it be known that his own personal coffers and the costs related to his royal lifestyle would not be exempted from the strict program of thrift. He announced his intention to sell off as quickly as possible all superfluous collections of jewels, silver, gold, and furniture that had accrued in the various residences and palaces of Brandenburg and Prussia in the previous decades and centuries. Indeed, in addition to silverware, countless gems, tables, cabinets, and chairs, he parted with all of his father's fine wines, the many now unnecessary litters and sedan chairs, and even the sumptuous coronation cloak from Königsberg. Of the twenty-four electoral and royal palaces and chateaus, he kept only six, selling or leasing the rest. These actions also quickly put handsome sums at his disposal, to spend how and when he saw fit, without needing to seek the acquiescence of a representative body or the estates.

At home, Frederick William I insisted that all the subjects of his lands recognize him as a sovereign, absolute monarch with full power to make decisions on his own authority. Likewise abroad he sought the respect of the great European powers and their rulers, so that he could continue building up his fledgling state as autonomously and free of military conflict as possible. The terms of the Peace of Utrecht were an early success in this direction, as they not only gave the Prussian monarch new territories but also provided his kingdom with the long-desired international recognition of France and Spain. Yet he was not satisfied with these felicitous developments. He also sought to enhance the reputation and the strength of the Prussian army, which had played no small part in securing the advantageous peace terms for the Grand Alliance.

Accordingly, in 1713 he invested a large portion of the money that had been saved by his radical austerity program in enlarging the royal infantry, adding to it 8,073 boys and fighting men. To fill the ranks, the king did not shrink from forcible recruitment measures. These were carried out so hastily that one British diplomat reported in amazement that the able-bodied sons of craftsmen were dragged directly from workshops by recruiters and officers. The cavalry was also augmented appreciably: 1,067 riders were added to this division of the army in only a few months. In this way, the royal troops quickly reached a new and formidable overall strength of 50,000 men. The Prussian king's army was now one of the largest in Europe. This was especially impressive considering that Brandenburg-Prussia was the tenth-largest European state in terms of territory and only the fourteenth largest in terms of population.

The fast and furious expansion of the Prussian army not only sent an unmistakable signal abroad, but it also powerfully changed the political climate at home in the lands ruled by Frederick William I. On April 21, 1713, the king issued an order regulating court ceremonial that gave clear preference to the highly decorated army at the expense of civil servants, the latter already having been downgraded in their numbers and their pay. In his eyes, military officers and common soldiers unquestionably formed the true backbone of the Kingdom of Prussia, and he wanted everyone to know it. Whereas the high chamberlain had once enjoyed prominence at court, his place was now taken by the field marshal. Similarly, chamberlains now ranked below colonels. As one perceptive observer of this transformation remarked, when one spoke of the court in Berlin, the reference was only to military men—"a novelty in every sense." Illustrating the new state of affairs, the king rarely appeared after his ascension without wearing the plain blue coat of a Prussian lieutenant or captain.

By consistently donning a military uniform and elevating military men in court ceremonial, the king almost completely wiped out the distinction between the civilian and military spheres—a distinction already blurred by Frederick I, who had unerringly and deliberately amplified his political sovereignty by arrogating all decisions in military matters to himself. The Prussian Crown, the state, society, the army—all melted into an indivisible, nearly organic unit that, at the king's command, was now animated and controlled by one single driving force, one undisputed, supreme authority. His will alone was to be law in Prussia, and it had to be respected by all his subjects without delay, happily, and with military obedience.

In lockstep, the mood, behavior, and even table manners of the Prussian court grew increasingly martial and decreasingly refined after King Frederick William I ascended to the throne. Indeed, the air became rough, uncouth, smutty, and vulgar. "Rogue," "buffoon," "rascal," "riffraff," and "scoundrel" were favorite epithets of the king. He commonly hurled them at his ministers, privy councilors, and diplomats, berating them thusly on an almost daily basis and with grim pleasure. Indeed, the cloddish "Soldier King" was wont to abuse them with far ruder expressions. Occasionally, he threatened to tan their backsides. This conduct was coupled with a downhome menu—he preferred pea soup, cabbage, pork belly, and bitter beer—rounding out the picture of an extremely crude, at times obscene, ruler. This is the image of the Prussian king that inevitably settled in the minds of his subjects and European neighbors. According to an especially trenchant characterization, penned by the philosopher Montesquieu while on a tour of Germany in 1729, "The king doesn't eat supper. He shuts himself up in his room with a few of his officers to smoke and drink beer.... He loves his soldiers, beats them up and then kisses them.... Being a subject of this prince is pure misery."

Few people knew or guessed that the boorish, primitive identity affected by Frederick William I essentially compensated for an inferiority complex that had haunted, oppressed, and at times even tormented him since his youth. The vigor and decisiveness with which he had begun his reign, instituting countless radical reforms at court and in the military, was mirrored by an equally strong, deep-seated insecurity over whether he was, or ever would be, a good, capable monarch. And yet, early on he had been regularly provided by his father with opportunities to prepare in practice for the duties of a sovereign ruler. For example, Frederick William I was sent on two extended trips abroad between 1700 and 1705, including longer visits to the Netherlands. In 1708, while his father took the waters for three long summer months in Karlsbad (now Karlovy Vary) in western Bohemia, the government of Brandenburg-Prussia was even transferred to him. One year later, he also distinguished himself militarily under Marlborough and Prince Eugene's command at the Battle of Malplaquet, where he developed a close, lifelong friendship with Leopold of Anhalt-Dessau and discovered his abiding passion for the art of war. Despite these many accomplishments, he was plagued his entire life by a low opinion of himself and his achievements.

This feeling of inadequacy, which had become a full-blown inferiority complex by the time he ascended the throne, was probably the reason why his royal guard regiment was filled specifically with exceptionally tall, beefy young men who had to wear absurdly high, indeed ridiculous, hats. The rather small and stout Frederick William I clearly felt at ease among these eccentrically dressed, gigantic grenadiers, and it gave him deep satisfaction to be able to order about these stringy soldiers, soon commonly referred to as "the long fellows" (*die langen Kerls*). He zealously assembled four companies of these oversize royal grenadiers, whom he recruited all over Europe. At least in this quirky, playful way, he was able to compensate for the gnawing self-doubt that critically undermined his self-confidence.

What was the source of the Prussian king's inner anguish, his lack of self-esteem, his profound feeling of insecurity about the meaning and validity of his own actions and desires? On the one hand, he seemed to have been born with an unsteady temperament given to extreme mood swings, making his life increasingly hard and turning him into a choleric, often irascible man. Yet, another, equally strong factor in the development of his fragile, difficult character was doubtless his rigorous Calvinist upbringing. It had a very different effect on him than on his father, whom the Reformed faith had provided with steady comfort, constancy, and an unswerving self-confidence. For King Frederick I, the theological dogma of predestination had acted as proof that he and Prussia were chosen by God. For Frederick William I, however, it had always been a nightmare. For he could not know which fate had been allotted him, meaning that he himself might not belong to the elect but rather to the damned.

Some relief for the agony in his soul was provided before he took the throne, when he met August Hermann Francke, a professor of Greek and Near Eastern languages at the University of Halle. Francke was not only an excellent classical philologist but also the leader of the Halle Pietists, a reform movement within Lutheranism that—with the consent of the patron of religious tolerance King Frederick I—had been a counterweight to the ruling Lutheran orthodoxy in the city on the Saale River since the 1690s. The Pietists, believing that Lutherans had long been concerned merely with liturgical superficialities and superfluous doctrinal disputes, instead concentrated their pastoral efforts on the spiritual needs of simple believers. In many places, they formed edifying discussion groups, simple Christian fellowship circles that could meet in private homes as a supplement to regular church attendance.

The main focus, however, was to teach Lutheran Christians to once again engage in practical piety (known in Latin as *praxis pietatis*)—that is, to live out their faith meaningfully in all aspects and realms of society. For this reason, the reform Lutherans in Halle around Francke self-consciously called themselves Pietists, despite the fact that this designation had originally been used by their opponents as a term of abuse. Francke's own religious ambition was to improve education for all social classes. Therefore, in addition to his work as a professor, between 1695 and 1698 he had founded various types of educational institutions for the poor, for orphans, and for wealthy burghers and aristocrats in Halle and in the neighboring suburb of Glaucha. They would soon gain international fame under the collective name of the Francke Foundations. What all these schools had in common was a central message, taught in every Pietist classroom: God's blessing would always be upon those who steadfastly stood by their fellow man or served the state in which they lived with sobriety, thrift, asceticism, and self-sacrifice, be they farmer, burgher, noble, or ruler.

This fundamental belief of the Pietists—that is, their ascetic sense of duty to all parts of society, which animated their steady commitment to the common good—mapped very closely onto the thrift and work ethic of King Frederick William I. But since the Pietists' enthusiasm for work had a peculiarly religious foundation, and since their writings always emphasized that good works were pleasing to God, the Prussian monarch learned from Francke to think of his grueling application to the welfare of the state in a very new way: as a (literal) royal road to salvation. This insight allowed Frederick William I to dispense with the dogma of predestination, which he now chided as a strange doctrine, without formally breaking with the Calvinist religious community of his forefathers.

On the one hand, this Pietistic understanding of the meaning of work was a liberation for him, an opportunity to escape his crippling fear of the fatal consequences of predestination. On the other hand, this new view of his office put him under immense pressure to succeed. The good work that now enjoyed such high status could only be performed at the head of the Prussian state by a capable, diligent, watchful, and, if necessary, strict, demanding, and ever-sovereign king who never ceased in his efforts. Was he such a ruler? Did he truly have what it took to do his duty with courage, confidence, and vigor? He was deeply uncertain.

This sense of insecurity had gripped him with fierce intensity in his father's dying hours. Terrified by his imminent ascension to the throne, he stole away from Berlin and went to Köpenick Palace, located ten miles away, where he tried to distract himself from the tensions mounting inside him for an entire morning. He returned to the Berlin City Palace by early afternoon, in time to receive a final blessing from Frederick I before he died, but he had to endure the latter's puzzled query: "Where have you been, my son?"

Fear, self-doubt, and insecurity continued to accompany Frederick William I after his father's death. Nevertheless, the day Frederick I died, it dawned on him suddenly, as if in a moment of inspiration, that the responsibility for expanding, developing, and solidifying the Kingdom of Prussia did not rest as fully and entirely on his shoulders as it had seemed to that morning in a fit of dejection and dread. For when he went to his wife's apartments on the afternoon of February 25, 1713, to bring to her news of the king's death, his eyes fell on his one-year-old son Fritz. As if beholding with fresh eyes the delicate young boy, who had just learned to walk, and as if the death of the grandfather affected the child more than anyone else, he said with a grave and fateful voice, "Today I will make you crown prince again."

It was as if to say, "I will make you the crown prince I once was, and, starting today, you will have to undergo the same anxious preparation for the high office of a Prussian ruler that I endured." Or else, "From this moment forward, you and I are indissolubly joined in our hopes and fears." At any rate, the words he had spoken soothed him appreciably. In young Fritz he saw a fellow defenseless toy of fate who, in his own particular way, would be required to satisfy the demands that the current situation was now placing on him as well.

At the same time, the new king's address to young Fritz was tantamount to passing a momentous verdict on the lad's childhood and upbringing. From then on, he would use all of the power at his disposal to force the boy to feel and act like the tough, stouthearted Prussian crown prince that he was supposed to be. Whereas his own father had given him breathtaking latitude in his childhood and youth to fathom his own abilities and talents, Frederick William I controlled and regimented the upbringing of Crown Prince Frederick around the clock. The first step he took in this direction, soon after ascending the throne, was to provide his son with a comprehensive introduction "to the military profession" that he believed was the bulwark of the Brandenburg-Prussian state. But whereas the king himself had discovered his enduring passion for military life as a young man in the War of the Spanish Succession thanks to a series of experiments and experiences of his own choosing, his son Fritz had no say in the matter. At the bidding of his father, he was forced to learn to love soldiering as a two-year-old boy. Later—when he had grown to be a man—this same Fritz lamented his early childhood in melancholic verse, noting that his "cradle lay amid the weapons of war."

> I was brought up in the thick of troubles,
> among the soldiery, without pomp and splendour
> by a stern and censorious father.

In fact, when Fritz was only two, his father began relentlessly pushing him to play with tin soldiers, toy cannon, and pistols. In addition, King Frederick

William I urged his son to beat out military marches on the drums at every opportunity. He was also to acquire a taste for military exercises as early as humanly possible. To this end, the king engaged two decorated officers from the venerable Prussian nobility to direct and monitor the crown prince's education: Field Marshal Albrecht Konrad Finck von Finckenstein, who had distinguished himself at the Battle of Malplaquet, and Colonel Christoph Wilhelm von Kalckstein, who had taken Moers. Their job was to make sure the boy was provided from his earliest days with professional military training. When only five years old, young Frederick had to independently command a company of "Crown Prince's Cadets," made up of 131 boys of the same age.

In addition to this wide variety of military play and instruction, Frederick also had to devote himself to extensive reading, writing, and arithmetic exercises that required no less discipline of him. Week upon week, he was educated by a court tutor all morning long and often in the afternoon till sundown as well. Even on Sundays, church attendance was preceded by thorough catechism training. Initially, Frederick William I engaged as tutor the Berlin Gymnasium teacher Hilmar Curas, who instructed the boy along with his sister Wilhelmine, three years his senior. In 1718, Curas was then replaced with Jacques Egide Duhan de Jandun, the thirty-two-year-old scion of a Protestant noble house in Champagne. The young Huguenot had enlisted in the Prussian army only a few years before, his courage and outstanding service leaving a lasting impression on the king. It was thanks above all to his military prowess that Frederick William I considered him especially competent to educate the crown prince. Frederick marveled at this fact many years later. "Seldom is a teacher chosen in the trenches," was his ironic comment on his father's unusual selection.

Yet Duhan was very well educated. He had received an excellent education in his youth from no less than Mathurin Veyssière de Lacroze, the royal librarian in Berlin and a close friend of the philosopher Leibniz. Ever since, he had fostered a strong love for the study of literature and philosophy. According to the express wishes of the king, however, the brilliant and bookish soldier was only allowed to impart very specific knowledge to his pupil. The crown prince was to be brought up in the Reformed faith of the House of Hohenzollern, but under no circumstances was he to learn of the doctrine of predestination that had so tormented Frederick William I. Furthermore, instead of the history of the Greeks and Romans, which the king believed to be good for nothing, Duhan was only allowed to teach the basic details of modern European political, diplomatic, and military history, especially the history of

Brandenburg and Prussia. And all instruction, without exception, was to take place in German and French.

Accordingly, the king strictly prohibited the crown prince from learning Latin, believing that a future ruler could very well dispense with knowledge of that ancient language. In his eyes, years spent studying Latin grammar and literature were nothing more than a careless and condemnable waste of precious time—time that could otherwise be spent learning useful things or working. It was nothing short of incredible, then, that this express educational ban was occasionally disregarded. The king flew into a rage when he learned that his son's teacher had disobeyed his orders, as Frederick would later relate to his private secretary Henri de Catt. He was just a boy and was working on his Latin "when suddenly my father entered the room."

"What are you doing there?"

"Papa, I am declining *mensa, -ae,*" I said in a childish voice which should have touched him.

"Ah, rogue, Latin for my son! Get out of my sight!" And he gave [my teacher] a volley of kicks and blows with his stick, accompanying him in this cruel manner into the inner room.

Terrified by his father's face, distorted as it was with rage, the boy took refuge under a table, thinking he was safe. But Frederick William I soon discovered his son's hiding place. "He took me by the hair, pulled me from under the table, and dragged me thus into the middle of the room, finishing by smacking my face several times" before thundering forth the threat, "'If I catch you again at your *mensa*, I will let you know what is what.'"

This terrifying episode testifies to Frederick William I's abhorrent manners and utter lack of self-control, which in turn were a direct result of an untamable, violent temper. Yet, as Frederick himself came to learn, the burst of outrage was not the badge of a dull hatred of learning. Indeed, long before becoming king, Frederick William I knew very well that Prussia's raison d'être extended beyond securing the material subsistence of its subjects. A Prussian king must also see to the intellectual welfare of everyone living in his lands. The state envisioned by Frederick I was to vigorously promote culture and education and thereby act as a shining example for other states to model themselves on. Therefore, it had to do whatever it could to provide a thorough education to members of all social classes, be they poor subjects or members of the royal family. To that end, on September 28, 1717, Frederick William I issued a decree that was one of the first of its kind in Europe: an "order . . . to parents, on pain of penalty," both in the cities and "especially in the countryside, . . . to send their children to school."

Frederick William I's ideal of universal compulsory education, intended to "remedy" the "gross ignorance" of the inhabitants of his lands, was animated by a different spirit from the one that informed his father's view of Prussia's educational mandate. Whereas Frederick I underwrote his elite Academy of Sciences and musically superb Royal Opera primarily to showcase his young state's cultural sophistication to the rest of Europe, his son preferred to benefit the masses, expanding access to basic knowledge to as many children as possible. His plan was guided by the simple pedagogical values of the Pietists, whose educational activity placed a premium on useful activity, hard work, and doing one's duty.

It was therefore a significant and highly symbolic act when Frederick William I ordered the demolition of the Royal Opera House. It had been built as an integral architectural component of Charlottenburg Palace in the days of Queen Sophia Charlotte, and Frederick William I himself had once performed there in an amateur production as a young boy. Now the king invited the citizens of Berlin to reuse the rubble to build a school. Would Leibniz have approved of his preference for the mass education of all social classes at the expense of promoting an artistic and scientific elite? The spiritus rector of the Prussian Academy of Sciences could no longer weigh in on these remarkable events. He had died on November 14, 1716, having just completed his seventieth year.

Frederick William I wanted to cultivate more in his territory than just the fallow talents of those growing up in simple or even crude circumstances. Always focused on practical utility, he also ordered the improvement of the vast tracts of waste- and moorland that dominated Havelland Luch, a large marshy area only forty miles northwest of Berlin. Starting in 1719, he had first-rate Dutch engineers lay out a series of ditches and canals to drain the interminable, muddy wetlands, so that new villages could be planted and churches built. The first colonists of the settlements that sprang up there thanked the Soldier King for this decidedly unmartial act of territorial expansion by placing a lavish inscription in his praise on the new church in the foundation named for him: Königshorst (literally "king's nest"). Even today, visitors can still read that "Frederick William, King in Prussia," proved himself to be an exceptionally "capable expander of his realm." For at his behest, many workers had taken "this previously bottomless swamp and abode of wild animals and toiled strenuously" to make it "arable" and "useful for raising crops and animals." The plaque claims that his work would never be forgotten.

At the same time as he initiated land reclamation efforts at home in Havelland Luch, Frederick William I bid final farewell to a very different kind of colonial undertaking. In 1720, he sold the Prussian trading settlement Groß Friedrichsburg to the Dutch West India Company. It had been founded by his grandfather, the Great Elector, on the Gold Coast of West Africa back in the seventeenth century. In the view of Frederick William I, the effort it would have entailed to develop the distant colony into a reliable generator of profit simply seemed too great and too risky. In contrast, he felt no compunction for the fact that Brandenburg-Prussia—the fledgling model state that, in the spirit of a more enlightened age, promoted education, science, and religious tolerance—had spent decades involved in the slave trade in West Africa.

Between 1683 and 1720, Groß Friedrichsburg had exported more than just gold, ivory, rubber, and ostrich feathers to the wider world. It had also transported 20,000 enslaved Africans, usually in abject conditions, to the Caribbean and thence to the North American mainland, where so many of them were forced to endure inhumane treatment and perform heavy labor on tobacco plantations. Frederick William I himself was the beneficiary of this practice. In addition to the 72,000 ducats that the Netherlands paid in exchange for Groß Friedrichsburg, twelve young African men were sent to Berlin, where they had to perform various services at the royal court.

The Prussian king called them *Mohren* (Moors), in line with the common linguistic usage of the time. Some became liveried servants of his children Wilhelmine and Fritz. Others had to play the trumpet or the drums in the Royal Military Marching Band. Finally, there were other Africans who served the king in a very particular way. In the evening after a long day of hard work, he liked to relax in the company of close friends and male family members to smoke his pipe. His Black servants had to hand out the necessary tobacco to the members of this Tabagie, or "smoking club" (*Tabakskollegium*). Before arriving in Berlin by way of London and Amsterdam, this exotic luxury good had to be harvested, dried, and packed by other enslaved West Africans, wretched cousins of the king's "court Moors" (*Hof-Mohren*). And no small part of this work was done in the British colonies of North America.

The first African slaves on the North American mainland were brought in the early seventeenth century by Dutch ships to the colony of New Netherlands, wedged between the English and French zones of settlement. Of course, other European seafaring nations had been involved in the Atlantic slave trade for a long time before that. Its origin was concomitant with the earliest Portuguese voyages of discovery to the West African coast in the mid-fifteenth century. It was Arab traders based in the Portuguese outpost of Arguin, established in 1445, who first supplied their European partners with pepper, gold, and Black slaves. They were paid in kind with horses, cloth, and wheat. This trade in "Saracens and pagans" was blessed by Pope Nicholas V in the bull *Romanus Pontifex*, issued on January 8, 1455, making it legal for Christians to "invade, search out, capture, vanquish, and subdue" them. As a result, thousands of Africans were sent to Portugal and southern Spain. Around 1550, there were already 10,000 Africans living in the Portuguese capital of Lisbon, forming 10 percent of the city's entire population. At the same time, about 6,000 Black slaves lived and worked in Seville, which had close economic ties to Portugal.

Due to the expansion of Portuguese and Spanish colonies in South and Central America and the exploding need for laborers on the sugarcane plantations created there, a swiftly growing number of African slaves came to the New World throughout the sixteenth century. With increasing frequency, English, Danish, Swedish, and above all Dutch middlemen got involved in the West African slave trade as well. As bitter rivals of the Portuguese and the Spanish, they set up their own outposts along the Gold Coast, concluding friendship treaties and commercial agreements with various local tribes. These agreements stipulated that the leaders of the African coastal states would regularly receive guns, iron, textiles, and liquor. In return, they promised their new European trading partners that they would send warriors deep into the interior of the continent to capture people. In this way, they would pay for the goods they received from Europe not only with gold and ivory but also with freshly kidnapped human beings offered up as slaves.

Starting in the 1620s, many of the enslaved Black Africans given in payment to Dutch traders were shipped to North America. By 1640, nearly 100 Africans lived in New Amsterdam, the capital of New Netherlands. This number represented 30 percent of the total population of the recently founded city. By the time the English captured New Netherlands in 1664 and changed its name to New York, there were 300 Black people living in the burgeoning settlement on the Hudson River. That gave the city of New York the largest slave population of any urban center in North America. At that time, however, most Black people lived on the sweeping plantations of the colony of Virginia. By 1665, English and Dutch slave ships had brought 1,500 Africans to this, the oldest possession of the English Crown on the North American mainland.

The lot of the slaves brought to North America was hard, their living conditions often oppressive and degrading. On the other hand, until the late seventeenth century, those in New York and Virginia could hope to improve their fate by virtue of their own hard work. Many Black slaves were freed after having performed especially harsh labor for a stipulated period of time. They were then allowed to acquire land and even a certain degree of wealth. In certain respects, therefore, African slaves were similar to the indentured servants who emigrated in large numbers from Europe. Such colonists could not afford the trip, so they formed agreements with American plantation owners or craftsmen before leaving Europe, trading a specific number of years of their labor in the New World in return for having their passage paid. They, too, only gained full freedom and the right to their own labor after having fulfilled the oppressive terms of their service.

A surprising number of African slaves trod the onerous yet ultimately liberating path that led through backbreaking work to freedom. Until 1670, one in every three Africans in Virginia was free. By the 1680s, however, fewer and fewer white colonists were arriving as indentured servants. At the same time, tobacco plantations in the southern colonies of North America were expanding in number and size, resulting in a massive labor shortage. In response, the colonial legislatures hastily passed numerous laws barring the way to freedom for African slaves and their offspring. From then on, the children of enslaved Black women irrevocably became lifelong slaves. Slaves had to toil harder and longer in the tobacco regions than ever before. What is more, they were under constant observation and forced to adhere to a gruesome regime. Even Sunday became a normal working day for them. There were only three days of rest per year: Christmas, Easter, and Pentecost.

Simultaneously, the transatlantic slave trade was growing by leaps and bounds. Between 1683 and 1720, more than 20,000 Africans were exported to the colony of Virginia alone. That is about the same number of slaves sent on the dread Middle Passage in the same period from the Brandenburg-Prussian colony of Groß Friedrichsburg. Yet this increase in human trafficking did not go entirely unopposed in the freedom-loving North American colonies. Not unsurprisingly, it was a group of citizens from the Province of Pennsylvania that, eight years after the founding of Philadelphia, publicly protested the now perpetual enslavement of Africans. A petitioned jointly authored by Garret Hendricks, Francis Pastorius, and the brothers Derick and Abraham op den Graef enjoined their fellow citizens to meditate on the following simple words of wisdom: "Here [in Pennsylvania] is liberty of conscience, which is right and reasonable; here ought to be likewise liberty of the body."

Members of the General Assembly in Philadelphia did not initially heed the spirited arguments of these philanthropists. The reason may have been that the elected representatives of the citizens of Pennsylvania—despite their insistence on their own political and religious freedoms—had no intention of ever leveling or dissolving the hierarchies and relationships of dependence that so thoroughly structured their colonial society. For example, none of them considered extending to women, who were utterly dependent on their husbands economically and politically, the same political rights and privileges that were so prized by men.

Furthermore, most young men also had to pass through a phase of broad dependence on older authorities before they could become truly free citizens. For the duration of his apprenticeship, which could last up to nine years, every novice craftsman had to pledge to his master that he would immediately and happily follow his every lawful command, that he would not marry, and that he would not leave service in his house at any time of day or night. Of course, these oppressive conventions and provisions—which existed in exactly the same form in Europe—met time and again with massive resistance in America. The gazettes of the American colonies were full of wanted advertisements printed by husbands, masters, and craftsmen hoping to find their wives, indentured servants, apprentices, or African slaves.

There may have been another reason that the majority of Pennsylvania's white citizens did not view slavery and the slave trade as all that great a scandal: The few hundred Black people living in the colony were mostly put to use as household servants, in which capacity they tended to suffer no appreciably worse treatment than white laborers. Very different was the situation of African slaves in Virginia, where, around 1720, many more than 20,000 of them were forced to perform grueling labor in the fields and tobacco plantations. There, too, the citizens were unwilling to give up their easy access to African slaves. For in Virginia—unlike in Pennsylvania—slavery had become an indispensable foundation of the colony's economic viability. Even if Virginia plantation owners had wanted to do otherwise, sheer economic logic counseled against even considering liberalizing the colony's strict slave laws.

One of the free citizens of Virginia who owned slaves was Augustine Washington. Just as King Frederick William I and his children, Princess Wilhelmine and Crown Prince Frederick, took it for granted that they were served in their palace by African "Moors," as a matter of course this proud and self-confident

Virginia planter sent his Black slaves to work in the fields to harvest a large crop of tobacco, which yielded high profits especially in Europe.

His grandfather John Washington, the son of an Anglican clergyman, had emigrated from England to America in December 1656 out of the sheer love of adventure. He married in Virginia and bought the Bridges Creek Farm in the colony's Westmoreland County. There he planted tobacco and had slaves work the fields. John Washington's oldest son, Lawrence, was born in 1659. He followed in his father's footsteps and even managed to add to the property he inherited. There was nothing remarkable about the fact that his own son, Augustine, born in 1694, continued his father's legacy after the latter's death in 1715. Nor was it strange that Augustine farmed the thousand acres he inherited in Westmoreland County using the labor of slaves, their number reaching as many as sixty-four. That was the way of things in Virginia.

One extraordinary aspect of his life as a planter, of which Augustine Washington and all other property-owning citizens of Virginia were acutely conscious, was their documented right to participate in the administration and government of the colony in concert with officials of the British Crown named in London. Very many forms of dependency were to be found in the fundamentally hierarchical societies of the European states and their American colonies. Therefore, the type of legislative self-government practiced by the landowning citizens of Virginia—which, outside the British North American colonies, existed only in the mother country of England—was a milestone in the history of human liberty. And since a far greater percentage of the population of Virginia had the right to vote than that of Great Britain, a man like Augustine Washington could only revel with pride and gratitude in his privileged position. Only the citizens of Pennsylvania enjoyed greater freedoms than Virginians did.

Augustine Washington put his freedom to use by actively working in government. In this, he followed in his father's and grandfather's footsteps. John Washington had been elected to the Virginia House of Burgesses in 1665. Not even two decades later, in 1683, his son Lawrence became a legislative representative of his fellow citizens. Augustine also had the ambition of becoming part of the Virginia assembly, but the first public office he held, to which he was appointed in 1721, was justice of the peace. In 1727, he was then named sheriff of Westmoreland County by the Virginia governor. In this capacity, he had not only to arrest criminals but also to ensure that legislative elections in his jurisdiction went ahead smoothly and according to the precise procedures outlined by the law. This office earned him a handsome supplementary income.

Yet the sedulous planter and sheriff Augustine Washington was not unduly wealthy. His property was not in the least comparable with the monstrous landholdings that some members of the British high aristocracy received from the monarch. For example, the Scottish peer Thomas Fairfax, sixth Lord Fairfax of Cameron, was recognized by the Crown in 1719 as the owner of an astounding 5,282,000 acres of land, located between the Rappahannock and Potomac Rivers in the direct vicinity of Washington's farm. This truly gigantic transfer of land took place in the reign of King George I, who, as elector of Hanover, ascended the throne upon the death of Queen Anne on August 1, 1714 (as stipulated by the Act of Settlement).

Nevertheless, Augustine Washington was assured of a very good income by his plantations, even if their size was dwarfed by Fairfax's holdings. Accordingly, he was able to enjoy a comfortable lifestyle and a well-organized household, managed to his great satisfaction by his wife, Jane Butler, whom he wed in 1715. Around their new farmhouse, built between 1722 and 1727, the Washingtons planted a sizable vegetable garden amid apple, peach, and cherry trees. They raised maize and wheat in addition to tobacco, and the grain they harvested was ground into flour in their own water mill, erected along a Potomac tributary known as Pope's Creek. Their table was typically set with homemade cornbread, fresh fish, oysters, crispy chicken, and goose. Wild game, which Augustine regularly hunted on his own lands, was also served, either boiled or roasted. Other than fresh water and homemade apple cider, the Washingtons drank a considerable quantity of wine from Madeira and Bordeaux.

Augustine Washington and his wife, Jane, shared this prosperity with their children. Their first son, Butler, who died shortly after birth in 1716, was followed between 1718 and 1722 by Lawrence, Augustine Jr., and Jane. All of these children, both sons and daughter, were required from an early age to perform chores in the house and on the farm. For example, Jane assisted her mother, whereas the boys helped their father fell trees for firewood. The children enjoyed a great deal of freedom, too. They rode horses, drove coaches, and practiced shooting a shotgun. They galivanted at fairs, playing billiards or enjoying rhythmic tunes on the fiddle. And they ran barefoot among the slave huts on the farm down to the riverbank, where they plopped down onto the grass to watch the boats laden with tobacco and other goods sailing over the Potomac, gliding smoothly or struggling depending on the wind. Much to their surprise, the year 1727 witnessed the birth of yet another brother—five years after their mother's last pregnancy—but he would depart this life not all that long after entering it.

For the planter, landowner, father, and freshly minted sheriff Augustine Washington, the summer of 1727 was a time of enhanced personal happiness and increased political responsibilities in the colony of Virginia, with the duties and challenges of a new office accruing to those of justice of the peace. Meanwhile, on the other side of the Atlantic, the Prussian Crown Prince Frederick was himself adapting to a new framework of altered responsibilities. Upon his confirmation, celebrated on April 4, 1727, after a solemn public examination in Berlin Cathedral, he had become a full member of the Reformed congregation. He was now permitted to take communion, as he had proved that he could truly grasp and embrace the Calvinist doctrines he confessed and recited. Incidentally, Frederick's training for his confirmation exam was attended by a strange and highly ironic event. In 1725, his religion teacher, the court chaplain Andreä, was dismissed for defying the wishes of the king and instructing the crown prince in the doctrine of predestination—the fundamental theological dogma of orthodox Calvinism, for which the Pietist Frederick William I felt nothing but fear and loathing.

Having reached his very idiosyncratic religious maturity, Frederick was considered so far advanced on his path to adulthood that his longtime tutelage at the hands of Duhan came to an end in the summer of 1727. From then on, his sole education consisted in military training under the long-serving Major Johann Wilhelm Senning. And his sole occupation was to command a battalion of Potsdam Grenadiers. Ideally, he would perform his duty so satisfactorily that his father could promote him with lightning speed to the rank of a Prussian lieutenant colonel, paving the way for a career of military glory and martial honor. Yet the plan was for Frederick to become not only a courageous strategist but also an upright officer. Accordingly, soon after Duhan's discharge, King Frederick William I engaged two veterans from Brandenburg as military companions for the crown prince: Friedrich Wilhelm von Rochow, a salt-of-the-earth lieutenant colonel from Brandenburg, and Dietrich von Keyserlingk, an urbane captain, steeped in philosophy and mathematics, from the Baltic region of Courland (now part of Latvia).

Being a full member of the Calvinist congregation and a high-ranking officer in the Prussian army did not, however, mean that the fifteen-year-old crown prince now suddenly felt freer and more independent than in his childhood and early youth. In the presence of Ulrich Friedrich von Suhm, an ambassador from Saxony in whom he confided with remarkable candor, he complained of the abhorrent slavery to which his father continued to subject him after his confirmation. The latter kept him under nearly constant observation day and night, and he prescribed his activities down to the smallest detail. More than ever, Frederick yearned for more autonomy, for just a little freedom.

Indeed, Frederick William I continued to be the absolute dictator of his oldest son's education and daily regimen. He constantly altered, augmented, and improved the fastidious schedule that the crown prince was required to follow without the least deviation. Again and again, the king even arbitrarily countermanded his own orders when they no longer seemed opportune to him. For example, he consented to Frederick's taking music lessons from the violinist and cathedral cantor Gottlieb Heyne. After first learning the correct use of chords, Frederick received instruction in simple basso continuo accompaniment and finally even studied formal composition. The king also allowed Frederick to learn to play the flute, which the musically gifted student soon mastered with great virtuosity. However, when the crown prince seemed overly distracted from all his other duties by his patently growing passion for music, Frederick William I strictly forbade him to continue pursuing it.

The crown prince was a very quick study. As one visitor to the royal court in Berlin observed, he was basically able to "grasp everything shown to him with the greatest of ease," such that he inspired the highest hopes. Nevertheless, he approached the educational program punctiliously designed by his father with little eagerness to learn any of it quickly or avidly. Indeed, in January 1727, only a few weeks before Frederick's confirmation, Colonel Kalckstein was forced to report to the king that the crown prince had profited little in the last eight months from the religious instruction provided by the court chaplain Noltenius. In response, the furious monarch ordered the weekly hours of catechism to be doubled.

Frederick's older sister Wilhelmine suffered similarly degrading micromanagement at the hands of their strict father, and she understood her brother's resistance to formal education all too well. Nevertheless, she urged the crown prince to improve himself. Having always had "the deepest affection for him," as she said, she felt called upon to at least encourage him to read good literature. And she was successful. Later, Frederick admitted that as a boy he had indeed wanted to do nothing during his lessons. "Then my sister [Wilhelmine], . . . seeing that I never sought to occupy myself and to read, that I only loved to gad about, she said to me one day, 'But, my dear brother, are you not ashamed to be gadding about? I never see you with a book in your hand. You neglect your talents.'" Clearly moved by these words, the boy began devouring books just because she recommended it. This enthusiasm grew over time, especially for novels.

One of his favorite books was the utopian bildungsroman *The Adventures of Telemachus, Son of Ulysses*, which François de La Mothe-Fénelon, archbishop of Cambrai, had written in 1695 for the grandson of King Louis XIV of France. In the novel, during his father's absence, Telemachus is taken on a long journey through various states by his tutor Mentor, who teaches him about their good and bad political systems. On the way, the two travelers must undergo many adventures. It turns out that Mentor is actually Minerva, the patron goddess of poets and the guardian of all knowledge, in disguise. It is with the help of her abilities that Telemachus ultimately overcomes all dangers. The novel also contains a coded critique of Louis XIV's authoritarian style of rule, for which the king did not forgive Fénelon. Indeed, the archbishop was forced to renounce his honorable office as tutor to the French prince after the book's publication. The crown prince of Prussia, however, was endlessly delighted by the élan, courage, longing for knowledge, and magnanimity exhibited by the fictional hero, with whom he wholeheartedly identified.

What is more, *The Adventures of Telemachus* spurred him on to read more and more novels. When his father discovered that he was spending time reading books that were not part of the official curriculum, the king explicitly forbade the illicit pursuit. Yet Frederick refused to renounce the ideal world of literature of which he had grown so fond; defiantly, he kept reading in secret. Many years later, he recalled the stratagem he commonly employed: "When my governor Marshal Finck and my valet were sleeping, I stepped over my valet's bed, and gently, most gently, I went into another room, where, near the fireplace, there was a night-light. Crouched over this lamp, I read."

To Frederick's gratification, he also received discreet assistance from his mother, Queen Sophia Dorothea. During his regular visits to Monbijou Palace, which was located on the northern bank of the Spree, in view of the City Palace, and which had served the Prussian queen as a summer residence since 1712, he was permitted to make free and liberal use of her excellent library. After the births of Princess Wilhelmine and Crown Prince Frederick, Sophia Dorothea bore her husband nine further children, the last in 1727, of which seven survived. She was clearly docile in the performance of her expected spousal duties. In other respects, however, she had little to do with her husband, whose decidedly coarse manner of life she rejected. At least within the confines of Monbijou Palace, she was determined to provide her children with a foil for the king's court, a safe space for subtlety of feeling and the enjoyment of art.

Duhan, who remained devoted to his former student, also fostered Frederick's hidden love of literature. In a house rented near the palace, he assembled a private library stocked with French translations of the major works of the great ancient writers Homer, Herodotus, Thucydides, Plutarch, Vergil, Ovid, Horace, and Cicero. With extraordinary artifice, the crown prince now led a double life. During the day, he did the bare minimum to fulfill his father's expectations, so that in the evening or at night he could find time to read without raising suspicion. He played the dutiful heir to the throne for the king, all the while secretly living the life of an aesthete with musical and literary ambitions. Giving voice to this essential core of his schizophrenic existence, in a letter to his beloved sister Wilhelmine, written only a few months after his confirmation, he signed himself "Frédéric le philosophe."

The more Frederick playacted for his father, the less he managed to convince the instinctively mistrustful king of his obedience, which was not always successfully feigned. Frederick William I regularly thought he glimpsed a conceited haughtiness or rustic pride in his oldest son's face that irritated and nauseated him. Once he confronted him about it violently in the presence of Minister Friedrich Wilhelm von Grumbkow. "I want to know what's going on in that tiny head of yours," the king said, repeatedly tapping Frederick provocatively on the brow. He then dressed him down: "I know you don't think like I do, and that there are people who plant contrary ideas in you and induce you to criticize everything. But they are scamps!" Now in a rage, the king accompanied these words with a fury of slaps to the prince's face. These became more and more aggressive as the king's sudden outrage swelled, ultimately raining down in a barrage of full-scale blows.

To such acts of violence and all other public castigations, which now became more and more common, the humiliated Frederick reacted with outer resignation and inner, quiet contempt. He made absolutely no attempt to defend himself, but that only provoked greater rage in his father. The crown prince's lack of resistance, which could have been seen equally well as an attitude of moral superiority, was interpreted by his father as an inexcusable failure of nerve. In his son's contorted, oddly grimacing face, he espied a soft, womanly weepiness. Accordingly, in one personal letter he belittled him as an "effeminate fellow," accusing him of being unable "to either ride or shoot" properly, of styling "his hair like a buffoon," and of wanting "to do nothing but follow his own mind."

Contrary to his father's recriminations, Frederick lacked neither courage nor grit. His extremely defiant behavior testified to a vast wealth of fortitude. On the other hand, he preferred to don a modish gold brocade dressing gown instead of the traditional Prussian military coat, which he contemptuously called a *Sterbekittel* (shroud). This, his favorite piece of clothing, which he wore like a second skin, was such a thorn in the king's side that the latter unceremoniously threw it in the fire one day. It instantly went up in flames. It was a symbolic act, as if the punitive monarch had sought to destroy Frederick himself, or at least to purify the spirit of his stubborn son in a purgatorial fire. This ghastly, ghoulish act intimated the horrors of which the autocratic monarch would one day be capable.

In light of the paternal humiliations perpetrated by the king and the puerile defiance persistently demonstrated by Frederick, it was almost inevitable that the two would develop a piercing mutual animosity toward one another. In a plaintive petition to his ruthless father, Frederick begged him to finally soften or suppress his gruesome loathing. Yet, as the French ambassador Konrad Alexander von Rothenbourg wrote to the court of Versailles, the Prussian crown prince possessed an equally boundless hatred for his father: "Il hait son père souverainement." As the situation came to an ever more drastic and ominous crescendo, the only remedy was ultimately for father and son to get as far away from one another as possible.

Frederick would have been content with being allowed to take a long tour of Europe with one of his governors. Italy was one of the places he longed to see most. And after all, as a twelve-year-old boy, even his strict father had been given generous permission by King Frederick I to spend several months in Holland as part of an educational trip. But Frederick William I prohibited the crown prince from taking journeys of that kind, if only because he did not trust him sufficiently. At most, Frederick was permitted to accompany his father and the Prussian high command on inspection tours of Brandenburg-Prussian territory between the Rhine and Weser Rivers. To his dismay, he always found himself under the thumb of the king on such occasions. Shorter trips in the vicinity of Berlin were much more common. Especially in the hotter months, the entire family would drive through the city gates and head south to nearby Königs Wusterhausen Palace, one of the king's favorite spots in summer. But even in Königs Wusterhausen, in whose expansive surrounding forests

Frederick William I could go hunting to his heart's content, the crown prince spent many hours of the day in the oppressive company of his father.

In the late summer of 1727, Gotthilf August Francke, the son of the recently deceased Halle professor August Hermann Francke, paid a visit to Königs Wusterhausen. Noticing the crown prince's conspicuously melancholic character, he spoke of it immediately to the king. In his view, the laconic Frederick was a "very sensitive soul." In response, the king complained quite openly to Francke that his oldest son's conduct was utterly reprehensible. Indeed, it was the opposite of the irreproachable behavior of his five-year-old brother, the perfectly obedient Augustus William. In a letter written at the end of August 1727 to an officer who had remained behind in Potsdam, Frederick echoed Francke's observations. He desperately needed "cheering up" in Königs Wusterhausen, he wrote, "to drive away my melancholy." At the same time, he crowed defiantly that he always chose to sit in the tree stand when it was time to go hunting, an activity that bored him. At least in that secluded place he could remain unobserved for a stretch. Once ensconced there, Frederick would pull a book from his pocket and read, while the hunting party would wonder why he hadn't shot anything. He likewise mocked his father's evening smoking ritual. "While the others smoke," Frederick remarked, "I entertain myself by cracking nuts." The performance was fit for the stage, so to speak, as it was a tried-and-true way to annoy the king and his friends.

Frederick did finally undertake one longer journey, which stood in brilliant contrast to the otherwise depressing humdrum of his everyday life. At the invitation of the king of Poland, the Prussian court spent January and February 1728 in Dresden, the capital of the Electorate of Saxony. Augustus II, elector of Saxony and king of Poland, known as "the Strong," entertained his guests with the rare pleasure of an intricate procession of parties, plays, and concerts. Nor did he neglect to present to them the loveliest ladies of his court. Frederick fell under the spell of a bewitchingly beautiful daughter of Augustus the Strong: the twenty-one-year-old Anna Karolina, the product of an extramarital affair between the king and a French wine trader from Warsaw named Henriette Rénard. To provide Anna Karolina with a life befitting her paternity, Augustus gave her a title of Polish nobility: Countess Orzelska. Frederick requested a portrait of the beguiling countess, which was promptly made at the behest of Augustus II by his court painter Louis de Silvestre. The picture arrived in Berlin in November 1728.

It was, however, not Frederick but his mother, Sophia Dorothea, who officially received the portrait. The Prussian queen, vigilantly on the lookout for a suitable wife for her son ever since his confirmation, kept track of his amorous infatuations. Yet she was not interested in a union between Saxony and Prussia. It was, instead, a Prussian-British double wedding that she sought to arrange. Her older brother George Augustus had ascended the British throne as King George II upon the death of their father, George I, in June 1727. Ever since, Sophia Dorothea had thought the time was ripe to fix two engagements: one between the Prussian crown prince and the English Princess Amelia, and the other between the Prince of Wales and Princess Wilhelmine. Even King Frederick William I was long receptive to the idea. Amelia, whom her parents called Emily, also warmed to the planned marriage with her cousin in Berlin, and she requested a portrait of Frederick. The plan was to provide Emily and Fritz with their own court in Hanover after their wedding, and to place them in charge of the Electorate of Hanover until Frederick took the Prussian throne.

It was an alluring prospect for Frederick. Marrying Emily would have meant finally escaping the permanent micromanagement and mistreatment he suffered at the hands of his father. Yet the marriage negotiations proceeded sluggishly all through 1729. By the early summer of 1730, George II and his advisers had still not reached a definitive decision, although Frederick had pledged to his uncle George in writing that winter that he would wed no woman but Amelia. On July 10, 1730, the Prussian king lost his temper. He had long considered his brother-in-law from the House of Hanover to be too proud. Now he summoned the British ambassadors Sir Charles Hotham and Melchior Guy Dickens and told them with regard to the prospective wedding, "Gentlemen, I've had enough of this stuff!" Offended, Hotham abruptly departed, and with that all talk of marriage ended.

Frederick was aghast. He had been robbed of his only hope of soon improving his situation, and, to make matters worse, he continued to be beaten and castigated publicly by his father. He confided to his sister that he was now so tired of the king's outrageous outbursts of violence and repugnant behavior that he would rather beg for his bread abroad than continue living like this. So he decided to escape Brandenburg-Prussia, cross through France, and go into exile in England. The English ambassador Dickens, to whom Frederick communicated his audacious plans, warned him not to make a hasty decision. He assured the crown prince that he would find no little sympathy in England, but that fleeing the Prussian court would have unforeseen political consequences. But Frederick would not be deterred. His resolve was unshakable. All he had to do now was find the right moment to put his plan into action.

To his great surprise, that moment seemed to come only a few days later. On July 15, Frederick William I departed on a journey around the Holy Roman Empire. On his sweeping tour, the king intended to visit the courts of Electoral Palatinate and the Electorate of Cologne, in Mannheim and Bonn, respectively. He spontaneously decided that his oldest son should accompany him on this expedition. Shortly before departing, Frederick discussed his escape plan with the young officers Hans Hermann von Katte and Peter Christoph Carl von Keith, both of whom had become close confidants in recent years. He asked them to accompany him to England, helping him find suitable routes and stopping points on the way through France. Katte initially stayed behind in Berlin to develop further contacts for their conspiracy. Keith, however, was unexpectedly transferred by the king to Wesel, on account of which his younger brother now had to accompany the crown prince on the journey to southwestern Germany. With no other choice, the younger Keith was now initiated into the escape plan.

On the way to Mannheim, the king had the Prussian entourage stop to view a few attractions of exceptional historical importance for the Empire, such as the imperial regalia in Nuremberg and the site of the Battle of Höchstadt, fought during the War of the Spanish Succession. Only afterward was the king of Prussia and elector of Brandenburg ready and willing to meet with the elector palatine. On the night before the last stage of the journey to Mannheim, the travelers crossed the Neckar River and took lodgings in the town of Steinsfurt, near Sinsheim. From there, the Rhine—and thus the German-French border—was only a few hours away at a swift gallop.

Frederick had to act. He ordered Keith to appear outside his quarters with two saddled horses at three o'clock in the morning on August 5. But when the crown prince rose and went out onto the street at the appointed time, his path was suddenly blocked by his companion Rochow, who had seen Frederick getting dressed. Thinking quickly, Frederick made excuses that reassured his suspicious chaperone, but he had to postpone the ride to France. Both men went back to sleep. Before doing so, however, the impeded escapee ordered Keith to have stage horses ready in Mannheim.

This time, Keith did not obey his young master. After arriving in Mannheim, he had such pangs of conscience that he sought out the king, fell at his feet, begged for mercy, and betrayed Frederick's plan. Fuming with wrath, Frederick William I ordered a detailed investigation that brought the intentions of Frederick and his accomplices to light in full detail. The older Keith, warned in time, abandoned Wesel and made for England. Frederick and Katte, however, were immediately taken into custody. The king personally interrogated his insubordinate son. He told him to his face that he plainly considered the escape attempt to be tantamount to "plotting desertion," and that it must be punished accordingly. Frederick William I also informed Queen Sophia Dorothea in writing that their eldest son had tried to desert.

In his assessment of what had happened at Steinsfurt, it was decisive that the king considered the design to flee to England not as an intended but as an actual desertion. Under Prussian military law, desertion was an extremely grave crime, potentially punishable by death. The Prussian king's wrath was boundless, extending even to those confederates of Frederick who had been ignorant of the plan but who had offered him active support in other illicit activities in the previous years. Sophia Dorothea was prohibited from any and all contact with her son. Princess Wilhelmine had her freedom of movement severely curtailed. And Frederick's former tutor Duhan, along with the Berlin bookdealer Ambrosius Haude—who had stocked the crown prince's secret library—was banished to Memel (now Klaipėda, Lithuania) without his pension. Frederick's library, which had grown to 3,775 volumes, was sent to Hamburg and then on to Holland, where it was auctioned off.

The fates of Frederick and Katte were to be decided by a court-martial presided over by the seventy-one-year-old Lieutenant General Achaz von der Schulenburg. Frederick William I was ready to reduce the sentence he passed, expecting it to be severe. But when, to his astonishment, the court insisted that "no deed had been done or actual escape attempted," and thus that the death penalty was out of the question, the king decided to intervene on the side of severity. As the absolute sovereign and thus, as he saw it, the source of all law in Prussia, he ignored the judgment of the high court and instead ordered Katte to be executed. He also held out the prospect of death for his son. Directly after the initial interrogations, which had taken place on the Rhine, the king had transferred Frederick to the massive hexagonal, red-brick fortress of Küstrin (now Kostrzyn, Poland) on the Oder River. Since then, Frederick had spent his days in solitary confinement in the moldy dungeon, enduring hours on end in the dark. Although still ignorant of Katte's sentence, Frederick clearly felt that his own life was in danger. Now, after so many years of arrogance and defiance, he begged contritely to be "informed in good time" should his beheading be ordered, so that he could prepare himself for death.

In England, these events were received with disbelief. All British observers were left nearly speechless—and not only due to the severity of the penalty, but especially because of the despotic arbitrariness with which Frederick

William I had disregarded the sentence of the court. Indeed, their own constitutional tradition had great respect for the verdicts of an independent judiciary. Now they knew what it meant when the will of the sovereign alone was the law in his state. They shivered at the Prussian monarch's mean-spiritedness. And they glimpsed a sinister, deeply disturbing streak in the nature of the Kingdom of Prussia and its political system.

Katte was executed on November 6, 1730, in Küstrin. The king, wanting to set a powerful pedagogical example, required Frederick to witness the deliberately staged decapitation of his friend. He hoped this would finally "cause him to do some serious thinking." Yet the blindsided crown prince had no time to reflect. Informed about the ruthless sentence only a few hours before Katte's killing, he seemed rather to go into a terrible state of shock. He screamed, wept, begged for Katte to be shown mercy. In vain. Frederick's friend was beheaded before his eyes. After the bodily tortures of his degrading imprisonment, and now with this further psychological torment, all the crown prince could do was collapse unconscious. Frederick had terrible nightmares and fever dreams for days after Katte's execution. The king was informed of his son's pitiable state, but he himself was deeply satisfied. He may have had to resort to violence, but he had finally earned the "respect" that the crown prince had always denied him. Frederick's haughty soul, against which his father had fought in vain for so many years, was deeply wounded. The reprehensible pride that the king had sought to conquer was likely broken forever.

And so, only two days after the execution, the mollified monarch released his son from his harsh captivity. By the end of November, Frederick was allowed to move into a house in the city of Küstrin, although he was still under house arrest there. He was to spend the entire year of 1731 in a bare room in the Küstrin War and Interior Office, devoting his energies to mastering the administrative duties of Prussian state officials. He assumed the role of an auditor, monitoring and keeping accounts pertaining to the draining of swamps, the collection of rents, and the surveying of land. Reading French literature and playing the flute were strictly forbidden. Furthermore, he was only permitted to read and write in German, not in the French language he loved so dearly. The crown prince complied with all orders and provided his father with regular reports about his activities as a civil servant.

On August 15, his forty-third birthday, Frederick William I personally went to Küstrin to pay his son a visit, after avoiding him for an entire year. Again, he appealed to Frederick's conscience. He expressed the hope that the severe punishment had killed off his oldest son's insolent obstinacy once and for all.

Frederick was under terrible strain, and these words were more than he could bear during the reunion. Sobbing and trembling, he fell at his father's feet. Interpreting this renewed collapse as a sign of voluntary submission, the king drew his son to him, embraced him, and solemnly pledged his forgiveness. As a sign of his clemency, he permitted Frederick to leave Küstrin on the weekends so that he could go on excursions in the outlying areas.

Frederick was not fully rehabilitated, however, until he agreed unconditionally to a marriage arranged for him by the king. The crown prince was to wed not an aesthetically minded, mercurial princess from England but rather the stuffy Lutheran Princess Elisabeth Christine of Brunswick-Wolfenbüttel-Bevern. She was a niece of the wife of the same name of Holy Roman Emperor Charles VI, who had been elected in 1711. The bride selected by the king would ensure enduring close ties to the imperial court in Vienna—clearly more important to Frederick William I than a tightly knit familial relationship with the British royal house. The Prussian king advertised to his son one further virtue of the Brunswick princess from the House of Bevern: She was "neither pretty nor ugly."

After a flurry of letters exchanged with his father, Frederick realized no later than the beginning of the following year that he would have to defer to the king in the matter of marriage as well. He had no other choice. As he remarked, marrying Elisabeth Christine, whom he had not even met, was "the price to be paid" for having his own court, and thus for breaking free of his father's overbearing control. On February 22, 1732, at the end of a long winter, he informed Frederick William I that their interests were now aligned in the matter of marriage. The letter achieved its purpose. Frederick was allowed to leave frosty, snow-covered Küstrin and return to Berlin. For him, it meant a return to life, a radical transformation, and a new beginning.

5

Education and Leisure
(1732–1740)

IT WAS on the afternoon of February 22, 1732, that Crown Prince Frederick informed his father that he would accede to his wishes and marry Elisabeth Christine of Brunswick-Wolfenbüttel-Bevern—the inescapable price for returning to normal life after spending a year of unhappiness and deprivation in Küstrin. At roughly the same moment, several thousand miles away in Virginia, where the dawn was just beginning to break, yet another son was born to the planter and sheriff Augustine Washington. It had been ten years since the birth of Augustine's youngest daughter, Jane. Eight weeks later, on April 16, the healthy, stout boy was baptized at home in the presence of the nearest neighbors. The minister had been called to the house to perform the ceremony, as the closest church was much too far from Pope's Creek Farm for a newborn to make the journey. He took the baby in his arms and solemnly spoke the words of the old Anglican rite, "Name this child." And the godparents answered according to the parents' wishes: George.

Young George Washington's entry into this world, and into the Anglican Church, was recorded by his parents in clear handwriting in the family Bible, along with the precise hour of his birth. Sadly, this joyous beginning of a new life was preceded by a major family tragedy. In the mid-1720s, George's father, Augustine, had found iron ore while digging on his property. He decided to mine it, smelt it in his own furnaces, and export it to Great Britain. In order to reach a mutually beneficial agreement with his trading partners across the Atlantic, he had even sailed to England in the summer of 1729. While in the mother country, he also intended to visit relatives of his father, as well as to get an impression of living conditions in Europe and how they compared with those in America. He accomplished a great deal during his lengthy stay in

Great Britain. But when he returned to Pope's Creek Farm on May 26, 1730, after nearly a year away, bitter news awaited him: His beloved wife, Jane, had died the previous November 24.

The widower was deeply saddened, but despite his sorrow he did not give himself much time to mourn. Not wanting his three children to be raised solely by slaves, he had to look for a new wife. In this he was not unlike many men of his age, who sought to remarry only a few months after their wives died—not out of coldness of heart, but purely for economic and family reasons. A sizable farm could not be successfully managed without a woman in charge, nor could a household with many children flourish without the care of a mother. Thus, by the end of 1730, Augustine Washington was on the lookout for a suitable wife. He chose twenty-three-year-old Mary Ball, a short, round neighbor blessed with a beautiful voice, and she received his sincere courtship gladly.

The daughter of Joseph Ball, a plantation owner who had immigrated to Virginia from England in the 1670s, Mary was orphaned early. By the age of twelve, she had lost both her father and her mother. In 1721, she moved to the estate of her attentive guardian George Eskridge, where she grew up. Eskridge, a distant relative of her mother, lived in Sandy Point, located only twenty miles from Washington's plantations. It, too, was situated along the western bank of the Potomac, near the mouth of the Yeocomico River. The distant neighbor and his family were well known to Sheriff Washington. Eskridge was not only a successful farmer but also a brilliant lawyer with a lengthy list of clients, and he had represented Westmoreland County in the House of Burgesses for several legislative sessions. Eskridge respected Sheriff Washington, and he had no objections to the latter's marrying his ward Mary Ball. The wedding took place on George Eskridge's estate in March 1731. And when her first son was born in February 1732, it was clear to the grateful Mary Ball Washington that the baby would be named after her faithful and dutiful guardian. Thus, on the day of his baptism in his parents' home, George Washington received the name of a distinguished Virginia legislator.

Of course, young George had no inkling as of yet just how important the House of Burgesses was for the life of the free planters and citizens settled in Virginia. He was still perfectly ignorant of British North America's hundred-year-old legislative tradition. Nor did he know anything of Philadelphia, the fastest-growing city in all the British colonies, which already boasted more than 8,000 residents and continued to welcome a steady stream of new arrivals from Europe. Like his older siblings, George Washington came of age in an isolated, rural world that seemed designed for the carefree, unrestricted play of small children. He was surrounded by chickens to tease and dogs to romp through the countryside with. Day in, day out, he observed the pigs, heifers, and cows, delighting in their grunting and mooing. From time to time, he was even allowed to ride a horse, his father poised protectively behind him in the saddle, holding him tight.

This father, who had already conscientiously raised two young boys—Lawrence, now fifteen, and Augustine Jr., now thirteen—cared for George with a kindness that was obvious even to neighbors. They, too, respected the six-foot-tall, athletic planter. He was known as an upright sheriff who had learned to maintain the civic, legislative order of their community because of his "kindly nature." Clearly, Virginians believed this friendliness to be a necessary quality for living justly and according to the law, whether as a public official or as the head of a family. Augustine's abiding kindness was also a joy to his new wife, Mary, who bore him a second child in June 1733, a little over a year after George's birth: a daughter named Elizabeth, whom they called Betty. Like her brother George, Betty Washington was born into a family full of children who enjoyed peace and stability thanks to the good marriage of their parents.

The same month Betty Washington was born, a wedding was celebrated in the heart of the Holy Roman Empire, in the Duchy of Brunswick-Wolfenbüttel. According to the gloomy prediction of the groom, Prussian Crown Prince Frederick, it was doomed to unhappiness. As arranged by his father, Frederick William I, he and Princess Elisabeth Christine were married on June 12, 1733. The location she chose for the ceremony was Salzdahlum Palace, located only a few miles north of the city of her birth, Wolfenbüttel. The magnificent Baroque structure was built between 1688 and 1694 during the reign of her great-grandfather, Duke Anton Ulrich of Brunswick-Wolfenbüttel, to resemble a smaller version of Versailles. While the bride joyfully helped to plan the opulent and solemn festivities attending her wedding, Frederick resigned himself glumly to the inevitable. Elisabeth Christine's father, Ferdinand Albert II of the House of Brunswick-Bevern, had asked her in early 1732 if she was interested in marrying the Prussian prince, to which she blushingly responded in the affirmative. Frederick, in contrast, as he bitterly and vigorously reminded Minister Friedrich Wilhelm von Grumbkow, had been given an ultimatum: He had to marry the girl within a year's time "whether I liked it or not." The wedding was thus nothing but "the price to be paid" for freedom that had been so painfully extorted from him in Küstrin. If anyone, forgetting this fact, were foolish enough to think the ceremony at Salzdahlum had anything to do with love, they should be forcibly reminded of a hard and fast truth: "Violence is ever at odds with love, and love cannot be won by force."

And yet, Frederick had to admit that he had no animus toward the princess. As he remarked to Friedrich Heinrich von Seckendorff, the imperial ambassador to Berlin, he bore her no ill will. He met Elisabeth Christine for the first time shortly after returning from Küstrin, when her family came to visit the Prussian court. He could not deny that the princess was "pretty," with "fine features and a handsome face." He also observed that she had an extremely good heart, although she could at times be much too shy, appeared clumsy and awkward, and occasionally emitted a goofy laugh. One could certainly make a worthy, pleasant, and attractive consort out of her, he pointed out. Nevertheless, Frederick held fast to his initial conviction, emphasizing that he would never be able to love Elisabeth Christine. But that did not matter to him. The marriage served primarily to liberate him from his father and finally let him preside over his own court and household. His last word in the matter was therefore clear and unequivocal: "Marriage will make me independent," Frederick wrote to Grumbkow, and "once I am, I will be sovereign in my own house." He closed the letter with a triumphant flourish: "Long live freedom!"

Despite internally distancing himself from the nuptials, the master of disguise made every effort to put on a good face for the wedding guests. Frederick therefore ironically referred to his marriage, which he did not personally take all that seriously, as "the Brunswick comedy." Fittingly, the evening before the ceremony, he was given the role of a lovesick shepherd in a play put on by the court, and he received great praise for his performance from all sides. Reinforcing his sense of acting a part in a production, the whole of Salzdahlum Palace seemed to him like one giant unreal stage for the farce of his own wedding, for it only pretended to be a mighty Baroque stone structure; in reality, the palace was a half-timber construction with a plaster veneer.

Nonetheless, Frederick participated with gusto in the banquet following the ceremony. After the twenty-one-year-old prince had wed Elisabeth Christine—four years his junior but much taller than him—the bride and groom and their assembled guests ate their fill from golden plates piled high with roast veal, venison stew, lobster, crab, trout, and salmon. As the bill for the fancy food was being footed not by the frugal and unrefined Prussian king but rather by the munificent father of the bride, Ferdinand Albert II, the hearty eaters at the head tables raved about the generously portioned culinary delights. The hosts also provided the feasting revelers with musical entertainment. There was a performance of George Frideric Handel's *Partenope*, a beautiful, humorous opera composed in 1730 that revolves around two princes' competition for the favor of the queen of Naples. Ferdinand Albert II also satisfied the Prussian king's preference for military over musical entertainment, staging a military parade by the Brunswick Guard. On June 16, the wedding guests assembled for the premiere of the opera *Lo specchio della fidelità* (The Mirror of Fidelity), by the Brunswick court singer and second Kapellmeister Carl Heinrich Graun. This comedy in song made an even bigger impression on the highly musical Frederick than had Handel's *Partenope*. After the performance, the entire Brandenburg-Prussian court set off on the return journey to Berlin.

After arriving in the capital on the Spree, the newlyweds first moved into a former government building across from the armory (*Zeughaus*) on the boulevard Unter den Linden, remodeled only a short time before as the Crown Prince's Palace (*Kronprinzenpalais*). But Frederick did not intend to live permanently in this new royal residence in Berlin. As he had stressed often enough, marriage provided him with the opportunity he had long yearned for to set up his own court wherever he chose. As now emerged, it was to be located in an isolated place, as far from the noisy streets of Berlin as possible—a considerable distance, too, from the palaces in Potsdam, Köpenick, and Königs Wusterhausen and above all from the physical presence of his father, who continued to instill in him feelings of disquiet.

In September 1732, only a few months after entering into matrimony with Elisabeth Christine, Frederick firmly entreated the king to buy Rheinsberg Palace for him as a wedding gift. It was located far north of Berlin, in a broad forest and lake district on the border with the Duchy of Mecklenburg-Strelitz. There, two days' journey from the Brandenburg-Prussian capital, on the southern end of a rush-bound lake called Grienericksee right near the mouth of the Rhin River, is where he wanted to live with his wife and set up their court. On the condition that at least one-third of the sale price of 75,000 thalers be paid for out of the princess's dowry, Frederick's father agreed to his resolute request.

After everything he had demanded of his son since 1730, King Frederick William I bluntly confessed that it would be necessary for the crown prince's court to be located very far away from his own—and remain strictly financially independent of it as well—if the formal reconciliation they had enjoyed since 1732 was to be maintained. He even tried to see a positive side to Frederick's planned departure, musing that they would now never get bored of one another. After extensive negotiations with the Huguenot owner of Rheinsberg Palace, Colonel Benjamin Chevenix de Beville, the king finally purchased the remote estate in the fall of 1733. At the same time, he commissioned his court architect Johann Gottfried Kemmeter to expand Frederick's new home, as economically as possible, into a residence befitting the young couple's rank.

As long as Rheinsberg was a construction site, with dilapidated walls being torn down and new ones laboriously put up, the crown prince and his wife could not live in the palace. Yet Frederick was unwilling to remain for an indeterminate length of time in Berlin, in the immediate vicinity of his father, under any circumstances. Therefore, only two weeks after the wedding, he moved to the garrison town of Ruppin am Rhinsee (now Neuruppin), close to Rheinsberg. It was the headquarters of an infantry regiment whose command he had been given upon being released from the Küstrin War and Interior Office as a fully rehabilitated lieutenant colonel. This "Crown Prince's Regiment" was composed of individual companies that, up until 1732, had been stationed in various smaller towns in Prignitz and Havelland. When the unit was founded, the king also created a place for Frederick to stay in Ruppin, joining two houses to form a kind of modest princely residence at the base of the town ramparts. This apartment, initially intended as Frederick's quarters when regularly visiting his troops, he now turned into a temporary home.

Elisabeth Christine was left behind in Berlin. On the one hand, even had he wanted her to accompany him, there was no way to create a comfortable lodging for her in his Ruppin officer's quarters, to say nothing of finding room for her court ladies or even the bare minimum of furniture she required. On the other hand, he felt absolutely no desire to have his arranged bride at his side at all times. Elisabeth Christine silently obeyed his wishes, although she was not happy about his decision. For she felt sincere and deep sympathy—indeed even love—for the man who would not and could not love her back. Frederick knew very well that his young wife was pained by her forced separation from him, but he disavowed all responsibility for her emotional state. It was his father and his closest advisers, he reasoned, who had pressed him to marry the princess from Brunswick. Therefore, it was not he but the king and his ministers who should be plagued by deep sorrow if his wife now found herself in the unhappiest marriage in the world.

Frederick William I, however, was not concerned in the least for his daughter-in-law's well-being when his son moved out to Ruppin. On the contrary, he was pleased that the crown prince now suddenly appeared willing—and content—to fulfill his military duties as regimental commander. Indeed, in the first letters he sent from Ruppin to Berlin, Frederick described a soldierly existence that sounded all-consuming, physically demanding, and happy. "I have just come from drilling, I am drilling now, I will drill later. That's all the news I have to report." And, "I would rather drill here from dawn till dusk than live like a rich man in Berlin." Although these reports pleased the king, they in no way provided a full picture of Frederick's daily routine in Ruppin.

Naturally, the crown prince had to perform his duties as lieutenant colonel in order to justify his long stay in Ruppin to the king and his court. And naturally, that meant that Frederick spent a large portion of his day drilling soldiers. He did not do it because he loved it, however, but rather out of necessity and not for one minute longer than necessary. Much more important to him was his time off-duty in Ruppin, in which, as he wrote to Grumbkow, he diverted himself "with reading and music." Every evening, he sat together with his devoted officers at a well-set table, eating fish and oysters from Hamburg and engaged in buoyant, leisurely conversation bubbling with wit. His greatest ambition, however, was to create a cloistered park in Ruppin where he could spend time alone, reading and thinking.

To this end, he had a small gate installed in the town walls to which he alone had access. This allowed him to escape from his quarters quickly and at any time, even at night, under the light of the moon, to a section of the ramparts that was surrounded by old elm, oak, beech, and hazel trees. As Bernhard Feldmann, a chronicler from Ruppin, recorded, Frederick had this secluded section of the ramparts planted with various kinds of trees and, at one end (near the Berlin Gate), adorned with a beautiful garden. This made the rampart a very pleasant, shady promenade full of nightingales. In the garden, Frederick himself raised melons, grapes, and cherries, which he proudly served to his officers in the evening. "God knows," Frederick wrote in a letter bound for Berlin from his idyllic park in Ruppin, "that I am as secluded at present as one can possibly be."

In Ruppin, he enjoyed peace, serenity, and a paradisical, oasis-like seclusion unlike anything he had ever known or had the power to create before. These conditions gave him ample time to reflect on the fear and anxiety he had felt in Küstrin and the effect the experience had had on him. The Prussian crown prince was thoroughly traumatized. He still had nightmares—not every night, but regularly. For that reason, his father had had the gallows for deserters removed from the Ruppin town square before Frederick took command of the

Crown Prince's Regiment. This spared Frederick a sight that would have devastated him, reminding him of his own and Katte's condemnation. Frederick
William I may have ordered Katte's execution, but this gesture, like the purchase of Rheinsberg Palace, clearly showed that he now sought to be mindful
of his son's sensitive nature. Nevertheless, in Frederick's eyes he remained a
horrible man whom, in order to protect himself, he had to avoid as much as
humanly possible.

On the other hand, Frederick ultimately came to the conclusion that, in a
higher sense, his father was not to be held responsible for the pain he had
caused him. The king was himself subject to a loftier power. While still imprisoned in Küstrin, Frederick had confessed to the Lutheran chaplain Johann
Ernst Müller that he believed in the doctrine of predestination, and that he
could not change his mind in this matter of conscience despite all the king's
efforts to convince him otherwise. In his discussions with Müller, the well-read
Frederick backed up his belief in part by citing Luther. In his 1525 treatise *On
the Bondage of the Will*, the Reformer had claimed no less strictly than Calvin
that the human will must be considered *servus et captus*, a "slave and prisoner"
of divine will. According to Luther, nothing happens without the knowledge
and participation of almighty God. No single human action is undertaken
freely but rather out of a necessity—*necessitas*—decreed by God. Through his
eternal, immutable, and infallible providence, God has ordained everything
that happens in the entire universe of his Creation, including human actions.
According to this Lutheran teaching, then, King Frederick William I was an
unfree instrument of divine will.

Interpreting his father's actions in the light of the doctrine of predestination
did not dissolve the trauma of Küstrin. Yet it did cause Frederick to come to
terms with his lot in life. If everything had to happen as it did, then it was
pointless to wrestle with one's fate for too long. Instead, Frederick now felt
called to make the best of his current life circumstances. If what he had suffered in Küstrin had a predestined significance, that did not mean Frederick
would ever grasp that significance. Much of the dramatic course of events of
1730 remained mysterious and inscrutable to him. Yet he had been spared. He
had survived. And as a married crown prince, he now enjoyed a freedom of
action that had long seemed unreachable, and that was slowly teaching him to
enjoy his life anew.

This theologically informed view of the grand scheme of things even allowed Frederick to recognize and respect his father's indisputable achievements as a builder and ruler of the Brandenburg-Prussian state. There was no

doubt that Frederick William I, though a crude monarch, was an industrious man. He devoted himself tirelessly to the common good, all the while continuing to lead a modest, frugal, and unpretentious private life. In the twenty years of his reign, he had permitted himself to build only one new royal residence: a plain, red-brick building called the Jagdhaus am Stern. This hunting lodge (*Jagdhaus*) was constructed south of Potsdam amid a forest crisscrossed by a system of paths shaped like a star (*Stern*). Both inside and out, it bore a striking resemblance to a plain Dutch townhouse; it looked nothing like a royal Prussian palace. Finished in 1732, the "Stern Hunting Lodge" (or "Star Hunting Lodge") would have been more at home on the streets and alleys of cities like Leiden and Haarlem, which Frederick William I had visited in his youth, than on the sandy soil of a pine forest in Brandenburg.

This simple lodge did more than serve the king's chief pleasure pursuit of hunting. Indeed, it was a useful prototype for houses in a large, Dutch-style neighborhood that Jan Bouman, a carpenter and shipbuilder from Amsterdam, began building for Frederick William I in the heart of Potsdam in 1733. This building project was meant to attract Dutch craftsmen to Potsdam, the idea being to strengthen the economic viability of the country by encouraging highly skilled workers to settle there. As a result, nearly 150 new Dutch-style houses closely resembling the king's hunting lodge quickly sprang up in Potsdam.

It was not only economic reasons that motivated Frederick William I to encourage new subjects to settle in his lands. Rather, he felt obliged to offer asylum to all upright people who were persecuted on account of their faith. When, in late 1731, the archbishop of Salzburg expelled all the Lutherans still living in his diocese, the Prussian king took the majority of them in. Within a few months, nearly 20,000 Lutherans from Salzburg made their way to Brandenburg-Prussia. This commanded great respect from the crown prince, who marveled that they preferred to leave their homeland rather than repudiate their religion. The Calvinist king then radically expanded Brandenburg-Prussia's policy of religious tolerance. The same year the Salzburg refugees arrived, he had a mosque built right next to Potsdam's Garrison Church. It was the first Muslim house of worship anywhere in Germany. The Prussian king believed that the twenty Turkish guards given to him the year before by Ferdinand Kettler, Duke of Courland, should be able to practice their faith in peace.

Thanks to these achievements, Frederick learned to see that the king was not only appallingly brutal, crude, cheap, and petty but could also be admirably caring, thrifty, frugal, and tolerant. Frederick William I was driven by very different impulses that at times could seem utterly incompatible with one another—impulses, according to Luther and Calvin, over which human beings, as creatures of an all-powerful God, had no control. Consequently, he had done awful things and good things too. Clearly, his actions were guided by highly disparate and ever-shifting passions of the soul.

Yet Frederick learned still more. Not long after taking up his post in Ruppin, he was astonished to realize that he himself, who had been bullied so often by his strict soldier father, may have been driven by contradictory impulses just like the king. For he came to see that he was not only the philosophically and artistically minded reader and flute player he had known himself to be. Contrary to all previous expectations, Frederick suddenly discovered in himself a genuine inclination for military life, a surprising passion for the art of war. It now assumed a status of equal importance to the intellectual and artistic interests he had cultivated for so many years.

The occasion that led him to discover this unexpected yet very real martial side of his character was the death of Augustus the Strong. The king of Poland and elector of Saxony departed this life on February 1, 1733, without first having managed to reconcile the hopelessly estranged noble factions of the elective kingdom of Poland. A large number of Polish magnates elected his son Frederick Augustus II as the new king of Poland, but a significant confederation of Polish nobles voted for Stanisław I Leszczyński, the father-in-law of King Louis XV of France. A military conflict quickly erupted between imperial troops, who supported the new elector of Saxony, and the French army, which sought to place the Polish candidate on the throne in Warsaw. French forces crossed the Rhine in October 1733, taking the fortress of Kehl in Baden after a two-week siege.

Thus began the War of the Polish Succession. In many respects, the early action reminded concerned observers of the outbreak of the War of the Spanish Succession, which three decades earlier had nearly destroyed the balance of power in Europe. Once again, French troops marched into German territory, resorting to arms to help a French-supported contender ascend the vacant throne of a European kingdom. Once again, the Holy Roman Emperor arrayed his own army against the French invaders. This time as well, the Habsburg monarch was supported in the endeavor by the Prussian king, who by the spring of 1734 had sent nearly 10,000 soldiers to the Rhine and the Neckar. And yet again, Prince Eugene, now seventy years old, was in command of the combined Austro-Prussian forces. It seemed like history was repeating itself.

Precisely these clear historical parallels brought the young Prussian Crown Prince Frederick into the arena. He was presented with the extraordinary opportunity to see with his own eyes what could be thought of as the uncanny reenactment of a key event in modern European history. In the spring of 1734, Frederick William I, as commander in chief of all Prussian troops, ordered the lieutenant colonel in charge of the Crown Prince's Regiment to join the Prussian units in Baden, and to conduct himself there as boldly as a soldier from Brandenburg should. Frederick did not have to be told twice. He left Berlin on June 30 and arrived at the headquarters on the Neckar on July 7. Soon thereafter, he met Prince Eugene, whom he found in extremely poor health.

Although the elderly Austrian war hero was no longer the man of earlier days, Frederick noticed immediately that "even the shadow of Prince Eugene instilled" an unsurpassed "awe" in every prince, general, and officer who came near him. For in the face of that experienced old man they could see all those famous battles, starting with the second Turkish siege of Vienna in 1683, where he had time and again demonstrated his bravery, his martial ability, and his proneness to victory. Never had Frederick seen anyone who emitted an aura so demanding of respect. He was especially impressed by the fact that no words of praise for the war hero were allowed to be spoken in the latter's presence. Prince Eugene's glory electrified Frederick, blazing like a "miraculous fire" in his breast, because it was real, based on stupendous accomplishments, and required no further flattery. It was an incomparable, awe-inspiring kind of glory that clearly could only be won on the battlefield.

The example of Prince Eugene had an incredible impact on Frederick. After meeting the Austrian commander, the clearly smitten crown prince confessed that he had a date with destiny. He of all people, after mocking military service for so many years, was now suddenly one of those who burned with enthusiasm for the soldier's calling. This self-assessment was no exaggeration. Indeed, he began seeking out audacious missions, playing the part of the risk-taker. Once, when reconnoitering a forest near Philippsburg on horseback, he and his companions came under fire. Yet the hail of bullets did not deter him from staying on his horse or continuing his conversation; the splintering trees did not faze him. In the days following, the report of his astounding sangfroid made quite an impression on the Austrian and Brandenburg-Prussian camps.

He could win no further spurs in close combat on the Rhine, however. On the one hand, the allied imperial troops preferred stalling tactics to dramatic assaults, seeking to keep their own losses to a minimum while protecting the southwestern regions of the Empire from further French advances. On the other hand, Frederick was called back to Potsdam in late August 1734 because his father was gravely ill. The king's doctors communicated to the crown prince that Frederick William I, though forty-six years young, had only fourteen days to live. And so, with a heavy heart, he left a region in which he would have preferred to stay longer—a place from which, not even four years earlier, he had sought to escape to England and abandon the Holy Roman Empire forever. Nothing could have been further from his mind now, and he obediently rode back to Brandenburg. As for what would happen to his father and himself, the heir to the Prussian throne, he left that up to a higher power. "God," he wrote to his sister Wilhelmine on September 2, "rules everything in the world and is the first cause of all events." God would "dispose according to his wisdom, as determined by his holy will."

Was Frederick really destined to become king of Prussia now, far sooner than he ever imagined? Was this truly his ineluctable fate? Upon his arrival in Potsdam on October 12, he found his father in a miserable state. Frederick William I was emaciated, could barely breathe, and feared his end was nigh. He immediately transferred the most important responsibilities of government to his son and retreated into quiet suffering. His illness was so agonizing that even Frederick felt sympathy for him. To his sister he admitted that he never would have thought the pain suffered by his apparently moribund father could grieve him so deeply. At the same time, having been invested with the authority of a king overnight, the crown prince also experienced unaccustomed exuberance in the first weeks of his regency. He even found that it was fun to exercise the powers of an absolute monarch, as he admitted in amazement to Alexander von Wartensleben. It was a confession of disarming candor.

Contrary to the prophecies of his doctors, the king's condition began improving in early 1735. The crown prince was in no way heartened by the news. "It's a miracle of the rarest kind," he remarked to his sister Wilhelmine. Agitated and enraged, he now harbored the deep suspicion that his father had faked the severity of his illness. "He improves when he feels like it. He gets sicker when it's convenient. In the beginning I let myself be fooled, but now I know better." Disgusted by the king's "beastly nature," Frederick was now forced to watch as his father reassumed all the duties of a monarch. With palpable resignation, he informed his sister that he would now have to stand aside for the almost fully convalesced Frederick William I for the unforeseeable future.

Frederick could not even return to the Rhine. After a short, mild war ending in the usual stalemate, the French king and the emperor had come to an agreement in 1735: Elector Frederick Augustus II of Saxony would be universally recognized as King Augustus III of Poland; in compensation, Leszczyński would be given the Duchy of Lorraine. In this way, a conflict of the dimensions of the War of the Spanish Succession had been avoided. While most people in Europe rejoiced, the Prussian crown prince grumbled loud and clear. First his father had suddenly recovered, and now the political situation had unexpectedly improved. When his father asked him if he would like to take a "pleasure trip" to the Prussian capital of Königsberg now that the war had been called off, he scoffed that "taking a trip to Prussia" was "only slightly more alluring than going to Siberia, but not by much." Nevertheless, having nothing else to do, he took up his father's offer. If nothing else, it was an opportunity to become thoroughly acquainted with the small realm on the Baltic Sea that had enabled his grandfather to attain a royal crown.

By November 1735, however, Frederick was back in Ruppin. The Rheinsberg renovations were almost finished, and it seemed that a portion of the palace would be habitable very soon, weather permitting. Therefore, the crown prince made all necessary preparations to move into his swanky new seigneurial domicile as soon as spring had sprung. Upon closer inspection, however, he was not completely happy with the work done by the architect Kemmeter. Frederick thus called upon the services of Georg Wenzeslaus von Knobelsdorff. Formerly a captain in the Prussian army, Knobelsdorff had been forced to retire for health reasons. As an autodidact and then as the protégé of Antoine Pesne, Frederick William I's court painter, he had become a landscape painter, landscape designer, and architect. In Rheinsberg, he was to serve as an artistic adviser, assisting in making the palace more elegant and better proportioned. Knobelsdorff had already helped Frederick with the layout of his park in the Ruppin ramparts. Now he gladly accepted Frederick's invitation. Before getting started, however, he was sent on a year's journey to study the buildings of Venice, Florence, Rome, and Naples, from which he was to return to Brandenburg with a wealth of new architectural designs.

In the first weeks of summer 1736, after sufficiently acclimating himself to Rheinsberg, Frederick invited his wife, her court ladies, many of his own companions, the extended princely household, and a considerable number of servants to join him there. In late August, Elisabeth Christine arrived at the palace in a remote corner of Brandenburg, whose purchase and renovations had been partially funded by her own dowry. The majority of the cost, we recall, had been borne by Frederick William I on the condition that his son and successor set up a proper court there with his young wife. The crown princess now came

FIGURE 5.1. Frederick's wife: Queen Elisabeth Christine (1715–1797).
Painting by Antoine Pesne, 1735 (akg-images).

to Rheinsberg with 130 courtiers in tow, most of whom resided outside the palace walls in the neighboring small town, significantly augmenting its population of 700.

Frederick was now more receptive than ever to Elisabeth Christine, perhaps because of the great joy he felt at living far from Berlin and being able to create a social setting entirely according to his own taste. He maintained that he had never been in love with her, as he underlined to a group of friends shortly before her arrival. On the other hand, he would have to be "the vilest kind of man" to not "earnestly esteem" her simply on account of this unavoidable shortcoming. She had "a very kind disposition," was "accommodating to the point of excess," and did everything "that my mere expression seems to indicate I want in order to make me happy." While he did not share the bedroom in Rheinsberg with Elisabeth Christine with the utmost passion, he was not emotionally absent either. For her part, she professed that she now finally enjoyed complete satisfaction with her husband, that she had been graciously accepted by a man whom she tenderly loved. Frederick was even wont to write little notes to her, telling her that he looked forward to embracing her or that he could hardly wait to take her in his arms and assure her he was hers alone.

Frederick William I's ministers, concerned with the continuation of the Hohenzollern dynasty, now inquired with increasing frequency when the crown princess was finally going get pregnant. In his replies, Frederick adopted an aloof, direct, almost scornful tone to inform them that he and his wife were in fact regularly sleeping together in Rheinsberg. In September 1736, he crowed crudely to Grumbkow, "If I work as hard as those bucks that are in rut at the moment, then what you hope for me could come to pass in nine months." Although Elisabeth Christine regularly presented with symptoms suggesting pregnancy, both her own hopes and the expectations of the royal court remained unfulfilled. Frederick, who had three younger brothers—Augustus William, born in 1722, the ten-year-old Prince Henry, and the six-year-old Prince Ferdinand—regarded his own lack of children with equanimity. He did not know why his wife had not yet conceived, but no doubt one of his brothers would eventually have children. If necessary, one of his "nephews or great-nephews" could be installed as his "successor." The crown prince, who had been bullied so fiercely by his own father, clearly felt no urgency to have a son of his own.

In Rheinsberg, Frederick was much more concerned with indulging his passion for music and philosophy, which still burned as brightly as ever. Indeed, he pursued these interests even more intensely than he had while living in Ruppin. He wrote poetry, played the flute daily, and composed several ambitious solo pieces and concertos for the high-pitched wind instrument. He did this just to pass the time, or so he claimed, with obvious understatement, in a long letter about his musical endeavors to his sister Wilhelmine, now married to the Margrave of Bayreuth. In addition, he organized theatrical performances, chamber concerts, and merry masquerades. He enjoyed all of these playful diversions in the company of a tight circle of professional musicians, amateur actors, and close confidants that he assembled before the year 1736 was out.

Two professional representatives of the fine art of music joined the court in Rheinsberg: the gifted flautist Johann Joachim Quantz and the composer Graun, whose virtuosity had so deeply impressed Frederick at his wedding in Salzdahlum. The crown prince's wittiest and most intimate conversation partners included the lively and eloquent Baron Dietrich von Keyserlingk of Courland, whom he had known since before his imprisonment in Küstrin; the proud, jocular, and pleasure-seeking French cavalryman Egmont von Chasot, who, after fighting a duel during the War of the Polish Succession, had fled the French army, crossed the Rhine, and sought refuge in the German camp, where Frederick immediately took a liking to him; his private secretary Charles Etienne Jordan, a widely traveled Huguenot well versed in literature; and Heinrich August Baron de la Motte Fouqué, a company commander from Anhalt who was also an accomplished amateur theatrical performer.

Frederick was finally free to spend his days with friends and musicians at his pleasure, and to pursue his manifold interests in their genial company as he pleased. Accordingly, he raved in one of his first letters from Rheinsberg to his old friend Ulrich Friedrich von Suhm, "I've never known days as happy as these." Frederick could be utterly himself in Rheinsberg. He fully indulged his inclinations, without paying much heed to courtly etiquette. At one wine-sodden bacchanalia, courtiers and even the otherwise straightlaced princess smashed glasses to smithereens, all just for the fun of it. As one astonished observer wrote, the amused prince "regarded the destruction with a cheerful, serene expression." When the jubilation and turmoil reached a crescendo, "in that moment he retired to his room" with Princess Elisabeth Christine.

In some of his letters, the exuberant and lighthearted Prussian crown prince took to calling his new palace in Rheinsberg Sanssouci (i.e., "No Worries" or, somewhat less formally, "Carefree Castle"). The inspiration probably came from Ernst Christoph von Manteuffel, a close friend of Frederick and quondam envoy from Saxony to the Prussian court, who had named his own manor in Farther Pomerania "Kummerfrey," a German analogue to the French sobriquet. In the same spirit, after moving into his secluded abode, Frederick had a catchy Latin phrase inscribed above the entrance gate as a kind of sublime dedication to himself: *Frederico tranquillitatem colenti*—"For Frederick and his cultivation of leisure." Yet the leisure that Frederick so ostentatiously prescribed for himself was in no way to be understood as an incessant, otiose idleness or as a never-ending musical scherzo, but rather as an ardently passionate, deadly serious study of philosophy and literature.

Frederick now possessed more hours, days, weeks, and months to call his own than ever before. He had so much precious time, and he intended to suck the marrow out of every single minute, proceeding deliberately, mindfully, and with singular focus. He wanted not only to enjoy life to the fullest but also to understand it better, grasping its deepest significance and fundamental framework. Every morning, he rose at four o'clock and spent the next six hours reading books of all kinds in his freshly stocked library. It was located in a tower of the palace, its windows affording a panoramic view of the surrounding lakes and forests. The remaining hours till noon were devoted to copying the most important passages he had read that morning into a notebook. After eating lunch, he dedicated the rest of the day to his occasionally raucous social life. Before going to bed, he often spent more time reading. Once, he even tried to ween himself off sleep entirely, but the willful experiment only lasted four days. Bloodshot eyes and stomach cramps taught him that restorative sleep was essential even for a very young man's survival.

When he had finally discovered what work schedule suited him best, and what combination of intense intellectual effort and total relaxation was most felicitous, he sought out a mentor to perfect the formation of his spirit, his power of imagination, and his literary taste. This teacher was also to save him from philosophical errors and fallacies. His heartfelt desire, as he wrote in a letter to Suhm, was that constant learning, careful study, and true philosophy would "enlighten me." He sought a torchbearer of modern science, a trailblazer spreading the light of knowledge, someone who could provide him with more wisdom and artistic sensibility than was afforded by the quartet of Keyserlingk, Chasot, Jordan, and de la Motte Fouqué. After short deliberation, Frederick—never one for humility—chose no less than the world-famous French poet and philosopher Voltaire, who enjoyed the reputation of being one of the greatest writers and thinkers of the Age of Enlightenment.

Voltaire, the son of a prominent lawyer in Paris, was born in 1694 and baptized as François-Marie Arouet. After a thorough education at the Jesuit school Louis-le-Grand, he studied law with the intention of working in his father's law office. Alongside his legal studies, however, he had always composed verse, including razor-sharp satires on unjust actions undertaken by the French government. In 1717, the state lost its patience with the young lawyer's invectives and sentenced him to eleven months in the Bastille. During his imprisonment, the poet, who now called himself Voltaire—an anagram of "AROVET L[e] I[eune]" (Arouet the Younger)—wrote a verse tragedy of the ancient Oedipus myth. After his release, it premiered in Paris under the name Œdipe, garnering rave reviews. Spurred on by the broad acclaim he received in the literary world, he published *La Ligue, ou Henri Le Grand* in Geneva in 1723, a historical epic intended to promote religious tolerance. It focused on King Henry IV of France, whose prudence and dedication to peace put an end to the French Wars of Religion in the sixteenth century. The purity of Voltaire's Alexandrine verse, the sophistication of his style, and the balance and harmony of his compositions won enduring poetic fame for the Jesuit-trained jurist.

This literary fame, however, provided him with no effective protection from the arbitrary power of the French state. After a fight with a high-ranking member of the French aristocracy, he managed to avoid a second stay in the Bastille only by escaping for a time to England, where he remained until the end of 1728. While there, he apprenticed himself to the outstanding philosophical, scientific, and political achievements of the Britons. The fruit of this period was his *Letters Concerning the English Nation*, whose first French edition appeared in 1734 under the title *Lettres philosophiques* (*Philosophical Letters*). This work portrayed the free society of England, based on legislative participation in government and wide-ranging religious tolerance, as the exemplary foil for the dogmatic, state-sponsored Catholicism of France. As a result, its author was convicted in 1734 of engaging in activities hostile to the state and religion and condemned to another prison term. The sentence was not carried out, but only because Voltaire managed to flee to Cirey, in the border region of Lorraine, where an admirer of his work, the Marquise du Châtelet, gave him asylum in her small chateau.

In this remote location, the two of them assembled a library of many thousand volumes and set up a scientific laboratory. It was there that Voltaire received a letter from Rheinsberg in the autumn of 1736, in which the Prussian crown prince requested that he send him all his works. For they were "treasures of the mind . . . and compositions elaborated with so much taste, delicacy, and art, that their beauties appear new each time they are reread." Frederick also wished to receive from Voltaire personal "instruction" in the "arts and sciences." For not only was the author of the *Lettres philosophiques* an "excellent poet," but he also possessed "an infinity of other knowledge" about all areas of philosophy and science.

Voltaire, who had been forced to flee Paris several times, was surprised and touched. Understandably, he also was very flattered by the overtures of a studious young man who was destined to be king of Prussia. He promptly replied to Frederick, consenting to aid him on his path to "loving the truth" and "detesting persecution and superstition." For "any prince who thinks in this way can bring back the golden age to his dominions." A few months later, Frederick sent his friend Keyserlingk to Cirey to find out under what conditions Voltaire would be willing to move to Rheinsberg. The poet, however, informed the crown prince that he intended to stay with the Marquise for the time being. Not even the gifts Keyserlingk brought—a portrait of Frederick and fine Hungarian wine—could change his mind. Still, Voltaire kept his promise to act as Frederick's mentor, sending a veritable flood of letters from Cirey to Rheinsberg in which he continually and progressively enlightened the Prussian crown prince about the most important aspects of good poetry, science, and political philosophy.

In these letters, Voltaire enjoined Frederick, eighteen years his junior, to devote himself immediately, thoroughly, and tirelessly to the odes of the Roman poet Horace, the greatest versifier of the Augustan Age. For they dealt with the question of human happiness in a more profound way than anyone had since. Even in the eighteenth century, Voltaire argued, Horace's practical wisdom was an important source of inspiration for all individuals seeking enlightenment. Therefore, it was also beneficial to regularly compose verse of one's own in Horace's style. Frederick should then supplement these efforts with a thorough investigation of the philosophy of the Englishman John Locke. In Voltaire's view, the paradigm of modern, enlightened philosophy was not Leibniz—who, while playing a large role in founding the Prussian state, was still esteemed too highly in Germany—but rather Locke, the theorist of the Glorious Revolution and the adviser to Pennsylvania's founding father, William Penn.

Locke was a "genius" in Voltaire's eyes. For he had based his political philosophy fully on a conception of human beings that adhered with the findings of modern anatomy and science. Whereas Leibniz described the human intellect (*intellectus*) as a faculty of the understanding independent of the senses, Locke claimed that all human concepts and ideas could only be formed by sense perceptions sent to the brain via the nervous system. In his *Philosophical Letters*, Voltaire had praised "Monsieur Locke" for the "more solid and more methodical" approach he had taken in his 1690 *Essay Concerning Human Understanding*, which argues "that the origin of all our ideas is from the senses." According to this Sensualist philosophy, all individuals are endowed with their own proclivities shaped by very different sensations, and these proclivities in turn give rise to very different preferences.

In order to aggregate the eclectic preferences and interests of individuals into a general political will—as Locke had explained in his *Two Treatises of*

Government—it was absolutely necessary for citizens to participate in government via legislative representation. This understanding of politics was shared by Voltaire, who had come to know and appreciate the British system of government during his sojourn in England. In his view, when a parliament elected by citizens participates in political decision-making, then no one is tyrannized, and everyone feels free and easy. It would therefore be highly desirable for legislative assemblies to be instituted in other parts of the world, as that would let the people participate in government and rein in the arbitrary rule of princes.

Voltaire believed that the prime example for the universal possibility of transplanting English parliamentarianism to another part of the globe was furnished by William Penn in America. For shortly after founding the colony of Pennsylvania, he transferred nearly all the prerogatives of an absolute monarch to the colony's settlers as represented in a legislative assembly. And indeed, these "wise and wholesome laws . . . have remained invariably the same to this day." The capital of Philadelphia continued to grow thanks to immigration from Ireland and Germany and was now, in Voltaire's words, "a very flourishing city." Pennsylvania was now home to a motley "body of citizens without any distinctions," all of whom enjoyed the exact same rights and privileges.

In one very specific sense, Penn had even further developed and optimized the social order of the English mother country: In Pennsylvania, universal tolerance reigned. Unlike in Great Britain, in the American colony all kinds of faith communities were given the space to freely and fully practice their own religion. No church was given special treatment of the kind enjoyed by the Church of England across the sea. Thanks to Pennsylvania's unique combination of religious tolerance and legislative self-government, "William Penn might . . . boast of having brought down upon earth the Golden Age, which in all probability, never had any real existence but in his dominions." For Voltaire, Pennsylvania offered the purest example of the applied political principles of the Enlightenment. And none of his readers could fail to note his enthusiasm for this English colony, which he considered to be a model even for Europe to follow.

For that reason, some people thought it necessary to warn Frederick about engaging with Voltaire uncritically. One of them was Manteuffel, who took pains to point out to Frederick just how subversive the *Philosophical Letters* were. He had recognized that Voltaire's ideal of political enlightenment, steeped as it was in British and American realities, did more than undermine the established order in France. Indeed, it likewise challenged the political system of the Brandenburg-Prussian state, in which parliamentary participation and citizen representation had no place. Frederick was nonplussed by these objections. He admired Voltaire for his courage, his independence of mind, his championing of tolerance, and especially his literary and rhetorical brilliance. Moreover, Frederick was discerning and confident enough to distinguish the doctrines of Voltaire that seemed most important to him from those that, upon due consideration, he decided not to adopt.

That being said, most of what Voltaire had to offer him in his letters and other writings was received by the Prussian crown prince as a treasured enrichment of his intellectual life. Once, he compared the shrewd teachings of the French philosopher to a very precious gift. As he wrote in a letter destined for Cirey, he felt like a penniless European colonist in the New World who had suddenly struck gold. Precious as any metal from America were, for example, Horace's odes. Just as Voltaire had advised, Frederick read Horace and composed his own verse imitating the Roman poet's style. He was now writing so much poetry so often that he jokingly referred to himself as suffering from *métromanie*—that is, he was "addicted to poetry." In homage to the ancient poet and his French mentor, he had the goddess Minerva painted on the ceiling of his study once Knobelsdorff had finished turning Rheinsberg into an even more lavish palace. In the painting, the Roman goddess of wisdom is depicted receiving a book on whose pages two names are legible: Horace and Voltaire.

Thanks to Voltaire's reading recommendations, Frederick also developed an enthusiasm for the philosophy of John Locke, which gave him brand-new insights into the potential and limits of human understanding. In particular, his study of Locke helped the Prussian crown prince to refine his understanding of human nature. In a certain sense, Locke's Sensualist philosophy even functioned like scientific confirmation of the doctrine of predestination preached by Luther and Calvin. Since human beings were molded by their sense perceptions and prisoners to their sensual nature, they could influence neither their temperament nor their taste. As a result, they had no choice but to accept themselves for who they were. Furthermore, they had to find a meaningful way to fill the place they occupied in human history and in the society in which they lived, embracing their unalterable fate and learning to trust that God had set the mechanism of the world at the beginning of all time with the precision of a "watch-maker." Human beings, Frederick now wrote to Voltaire, have the freedom of "the hand which marks the hours." They have a certain range of movement, and they can undertake certain actions, but they are "moved by hidden works." Everything that happens is directed by God. And thus, Frederick concluded, "if God directs events according to His will, He necessarily directs and governs men."

Other than performing regular inspections of his regiment in Ruppin and taking a trip to Holland in 1738, Frederick spent all his time warming himself by the light of reason in Rheinsberg. By 1739 at the latest, under Voltaire's tutelage he had firmly grasped that his own temperament drove him to prepare himself, through tireless reading and keen concentration, for the kingly office that was his personal, providentially predetermined fate. He had to study day and night, so long as he still had free time to devote to education and leisure. For his father, who took ill more and more often, doubtless could not have long to live.

From now on, Frederick focused his gaze firmly on the moment when he would succeed the increasingly enfeebled monarch. With what might be called presumption, he had the ceiling of the Hall of Mirrors designed by Knobelsdorff painted with a scene depicting the future of Prussia after his ascension to the throne. In a letter dated October 30, 1739, Baron von Bielfeld described a scene from Rheinsberg: "The famous Pesne is working on the ceiling painting which depicts the rising sun. On one side is night, shrouded in a thick veil, surrounded by its sad birds." But the night is receding "to make space for the dawn." This painting was doubtless an allegory: With Frederick as king, the sun of the Enlightenment would shine brighter than ever in Brandenburg-Prussia.

Nevertheless, it emerged that same year that Frederick's conception of political enlightenment differed greatly from the ideal of an enlightened polity sketched by Voltaire. Contrary to Manteuffel's misgivings, the Prussian crown prince did not follow the advice of his French teacher in every respect. Indeed, Frederick was now writing his own work of political philosophy, one that could be understood as a direct response to Voltaire's *Philosophical Letters*. The text was formally designed as a rebuttal to Machiavelli's *Prince*, the infamous treatise, first printed in 1532, that argued that the primary goal of princes is to increase their own power, at the expense of their own people's happiness if necessary. Yet Frederick's *Anti-Machiavel* often also made conspicuous reference to Voltaire, both in its content and in its style. For example, in his *Philosophical Letters* Voltaire had stirringly proclaimed that, in championing political enlightenment, he was "venturing to take the side of humanity." A very similar sentence appears in Frederick's *Anti-Machiavel*: "I venture to defend humanity against this monster, whose aim is to destroy it."

The monster that Frederick aimed to conquer was the tyrannical state, the opposite of an enlightened political system. Yet the heir to the Prussian throne had a very different understanding of what made a tyrant than his French mentor did. The two men agreed that an enlightened state could only be established on the foundation of religious tolerance, and that the government of such a state had to promote "all the arts and all the sciences" and the general welfare as unselfishly as possible. But whereas Voltaire saw freely elected parliaments as the best and only defense against arbitrary rule, Frederick believed that states with parliamentary systems of government were always wracked by a hopeless "competition among an infinity of wills," and that this strife would eventually drive a country into chaos and must sooner or later destroy it. For that reason, "the ruler of a country" should never be invested with authority "through the election of the people who hold power."

Instead, it seemed best to Frederick for the ruler to be chosen "through succession," since "hereditary kingdoms are the easiest to govern"—much easier than those whose authority depended on the confidence, to say nothing of the vote, of a parliament. Only an absolute ruler—in particular an enlightened one—could truly be the "first servant" of his people and, by virtue of his prudence, perform the difficult task of combining "all their separate interests into a single common interest." This was only possible, of course, "if his will and his power truly manifested his benevolence." Consequently, nothing made a monarchy stronger than the profound and indivisible unity of all its parts. Creating this unity must therefore be the goal of a wise prince. Ultimately, enlightened and wise princes can govern a state better than the people, who are always easily deceived.

Frederick claimed that states are ruled best by monarchs who "see with their own eyes" and "themselves govern their states"; who "administer domestic matters, as they do foreign affairs"; and who issue "all decrees, all laws, all edicts." The monarch should also be "the lord chief justice, supreme commander, and minister of finance," and he should deal with "all affairs touching on government policy" without disturbance from others. There is no doubt that Frederick had the Prussian ideal of the benevolent dictator in mind. This model of an uncompromisingly absolute monarchy in the service of the common good had informed the approach to government taken by his grandfather, Frederick I, and his father, Frederick William I. Frederick intended to adopt their exemplary standard when he became king. Indeed, in 1734 he had already gotten a taste for how satisfying it could be to rule as an absolute monarch in

Prussia. That is one reason why he rejected England's parliamentary system of government, where the king had "to be fearful of his people." And for the same reason, he was not receptive to Voltaire's praise of the American colony of Pennsylvania.

As for that colony's founder, William Penn, whom Voltaire had esteemed so highly, all Frederick could say was that the odd Quaker was first and foremost "the founder of a sect," a dreamer and no enlightener. And there was no mistaking that very "many sects" had a great affinity with "fanaticism"—never a good foundation for an enlightened polity, which had to be constructed rationally. Having delivered this abysmal appraisal of Penn's achievements in America, and having elaborated his argument for an absolutist kingdom, Frederick felt optimally prepared to ascend the Prussian throne whenever the time came. More sure of himself than ever, Frederick proudly put the finishing touches on his *Anti-Machiavel* in February 1740. That same month, he sent the manuscript to Cirey. Then he waited expectantly for Voltaire's judgment.

Not far from the colony of Pennsylvania, for which the Prussian crown prince showed so little interest, the planter's son George Washington began exploring his American environment with growing independence. Since remarrying, his father had moved the family within Virginia twice and at short intervals, thus expanding George's horizons at a very young age. In 1735, Augustine Washington bought a one-and-a-half-story farmhouse in Epsewasson, forty miles north of Pope's Creek. He liked it better than the estate that he had built and where George was born. Three years later, the Washingtons improved their living situation yet again, this time moving to a larger farm on the Rappahannock River in sight of the city of Fredericksburg, the seat of the new Virginia county of Spotsylvania. At first, they simply called it Washington Farm, but it was soon renamed Ferry Farm because of the nearby river ferry.

When they moved to Ferry Farm, George was the oldest child still living at home. His sister Jane had died at only thirteen years of age, and his two older brothers, Lawrence and Augustine Jr., had been attending school in Great Britain since the early 1730s. The two boys, now almost fully grown, were learning Latin at the Appleby Grammar School in Cumbria County in northwestern England. Since the early days of the colony, it had been customary for the wealthier planters to send their oldest sons to the mother country to finish their education. George, too, looked forward to the day when he would sail across the ocean and, following in his brothers' footsteps, go to school in

England. For now, though, he had to help his parents care for his younger siblings. Betty had been followed by three boys: Samuel in 1734, John Augustine in 1736, and Charles in 1737.

Starting in 1738, George's own education was overseen by a private tutor who gave him regular lessons at Ferry Farm. The city of Fredericksburg, founded only a few years earlier, still did not have a decent public school. George's tutor focused on reading, writing, and arithmetic, as only a solid elementary education would qualify the boy for acceptance to school in England one day. George learned his ABCs by spelling out Bible stories and shorter articles from *The Virginia Gazette*. Founded on August 6, 1736, this newspaper was printed in Virginia's capital of Williamsburg. The city had been founded in 1633 close to Jamestown and initially called Middle Plantation. It was renamed Williamsburg in 1699 in honor of William III when it became the seat of the colonial legislature. *The Virginia Gazette*, the first regularly appearing periodical in Virginia, was only the second newspaper after *The South Carolina Gazette* to be published south of the Potomac. Each issue of *The Virginia Gazette* was headed by the slogan, "Containing the freshest Advices, Foreign and Domestick."

George regularly spoke to his teacher about the texts he had read from the Bible and the newspaper. These conversations were intended to do more than test the knowledge he had gained, though. They were also an important tool for ensuring that the boy developed a more elevated manner of speaking. Since the children of Virginia planters commonly associated with the children of slaves, many educationally minded residents of the colony feared that the unrefined speech of Black slaves might be adopted by the offspring of white colonists. Another opportunity to hear elevated rhetoric, very different from the casual jargon of the streets, was available to young George Washington when he accompanied his parents to church on Sunday. Of course, there was nothing in the Anglican minister's sermons that might have caused George to question the commonly accepted practice of slavery.

George did not possess any books of his own when he began his elementary education, although he did have access to the Bible and the Book of Common Prayer at home. The latter had regulated Anglican worship since 1662, containing all the rules and rites for morning and evening prayers, baptism, communion, confirmation, marriage, and burial. The Washington family bookshelf also contained *Every Man His Own Doctor: or, The Poor Planter's Physician*, a layman's medical guide intended for home use. Published anonymously in Williamsburg in 1734, by 1740 this primer on home and emergency medicine was the most widely diffused book in the pioneer society of settlers after the

Bible and the Book of Common Prayer. According to its wry preface, it was intended above all for the use of poorer farmers who could not afford to be killed by a doctor, "for our doctors are commonly so exorbitant in their fees, whether they kill or cure." It promised "to lead the poorer sort into the pleasant paths of health, and when they have the misfortune to be sick, to shew them the cheapest and easiest ways of getting well again." It covered everything from rattlesnake bites to an abiding cough.

What George Washington absorbed in his first years of schooling was directed toward very pragmatic, everyday needs. Yet by reading *The Virginia Gazette*, he also became acquainted with the exceptional virtues of Virginia and the other American colonies, in which Voltaire had even seen the promise of a new golden age. The newspaper may have been published in a strongly Anglican atmosphere, but its pages still instructed readers that those who departed from the teachings of the Church of England should enjoy wide tolerance as long as they were good citizens—and not only in Pennsylvania but also in Virginia. Such good citizens, who could vote for legislative representatives to sit in the House of Burgesses in Williamsburg, included all white men who owned either 100 acres of farmland or a house in the city. Freed slaves and Indians, however, did not have the franchise, regardless of whether they owned land or a house. Finally, George Washington learned early on that farmers of little or middling wealth made up the majority of the white population. The impossibly rich Lord Fairfax of Cameron, with his over five million acres of land, was an exception. The lifestyle enjoyed by the Washington family was the norm for the white settlers of Virginia.

Thus, George Washington was an average American boy, whose experiences, both during his lessons and in his hours of leisure, were no different from those of countless other Virginians of his own age. Just like his older brothers, he enjoyed playing billiards and went to the fairs in Fredericksburg and Williamsburg. A passionate rider of horses from an early age, he later developed an interest in the horseraces that, by 1740, had become increasingly popular. Many planters had their own racetracks where high bets could be placed on favored sprinters or promising underdogs. George's enthusiasm for elegant, powerful, fast horses was never quite as strong as his love of dogs, though. The latter were not only faithful companions in everyday life but also indispensable escorts for hunting, a favored pastime of American farmers that combined athletic activity with the procurement of food.

Virginia offered a rich pageant of animals to hunt: deer in great number, bears, buffalo, wolves, foxes, panthers, wildcats, elk, and rabbits, as well as raccoons, possums, beavers, and otters, not to mention the numerous turkeys and partridges or the tasty wild geese, swans, cormorants, and ducks inhabiting the colony's countless bodies of water. Washington especially loved hunting for waterfowl with his hounds, and he regularly shot mallards. Duck hunting taught him to handle a gun—the use of which was a right guaranteed to every citizen in America. Guns were a symbol of power and boldness, but they were also a sign of a free man who knew how to defend himself. At a young age, George Washington learned that "my inclinations are strongly bent to arms." In the spring of 1740, however, he was still far too young to even guess the important role he would play in American history by taking up arms.

6

Glory and Ordeal (1740–1754)

WHILE THE young George Washington was discovering the pleasures of hunting on the reed-lined banks of American waterways, the life of the most passionate and privileged huntsman in Brandenburg-Prussia was nearing its irrevocable end. The decrepit monarch Frederick William I felt death approaching. Soon, he realized with unfazed composure, it would finally release him from the excruciating pain that attended every breath. The Prussian king resigned himself serenely to his fate and asked to be taken from Berlin to quiet Potsdam. As he was placed in his coach outside the large, gray City Palace on the Spree on April 27, 1740, he called out wistfully, "Goodbye, Berlin. I am going to Potsdam to die."

Underlining just how earnestly he meant this performative farewell to his earthly existence, the king gave his "beloved hounds" to Prince Leopold I of Anhalt-Dessau. As he told his friend, "I am done hunting in this world, and my oldest son is no lover of hunting, nor will he ever become one." On May 26, he sent a letter to this son in Rheinsberg informing him that he was sure to die within a few days and expressing his ardent hope to embrace the heir to the throne one last time before he did so. Immediately upon receiving this heartfelt request, Frederick rode hard to Potsdam. His father, sitting in a wheelchair, espied him from afar on the afternoon of May 28. He received his son with outstretched arms, and Frederick, crying in shock, kneeled at his side.

In front of the simple oakwood coffin in which he wanted to be buried, the king explained to his son the next day "what I want you to do with my body when the Almighty takes me to himself in the great beyond." However, it was not only his funeral that Frederick William I discussed with his son. He also had the young man promise to care as conscientiously and faithfully for Brandenburg-Prussia as he himself had done since 1713. In particular, the strength of the army, whose size had doubled during his reign, should be further enhanced, for it was a vital pillar of the state. Thanks to his life-changing experiences in the War of the Polish Succession, the once so unsoldierly Frederick was able to pledge this easily and credibly. His son having vowed to fulfill his heartfelt wish, the king then exclaimed in great satisfaction, "He promised that he will maintain the army, and I am sure he will keep his word. I know now that he loves the troops."

On May 31, 1740, at three o'clock in the afternoon, the pious Frederick William I passed away peacefully and quietly. One hour before, he had grabbed a mirror with his last bit of strength in order to see the marks of death that now began to imprint themselves on his face. The next day, his body was laid out in the Potsdam City Palace, where the royal household, his wife, and his children gathered round, each with very different emotions. They now bade farewell to the mortal remains of the man who had put his indelible stamp on all of them—as on the state he ruled—in the fifty or so years he had lived. Especially torn up was his successor, Frederick, in whom, as he wrote to Voltaire on June 6, a "whirlwind" of emotions was raging.

Frederick was now king. He assumed the duties of the office immediately on the afternoon of May 31. He dispensed with an elaborate coronation ceremony as resolutely as had his deceased predecessor. Yet, although he had awaited this moment for years, he was now forced to discover that one can only prepare oneself so much for such an occasion. Taking control of the government, and thus shouldering its responsibilities, suddenly seemed to him like a heavy burden. Everything was different now. Still, he consoled himself in another letter to Voltaire with the equally "singular thought" that he would from now on "serve my fellow citizens," and he would do so in the manner recently described in his *Anti-Machiavel*.

Indeed, the residents of Brandenburg-Prussia seemed to have high expectations of their new ruler. The people of the capital of Berlin enthusiastically welcomed their king, who now assumed the name Frederick II. They jubilantly received his first decree, in which he promised "to make all of our subjects happy," for he essentially wanted "to make no distinction" between their interests and his own. He intended to rule in an enlightened manner, with clemency, and to give his subjects justice at all times. In line with these sentiments, in the month of June he instituted three sensational reforms: Brandenburg-Prussia's policy of religious tolerance was further expanded, censorship of the press was largely ended, and torture during criminal interrogations was forbidden.

In his youth, he had been forced to hide his own religious convictions from his father, was not permitted to read everything he wanted, and had suffered traumatic mental anguish during his imprisonment in Küstrin. Now he sought to guarantee to his people those very freedoms and rights that the departed king had withheld from him. "All religions must be tolerated," Frederick proclaimed, and "everyone should find their own bliss." He believed that "all religions are equal and good as long as those who profess them are honest people." Therefore, he even expressly allowed mosques to be built in case any "Turks" should decide to settle permanently in Berlin. Furthermore, he stressed "that gazettes, if they are to be interesting, must not be censored." The abolition of torture, however, was not made public but rather communicated to the justice minister, Samuel von Cocceji, in a secret decree. Frederick did not want to embolden potential criminals.

The Prussian king, still only twenty-eight years old, also made very personal gestures of clemency and forgiveness to people who had been seriously harmed by his father. His former tutor Duhan, who had been banished to Memel after the crown prince's failed escape attempt and had not set foot in Brandenburg since 1730, was now allowed to return. Only three days after taking the reins of government, the new king wrote him a moving letter. "My fortune has changed, dear friend. I await you impatiently. Do not make me wait too long." Then there was Christian Wolff, a former philosophy professor in Halle. In 1723, the Pietist Frederick William I had ordered him to leave the city within forty-eight hours, concerned that Wolff's open enthusiasm for the ancient Chinese philosophy of Confucius would lead to the spread of atheism in Brandenburg-Prussia. The new king considered this fear utterly unfounded, and he now called Wolff back to the university town on the Saale River. Finally, Frederick made token restitution to the father of his lost but not forgotten friend Katte, Hans Heinrich von Katte, raising him to the rank of count. He also gave him a portrait of himself painted by Antoine Pesne, in which the radiant young ruler looks out at the viewer with clear eyes.

The most beautiful manifestation of Frederick's desire to provide the greatest number of subjects with the greatest possible joy and pleasure came in the form of changes he made to the city of Berlin. For example, he tasked Georg Wenzeslaus von Knobelsdorff with removing the fence from the royal hunting grounds known as the Tiergarten, located outside the west city gate, and turning it into a park. The wooded area was then to serve the capital's residents as a place to relax and stroll. Since he himself had no love of hunting, it was an easy way to please the people.

Frederick also put Knobelsdorff in charge of building the new royal opera house on Unter den Linden. This project matched his own interest in music with the local population's demand for sophisticated entertainment. The opera house was to have 3,000 seats, making it the largest music theater in the world. From the outset it was clear that it would be a freestanding temple to the muses in the heart of the city, and thus that a broader public, unassociated with the royal court, would have access to the same high-quality music as the king. In August 1740, Knobelsdorff began surveying the site and even started digging the opera house's foundation.

Voltaire was impressed with the cheerful and generous spirit with which the young monarch inaugurated his reign. True, the Prussian king had argued in favor of a much more limited understanding of enlightened government in his *Anti-Machiavel* than could have suited the French poet, whose own ideal was English and American parliamentarianism. But clearly, Frederick's political manifesto was characterized by the very same will to promote his subjects' "humanity" and "happiness" that he was now earnestly putting into practice in his realm. Consequently, when Voltaire received Frederick's request in August 1740 to prepare his manuscript of the *Anti-Machiavel* for publication, the Frenchman immediately agreed. A version of the text, edited by Voltaire, appeared in September.

That same month, the first personal meeting between the king and his philosophical mentor took place. During a long inaugural journey around his realm, Frederick visited Brandenburg's possessions Kleve, Mark, and Ravensberg in the Rhine region of Westphalia. From there, he took a short detour to Strasbourg in late August under the alias Count Dufour. Before returning to Berlin, he spent several days in Moyland Castle, outside Kleve. In this medieval water castle, which his grandfather Frederick I had acquired in the late seventeenth century, he now received in the second week of September the man with whom he had enjoyed a very intimate correspondence for four years. Frederick and Voltaire had actually planned to meet halfway between Lorraine and Westphalia, in Brussels or Antwerp. On the appointed day, however, the monarch was in bed with a high fever. Thus, the French poet unceremoniously sought out the indisposed Prussian king at his sickbed on September 11.

When Voltaire was ushered into Frederick's chambers in Moyland Castle, a small study with bare walls lit by one candle, he discovered a small cot. On it lay the king in a blue dressing gown; he was much smaller than the poet had expected. Sweating and shivering under a coarse blanket, he let his French visitor take his pulse as naturally as if the philosopher from Cirey had been his personal physician for years. The feeble Frederick was somewhat shy at first. Ultimately, however, a longer conversation developed, about which both men wrote excited letters to friends in the fall of 1740.

Frederick wrote to his confidant Jordan in Rheinsberg that he had finally "seen this Voltaire whom I had been so eager to meet." As expected, he had been captivated by the Frenchman's "mind," which "was always working." At a pace of almost once a minute, he let loose a "flash of brilliance." Weeks after the encounter, Frederick still admitted, "All I could do was admire him and remain silent." Sighing, he added, "Madame du Châtelet is lucky to have him." For his part, Voltaire was also impressed by Frederick. Alone the king's voice, which many other contemporaries described as wonderfully soft, melodious, and mellifluous, won him over, especially since it spoke such flattering words.

To Pierre-Robert Le Corneille de Cideville, a friend dating back to his student days, Voltaire wrote on October 18 that Frederick was "one of the most amiable men in the world." Indeed, he could be "the delight of society if he were not king." For he was "a philosopher but not exacting, full of gentleness, friendliness, and pleasantness who forgets that he is king as soon as he is among friends." At times, Frederick seemed like such a normal person that Voltaire could only "recall with difficulty" who exactly was lying in bed before him: "a sovereign with an army of a hundred thousand men."

Only two days after Voltaire made this observation, an infamous death occurred that caused the well-oiled Prussian army to be mobilized and sent into action within a few weeks. After eating a dish of sauteed mushrooms that turned out to be poisonous, the fifty-five-year-old Holy Roman Emperor Charles VI suddenly and unexpectedly died—without a male heir to his Austrian possessions. Frederick received this news on October 26, and it deeply dismayed him. As he informed Voltaire, "The Emperor is dead. His death alters all my pacific ideas."

Referring to the recently begun construction of the opera house in Berlin, the king explained to his French correspondent that soon "it will be rather a matter of cannon-powder, soldiers, and trenches than of actresses, of balls and stages." Charles VI's death created a power vacuum in the Empire, and Frederick thought it prudent to occupy Austrian territory as quickly as possible in order to protect vital Prussian interests. In fact, he ordered his troops to do just that by the end of November or December. Due to this unilateral decision made by Frederick, Voltaire would later remark laconically that a "plate of mushrooms changed the destiny of Europe."

What motivated Frederick, the elector of Brandenburg and king of Prussia, to dare a surprise invasion of Austrian territory just because the Habsburg head of the Holy Roman Empire had died sooner than expected? Why did it even occur to him to enduringly undermine peace in Europe with this audacious and highly risky stratagem? His thought process can be divided into three stages. When he received news of the emperor's death, Frederick was initially panic-stricken about what could happen to Prussia if the Habsburg empire fell apart. This fear then merged with an overpowering urge to enforce old Hohenzollern claims to the Habsburg-controlled Duchy of Silesia, by force of arms if necessary. Finally, this desire was further fueled by the yearning for glory instilled in him by Prince Eugene.

Three years before the death of the last male Habsburg, Frederick had voiced concerns in a letter to Grumbkow: "If the Emperor dies in the next few days, what upheavals the world will know! Everyone would want a portion of his realm, and we would see as many factions arise as sovereigns." Charles VI had issued the Pragmatic Sanction on April 19, 1713, decreeing explicitly that a woman could ascend the throne in Austria. Nevertheless, Frederick did not believe that Maria Theresa, the emperor's eldest daughter, would be recognized as the universal heir to the Habsburg *Erblande*, or hereditary lands. He assumed that all the major territories possessed by the House of Austria within the borders of the Holy Roman Empire—the Austrian Netherlands, the Archduchy of Austria, and the Kingdom of Bohemia along with its appendages Moravia and Silesia, which had been attached to it since the Middle Ages—would soon excite the covetousness of several German princes.

As if on cue, the electors of Bavaria and Saxony disputed Maria Theresa's status as sole heir. In the name of their wives, Maria Amalia and Maria Josepha, both nieces of the deceased emperor, they asserted that they had equal claim to the Austrian territories. Frederick was now worried that Saxony would seek to add Bohemia, including Moravia and Silesia, to the crown of Poland it already possessed, either by a legal path or by taking unilateral military action. So threatening was the prospect of a massive Polish-Bohemian-Saxon realm right on the border with Brandenburg-Prussia that Frederick now believed he himself must take possession of Silesia as quickly as possible.

Justification for this frantic thought process was provided by passages that he had published just a few weeks before the emperor's death in his *Anti-Machiavel*. In chapter 26, he had explained to the world in no uncertain terms that "there are precautionary wars, which princes are wise to undertake. It is true that they are in fact offensive, but they are, nonetheless, just wars." For "when the excessive might of a power seems about to overflow, . . . it is wise to build dykes against it, and to check a raging torrent, while one is still capable of it." A watchful prince will act "when he has the option of choosing between an olive branch and a wreath of laurels, rather than waiting until matters become desperate." To preserve peace in one's own realm and promote the happiness of one's subjects, Frederick argued, a king must sometimes resort to a preemptive strike.

He now acted on the basis of these premises. The king needed only one month to deploy his regiments in sufficient strength. On December 13, he headed first in the direction of Frankfurt an der Oder and then south to Crossen (now Krosno Odrzańskie, Poland), a town in Brandenburg on the Silesian border. Thence, on December 16, he marched at the head of his 20,000 troops into the defenseless duchy. During the advance, he personally issued all the principal military commands. For in Brandenburg-Prussia, as he explained to Prince Leopold I of Anhalt-Dessau, "the nature of the government seems to demand that all regiments be directed by me alone." The invasion shocked the world, and it went off almost without a hitch. By the beginning of 1741, the young Prussian king had taken nearly all of Silesia.

Frederick may truly have considered this precipitous attack on Silesia to be an unavoidable act of self-defense, but he also believed he would only be able to hold on to the duchy permanently if he managed to gain recognition for past legal claims to this Austrian territory. Naturally, he assumed that his claims were indeed rightful. There were documents from 1537 stipulating that the Silesian principalities of Liegnitz, Wohlau, and Brieg (now Legnica, Wołów, and Brzeg in Poland) would fall to the House of Hohenzollern when the ruling Silesian dynasty died out. The legality of these claims had been challenged by Emperor Ferdinand I back in the sixteenth century, but that did not impress Frederick one bit. He sent the Prussian *Oberhofmarschall* Gustav Adolf von Gotter to Vienna to emphatically argue his case to Maria Theresa.

If anyone thought the daughter of Charles VI would submit meekly to Frederick's brash military performance and casuistic argumentation, they were dead wrong. Other German rulers, such as Landgrave William VIII of Hesse-Kassel and Prince Leopold I of Anhalt-Dessau, may have bought the king's argument that he had invaded Silesia to defend his country and his rights, but the twenty-three-year-old Austrian archduchess would not be deprived of her inheritance by anyone. Refusing to engage in any discussions with Frederick or his ministers, she sent troops of her own to the occupied territory, bringing the fight to the king.

Frederick was surprised by Maria Theresa's fierce resolve. On the other hand, her inflexibility finally gave him the opportunity to attain illustrious prestige as a battlefield commander. During the invasion of Silesia, he had quietly admitted to Voltaire that the obsession with military glory was in reality "a great folly." And yet it was "a folly too difficult to banish when once we dote on it." Indeed, Frederick was now truly gripped by the yearning for glory. Thus, in February 1741, he wrote to Jordan that he "love[d]" the imminent "war" with the Austrians "on account of the glory" to be won. Furthermore, he did not doubt in the least that the duel with the archduchess's army would have a felicitous outcome. As he frankly admitted to his friend in Rheinsberg, he felt an inner satisfaction at the thought of one day seeing his name sparkle brightly in the newspapers and the history books.

Prussian and Austrian forces—which theretofore had always fought side by side—first clashed on April 10 near the town of Mollwitz. As Frederick had predicted, Maria Theresa's troops had the worst of it in the fighting against the king's numerically superior regiments. Yet it was not he who shone brilliantly in the glistening snow as commander. The Prussian victory was won by the valiant Field Marshal Kurt Christoph von Schwerin. Frederick had withdrawn from the chaos of the battlefield to save his life. As a result, he thought of his first pitched battle as a personal debacle. Such deeds, he knew, did not get one's name in the papers.

Nevertheless, the Prussian triumph at Mollwitz provoked quite a furor in the Empire. The electors of Bavaria and Saxony broke off their laborious talks with Austria and, following the model of Frederick's troops, sought a military resolution to the issue. With the support of France, which had a profound interest in weakening its traditional foe Austria, Bavarian units marched into Linz in September. Meanwhile, the rulers of Saxony-Poland and Bavaria came to a "partage agreement," in which they calmly divided up the rest of unoccupied Austrian territory between themselves. In November, Elector Charles Albert of Bavaria invaded Bohemia. He then used this newly won position of power to have himself elected Holy Roman Emperor on January 24, 1742. As Charles VII, he was the first non-Habsburg emperor since 1437. In his capacity as elector of Brandenburg, Frederick, who turned thirty on the day of the imperial election, was one of those who cast a vote for the ambitious prince from the House of Wittelsbach.

Despite these depressing developments, the Austrians continued to fight. On May 17, 1742, they gave battle to the Prussian king yet again, this time in Chotusitz in Bohemia, where Frederick had gone to support the Bavarian army. This time the king displayed heroic courage. Personally leading a dynamic infantry attack, he put to flight the gradually advancing opponent. Finally, he had proved himself in battle and won personal military renown. This made it all the easier for him to make Maria Theresa an immediate offer of peace, on the condition that Austria permanently renounce its claim to Silesia and recognize it as a Prussian province. She had no choice. With the aim of gathering her strength and continuing the war against Bavaria and Saxony, she agreed to a preliminary peace with Frederick brokered by Great Britain. It was signed in Breslau (now Wrocław, Poland) in June 1742.

By unilaterally withdrawing from the fighting, Frederick alienated not only the new emperor but also the elector of Saxony. This did not bother him in the least, though, as the latter, in his capacity as king of Poland, had always seemed to him the most dread competitor for power and influence in Silesia. Having gotten what he wanted, the Prussian king now paid no mind to the continuing conflict between Saxony, Bavaria, and Austria. He longed above all to return to his "beautiful and peaceful beech trees" in Rheinsberg, as he communicated to Jordan in florid prose. Experience, however, was about to teach him that one who recklessly starts a war and then unexpectedly abandons his allies cannot so easily withdraw from the fray.

Its army freed up thanks to the peace with Prussia, Austria now moved deftly and with astounding speed to improve its position, conquering the Electorate of Bavaria in the course of 1743. It received aid in this endeavor from the British, who still needed the House of Habsburg as an ally in central Europe in the global competition with France. Emperor Charles VII was expelled by the Austrian army from his home territory of Bavaria and pushed all the way back to Frankfurt am Main. His French confederates had to withdraw across the Rhine. By 1744, Maria Theresa's military strength had been so fully restored thanks to the assistance of George II of England that the Prussian king now earnestly began to fear fierce retaliation from her. Once again, he reacted to a perceived threat with a preemptive war.

Blatantly disregarding the terms of the Treaty of Breslau, on September 16, 1744, Frederick led a massive army of over 60,000 men into Bohemia, a hereditary Austrian territory that had been left undefended. He occupied the capital of Prague, although he was not quite sure how to play this easily won bargaining chip. Then the king of Saxony-Poland, fed up with Frederick's constantly shifting plans and alliances, cut off the Prussian supply lines. As a result, Frederick was forced to make a winter retreat to Silesia, without having gained anything from his invasion of Bohemia. What is more, by disregarding the very peace treaty he had signed, he lost a great deal of credibility. Friend and foe alike now considered him utterly unpredictable. When Emperor Charles VII died on January 20, 1745, Frederick's situation took a dramatic turn for the worse.

On April 22, the new elector of Bavaria, Maximilian III Joseph, officially allied himself with Maria Theresa and promised to support her husband, Francis Stephen of Lorraine, in the upcoming imperial election. The Prussian king was now opposed by an alliance consisting of Austria, Bavaria, Saxony, Hanover, and Great Britain. In May, it proclaimed its intention to help the archduchess reconquer Silesia. It was all or nothing now for Frederick. In the past, he had often imagined that he was fighting for his survival in the battles against Austria. Now he really was. And since he believed that the Prussian state, ever since its founding in 1701, had always depended entirely on the person of its all-deciding, all-powerful king, the fate of the country was inseparably linked to his own. It made sense, therefore, when on April 27 he wrote to his foreign minister, Heinrich von Podewils, that either he would hold his own against Austria and its allies or, if he failed, he wished "to lose everything and have the Prussian name buried with me."

It may have been this all-or-nothing approach—in addition to his belief in providence, to which he constantly gave voice in this period—that spurred him on to outstanding military accomplishments and ultimately to victory. An army of 72,000 Austrian and Saxon soldiers under the command of Maria Theresa's brother-in-law Charles of Lorraine was now advancing on Silesia. Seeing an opportunity, the Prussian king made a surprise night attack on the enemy camp at Hohenfriedberg (now Dobromierz, Poland). Before dawn on June 4, 1745, Frederick engaged Charles's numerically superior force. Amid intense fighting, he himself gave the command for a decisive Prussian cavalry charge, led by his friend Egmont von Chasot, that broke the ranks of the Austro-Saxon regiments and drove them into immediate retreat.

Exuberant at the victory he had won with such unparalleled boldness, Frederick pursued the enemy troops in the following weeks all the way to Bohemia, where he beat them a second time at the Battle of Soor on September 30. Finally, the Prussians broke a last, desperate defensive effort by the now obviously weakened Austro-Saxon army at the Battle of Kesselsdorf, near Dresden, on December 15. Three days later, Frederick marched into the Saxon capital. On December 25, a new peace treaty was signed there by Prussia, Austria, and Saxony. Its terms were dictated by the king. Frederick belatedly gave his assent to Francis of Lorraine's election as Holy Roman Emperor, which had taken place back in September, thus also recognizing the latter's wife, Maria Theresa, as empress. For himself Frederick kept Silesia as a fully Prussian province, now formally detaching it from the Holy Roman Empire. Many contemporary jurists were of the opinion that the king had indeed withdrawn Silesia from imperial dominion.

In doing so, Frederick doubled the amount of territory that his still young, indeed parvenu Kingdom of Prussia controlled between Poland and Germany—and which, now more than ever, he could rule according to his own whim without respect for imperial law or obeisance to Poland and Bohemia. In addition, Saxony had to pay Prussia one million thalers in war reparations. It also had to allow Frederick's army, which had suffered a great many casualties in the victorious battles of the previous five years, to refresh its ranks by impressing Saxon men into service.

When Frederick returned from Saxony to Berlin on December 28, 1745, he was enthusiastically received by the people of his capital on the Spree. Many buildings and streets were illuminated festively in his honor, and cheers resounded in which the king was hailed for the first time as "Fridericus Magnus," or "Frederick the Great." The fact that in five years he had never been beaten despite most recently having to fight against a seemingly overwhelming alliance appeared to the Berlin populace as nothing short of astonishing. As a general, their king had achieved something truly great. Frederick himself was quite surprised that a musically and philosophically inclined king such as himself had risen to be one of Europe's most impressive military leaders. "Who would have thought," he candidly mused, "that providence would choose a poet to upset the political order of Europe and turn the calculations of its kings on their head?"

The warrior-poet Frederick also had to ask himself critical questions about the bloody price of the greatness he had won on the battlefield. No one formulated them as precisely or as combatively as Voltaire, still his treasured philosophical mentor. Indeed, 25,000 men had been killed or wounded on the Prussian side alone in the five battles Frederick had fought since he had marched into Silesia and unleashed the War of the Austrian Succession. The number of fallen, maimed, and wounded soldiers corresponded to one-quarter of the population of Berlin. How could a king who had promised to bring his people joy and happiness justify so much bloodshed?

Frederick responded to Voltaire with a metaphor: "Any man who makes up his mind to pull out a decayed tooth will give battle when he wishes to end a war." Prophylactic battles remove a threatening neighbor's ability to ruin one's own strength and well-being. "At such a time, to shed blood is to spare it." Furthermore, had he not also thrown himself into battle time and again, undaunted by death, and just like an ordinary soldier put his own life on the line for the future of Prussia? Had his actions not guaranteed the continued existence of the fledgling state that was providing its people with a more enlightened lifestyle than any other polity on the globe?

To underline the sincerity of his words, as soon as the Treaty of Dresden was signed, he redoubled his efforts to develop the Brandenburg-Prussian state, determined more than ever to turn it into a kingdom of the Enlightenment. The opera house in Berlin had been finished and opened during the short cessation of hostilities in 1742 after the initial Treaty of Breslau. Now, in January 1746, he had a small "Temple of Peace" erected right across from the prestigious opera. It was an expression of his gratitude for the end of the war and the renewal of peaceful cultural life. The following year, he then had the seat of Leibniz's brainchild, the Academy of Sciences, rebuilt bigger and more beautiful than before. The original building had fallen victim to a devasting fire in 1743. Along the grand boulevard Unter den Linden, Jan Bouman, Frederick's chief architect in Berlin, created an elegant structure for the academy that included a planetarium and an anatomical theater.

Under Frederick's judicious aegis, the revivified academy experienced a resurgence of activity. While other scientific societies in Europe—such as the Royal Society in London and the Académie des Sciences in Paris—limited their work to a few specialized disciplines, the academy in Berlin was devoted equally to the sciences and the humanities. The king considered astronomy, physics, anatomy, medicine, rhetoric, poetry, history, philosophy, and theology to be disciplines that built upon one another, interconnected pursuits of the human mind. Since an academy with such a universal program of research could only have a true polymath at its head, Frederick initially asked Voltaire to direct the reorganized institution.

When the philosopher from Cirey declined the invitation, Frederick named the mathematician Pierre-Louis Moreau de Maupertuis as president of the academy in May 1746. Maupertuis had gained fame thanks to an expedition to Lapland during which he had measured the shape of the earth, determining that it was an oblate sphere. In doing so, he empirically demonstrated a similar hypothesis by Isaac Newton. Maupertuis put his stamp on the academy, instituting French as its working language and raising the imperative of free debate in all moral and theological questions to the ultimate standard of scholarly discussion. Thanks to his tireless engagement and interest in the most pressing questions of modern science, the academy achieved new luster.

Frederick did not only devote his efforts to the arts and the sciences, however. In the wake of the Treaty of Dresden, he also felt more obligated than ever to bolster religious tolerance. For he was now in the process of integrating a new province into his dominion, Silesia, whose population was overwhelmingly Catholic. The gesture he made to welcome the Catholic Silesians as new subjects was grand indeed. On November 22, 1746, he gave generous permission to all Catholics in Brandenburg-Prussia to build a cathedral in Berlin, one "as big as they want or are able to make it." The site he provided to them was right next to the opera house and was thus a prestigious location in the heart of the city. The cornerstone was laid on July 13, 1747. The splendid church was to resemble the Pantheon in Rome, fronted by columns and crowned with a massive dome. The new Berlin cathedral was consecrated to Saint Hedwig of Andechs, the patron saint of Silesia; she had also been its duchess from 1201 until her death in 1243.

Frederick, in need of peace and quiet after the arduous acquisition of Silesia, also rewarded himself with a new palace. Magnificent yet intimate, he had it built in a secluded location west of Potsdam. He envisioned it as a summer house surrounded by a park and garden, for use exclusively in warmer months. He had discovered the site while riding on the Wüsten-Berg, a bald hill south of the village of Bornstedt. The vantage from this rise, utterly cleared of trees, provided a broad vista over Havelland that the king found simply entrancing. On August 10, 1744, he ordered a vineyard planted on its southern slope. The hill selected by Frederick was leveled, then raised, and finally furnished with six inwardly curved terraces to optimally catch and retain the warm sunshine vital to the growth of the vines. In addition to the grapes, whose varieties came from all over Europe, Frederick had fig, plum, peach, apricot, and cherry trees planted in over 150 semicircular niches in the terraces.

Atop the no longer bald but now fruit-bearing hill, construction began in 1745 on a one-story palace, which, in a gesture of tender but massive understatement, the king referred to as a vineyard cottage. His friend Knobelsdorff was once again the architect. On the basis of sketches and precise instructions provided by Frederick, he created a Rococo masterpiece that perfectly united intimacy and grandeur, simple living spaces and a ballroom surrounded by marble columns and crowned with a cupola. In summer 1747, the palace was far enough along that the king could move into a few rooms. And since it embodied so much lightness and cheer, Frederick gave it a name that in the past he had playfully applied to Rheinsberg. In golden letters, above the southern terrace of the summer palace, he had inscribed on the facade, "Sanssouci."

The carefree lust for life in which he planned to indulge at the new Sanssouci Palace was also depicted in countless pictures by the court painter Pesne. Some of them even featured priapic scenes with cooing doves, satyrs and nymphs, rams mounting sheep, and men embracing women, all swooning with pleasure. However, Frederick did not invite his own wife, Elisabeth Christine, to Sanssouci. After a phase of intimacy in Rheinsberg, the years of war—and attendant periods of long separation—had created an unbridgeable distance between them. Nor did Frederick any longer expect his wife to produce an heir. Thus he informed his next-youngest brother, Augustus William, aridly, "You are my sole heir." From now on, Elisabeth Christine had to live alone in Schönhausen Palace, located north of Berlin. The women who now attracted and enchanted Frederick were Italian and French dancers at the Berlin Opera. Charming portraits of these fetching beauties also graced the walls of Sanssouci.

Everywhere to be seen in the majestic palace atop the vineyard was also the shining sun of the Enlightenment. One, in gilded stucco, shone from the ceiling in the circular palace library, shedding its highly symbolic light on the king as he read or wrote. After the clash of arms in the bloody battles of Silesia and Bohemia, Frederick could once again play the part of the pure philosopher and poet in Sanssouci's reading room, which he had modeled on the tower library of Rheinsberg. He delighted in composing odes and epistles in which he inscribed his experiences of the previous years, giving them a philosophical interpretation. The king now signed all of his written works with the sobriquet "Philosophe de Sanssouci."

Frederick wrote numerous poems, even collecting a selection of them for his closest friends and printing it under the title *Œuvres du Philosophe de Sans-Souci* (Works of the Philosopher of Sanssouci). Time and again, he emphasized in these poems that, despite occasional, unavoidable wars, people were living in a "century of Enlightenment," *dans le siècle des lumières*. As he saw it, the philosophical ideas of Locke, Newton, and Voltaire, the latest advances in science, and respect for the importance of religious tolerance were spreading daily—and this was in no small part thanks to him as king of Prussia. His poetry praised the renewal of the Berlin Academy of Sciences, the building of the Berlin Opera, and the freedom of conscience and taste that reigned in

Brandenburg-Prussia; these were the most important cultural achievements with which he had enriched his lands in peacetime.

He still maintained that a truly enlightened kingdom could only be ruled by a wise king who had sole authority, free of parliamentary limitations, over every detail of government and administration, over the validity of judicial verdicts, and over questions of war and peace. As he explained in a letter to his general Asmus Ehrenreich von Bredow, zealous republicans—those who clamored for the complete self-determination and freedom of the people—ran the constant risk of plunging their commonwealth into chaos thanks to incessant debates, constant voting, endless controversy, and internal strife. For, in Frederick's opinion, the majority of the population was full of prejudices, "ignorant and stupid, and does not know what is at stake in the decisions it makes." Ultimately, it judged and complained without understanding, was fickle and easily deceived. As a result, the principles of the Enlightenment could only be made a reality by an avant-garde elite under the auspices of a monarchical state. Just how quickly an enlightened despot could advance his state was obvious to anyone who glanced at Brandenburg-Prussia.

Frederick was now extremely conceited. In an ode written in the spring of 1748 and entitled "The Present War" (*La guerre présente*), he portrayed himself as a king who cared uprightly and peacefully for the good of his country while other European monarchs continued to prosecute the seemingly endless war that he had exited in December 1745. He sent the ode to Voltaire, who praised him for his poetic productivity in Sanssouci. Yet he also replied with a clear criticism of the Prussian monarch, saying his self-portrayal as a prince of peace could convince no one. Indeed, Frederick was the one "who began the quarrel" all on his own in 1740 and "who won, with weapon in hand, a province and six battles." "Sire," Voltaire admonished him reproachfully, "your Majesty writes beautiful verses, but you laugh at the world."

Frederick was entirely correct, however, when he noted in his poetry that the kings of Great Britain and France had to make peace in order for the War of the Austrian Succession to end on all fronts. Indeed, the war that King George II of Britain had undertaken with Austria against his competitor France was being fought not only in Europe but also, and almost even more fiercely, in America. There, it was for good reason called King George's War. Spain had made common cause with France in May 1741, and since then the British had been fighting in a wider theater in North America than in Europe. The geographic zone in question was gigantic, stretching from the Spanish Caribbean to New France in Canada.

George II fought this war with firm resolve, hoping to protect and, if possible, to expand the northern and southern borders of Britain's colonies. The repercussions of the conflict were felt directly by the Washington family. George's oldest brother, Lawrence, who had returned to Virginia from his long period of schooling in England right before the outbreak of the War of the Austrian Succession, was a captain in the Virginia militia. He was sent to the Caribbean, where he was to lead the American expeditionary corps in support of regular British troops in the fight against the Spanish.

Lawrence served in the British fleet under the command of Admiral Edward Vernon. In the summer of 1741, he sent a letter full of vim and vigor to his father from Jamaica, proclaiming that he had already grown accustomed to the clamor of battle and was now able to ignore the thunder of the cannon even in situations of the greatest danger. What the cool and proud Lawrence Washington could not stand, however, was the condescending attitude of mid-ranking British naval officers. They did not give the American regiments the respect or the treatment they deserved, despite the fact that the Virginians gave their all to the British endeavor. However, he admired the charismatic Admiral Vernon.

In the fall of 1742, it emerged that Edward Vernon's fleet, despite making all conceivable efforts, lacked the necessary firepower and was thus not strong enough to undertake the planned attack on the Spanish island of Cuba. In consequence, the British changed their war strategy. They redeployed their forces to the north and sent the Virginians home for the time being. Thus, Lawrence Washington returned home—not in triumph, perhaps, but still as a battle-tested young man. In his brother George's eyes, he was a bold hero. In difficult circumstances, Lawrence had commanded the Virginia militia and voluntarily gone to war, and he had not been intimidated by cannon fire. Even the governor of Virginia, Sir William Gooch, was impressed by the pluck that Augustine Washington's oldest son had shown in the Caribbean. Therefore, at the beginning of 1743, Gooch named this promising young man commander of the Virginia militia, this time with the elevated rank of major.

Lawrence did not have long to glory in his promotion, however. That same spring, his father fell seriously ill and, sensing his death was near, to the dismay of the entire family drew up his last will and testament. After being confined to his sick bed for a few days at Ferry Farm, which not too long before he had built with his own hands, he died on April 12, 1743. Lawrence was devastated.

For his eleven-year-old brother, George, however, the sudden loss of his be-loved father was a much harsher blow. His mother, Mary, would doubtless continue to care for him, but who would now give the fatherly advice that was indispensable to a young American colonist who planned to be a planter or a soldier? It was Lawrence who took on the role of guiding his younger brother to adulthood.

Lawrence was a judicious and dependable mentor to his new charge. From his father he had inherited a gently sloping hill north of Ferry Farm on the Potomac River, on which he now built a stately house. In memory of the ad-miral he had admired so much on the Caribbean expedition, he named his new estate Mount Vernon. The up-and-coming major and planter now seemed a good marriage prospect in the eyes of wealthy Virginia plantation owners seeking husbands for their daughters. And on July 19, 1743, Lawrence married his fifteen-year-old neighbor, Anne Fairfax, who brought with her a dowry of 4,000 acres of land. The young girl was the daughter of Colonel William Fair-fax, who managed the five million acres of property owned by his cousin, Lord Thomas Fairfax of Cameron, as the latter lived in Great Britain. William Fairfax occupied the elegant Belvoir Manor on the western bank of the Potomac.

Thanks to his own landholdings and his connection to the aristocratic Fair-fax family, Lawrence Washington had the financial resources to send his youn-ger brother to school for a few more years, albeit not in England. With the consent of his mother, he was taught by a certain Mr. Williams who ran a school on Pope's Creek near the old Washington farm. That was now the resi-dence of George's second-oldest brother, Augustine Washington Jr., who had returned from England shortly before their father's death. George was a keen student. He showed great aptitude for mathematics and especially for geom-etry, with its two- and three-dimensional measurements. Yet he was also an avid reader of Enlightenment literature. One of his favorite authors was Joseph Addison, a member of the House of Commons and a journalist who had died in 1719. The brilliant parliamentarian had published *The Spectator*, a newspaper that appeared in 555 issues in its first run between 1711 and 1712. George studied this periodical intensely through number 143, in one of the countless reprints that floated around the English-speaking world.

Via Addison, who cited no political thinker as often as Locke, the young George Washington became increasingly acquainted with the arguments the British had used since 1688 to praise parliamentarianism as the guarantor of their freedom, both in the mother country and in the American colonies. His sense of the significance of legislative self-government was then heightened in

1744, when his dashing brother was elected to the Virginia House of Burgesses. Since the election of great-grandfather John as a burgess in 1665, the Washington family now entered its fourth generation of almost continuous membership in the colonial legislature.

George was deeply impressed by his brother's new political office, but Major Lawrence Washington still shone in his eyes primarily as a soldier. Thus, at the age of fourteen, when he began to consider what career path to follow, he was all too easily convinced by Lawrence to try his luck in the Royal Marines. The British were still fighting the War of the Austrian Succession, and their naval forces had recently won sensational victories against the French off the coast of Canada. In June 1745, for example, the British fleet had besieged the French fortress of Louisbourg, located on an island in the mouth of the Saint Lawrence Seaway, and forced it to capitulate. That put into British hands a mighty Canadian fortification that, since its construction in 1719, had represented a massive threat to the peninsula of Nova Scotia and the bordering colonies of New England.

When George Washington's mother heard of his plans to join the navy in late 1746, she disapproved and refused to relent. The resolute widow had not remarried after the death of her husband, and since then she had managed Ferry Farm on her own, with marginal success at best. She ignored the arguments her stepson Lawrence made in favor of George's preferred career. Instead, she asked her brother Joseph Ball, who lived in England and was always glad to shower his sister with male advice, to write George a sober letter highlighting the senselessness of his yearning for a life on the high seas.

Joseph Ball answered on May 19, 1747. He predicted that the war, from which the Prussian king had withdrawn in December 1745, would soon come to an end in America as well. Peace would come, he hoped, within a year. There would not be nearly enough time to work his way up from a "common sailor" to a high officer's rank. And anyway, to receive "any considerable preferment" one needed the support and intercession of highly placed men, and that would be hard for George to come by. On the other hand, as a Virginia planter—even if of no great wealth—he would enjoy the honorable "liberty of the subject" in a few years. And that was much more desirable than the hard work aboard a warship, where he would have to toil "like a Negro, or rather, like a dog."

Her brother's deliberately harsh advice strengthened Mary Ball Washington's resolve to relieve her oldest son of his urge for naval glory as quickly as possible. Instead, she hoped to interest him in a peaceful occupation in the countryside, one that would also be useful to him as a farmer. In the spring of

1747, George had put his gift for geometry to use by assisting a neighbor with surveying work. Now she advised him to focus on perfecting his abilities in that sphere. Carrying a compass and a measuring rod known as a Jacob's staff, which resembled the sextant used at sea, he excelled at calculating angles and distances at long range, even in hilly or forested terrain. The art of surveying that he mastered so well was extremely important in the American colonies, as it was necessary for creating the maps on which property was outlined with great precision and thus with legal certainty for sale to newly arrived settlers.

George respected his mother's wishes, and even Lawrence had to bend to her will. In the end, it was she—and not his older brother—who was the boy's guardian. George may have been saddened at not going to sea, but that did not stop him from enjoying his ever more numerous surveying trips into the fields and forests of Virginia, especially since they paid very well. On August 8, 1747, he recorded in his notebook the surveying of a parcel at the Oldfield school-house. Two months later, he entered the receipt of his ample wage: a cash payment equivalent to the price of 400 pounds of tobacco. By February 1748, he had received so many public commissions that not only his wallet but also his reputation as a surveyor had swelled appreciably.

When he was engaged for surveying duties by the Fairfax family that month, it was thus not only because of the private ties he enjoyed to Belvoir thanks to Lawrence's marriage. George was asked to accompany James Genn, who had served the Fairfaxes as a surveyor for many years, on an excursion to the Shenandoah Valley. The region between the Appalachians and the Blue Ridge Mountains belonged to the gigantic Fairfax holdings in western Virginia. In mid-March 1748, George set off on his first long journey as part of a survey-ing crew. The group was also joined by Colonel William Fairfax's twenty-two-year-old son George. George Washington was only sixteen at the time, but he was very athletic and nearly six feet three inches tall.

During the monthlong trip, Washington wrote in his journal every evening before going to sleep, carefully chronicling what he had done in the foregoing hours. Seldom did his entry read, "Nothing remarkable happened." Most of the entries record things that were new to him. One of the most exciting was an unexpected encounter with thirty Indians who were on the warpath and carried a freshly taken scalp. "We had some liquor with us of which we gave them part, it elevating their spirits," Washington noted. He then expressed his amazement that this gesture of peace and friendship was repaid by the Indians with a war dance, which he went on to describe in detail: "The manner of dancing is as follows: they clear a large circle and make a great fire in the middle, then seat themselves around it. The speaker makes a grand speech telling them in what manner they are to dance. After he has finished, the best dancer jumps up as one awakened out of a sleep and runs and jumps about the ring. In a most comical manner, he is followed by the rest." This noteworthy spectacle was accompanied by "their musicians," who beat on "a pot half of water with a deerskin stretched over it." They keep on incessantly "drumming all the while the others is [sic] dancing."

Almost as exotic as the Native Americans was a group of European settlers that he and his companions stumbled upon several days later in an area bordering the uninhabited wilderness. This group of "men, women, and children" gave no thought at all to getting permission to buy the property. Rather, they belonged to the growing number of colonists known as "squatters," who settled on unimproved, unsurveyed land in the hope of being allowed to buy it from the Crown or its owner at a very low price in the future, after years of living on it. The squatters Washington saw had clearly come from Switzerland or Germany, for "they would never speak English but when spoken to they speak all Dutch"—that is, German. They seemed to him "as ignorant a set of people as the Indians."

Naturally, his days in the Virginia hinterland were mostly spent in arduous labor. He surveyed several hundred acres of land, dividing them into parcels that were especially well suited to settlement. Time and again, he waxed lyrical about the "richness of the land" that spread out before him in the sweeping Shenandoah Valley. And he raved about the maple trees, which he called "sugar trees" because of the sweet syrup that could be tapped from them. The forests were also full of "wild turkeys," which Washington, the avid hunter, shot in large numbers. The birds were then defeathered and roasted in the evening over the campfire. Each man exhibited his own method of preparing the delicacy, as "every[one] was his own cook." Tired after a long day's work and full from dinner, they quickly fell asleep in a "tent" or "the open air."

The return journey was difficult, as it rained frequently now that it was April. The trails were very soft. To traverse certain stretches, it was easier for the horses to swim through rivers and the men to paddle alongside them in canoes. One especially muddy path seemed to Washington "the worst road that ever was trod by man or beast." Two days before the journey's end, a rattlesnake appeared on the path, and the group had to carefully navigate around it. The surveyors were happy to get back to the bosom of their families. Washington spent the first days after his return from the wilderness with his brother Lawrence at Mount Vernon. And Fairfax, with whom George had forged a close friendship during the surveying tour, returned safely to Belvoir.

The same day that the Fairfax surveying expedition came to a successful conclusion, a peace congress began in the Free Imperial City of Aachen (also known as Aix-la-Chapelle) that would finally bring about the long-awaited conclusion to the War of the Austrian Succession. Washington's uncle Joseph Ball thus turned out to be correct when he conjectured in May 1747 that peace would come within a year. After only five months of negotiations, the peace treaty was signed in October 1748. In the final phase of the war, the Austro-British army suffered several losses to French troops in the Austrian Netherlands. As a result, the British agreed to restore the Canadian fortress of Louisbourg to France; in return Flanders returned to Austrian control. In addition, Maria Theresa was finally recognized by all European powers as the sole heir to the Habsburg territories—except for Silesia, which the Peace of Aachen formally recognized as belonging to Frederick the Great, the true winner of the war.

The terms of the Treaty of Aachen largely met with approval in Europe, but the British colonists in America were angry that the fortress of Louisbourg, taken at great cost only three years prior, had to be given back to New France. Yet the peace treaty meant an end to all hostilities in North America, and so it was also celebrated all over the British colonies, from Boston in New England to Philadelphia, Pennsylvania, to Williamsburg, Virginia. The most lavish celebration of the Treaty of Aachen took place in London's Green Park. Over 10,000 people enjoyed a majestic fireworks display over the River Thames, accompanied by the kettledrums and trumpets of the *Music for the Royal Fireworks*, which King George II had commissioned from George Frideric Handel.

In this time of general public rejoicing, a private celebration also took place in Washington's orbit. Yet while everyone else enjoyed the festivities, the young surveyor came away with an unexpected shock. On December 17, 1748, his new companion George Fairfax married eighteen-year-old Sally Cary, several months after meeting her in Williamsburg. The groom invited relatives and friends, including Washington, to his home so he could introduce his new wife. But when the usually imperturbable young surveyor saw the bride, he came unhinged. On the spot he fell in love with the woman, who seemed to be the most beautiful he had ever seen—and who now, to his great sorrow, was wed to one of his best friends.

The many visits he made to Belvoir from Mount Vernon in 1749 were attended by a mixture of happiness and pain. On the one hand, he enjoyed every minute he was able to spend in the presence of the attractive Sally Fairfax. As he later wrote, she dazzled with "her charms" and "her amiable beauties," radiating gaiety, a fine sense of humor, and levity. She was the granddaughter of a president of the College of William and Mary, which had been founded in 1693 and which, along with the New England colleges Harvard and Yale, was among the most important institutions of higher learning in the American colonies. Her father had attended Trinity College, at Cambridge University in England. These two men had given Sally an excellent education as well. She read highbrow literature, spoke fluent French, was musical, and moved with grace. Her expressive eyes could sparkle with élan. Yet Washington was not destined to consummate his desire for this vivacious brunette. With a keen sense of prudence, responsibility, and above all conventional morality, she maintained a strictly platonic relationship with him.

Nevertheless, his mere proximity to her—and his frequent visits to the grand, dignified interiors of Belvoir—brought about a remarkable change in his behavior. He paid more attention to good manners and clothing, even developing his own design for an elegant coat reaching "down to or below the bent [sic] of the knee." And he regularly participated in a reading group led by Colonel William Fairfax, where he became acquainted with further writings of Addison owned by George and Sally. He greatly admired Addison's *Cato*, a tragedy first performed in 1713 that celebrates the republicanism of ancient Rome as the precursor to British parliamentarianism. *Cato* had many admirers in Europe. In part because of the ideal of freedom it extols, Voltaire considered it the best English tragedy of all time. Washington also sympathized with the tragic hero of the piece, the senator Marcus Porcius Cato. Determined to defend the liberty of the Roman Republic to the death, he lost his life in 46 BC in the fight against the usurper Caesar. The fact that the subplot of the tragedy deals with the Numidian Prince Juba's secret love for Cato's daughter Marcia made it even more attractive to Washington.

The romantic strings of his soul that Sally made sing, however, did not entirely overpower the rational, soberly calculating part of his character. Although he admitted in a letter to a friend in 1749 that it was difficult for him to rein in his feelings—"burying that chaste and troublesome passion in the grave of oblivion or eternal forgetfulness"—he did restrain his desire so as not to endanger his good relationship with the Fairfax family. He continued to receive well-paid commissions from William Fairfax to survey sprawling tracts of Virginia land. The colonial legislature in Williamsburg also provided Washington with several months of very profitable employment as a surveyor. In May 1749, the House of Burgesses decided to build a port on a sixty-acre plot of land at the headwaters of the Potomac River, as a means of expanding the capacity to export tobacco to England. Washington was commissioned to survey a section of the parcels and to draw the plan of the city. The new port was to be called Alexandria, after the previous owner of the site, John Alexander.

Washington was now earning so much money as a surveyor that he could afford better clothing, fine horses, and luxury bridles. In October 1750, he then bought his very first pieces of property. One of them, containing 550 acres, he had surveyed himself the previous year in the Shenandoah Valley. In addition, the journeys he undertook for work improved his acquaintance with the colony of Virginia. Sometimes he lived with his mother at Ferry Farm, but he preferred to stay with his brother Lawrence at Mount Vernon. Washington continued to enjoy a period of unadulterated success as a routine surveyor until the summer of 1751. Then, however, his oldest brother fell gravely ill, suddenly and irrevocably changing the life path George was traveling.

Lawrence had suffered from a chronic cough since the fall of 1748, which in the winter months worsened and sapped his energy. When his condition deteriorated seriously in the spring of 1751, the burgess, major, and planter decided to spend the next winter not in icy Virginia but rather in the warm climate of the Caribbean that he had come to appreciate while sailing with Admiral Vernon. He chose the island of Barbados, whose air had a reputation for being especially beneficial to those with lung problems. Lawrence did not want to travel all alone to the Caribbean, so he asked his younger brother George if he would like to accompany him. In part out of a desire for adventure, in part out of sincere concern for his favorite brother's welfare, he agreed. Nor was his mother opposed to the plan. She was sure George had lost all interest in the naval career to which he had once aspired.

The ship that brought Lawrence and George Washington to the Caribbean sailed out of the Potomac and into the open sea on September 28, 1751, reaching the port of Bridgetown, the capital of Barbados, five weeks later. The day after their arrival, Lawrence sought out an experienced pneumologist, who held out hope that his condition would improve. On November 6, the brothers moved into fine lodgings in a captain's house with a view of the sea. Washington was thrilled with the bay vista from his window. He could hardly get enough of the tropical vegetation and the colorfulness of the fruits and blossoms. As he noted in his diary, the "prospect" of Barbados "by land . . . and by sea" was incredibly "pleasant." He was even able to indulge his artistic and literary proclivities there: Bridgetown had a theater where he took in a tragedy on November 15.

Two days later, however, he suddenly fell ill with a high fever. The symptom was then joined by a headache, back pain, and nasty chills. When, on

November 20, he developed spots and pustules all over his face, the diagnosis was swiftly made: Washington had smallpox. Apparently, he had been infected right upon stepping ashore on the Caribbean island. For one whole week, he fought the life-threatening illness. Then his fever abated, and the pustules began to dry out. Washington was relieved and thankful. Patiently and with great fortitude in the face of suffering, he had overcome the disease that, as he wrote in his diary, had "strongly attacked" him. Nor would he ever get smallpox again, as he had now developed a natural immunity to the insidious illness. The memory of this painful victory would remain with him his entire life, in the form of prominent pockmarks on his forehead and cheeks.

By mid-December, Washington was once again able to stroll through Bridgetown as a fully healed man. On the other hand, his brother's condition had not distinctly improved since their arrival in Barbados. Shortly before Christmas, therefore, when they had planned to sail back to Virginia, Lawrence decided at the last minute to remain on the island for several more months. He asked George to return home alone and see to the most important affairs at Mount Vernon for him. After an unusually stormy voyage, Washington touched land in Virginia on January 28, 1752. Before going to his brother's estate, however, he first rode to Williamsburg to personally deliver a few important official letters from Barbados to the recently installed governor, Robert Dinwiddie. The two men developed an immediate liking for one another, and the governor made sure to remember the name of the reliable young letter-carrier in case of future need.

While awaiting his brother's return, George Washington devoted himself once again to surveying work, bought more land, and had a small party to celebrate his twentieth birthday. After the long trip to the Caribbean, which had vastly expanded his horizons, and the ordeal of surviving smallpox, he was now endowed with a prodigious thirst for action and an equally powerful sense of self-confidence. He felt young, courageous, and strong. Throughout Lawrence's absence, he managed his brother's affairs at Mount Vernon conscientiously. He also regularly rode over to Belvoir to spend as much time as possible with George and Sally Fairfax.

In the summer of 1752, Lawrence finally returned. His letters, which announced his arrival weeks ahead of time, were constant bearers of depressing news. His cough was worse than ever, and his stay in Barbados had been good for nothing. In his final pessimistic missive before his return voyage to Virginia, he announced that he would now just "hurry home to my grave." When George embraced his haggard brother at Mount Vernon, he knew that

Lawrence had not been exaggerating. On June 20, the unfortunate young man made out his will. On July 26, his exhausted lungs took their last breath. Lawrence was survived by his grieving wife, Anne, and their only daughter, Sarah, not yet two years old. George, as his deceased brother's closest adult heir, had to take care of them.

Upon Lawrence's death, his post as major of the Virginia militia had fallen vacant, and George intended to have it. It seemed natural to him that he would apply to the governor of Virginia to assume the military rank previously enjoyed by his brother. He was no longer drawn to a career in the Royal Marines, but he still burned with a passion for firearms. Governor Dinwiddie was well disposed to him, and, as the new year dawned, he acceded to his wish for military distinction. On February 1, 1753, the younger brother of the deceased Lawrence was himself appointed Major Washington. He received an annual salary of 100 pounds, a considerable supplement to his income as a surveyor.

It did not take long for the freshly appointed Major George Washington to be tested. In the spring of 1753, French units from Canada advanced into the Ohio Valley, west of Pennsylvania, and began to build a series of strong forts between the southern coast of Lake Erie and the Ohio River. They intended to use these bases to gain control of the region before the British. Up to that point, the densely forested Ohio country had not been an object of European colonization efforts. Only Indians and fur traders met there to exchange goods. The French had had designs of establishing a corridor between their far-flung settlements in Canada and Louisiana since the beginning of the century. If they now managed to occupy this region permanently, then British plans to expand their colonies westward were doomed to failure.

The French believed they were not breaking the terms of the Treaty of Aachen by building the forts, and Indians who hunted in the Ohio Valley initially tolerated them. In contrast, nearly every colonial government in British North America was dismayed by the French encroachment. Governor Dinwiddie sought advice directly from the Crown in London. The letter in response was signed personally by George II and arrived in Williamsburg in October 1753. The monarch urged quick, decisive action. He asked that a suitable emissary be sent to the Ohio Valley to demand that the French withdraw immediately.

When Washington heard from George Fairfax that the governor was looking for a reliable and cool-headed messenger to inform the French of the king's opposition to their occupation of the Ohio Valley, he rode to Williamsburg without delay to volunteer for the delicate mission. And indeed, Dinwiddie gave Major Washington the honorable commission on October 30, 1753, although the latter was only twenty-one years old and bereft of any military experience. Washington was to seek out the commander of all French soldiers in the Ohio country—Captain Jacques Legardeur de Saint-Pierre—and hand him a strongly worded note of protest enjoining him to cease building the forts. Years later, Washington recalled it was highly unusual to entrust such important diplomatic business to so young and inexperienced a man as himself.

On November 15, the major set off for the Ohio Valley with six companions. The group included a Dutchman fluent in many languages, Jacob van Braam. He was to translate for Washington, who was ignorant of French. Furthermore, the surveyor Christopher Gist was to serve as the party's scout. He was one of the few British colonists who knew the woods of the Ohio country well enough to show Washington the way to Legardeur's residence, Fort LeBoeuf, located a few miles south of Lake Erie. On the way to the French commander, the Virginians conferred with chiefs of the Shawnee, Mingo, and Delaware Indians who were hunting in the Ohio Valley and were friendly—or at least not hostile—to the British. The Mingo chief Tanacharison confided to Washington bitterly that the French had forcibly constructed forts and unjustly built large houses on Indian land. Furious, Tanacharison had resolved to accompany the British and convince Legardeur on behalf of the Native Americans to stop building forts.

Washington, Gist, van Braam, Tanacharison, and their companions reached Fort LeBoeuf amid a heavy snowstorm on December 11. Chilled to the bone, they were formally greeted by the commander and invited inside to warm up. He catered to their needs as well as he could. At the same time, he made it perfectly clear that he had no intention of abandoning the French post in the Ohio Valley. Legardeur immediately gave Washington a letter for Dinwiddie containing his formal written refusal. The major quickly realized that further negotiation with Legardeur would simply be a waste of time. Tanacharison remained at Fort LeBoeuf to try to convince the commander to change his mind, but Washington left on December 16 to bring Legardeur's letter to Dinwiddie.

The winter had become savage. Washington, his company, and their horses were confronted with deeper and deeper snow on the return journey, severely sapping their energy. Shortly before New Year's Day, Washington noted that "the cold was so extreme severe that Mr. Gist got all his fingers and some of his toes froze [sic]." Even more dangerous was an ambush laid by Indians allied with the French. These "French Indians," as Washington called them, belonged to the Chippewa or Ottawa tribe. At a distance of "not fifteen steps," they shot at the major, missing him by a hair's breadth. Only with difficulty and against heavy opposition did Gist and Washington manage to put the Indians to flight and take the shooter "into custody." The captive turned out to be an inconvenient burden on the arduous return journey, though, so he was released a few hours later without his weapons in the safety of darkness.

On January 11, 1754, Washington reached Belvoir Manor, where he spent one full day recovering from the hardships he had just suffered. Only on January 16 was he able to hand Legardeur's letter to the governor in Williamsburg. When Dinwiddie read that "the rights of the king [of France] . . . to the lands situated along the Ohio are incontestable," he was not surprised. Indeed, he had expected precisely such an answer. Now, with this unambiguous letter in hand, he could call the British government and his own people to take up arms again against the French, whom he trusted no more after the Treaty of Aachen than he had during the War of the Austrian Succession. Washington had extraordinarily impressed the governor as a doughty messenger, and so Dinwiddie allowed him to write a report of his difficult undertaking and publish it in all the gazettes in the colonies. This report appeared a short time later in many European newspapers as well. For the first time, the world was able to read that a certain Major George Washington had gloriously acquitted himself on the North American continent.

7

Might and Right (1754–1762)

THE DEMAND to immediately quit the Ohio Valley, issued by King George II in distant London and delivered personally by George Washington, was defied by the French. The situation was not easy for Governor Dinwiddie to handle. What should he do? Should he write to England again asking for new instructions? That would take months, and all the while the French would be able to build numerous new forts. Or, without consulting with the king, should he seek on his own authority to take the portion of the Ohio country for the British that was not yet occupied by French soldiers? After intense discussions with his council, he sent an army of 200 volunteers under the command of Washington to the confluence of the Allegheny and Monongahela Rivers (which formed the headwaters of the Ohio), with orders to oversee the construction of a British fort on that spot.

Since the expedition had to be funded by tax money, it required the approval of the Virginia colonial legislature. Dinwiddie convened a special session of the House of Burgesses. On February 14, 1754, the representatives of the people granted the sum of money he requested, but they also reserved the right to be informed at all times of all troop movements and further military expenditures. They did not want to give Dinwiddie the opportunity to attack the French without their knowledge. They had no intention of violating the terms of the Peace of Aachen.

Promoted to the rank of lieutenant colonel, Washington now had to perform the laborious task of recruiting a sufficient number of militiamen to protect the British fort. Meanwhile, in late February, a small advance unit of experienced carpenters got to work at the forks of the Ohio River, 180 miles northwest of Alexandria. The new British military base was quickly constructed. Even the Mingo chief Tanacharison helped the Virginians. Despite remaining with the French commander Legardeur the previous year, he had been unable to persuade him to leave the northern Ohio Valley. In a symbolic act, Tanachari-son raised the first post of the wooden stockade, proclaiming that the fortifica-tion was from now on the common property of the English and his tribe. By mid-April, the fort and its defensive palisades had been completed.

Just as the British were mounting the gate on their new fortification, canoes bearing 500 French soldiers and eighteen cannon appeared on the river before them. When the French came ashore, their commander, Captain de Con-trecœur (Legardeur's successor), requested to speak with the workers. He explained that the governor-general of New France, the Marquis Duquesne, had issued orders several weeks earlier for a French fort to be built at precisely this location. If the British did not clear out voluntarily, he would have to use force. Considering the adversary's far superior numbers, the Virginians had no choice. They had to surrender the fort. The French named it Fort Duquesne in honor of the governor-general and reinforced it as a stone stronghold.

Washington did not set out for the Ohio Valley from Alexandria until early April, and he was only accompanied by 160 militiamen instead of the envi-sioned 200. On April 20, right after crossing the Appalachians, he received the depressing news of the French capture of the British fort. He briefly consid-ered whether he should return to Alexandria or Williamsburg in order to in-form the governor of the sudden change in the situation. But he decided to press on with his men. If no British fort could be erected on the spot foreseen by Dinwiddie, the plan could surely be put into action in another location not too far distant. What mattered was for the British legal claim to the Ohio coun-try to be staked, ideally by the construction of a fort. Thus, Washington or-dered his Virginians to build a new British fort on the northern rim of the Appalachians, only forty miles south of Fort Duquesne.

The work had just begun when Washington was visited by Mingo warriors on the evening of May 27. Sent by Tanacharison, they informed him that their chief had just spotted a camp of more than thirty French soldiers only a few miles from the new building site. Washington should come with them to Tanacharison and then scout out the French camp with him. The alarmed lieutenant colonel did not hesitate. That same night, he rode with forty-seven armed militiamen through the pouring rain to the nearby Mingo position, conferred with Tanacharison, and was led to the French camp by the chief and his bravest warriors. Washington and Tanacharison observed the French in the early-morning hours of May 28 as they were preparing breakfast.

The breaking of a branch alerted one of the French soldiers to the discon-certing fact that the camp was surrounded by Virginia militiamen and Indian warriors. He instinctively grabbed his gun and called his comrades to arms. A shot rang out. Washington reacted immediately. He ordered his men to raise their weapons and shouted, "Fire!" Again the command was given. The two English salvos left several Frenchmen on the ground. Thereupon followed an intense skirmish lasting about ten minutes. Washington stopped his men when he saw that the wounded French commander, Jumonville, had ordered his own troops to cease firing. He was waving at the British, inviting them to call a truce.

The Dutchman van Braam, again serving Washington as a translator, approached Jumonville. Before they could commence discussions, however, the Indians were ordered out of hiding by their chief, threw themselves upon the wounded French soldiers, and killed them instantly. Tanacharison was not in the mood to talk peace. He wanted to fight. In French he yelled at Jumonville, lying defenseless before him, "Thou art not yet dead, my father!" and struck his head with "several hatchet blows" until it broke open, blood and brains flowing freely from the wound. Then he pulled the gray matter out of the skull and bathed his hands in it. Finally, he and his warriors scalped the dead Frenchmen and disappeared back into the forest.

Washington's blood froze in his veins as he observed the Indians' startling assault. Beholding the ghoulish scene, he was in a state of momentary shock. All he could do was put himself and his men between the remaining uninjured French soldiers and the attacking Mingo warriors. By the time he fully regained his senses, the massacre was over. All that remained for the distraught lieutenant colonel to do was return to the construction site. He ordered the fort to be rapidly completed, reckoning that massive French retaliation was bound to come sooner or later. He sent the French prisoners to Dinwiddie, informing him in a letter of May 29 about what had happened and requesting reinforcements. Five days later, the fort was finished. Washington named it Fort Necessity, reflecting the moment of great emergency and pressing need in which it was constructed. On June 2, he had devout prayers read aloud in the fort, begging for salvation from the desperate situation.

While his letter was on its way to Dinwiddie, the news was making the rounds of all the British colonies that the French had taken Fort Duquesne at the forks of the Ohio River in April. The bold officer from Virginia named George Washington, who was still remembered for his newspaper article of January 1754, had suffered yet another defeat. In Philadelphia, a prominent member of the Pennsylvania colonial legislature commented on Washington's misfortune in the periodical he published, *The Pennsylvania Gazette*. The editor and author was Benjamin Franklin, the self-taught amateur scientist who two years earlier had invented the lightning rod, earning for himself international renown as an ingenious experimenter and trailblazer of the Enlightenment. As readers of the *Gazette* all over the colonies learned, Franklin did not blame Washington for retreating from the French. Instead, he criticized the lack of action taken by all the other British colonial governments. In his view, they had not yet grasped that now was the time for energetic, concerted action if the French were to be successfully opposed.

As Franklin argued, the arrogant presumption with which the French treated Washington and the royal governor was all too predictable. For the British colonists were simply not united enough in their approach. At fault for the unchecked French advance into the backwoods of Virginia and Pennsylvania was "the extreme difficulty" of getting so many different American "governments and assemblies to agree in any speedy and effectual measures for our common defense and security." In contrast, thanks to the centralized administration of New France, "our enemies have the very great advantage" of being "under one direction," that of General Governor Duquesne. If the British colonies did not finally form a true political union against the French threat, the result would inevitably be "the destruction of the British interest, trade, and plantations in America."

Franklin was not the only one to describe the situation in such dire terms. In the halls of power in Whitehall back in London, there was also a fear that a lack of cooperation among the British colonial governments would soon encourage the French to endeavor even more audacious encroachments. As a result, the Board of Trade, which was responsible for British colonial policy, ordered Governor James De Lancey of New York to convene a congress at which representatives from all the British colonies would gather to formulate a long-overdue common defense strategy. De Lancey set things in motion immediately. On June 19, 1754, he greeted the delegates he had invited from the various colonies in the city of Albany, at the headwaters of the Hudson River, and formally opened the discussions.

The Albany Congress was the first significant meeting of representatives from all the colonies. Its leading voice belonged to Benjamin Franklin, who attended as a delegate from Pennsylvania. He sought to convince the other participants that the most effective path to their mutual defense and safety could only be to create a union of the various colonies as swiftly as possible. Franklin did not argue for a centrally organized government. He had recently devoured an English translation, published in 1748, of *The Spirit of the Laws* by the French political philosopher Montesquieu, which praised federalism as the political form of the future. As a prime example of federalism, Montesquieu pointed to the Holy Roman Empire, a large state made up of various electorates, duchies, counties, and city-republics. In line with this concept, Franklin conceived of the union of the American colonies as an overarching state, composed of individual states, that would remain a part of the British Empire.

Franklin's "Plan of Union" called for the Crown to designate an American "president general" who would guide the policy of the new American union in consultation with a "grand council to be chosen by the representatives of the people of the several colonies," consisting of up to forty-eight members. At the same time, all the colonies joining the union—Massachusetts, New Hampshire, Connecticut, Rhode Island, New York, New Jersey, Pennsylvania, Maryland, Virginia, North Carolina, and South Carolina—would "remain in their present state," retaining their current constitutions and colonial legislatures. In this way, at both the federal level of union and the level of the individual colonies, American government would always be legitimized by elections and the work of legislatures. Believing that Philadelphia was the cultural, political, and geographical center of the colonies, Franklin proposed that the city on the Delaware River be both the union's capital and the meeting place for the grand council.

Franklin's concept for a unification of all the British colonies was enthusiastically approved by all the delegates. They immediately forwarded his constitutional design to the colonial legislatures and the Board of Trade in London, requesting that it be quickly ratified. But neither the legislatures nor the Crown gave serious and thorough consideration to the far-sighted plan—a plan that, if it had been acted upon, as Franklin later mused, very probably would have changed the course of American history. For "the colonies so united would have been sufficiently strong to have defended themselves; there would then have been no need of troops from England; of course the subsequent pretense for taxing America, and the bloody contest it occasioned, would have been avoided." As it was, while the Albany Congress was sitting, events took place in the southern Ohio Valley that left the British Crown no time to wait for the protracted process of legislative ratification.

In mid-June, as the Albany delegates were commencing their deliberations, the requested reinforcements had finally arrived at Fort Necessity. They included 200 Virginia militiamen and about 100 British regulars from Carolina. Lieutenant Colonel Washington now had more than 400 men to defend his new base. The fresh arrivals also brought him news of his promotion to full colonel; Governor Dinwiddie clearly wanted to boost Washington's courage and powers of perseverance. On June 28, however, Indian scouts brought him the gloomy news that a detachment of French soldiers over 1,000 strong had set out from Fort Duquesne. They were intent on two things: exacting revenge and forcing Washington and his men back over the Appalachians to Virginia. The leader of the hot-blooded French force was Captain Louis Coulon de Villiers, the older brother of Tanacharison's victim Jumonville.

Washington had no choice but to dig in at Fort Necessity and wait for the French to come. In the late afternoon of July 3, French units arrived at the new British fort, advanced upon it immediately, and opened fire. The attack lasted into the evening, leaving many holes in the thin palisades and nearly one-third of Washington's soldiers dead. Only with the onset of dusk did de Villiers cease fire and offer Washington the possibility of abandoning the fort in safety. In return, however, he required the signing of an unconditional surrender. In the absence of any real alternative, Washington relented, signed the humiliating document, and departed from Fort Necessity with what remained of his wounded and exhausted troops. The French set fire to the fort straightaway. It was not until early August that Washington arrived back in western Virginia. From there he sent Dinwiddie a letter detailing his renewed misadventure. He dramatically described the condition of his soldiers, who had returned from the Ohio country thoroughly beaten, "naked," and "without credit even for a hat."

Washington's report dismayed not only Governor Dinwiddie in the colony of Virginia but also the British government in the mother country. When news of the destruction of Fort Necessity reached London in early September, Prime Minister Thomas Pelham-Holles cried out in horrified anger that all of North America would soon be lost if French aggression continued to be tolerated with impunity. In order to not completely fall behind the French, the British government felt compelled to respond to the building of forts in North America with all possible force. What had begun as a verbal legal dispute, sparked by the delivery of Dinwiddie's note of protest to the French commander Legardeur in November 1753, now seemed impossible to resolve by peaceful means. And since there was no neutral, authoritative arbiter to decide in favor of the French or the British, only arms could now decide who would enjoy lasting authority over the Ohio Valley.

At the behest of the Duke of Cumberland, who was the second-oldest son of the British king and the most powerful military leader in Great Britain,

Major General Edward Braddock was sent to Virginia with two regiments of Irish infantry in January 1755. His mission was to drive the French out of the Ohio country for good by attacking their most important forts. As the commander in chief of all British soldiers and militiamen in America, it was also Braddock's job to weld the colonies together into a coherent unit, at least as far as the current military operations were concerned. This was to be done without founding the federal union conceived at Albany.

Braddock arrived in Virginia in February 1755, his two regiments following one month later. He lost no time in seeking out men who wanted to cooperate with him. He met with Franklin in Maryland, who offered to provide the major general, in exchange for just compensation, with 150 coaches, the 600 horses needed to draw them, and the requisite drivers, in an effort to improve the transportation of troops and munitions. Braddock gave Franklin 800 pounds, which the latter raised to 1,000 pounds using his own funds. That was enough to convince a sufficient number of farmers in Pennsylvania to rent out their wagons and horses for the campaign. Despite the English general's great eagerness, Franklin regarded him with skepticism. For when he anxiously advised Braddock that an advance through dense American forests was different from a march across European pastures and fields, the latter only smiled condescendingly.

The general also arrogantly dismissed the representatives of Native American tribes who came to him to develop a common battle plan against the French. In his view, it was "impossible" that "savages" could "make an impression" in a fight against a European opponent. Offended, the chiefs of the Shawnee and the Delaware withdrew all their support from the British. Only a few Mingo remained at Braddock's side—although without Tanacharison, who had succumbed to pneumonia the previous fall in the Pennsylvania backwoods. The British major general reacted differently when he received a letter from Washington in March in which the Virginia colonel offered to act as his aide in the imminent campaign against the French. Braddock accepted, as Washington knew the difficult terrain on the way to the Ohio Valley better than any other American militiaman.

Contrary to all expectations in London, Williamsburg, and Philadelphia, Braddock and Washington's march on Fort Duquesne ended in disaster. Franklin had not erred in his negative appraisal of the know-it-all commander. His advance over the Appalachians was much too clumsy and relied on cutting a brand-new path through the woods. In early July, he was ambushed by forewarned and well-prepared French troops. Braddock was shot through the lung and died of his wounds. Washington, barely escaping the barrage of bullets alive, ordered a hasty retreat. Of the 1,100 British regulars, over 700 had been killed. The rest fled to Philadelphia.

On the way, Braddock's body was buried in the middle of the road so that the wagons passing over it would erase all trace of the grave, thus making it unrecognizable to pursuers. Braddock's mortal remains were not to be discovered and desecrated by Native Americans allied with the French. The Virginia militia chaplain had been severely wounded, so it fell to Washington to preside over the burial. Despite being involved in yet another fiasco, Washington was celebrated as a hero by Dinwiddie for leading the survivors safely back to Pennsylvania and Virginia. Washington himself, as he later wrote, never forgot "the shocking scenes" of the defeat, "the dead—the dying—the groans— lamentation—and cries" that would have been "enough to pierce a heart of adamant."

The debacle suffered by Washington made a deep impression 3,000 miles away from the Ohio Valley as well. The British prime minister, his cabinet, and the king were horrified by the devastating news from America. Concern also began growing that the Treaty of Aachen—which was regarded as an extremely fragile truce to begin with—would not hold, and that the battles in the Ohio country would expand into a wider global and European war over the possession of America. George II, who was also elector of Hanover, believed his hereditary domain in Germany to be directly threatened by France, the far superior power on the Continent. Who might come to its aid in the case of war?

The king no longer wanted to rely on Austria, seeing as how he had come away with nothing as an ally of Maria Theresa in the War of the Austrian Succession. To secure Hanover's safety, it now seemed wise to conclude a pact of neutrality and common defense with the king of Prussia. Venerated since 1745 as Frederick the Great, he had integrated Silesia into his realm with the assent of all the European powers, and he had increased the size of his army to nearly 150,000 men. Negotiations began in the summer of 1755. The British king took up residence in Herrenhausen Palace in Hanover, where he received Frederick's envoy, General Karl von Winterfeldt. They held extensive discussions about Brandenburg-Prussia's willingness to enter into an agreement with Great Britain.

Frederick was ecstatic about the British monarch's overture. Indeed, it was a source of deep satisfaction, as it showed how much higher Prussia's standing and his own personal prestige had risen in Europe since the Treaty of Aachen. Of course, Frederick's current fame was based not only on his military feats but also on his reputation as a brilliant, enlightened ruler. What is more, he had managed to attract the greatest Enlightenment figure in Europe to his court, at least for a time. Voltaire's beloved companion Émilie du Châtelet had died in childbirth in the fall of 1749. And so, after many repeated requests, in July 1750 he finally accepted Frederick's invitation to visit Potsdam.

When Voltaire arrived in Sanssouci, he found that the king kept company with some of the most radical and provocative thinkers of the European Enlightenment. Having been expelled from most of the neighboring states on account of their controversial ideas, they had found refuge with the extraordinarily tolerant Prussian monarch, who esteemed them as provocative conversation partners. One was Frederick's personal physician, Julien Offray de La Mettrie, whose *L'homme machine* (*Man a Machine*), published in Holland in 1747, claimed that *soul* was just an empty word. Another was the writer and philosopher Jean-Baptiste de Boyer, Marquis d'Argens. In 1748, he had published a scandalous novel entitled *Thérèse philosophe* (*Therese the Philosopher*) that took obvious glee in describing pornographic scenes.

Frederick did not share all the views and proclivities of his interlocutors. In his mind, however, guaranteeing freedom of speech meant allowing the expression of materialistic and mechanistic ideas as well as erotic and lascivious thoughts. He himself had plumbed the pleasures of orgasm in a poem entitled "The Ecstasy" (*La Jouissance*). With deep sensitivity, his expressive verses described a young man "trembling in excitement" for his beautiful, well-proportioned bride. The "ecstasy of their senses" that attended their wedding night included

> Kissing, enjoying, feeling, sighing and dying
> Reviving, kissing, then back to pleasure flying.

Finally, "breathless and worn out," it was the "lovers' happy destiny" to fall into a blissful sleep. In a letter to Voltaire, Frederick confessed that this description of lovemaking was based on the reliable foundation of his own experience. Maupertuis, the president of the Berlin Academy of Sciences, was another regular contributor to the libertine discussions at Sanssouci. No longer part of the king's inner circle, however, were his friends Jordan and Keyserlingk. Those mainstays of his Rheinsberg days had died, to Frederick's great sorrow, in 1745.

Voltaire was smitten by the easygoing social atmosphere of the Prussian king's court. The uninhibited discussions suited him. "Nowhere in the world did people ever speak more freely of all the superstitions of men," he recalled later, "and never were these treated with more mockery and contempt." Only God was spared. This libertinism led at times to homoerotic play between the sexually open Frederick and some of his young cadets, but that did not bother the French philosopher. Voltaire also endorsed the Prussian king's clemency for a young man sentenced to death by a provincial court in Brandenburg for an adventure with a female donkey. This was a very humane gesture, considering that sodomy was a capital offense almost everywhere in Europe at the time. In Voltaire's recounting, the Prussian king personally overruled the judge's sentence, writing under the ruling that he guaranteed "freedom of conscience and prick" in his state.

Although Voltaire endorsed Frederick's legal intervention in this instance, where mercy trumped law in a gesture of royal magnanimity, in general he considered it highly problematic that the king desired to make the Prussian judiciary more and more dependent on the monarch's goodwill. Frederick had also read Montesquieu's *Spirit of the Laws*, and he knew the doctrine of the separation of powers elaborated in that work's eleventh book. Yet he did not consistently adhere to this key insight of the political philosophy of the Age of Enlightenment. Montesquieu argued that, in a free state, "to prevent the abuse of power, it is necessary that by the very disposition of things power should be a check to power." Yet Frederick, as an absolute king, preferred not to follow this precept.

In his *Dissertation on the Reasons for Establishing or Repealing Laws*, read out on January 22, 1750, at the Berlin Academy of Sciences, he criticized England for the fact that "the king's power finds itself ceaselessly in conflict with that of Parliament," calling it a singular "deficiency in governance." In a supercilious tone, he thus observed "that England, more than any other kingdom, is in the position of needing reform of its laws." He thought it was just plain wrong that the "turbulent and stormy government"—both in England and in the British colonies in North America—"changes its laws endlessly, by Act of Parliament, as circumstances and events require."

Thus, in his *Politisches Testament* (*Political Testament*), written two years later, he observed that, in the courts in his lands, only the laws should speak and the ruler should be silent. Yet he also reserved for himself the right to personally monitor how judges performed their duties. Ultimately, in Prussia all aspects of government should be guided by one wise hand, just like horses pulling a chariot, so that the prince can accomplish everything he decides to do. Just like his father had in Katte's trial, Frederick was able to ignore the judgment of his courts when he deemed it proper and useful. In Prussia, there were no constitutionally ordained institutions to stop him.

Nor should there ever be. Instead, Frederick ordered his justice minister and grand chancellor Samuel von Cocceji to institute a judicial reform, whose aim was to further rationalize and above all to standardize the system of courts and jurisdiction in his lands. Berlin was now the seat of the highest court of appeals for all the territorial units of the larger Brandenburg-Prussian monarchy—which now also included far-off Emden, an important North Sea port in the county of East Frisia that had accrued to Frederick during the War of the Austrian Succession. In the wake of this judicial reform, there were de facto no longer any provincial courts independent of and unsupervised by the king.

Montesquieu had visited Germany in 1729, at which time he described King Frederick William I as a crass, beer-guzzling, tobacco-smoking despot who exercised "a frightful tyranny over his subjects." He was deeply mistrustful of the Prussian style of autocratic monarchy. His preference was for English parliamentarianism, which he esteemed as much as Frederick disparaged it. In contrast, the Prussian model of enlightened absolutism seemed to him hardly different from the stiff, centralist, and often despotic form of government in absolutist France that he despised. Frederick the Great, who in war and peace had often flouted established law, thus seemed to Montesquieu "the greatest madman who ever lived," as he wrote in a confidential letter to a French friend.

Voltaire's understanding of enlightened government was much closer to Montesquieu's ideas than to the Prussian king's visions. He did not think Frederick was crazy, but he did begin to distance himself from him in 1752. The king, it was true, was a supporter of free speech. Yet he dominated the discussions in Sanssouci, often unbearably interjecting contemptuous comments that spared no one. Occasionally, his courtiers spread rumors about what he said about them behind their backs. Voltaire was deeply hurt when he learned from La Mettrie that the king supposedly considered him no more than an "orange" to be squeezed for French verse and philosophical knowledge: "One squeezes the orange and then one throws away the peel." Once, when Voltaire was given another batch of the king's French poetry to correct, he sighed, "Will he never get tired of sending me his dirty linen to wash!" Maupertuis told Frederick about the episode, on account of which the French philosopher felt compelled to write a malicious invective denouncing the president of the Berlin Academy of Sciences. Frederick was so furious that he had Voltaire's tirade against Maupertuis publicly burned on Christmas 1752. "Your conduct deserves chains," he barked at Voltaire.

The king then carried out this threat the following year. In March 1753, he had permitted the utterly exasperated Voltaire to leave Potsdam and return to France. Shortly thereafter, he discovered that Voltaire had taken with him a privately printed copy of his poetry collection *Œuvres du philosophe de Sans-souci*. Frederick was in the habit of giving this book to his closest friends, but he insisted that everyone who left Sanssouci give it back to him first. The poems contained some biting invectives against other European monarchs and their ministers. Now Frederick feared that Voltaire might be indiscreet with them, so he had the French philosopher arrested during his stopover in Frank-furt am Main by two Prussian officials residing there. Voltaire protested his arrest in a letter to Maria Theresa's husband, Emperor Francis, arguing that Frankfurt was not a Prussian possession but rather a free imperial city. But no one came to his aid. The citizens of Frankfurt did not want to risk a falling out with Frederick the Great. Only after surrendering the volume of poetry was Voltaire released on July 6, 1753.

After that, the written correspondence between Frederick and Voltaire came to a standstill for more than a year. And when it was renewed, it took a long time for the letters of the two men, who could not seem to quit each other, to resume a friendly tone. Voltaire admitted that he was "angry" with Frederick but also "enchanted" by him and thus could not "live with you or without you." By 1755, then, Frederick once again felt he had a clear conscience. Indeed, he was even cockier than before. In June, as Washington was accom-panying Braddock on his calamitous march to the Ohio Valley, the Prussian king was traveling incognito on a vacation in Holland. Wearing a black wig and a cinnamon-colored robe, he posed as the Kapellmeister to the king of Poland. He lavished in the summery landscape between Utrecht and Amsterdam, lei-surely watching it slip by him from aboard a houseboat.

It was in the months after Frederick returned from this rejuvenating journey that his envoy Winterfeldt negotiated the pact between England and Prussia with King George II. The intense diplomatic talks were a success. In August 1755, the British alliance with Austria was dissolved. In its place, Great Britain signed the Convention of Westminster with Prussia on January 16, 1756. The two pow-ers pledged not to attack one another and to keep their respective allies from attacking as well. Frederick believed that this agreement with Great Britain would further strengthen his position in Europe. Only a few months later, how-ever, this overly optimistic assumption would be deeply disappointed.

Wenzel Anton, Count of Kaunitz-Rietberg, the head of the Austrian chan-cery, did not simply sit by and watch as the European system of alliances was rearranged. Instead, he completed the process to Austria's advantage with a series of clever diplomatic moves. The previous year, he had lectured Emperor Francis and Empress Maria Theresa that Prussia "must be thwarted." In his eyes, the Prussian kingdom was a superfluous, thoroughly artificial construction and a source of constant unrest that upset the delicate balance of power in the Empire's federal constitution. Kaunitz saw the Anglo-Prussian pact as a golden opportunity to reset the diplomatic chessboard in Europe. By the summer, he had persuaded France, Russia, and Sweden to forge an alliance of common defense against Great Britain and Prussia. After 250 years of opposing each other in every conflict and war, Austria and France suddenly found themselves on the same side. Contemporaries viewed this precipitous shift in alliances as nothing less than a diplomatic revolution.

No one was more surprised and dismayed by this development than the Prussian king. Unexpectedly, he was now faced by an overwhelming alliance that had two times as many troops at its disposal as Prussia: at least 80,000 from France, 80,000 from Austria, 80,000 from Russia, 20,000 from Sweden, and 20,000 from Saxony—all in all, 280,000 men. In contrast, Prussia had 150,000 soldiers, and Great Britain, mired in military conflict in America, was able to provide financial but not military assistance for the time being. As in the fall of 1740, Frederick was overwhelmed by panic and anxiety. He believed that Prussia's very existence was imminently threatened by an attack from the hostile alliance. Maria Theresa informed the king that her new diplomatic stance was not intended to cause harm to anyone, but he was not reassured. Upon receiving the message from Vienna, he wrote laconically to Duke Charles William Ferdinand of Brunswick, "I have received the answer and it is worthless."

To preempt the plot he feared from his adversaries, Frederick ordered his troops to mobilize on August 2. On August 26, the Prussian king then gave the command for an attack on the Electorate of Saxony, considering it the principal region from which enemy troops could be deployed against Brandenburg. Explaining his actions to the Duke of Brunswick, he wrote that day, "Since I now lack all security, both at present and in the future, arms are the only path left to me to foil the plans of my enemies." This justification perfectly paralleled the logic of preemptive attack that Frederick had cited in 1740 to legitimize his invasion of Silesia. And once again, true to the autocratic tradition of the Prussian mode of government, he made a unilateral decision. Incidentally, he ignored the counsel of his younger brothers Augustus William (the designated heir to the throne) and Henry, who at the age of thirty-one was already an experienced officer.

On August 29, Frederick invaded Saxony with three columns of troops. The Saxon army was warned and drawn up at the last moment, but he managed to trap and besiege it at Pirna, on the Elbe River. To cut off an Austrian relief army sent to liberate the Saxon troops, the king advanced on Bohemia with 28,000 men. On October 1, he dared to attack a larger force of 35,000 Austrians at Lobositz (now Lovosice, Czech Republic). Warned by his anxious officers of bullets whizzing close by, Frederick waved them off with the blunt remark that he was not there to avoid them. With visibility obscured by thick fog and the smoke of gunpowder, both sides suffered severe losses. The battle went to Prussia, however, which succeeded in stopping the Austrian advance. Frederick withdrew to Saxony, where he restocked his decimated army by impressing 18,000 Saxon soldiers who had surrendered at Pirna.

The two armies went into winter quarters in November, where they hatched plans for the coming spring. Meanwhile, the Imperial Estates met at the Diet of Regensburg to discuss the Prussian king's brazen course of action. Whereas it had been possible to view the Prussian occupation of Silesia in 1740 as a conflict between sovereign states, Brandenburg's invasion of Saxony was a blatant violation of the imperial constitution. The majority of the Diet found that, rather than adhering to established law, this time the Prussian king had been motivated by unsanctioned considerations of power. Accordingly, Imperial Chancellor Kaunitz labeled Frederick's invasion a perfidious ambush that injured the emperor's sovereign authority and the majesty of the Empire, as it threatened to overthrow the constitution of the Empire and to do equal violence to the Imperial Estates. As a result, the Holy Roman Empire declared war on the aggressor Frederick on January 18, 1757. Of the German princes, sixty voted for the decree and only twenty-six opposed it. The only prince-elector to support Frederick was King George II, in his capacity as elector of Hanover. He disapproved of the Prussian king's unilateral action against Saxony, but he was bound by treaty to support him.

While an imperial army was slowly being formed in the spring of 1757, in April Frederick led 64,000 troops in a renewed attack on Austria's province of Bohemia. Once again, his swift offensive maneuver caught the Austrians by surprise. Their forces were not yet fully deployed, and their allies left them waiting. In consequence, the main Austrian army suffered a devastating defeat at Prague on May 6. The survivors only barely escaped inside the city, where they were trapped and besieged. Some of the Austrians gave up the cause completely. Even the court in Vienna recognized the gravity of the situation, unceremoniously canceling Empress Maria Theresa's birthday party (planned for May 13) after receiving the news from Prague.

For his part, Frederick feared the war might last a long time. So he turned now to justifying his invasion of Saxony and Bohemia to his critics in the Holy Roman Empire. In the early summer of 1757, he published his *Rechtfertigung meines politischen Verhaltens* (Justification of My Political Actions). The tract blamed the war on the British and the French. They had brought matters to a bloody head in their American colonies and then orchestrated the shifting of alliances that had produced such lamentable consequences in Europe. Everyone knew, as Frederick had written earlier to his sister Wilhelmine, that "the war" tearing Europe apart "began in America," and that the dispute between the English and the French over a few obscure parts of Canada was the impetus of the bloody conflict that had sunk his own part of the globe into deep mourning. Despite the vast ocean between them, North America and Europe were not far enough apart to prevent a political fire in one place from spreading to the other.

Transatlantic communications were so good that the first tidings of Frederick's victory at Prague reached the American colonies by early August. The news was immediately published in all the papers. An especially thorough report was printed in the August 4 edition of *The South Carolina Gazette* in Charleston. It was read by an associate of Washington who lived there, George Mercer, who immediately sent the Virginia colonel an enthusiastic letter celebrating Frederick's magnificent victory in Bohemia. As Washington read when he received Mercer's letter in late August 1757, "We have advice here, and it seems well attested, that the Austrian army met with a total defeat." As Mercer reported, "Above two hundred pieces of cannon and all their field equipage fell into the hands of the Prussians," who then "immediately entered Prague sword and hand." Considering the sensational boldness of Frederick's dashing attack, Mercer assumed that Washington would have already learned of the Prussian king's victory from other sources "e'er you see this."

The inhabitants of Britain's North American colonies celebrated Frederick the Great's military successes so unreservedly because of their own desperate situation in the fight against the French. Braddock's disastrous defeat had in no way been the last in the series of unexpected failures that had begun with Washington's abortive mission to the Ohio Valley. Washington was miffed by the surprisingly clear superiority of the French, describing it in 1755 as one of those "powerful dispensations of Providence" that he could not begin to understand. This situation had not changed in the least by 1757. Therefore, news of Frederick's victories in battle against Austria—France's most important ally—was music to the ears of the demoralized British colonists.

It was primarily inhabitants of the Virginia and Pennsylvania frontier who had suffered the worst attacks since the autumn of 1755. Time and again after Braddock's death, Native American tribes allied with the French had raided the western border zones of the British colonies, leaving gruesome carnage in their wake. Not even radical pacifist settlements were spared, such as the German Pietist foundation of Gnadenhütten in Pennsylvania. In light of this nasty situation, even the peace-loving Quakers in the Pennsylvania General Assembly approved a fresh defense budget of 60,000 pounds to finance a new militia organized by Franklin. The Virginia House of Burgesses also increased its colony's military budget, immediately allocating 40,000 pounds to finance a regiment of 1,000 militiamen. Washington was named colonel of this regiment and given a somewhat ponderous honorary title: Commander in Chief of all forces now raised in the defense of His Majesty's Colony.

Only twenty-three years old, the commander in chief was clearly flattered that this supreme command had been forced upon him by the vote of the people of Virginia, even though he had not pushed for it this time. Governor Dinwiddie likewise thought him capable of taking all necessary measures to protect Virginia, both defensively and offensively, on his own authority and according to his own judgment. This powerfully demonstrated how much confidence people in the colony had in him and how much they respected him. However, the reputation he enjoyed did not make him conceited but rather sharpened his sense of responsibility for those under his command. The renown he had won so far only spurred him on all the more forcefully to fulfill the expectations people had of him.

Having recruited his regiment, the first thing Washington did in 1756 was balance out the very healthy pride of the militiamen with an equal dose of indispensable discipline. Unlike European armies, whose ranks were full of soldiers who had been pressed into service, the American militias were overwhelmingly composed of volunteers who refused to be ordered around against their will. According to Washington, the average soldier of a standard American unit had his own raw understanding of the tactics to be employed and thus all too often presumed to give orders on his own. But in order to survive a heated battle, even confident men had to learn to follow the wise orders of an experienced commander. "Discipline," he told his regiment, "is the soul of an army. It makes small numbers formidable, procures success for the weak, and esteem to all."

Accordingly, Washington strictly punished disobedience. He had incorrigible drunkards whipped. He did not abolish the death penalty for deserters.

On the contrary, he considered it an effective means of deterrence. In general, however, he provided for his regiment like a doting father. He even designed the elegant uniforms worn by his Virginia officers: "the coat blue, faced and cuffed with scarlet, and trimmed with silver." In addition, he used his good standing with Dinwiddie to regularly press for his militiamen to be given the same pay for their service as was received by the regular soldiers of the British army. His officers rewarded his steady advocacy on their behalf by praising him publicly as an outstanding commander, indeed as an upright friend and agreeable companion of his regiment.

It was not only the militiamen whom Washington took care of. He also did everything in his power to secure the open western border of Virginia, thus providing increased protection for civilians and farmers. Most of the settlers on the frontier were hopelessly exposed to surprise attacks by Indians allied with the French. Many had moved back to the interior of the colony in recent months. As Washington glumly wrote to the Speaker of the House of Burgesses, it was a "vast extent of land we have lost since this time twelve-month."

Washington resolutely sought to stem the fatal tide of settlers fleeing the Virginia frontier, building a series of forts intended to finally rid the region of Native American attacks. The mass exodus of colonists simply had to be stopped. For that to happen, the new palisade forts needed to be garrisoned by a sufficient number of militiamen to go out and deal with raiding Indians. The colonial legislature approved funds in the summer of 1756 to recruit another 1,500 soldiers.

Washington himself oversaw the building of the largest Virginia fort. He had the impressive defensive structure built near the city of Winchester, in the middle of the Shenandoah Valley about fifty miles northwest of Alexandria. He made Winchester his headquarters, renting a large house there and decking it out with tasteful furniture and elegant decorative pieces befitting a high-ranking dignitary. Washington was now a military figure of considerable respect who enjoyed solid support from the legislature, and he intended to live accordingly. At the same time, he was precisely aware and respectful of the limits of his rank and standing. For example, right after the new fort near Winchester was finished, he named it Fort Loudoun, dedicating it obsequiously to the new commander in chief of all troops in British North America, John Campbell, Earl of Loudoun, who had just arrived from England.

Thanks to the mere presence of the regiment recruited, disciplined, and commanded by him, by year's end fewer people were leaving the frontier than twelve months prior. In light of this achievement, Washington, as ambitious as ever, now burned for another promotion. He set his sights on a regular officer's commission in the British army. Hoping for support from Lord Loudoun, the self-assured Washington sought a personal interview with him where he could make a report of his successes. When Loudoun invited all the governors of the British colonies to Philadelphia to discuss the situation in February 1757, Washington asked Dinwiddie if he could accompany him. The Virginia governor obliged. "As you seem so earnest to go," he wrote to Virginia's highest-ranking military officer, "I now give you leave."

The encounter with Lord Loudoun turned out to be a singular disappointment for Washington. Despite the American's undeniable successes, despite the discipline he had managed to instill in his militia troops, the British commander in chief was simply unwilling to treat American soldiers like a regular British regiment. He refused to give the Virginia militiamen the same pay as regular British troops, nor would he consider a commission for Washington. Indeed, Loudoun treated the Virginia colonel with dismissive contempt, letting him know that he considered his achievements in no way sufficient for promotion to the upper ranks of the British army.

Loudoun's response was not only a surprise to Washington but also a source of growing resentment. Letting off steam, he wrote a long letter to Dinwiddie on March 10, 1757, in which he denounced Loudoun as an arrogant commander who disappointed and discouraged willing militiamen, thoughtlessly "nipping in the bud our rising hopes." The new commander in chief's contemptuous behavior was therefore "in the highest degree dispiriting," especially for him, since he had "thrown [himself] out of other employment" as a surveyor in order to pursue a career as a soldier. Furthermore, he had pursued that career with single-minded devotion, a professional ethic, and a sense of duty. Now he had to admit that he had made a mistake, carelessly "wasting the prime" of his life "in a service the most uncertain and precarious." This sad recognition was the object of many a "melancholy reflection." For the life of him, he could not fathom why "being Americans should deprive us of the benefits of British subjects, nor lessen our claim to that preferment."

Governor Dinwiddie had done a great deal for Washington, promoting him four times in the Virginia militia (with the approval of the House of Burgesses) and even naming him to the highest possible rank in that system. This time, however, he could offer no help. He lacked the authority. He also distanced himself from Washington now. He merely shrugged his shoulders at the latter's lament that the Americans were all too often treated as inferiors by the officers sent from the mother country. And in the summer of 1757, when Loudoun sent

400 Virginia militiamen to South Carolina without first consulting Washington, Dinwiddie did not intercede.

This infringement of his authority was yet another tough blow for Washington, utterly disillusioning him. In younger years, he had given up hopes of a career in the Royal Marines on the advice of his uncle, who argued that as an American he would not be able to rise to the upper ranks. Now he was forced to realize that there was no place for him at the top of the hierarchy of the British army either. He who had always judged the militiamen of his own regiment strictly on their performance now became aware that the regular British army was not a meritocracy. A commission in the British officer corps corresponding to his talents would always be withheld from him.

This insight scuttled his deepest yearnings. It went beyond damaging his sense of dignity and honor, even doing him physical harm. In August, Washington contracted a dangerous bacterial intestinal infection that lingered for several weeks. When he came down with a high fever in November, the army medic confined him to his bed. In January, Washington was able to walk again, but he still considered his health to be severely impaired, especially since he had suffered from a debilitating cough since late December. He feared the same fate might be in store for him as the one faced by his prematurely departed brother Lawrence. But then he made a manful decision that provided him with immediate and obvious relief. He wrote to British Brigadier General John Stanwix, a close friend of Lord Loudoun, that he was seriously considering the idea of "quitting my command" even if he did fully recover, seeing as how "I now see no prospect of preferment in a military life."

With this letter, Washington had taken charge of the situation. It was doubtless better to announce his departure from military service on his own accord than to suffer further humiliation at the hands of narrow-minded, snotty superiors. And while it hurt to relinquish his hopes for a commission, at least it opened up vistas for new and perhaps even more honorable employment in the service of the colonial American society of whose freedom-loving ways he was so proud. For months he had been not only sick but maudlin and full of self-pity. Now he had overcome his own demons and regained his spirits. He had learned to submit to the immutable realities of the day, and he was ready to start over. By March 1758, he had recovered completely.

Before officially exiting military service, he stood as a candidate to the House of Burgesses from the city of Winchester. He wanted to see whether the great respect he had earned from the colonists as the commander of the

Virginia Regiment could be parlayed into a civil career as a legislator. On July 24, election day, he was given an overwhelming vote of confidence. He received 309 of 396 total ballots cast. One of Washington's enthusiastic supporters ascribed his massive electoral victory primarily to his humane and just treatment of each and every one of the militiamen under his command, as well as to his unflagging, burning zeal for the common good.

The decision to give up his military career did not make Washington a social outcast. Rather, it drove him into a new realm of civil responsibility where he now served as a conscientious legislator. In the process, he had learned a valuable lesson: that voluntarily giving up a cherished goal could at times bring with it unexpected gains, as a new field of endeavor could contain many treasures as yet unnoticed. Seeing how quickly a promising perspective had opened up after he had abandoned the path to a commission, in the fall of 1758 he decided to bury yet another unfulfilled dream: his love for Sally Fairfax. This left him free to marry a woman who was actually available.

During his period of convalescence, Washington had met a friendly widow named Martha Dandridge Custis in Williamsburg. She was one year older and possessed 1,000 acres of fertile farmland. Her physique was very different from Sally Fairfax's, not thin and elegant but rather short and plump. In the previous four years, she had given birth to two children, John and Martha, to whom she was a good mother. She radiated a soothing warmth that gave Washington a feeling of security. Soon enough, this woman who had so unexpectedly entered his life became the object of his sincere affection. Likewise, she took a fancy to the much taller, handsome man who was so well liked all over Virginia. When he proposed marriage, she accepted without hesitation.

For Washington, the imminent prospect of marital bliss also meant the end of the feelings he had long nourished in his heart for Sally. In September 1758, he wrote the first great love of his life two deeply moving letters in which he confessed to her that he still felt the beguiling "force of her amiable beauties." Despite "the animating prospect of possessing Mrs. Custis," he would never be able to erase "the recollection of a thousand tender passages" with her at Belvoir. Alluding to Joseph Addison's poignant drama *Cato*, he compared himself to the Numidian prince Juba, who was never able to openly live out his secret love for Cato's daughter Marcia, alias Sally. Yet every individual had their own unalterable "destiny," and a mature person had no choice but to accept it with steadfastness. For not even "the strongest efforts of human nature" could "resist" what providence had foreordained. For that reason, from now on he would try "to conceal" his feelings for Sally.

FIGURE 7.1. Washington's wife: Martha D. Custis (1731–1802). Anonymous engraving, after a painting (1757) by John Wollaston (akg-images).

Before marrying Martha Custis and officially tendering his resignation from the militia, in November he took part in one final armed conflict with the French. At that point, the course of the war in North America had turned in favor of the British. The cause of this substantial change in fortune was a bold shift in strategy insisted on by Prime Minister William Pitt over and against the opposition of high-ranking officers. When Lord Loudoun failed as commander in chief of British forces in North America, Pitt divided over-all command in the summer of 1758 among three younger and much more talented officers—John Forbes, James Wolfe, and Jeffrey Amherst. Since then, they had closely coordinated the efforts of British and militia regi-ments. In addition, at massive cost Pitt had increased the number of troops to 50,000. The 16,000 French soldiers in Canada were simply no match for them.

Highly symbolic of the now decisively altered balance of power was the conquest of Fort Duquesne, which the British then renamed Fort Pitt after their prime minister (it later became Pittsburgh). The victory went to Brigadier General Forbes at the head of 7,000 soldiers, among whom was Washington, on November 12, 1758. Many years later, Washington claimed that his life had been in greater danger during that attack than ever before or since. For a mo-ment he had found himself between two contingents of his own soldiers. They mistakenly took aim at one another and only missed him by a hair's breadth. But fate—the fate he so often invoked—clearly meant for him to live on, to get married, to sit in the Virginia House of Burgesses, and to live the life of a country gentleman.

After resigning from the militia in December and marrying Martha Custis on January 6, 1759, Washington moved into Mount Vernon, the estate previ-ously owned by his deceased brother Lawrence. It was now permanently rented to him by his sister-in-law Anne. After the death of her only daughter, Sarah, who had not even reached the age of five, Anne attached so many sad memories to Mount Vernon that she no longer wished to live there. Instead, she and her new husband, George Lee, resided several miles to the south at his ancestral family home of Coles Point. Washington was free to expand and remodel Mount Vernon according to his own taste.

Washington happily adapted to his new life as a freshly married husband, first-term legislator, and proud member of the gentry. Yet in a farewell letter to his old Virginia Regiment dated January 10, 1759, he confessed very frankly that he could only think back on his time as their commander "with grief" and therefore "must strive to forget" that fulfilling period of his life. Despite the wistfulness that came over him when he mused about his own unused talents as a military commander, he still managed to be sincerely enthusiastic about the many victories that the British were now able to win against the French in North America under the leadership of their new generals. The high point of a long series of successes, and the decisive blow to the French troops, was the seizure of the Canadian capital of Quebec on September 13, 1759. Major General James Wolfe won the day but lost his life in the battle.

When this news reached Washington seven days later, he wrote, "The scale of fortune in America is turned greatly in our favor." And since he was so impressed by the British triumph, on September 20 he ordered from the London merchant Cary & Company a small bust of the Duke of Marlborough. One of the greatest English military heroes of all time, he had won glorious, decisive battles for Great Britain half a century earlier in the War of the Spanish Succession. At the same time, Washington ordered a much more imposing bronze bust—forty-five centimeters high and ten wide—of the man he believed was the greatest contemporary general: the king of Prussia. He intended to place the bust in a part of Mount Vernon where he spent substantial time, so that he would be reminded of Frederick the Great's amazing strategic abilities every time he passed by.

Time and again in the previous months, Washington had received letters from friends and acquaintances that brilliantly recounted the bold feats of the Prussian monarch. George William Fairfax, who had gone to London at the outbreak of the war, reported to Washington that the British Parliament had passed "a firm resolution to aid the victorious king of Prussia" by providing him with financial contributions in his fight against France and Austria. As an ally, Frederick had "surpassed all expectations." From a New York acquaintance, Washington received various newspaper articles containing extensive reporting about the brave king of Prussia, who, even when outnumbered, had attacked and conquered the troops of the enemy alliance.

Washington and the American colonists warmed so heartily to Frederick the Great because his stupendous victories increasingly forced the French to retrain the focus of their military efforts away from Canada and onto the European theater of the war. In doing so, he took the pressure off the British in Europe, allowing them to follow Pitt's strategy of doubling down in America. Frederick may have ruled the Kingdom of Prussia as an absolute sovereign without any legislative participation by his subjects, but his audacious generalship and steady victories were a decisive factor in protecting the parliamentary constitutions of the British colonies from the threat of French encroachment. On this account, the American colonists were enormously thankful to Frederick, even though Prussia embodied the opposite of their ideal of freedom. Therefore, Washington could only nod assent when William Pitt, referring to Frederick's assistance, exclaimed after the capture of Quebec that "America was conquered in Germany." Washington was thus all the more crestfallen

FIGURE 7.2. Pennsylvania German Fraktur with a portrait of "Frederick the IId, King of Prussia." Watercolor and ink on laid paper by an anonymous artist, mid-eighteenth century (Mennonite Library and Archives, Lancaster, Pennsylvania).

when the news spread in the American colonies that the Prussian king unexpectedly found himself in an extremely precarious position. "We are in pain here for the king of Prussia," Washington wrote in a letter in August 1760. For the king's life and the very existence of Prussia were now clearly in the gravest danger.

What had happened? After the siege of Prague had begun, an Austrian relief army under the command of Count von Daun had unexpectedly succeeded in advancing ever closer to the iron ring of Prussian troops around the city. Daun opted for caution. Instead of attacking the Prussian soldiers besieging the Bohemian capital, he took up a position only a few miles east of Prague on the heights above Kolin (now Kolín, Czech Republic). His plan was not to strike hastily but rather to bide his time and get the lay of the land. Frederick chose a different tack. Having so often taken his opponents by surprise and conquered them by recklessly rushing in, he sought a speedy resolution here as well. On June 18, 1757, he attacked Daun's numerically far superior army at Kolin. Due to a misunderstanding, the right wing of the advancing Prussian army attacked too soon. As a result, Frederick's artfully composed battle plan went up in smoke. The Prussian advance came to a halt, became confused, and then broke under Austrian artillery fire.

Forced to retreat, numerous Prussian units got entangled in fights that cost many casualties. Even the siege of Prague had to be broken off. Frederick's almost mythical aura as an invincible general dissipated at a stroke. Dashed, too, was the hope he had nourished at the war's outbreak of overpowering the Austrians before the French and the Russians could join the fray with full force. Instead of waging a short and lively war as he had hoped, in one single unsuccessful attack he had robbed himself of all the advantages previously gained.

Frederick's brother Henry blamed the king's senseless haste for the defeat suffered in Bohemia. Instead of keeping Daun pinned in Kolin until Prague had capitulated, Frederick had gone for it all much too soon. Later, Henry noted critically, "All my brother ever wanted was to give battle. That was his entire art of war." Yet the Prussian king was more than just a danger-be-damned general who saw offense as the best defense. Indeed, he was also a stubborn and determined warrior who refused to give up. His spirit of resistance never broke—not when Russians temporarily occupied East Prussia after the Battle of Kolin, and not even when a brash band of 3,400 Austrians surprised Berlin and made off with 200,000 thalers.

Frederick rose to the occasion. In late 1757, at the Battle of Rossbach in Saxony and the Battle of Leuthen (now Lutynia, Poland) in Silesia, he not only defeated the imperial army but also put a massive French force to flight that was twice as big as the Prussian army. In August 1758, Frederick checked the Russians at Zorndorf (now Sarbinowo, Poland), east of Frankfurt an der Oder. The price of the victory he won there was paid with a great deal of blood,

FIGURE 7.3. Snowbound battle: Frederick the Great with his generals
at the Battle of Leuthen. Painting by Adolph Menzel, 1861
(pbk/Nationalgalerie SMB/Klaus Göken).

leaving one-third of the Prussian troops dead or wounded. Nevertheless, with
only 36,000 men, Frederick managed to win the field against the 45,000 soldiers arrayed by Empress Elizabeth. It was these totally unexpected successes
that the American colonists celebrated so jubilantly.

Then the tide turned. After fighting off the Russian army, Frederick pursued
the Austrians, who had retreated to Saxony. On October 14, 1758, he was surprised by the Austrian army in a night attack while bivouacking at Hochkirch
in Upper Lusatia. When the village clock struck five, the Prussian camp was
invaded. In fierce combat at close quarters in the dark, the Prussians lost nearly
9,000 soldiers and 102 pieces of artillery. With difficulty, the Prussian units
managed to extract themselves from the fighting, and in the following snow-
covered months they recovered their strength in winter quarters. But in 1759,
the king could only field 100,000 troops. He was no longer a match for the
combined army of Austrian and Russian forces.

The joint Austro-Russian attack on the decimated Prussian army took place
on August 12, 1759, at Kunersdorf (now Kunowice, Poland) near Frankfurt an
der Oder. The Prussians were simply overrun by the enemy cavalry. The battle

was a catastrophe for Frederick. Two horses were shot out from under him. He was struck by bullets, one of them boring through his uniform and lodging itself in his snuffbox. After his troops fled in disarray, there were only about 3,000 men around him as dusk fell. There was no relief army. The Prussian capital on the Spree was fully exposed to the enemy. Fredereick feared the destruction of his fatherland, and it was something of a miracle that it did not take place right then and there. To the Prussians' disbelief, instead of advancing on Berlin, the enemy marched south to occupy Silesia. On September 1, the dumbfounded king wrote to his brother Henry, "I proclaim to you the miracle of the House of Brandenburg." For "just when the enemy had crossed the Oder and could have waged a second battle and ended the war," it turned around and "marched away."

The king was given a second lease on life thanks to his adversary's inexplicable mistake. Nevertheless, his situation continued to be desperate if not downright hopeless. Until the spring of 1760, merely managing to persevere through a time of such great insecurity seemed to him a success. In this very difficult period, as he wrote to the Marquis d'Argens, his "old good humor" would "flare up from time to time," but it would just as quickly die out "because there are no embers to feed it." Only forty-eight years old, he felt prematurely aged. "If you were to see me," he lamented to d'Argens, "you would no longer find a trace of who I used to be. You would see a gray old man, missing half his teeth, without cheer, without fire, without imagination." And he felt increasingly alone. In the previous three years, his mother Sophia Dorothea, his favorite sister Wilhelmine, and his most capable and faithful generals Schwerin and Winterfeldt had either died peacefully in bed or fallen on the battlefield.

Washington and the British government—which now seriously considered sending Frederick to a retreat on the Ohio—were not the only ones who felt the Prussian king's pain. He also had admirers in the Holy Roman Empire, and many of them feared for the man who almost overnight had become the bent figure now known as "Old Fritz" (Alter Fritz). Although an imperial war had been declared on him at the Diet of Regensburg in 1757 in response to his occupation and harassment of Saxony, the Prussian king still enjoyed a great deal of support among broad swaths of the German people for his intrepidity in the fight against the Russians and the French. One of his most ardent admirers was Johann Wolfgang Goethe, then only ten years old, the scion of a leading Frankfurt family. Later, in his memoirs, he would vividly describe how "Fritzian" he had been as a boy and how he had "rejoiced undisturbed in the Prussian victories, which were commonly announced with great glee." Ever since the beginning of the war, he had been fascinated by "the personal character of the great king."

The great resonance that the Prussian victories found among the German public is illustrated very well by the *Preußische Kriegslieder* (Prussian War Songs) published in 1758 by Johann Wilhelm Ludwig Gleim, a poet and secretary of the cathedral chapter in Halberstadt. In one poem, Empress Maria Theresa is urged to reconcile with Frederick the Great:

> Heroine, him you cannot conquer,
> Only God could work that wonder!
> Go and show him a friendly face,
> Please make peace apace!

Gleim's emotive rhymes achieved swift popularity in the Empire. The young Goethe copied them into his notebook. Later, he confessed that he "copied the songs of triumph, and almost more willingly the lampoons directed against the other party, poor as the rhymes might be." Yet he did not conceal the fact that the Prussian king, while enjoying the unbroken "enthusiasm of his worshippers," also suffered the increasingly bitter "hatred of his enemies." In the "image of Frederick," some saw a bold powerbroker to be revered, whereas others despised him as a reckless lawbreaker.

In 1760, Frederick described himself as a vagabond who currently had neither house nor home, always dwelling where it pleased his enemies. Yet these very enemies were still oddly indecisive and divided about what the future had in store for Frederick and Prussia. Two years earlier, the king had proclaimed with the force of a seer, "Their large number has become their undoing. Each one is depending on the other: the commander of the imperial troops on the Austrian general, the Austrian general on the Russian one." Lulled to sleep by "flattering hopes" and "solid faith in their future plans," they foolishly believed they were "masters of time" and "missed many good opportunities." This situation had not changed. They had not dealt him the death blow, and so now he gathered together one last contingent of troops. He attacked Dresden in July, Liegnitz (now Legnica, Poland) in August, and Torgau in November, signaling to his adversaries that he had not yet capitulated.

In 1761, his fate seemed sealed despite these renewed shows of force. The Austrians had been in full control of Upper Silesia since October. In addition, the Russians had conquered Kolberg (now Kołobrzeg, Poland) in December, thus adding all of Farther Pomerania to their possession of East Prussia. In essence, all the king had left were the core Brandenburg territories of

Mittelmark, Magdeburg, and Altmark. His future looked gloomy. The game would be up in 1762. And it was almost unimaginable that it would be decided in his favor. Yet this universal assumption turned out to be false. On January 5, 1762, the Russian Empress Elizabeth died as the result of a stroke. Her nephew and successor, Tsar Peter III, immediately and unconditionally took the side of the Prussian king, whom he had long admired.

Frederick viewed this sudden and unforeseeable shift in alliances as yet another miracle. For it provided him with new, unimagined military possibilities, and it instantly saved him and Prussia. Peter III promptly returned all Russian-occupied territory to Frederick and signed a peace treaty between their two states. In the summer of 1762, the Swedes and the French, now beaten in Canada, also withdrew from the anti-Prussian alliance. Austria was left isolated and without financial reserves. That put an end to a global war that had lasted for seven years and cost Prussia alone 400,000 lives. All that remained was for a formal peace treaty between Prussia and Austria to be negotiated.

8

Autonomy and Independence (1763–1770)

A TRUCE was agreed between Prussia and Austria a few months after the anti-Prussian coalition had been broken. Only then, in January 1763, did the real peace talks begin in earnest between the two long-standing antagonists. They took place in Saxony at Hubertusburg Palace, located in Wermsdorf near Grimma and Riesa. Empress Maria Theresa was represented by her Privy Councilor Heinrich Gabriel von Collenbach, and King Frederick the Great by his envoy Ewald Friedrich von Hertzberg. The two rulers endowed their negotiators with full authority to hammer out the agreement, but ultimately they both hoped for something that substantially resembled the terms of the 1748 Treaty of Aachen. Both sides desired a complete and legally binding return to the prewar status quo. And indeed, in the twenty-one meticulously elaborated articles of the Peace of Hubertusburg, Austria relinquished all the Prussian territories that it had conquered or occupied in the previous seven years. For the third time (after 1742 and 1745), Silesia was recognized in an international treaty as belonging to the Kingdom of Prussia. Even the County of Glatz (now Kłodzko, Poland) with its fortress, which was located in the border area between Silesia and Bohemia and which Maria Theresa would very much have liked to keep in her domain, was yielded to Frederick the Great and had to be evacuated by the Austrian army immediately. In return, Prussia promised to make no reparations claims for the losses it suffered during the war. In addition, the agreement included a secret article: The Prussian monarch guaranteed he would support Maria Theresa's oldest son, Joseph, in the upcoming imperial election (to be held on March 27, 1764, in Frankfurt am Main, with the intention of designating a successor to Emperor Francis I while he was still alive).

Moreover, important concessions were made to Saxony, Austria's most faithful ally. Since 1756, the electorate had been the victim of Prussian invasion, then occupation, and finally shameless exploitation. Now Prussia promised its neighbor to the south that it would immediately withdraw all its troops. Additionally, all Saxon prisoners of war, hostages, and forced recruits were to be immediately released by the Prussian army. In light of the de facto cessation of hostilities and especially the restitution paid to Saxony, the Diet of Regensburg consulted with the imperial court and announced on February 11, 1763, that it was ready to sign a treaty formally ending the imperial war against Brandenburg-Prussia. By adopting a position of general neutrality, the Empire played a significant and fitting role in promoting the Austro-Prussian peace talks.

The treaty was signed by the negotiators on February 15, reestablishing the framework of peace in the Empire and in all of Europe that had existed before Frederick's surprise invasion of the Electorate of Saxony. Only in America did one of the players win territory, with Great Britain taking Canada from its archrival France. The province was legally transferred from the French to the British in the Treaty of Paris, negotiated in parallel with the Peace of Hubertusburg and signed on February 10, 1763. In Europe, however, the unspeakable bloodshed and painful conflict that everyone now called the Seven Years' War had essentially changed nothing. The war had cost more than one million lives, leaving many contemporaries to shake their heads and wonder why this baffling sacrifice had even been made. There was no satisfactory answer. In light of the monstrous losses, Ernst Ahasverus Heinrich von Lehndorff, chamberlain to the Prussian Queen Elisabeth Christine, spoke in his diary of the "madness of humanity"—"and all that just to see the rulers back in the old *status quo.*"

Despite the restoration of prewar borders in Germany and the rest of Europe, one thing had changed, and dramatically so: the prestige and the aura of the Prussian king. Frederick had been known as "the Great" since 1745, in recognition of the fact that he had suffered not one defeat in the Silesian Wars. Now his reputation took on mythic proportions. Against all likelihood—and indeed, quite mysteriously—he had survived the Seven Years' War both politically and physically, even though his cause had seemed utterly lost not once but twice (in 1759 and 1761).

People in Europe and Germany in particular were amazed that the three combined continental superpowers Austria, France, and Russia, each of which had twenty million or more inhabitants, had not been able to subdue

Brandenburg-Prussia, which had not even five million inhabitants and could rely only on financial support from England. No doubt, the unity of political and military authority vested in the person of the absolute king was one of the decisive reasons that Frederick had been able to pursue a risky, all-or-nothing offensive strategy that made him utterly unpredictable to his opponents. Apart from all that, however, it was "the worth, the dignity, and the stubbornness," as Goethe dubbed it, that special mix of pride, steadfastness, and defiance that so characterized Frederick, that even made it possible for the audacious monarch to endure the extreme emotional strain of the war years, including in periods of profound hopelessness.

As a result, the citizens of Berlin were more enthusiastic than ever at the end of March as they decorated their city with victory arches and lights to celebrate the signing of the Peace of Hubertusburg, preparing a triumphal reception for their exceptional ruler. Yet Frederick refused to participate in the festivities planned for the day of his arrival. He was in a depressed mood that clearly prevented him from receiving the cheers of his subjects. His melancholy was entirely understandable. For after the king had ratified the Peace of Hubertusburg on February 21 in Dahlen Palace in Saxony, he had ridden in his coach in the direction of Silesia and then along the Oder River to Kunersdorf. On March 30, a gray and rainy day, he viewed the battlefield where, on August 12, 1759, he had suffered his most devastating defeat. That one awful summer day during the Seven Years' War had cost more than 35,000 dead and wounded.

Did the thunder of cannon, the beating of galloping hooves, and the cries of the dying echo from far off in his ear? Was he now more sensitive than he had been able to be during the chaos of the battle? Did his inner eye now see the true dimensions of the slaughter for which he was ultimately responsible? However that may be, when Frederick arrived that same day in Berlin, lost in his ruminations, he refused to greet the masses of people who had waited hours to see him. Instead of taking his place in the ceremonial coach that had been prepared for him, he paid a cursory visit to the Berlin city authorities at Frankfurter Tor and then drove through the emptiest, unlit streets of the capital to the City Palace. There he dined with his wife, who had not seen him in a very long time. On that occasion, Elisabeth Christine's chamberlain was witness to a moment of bitter sarcasm that erupted from Frederick. Upon seeing his queen for the first time in seven years, he greeted her tersely, "Madame has gotten fatter." Then he spent the rest of the meal speaking to the court ladies.

But what of Frederick himself? What transformations had taken charge of his body and soul in the course of the partly catastrophic events of the Seven

Years' War? He had certainly not lost his emotional side entirely. He still wrote passionate poetry, philosophized, made music, and exchanged charming letters with Voltaire. The mockery he delighted in, however, became nastier, more offensive, and more hurtful. Perhaps the war had kept his nerves so permanently on edge that he was now constantly irritable. Physically, he had aged ahead of his years, with a deeply furrowed brow, clear wrinkles around his eyes, and a thin-lipped mouth.

As if in search of himself, in the summer of 1763 Frederick made the surprising decision to have his portrait painted. At the site of his wedding, Salzdahlum Palace, he sat for Johann Georg Ziesenis, who was court painter in Hanover. It was the first time in a quarter-century that the king had permitted anyone to paint or draw his likeness from life. This was a remarkable exception. The painting that resulted from this sitting in Salzdahlum shows Frederick not in the stance of an imperial ruler but rather in the much more modest pose of a sensitive, fragile mortal. There is no crown on his head, no regalia in the background. Wearing a plain blue coat, he regards the viewer almost a bit shyly—but also with a trace of scorn emanating from his clear, large, penetrating blue eyes. When the first copies of this portrait made the rounds in Germany and then in England, it was generally considered a sensation that the hero of the Seven Years' War had allowed himself to be portrayed in such a human, touching way. From a letter from his younger sister Philippine, which she sent only a few months after the painting was finished, Frederick learned that all the world seemed eager for a copy of his picture.

Who he was, however, was to be displayed to the world above all in the building program he now resumed in Berlin and Potsdam. Across from the opera house on Unter den Linden, he had a palace finished that had been begun many years before the war as a new residence for the king. Now it was completed as a stately home for his brother Henry, fronted by six mighty Corinthian columns and flanked by two wings. This new residence in Berlin for Henry, who had lived mostly at Rheinsberg Palace since Frederick's ascension to the throne, formed the northern end of a spacious, elegant architectural ensemble that was named the Forum Fridericianum after its benefactor.

The new royal palace that was not built in Berlin rose instead in Potsdam. In May 1763, the first warm month after the end of the war, Frederick had construction begun at the western end of Sanssouci Park under the direction of the architect Karl Philipp von Gontard. In only six years, a colossal structure was built whose entire length measured 220 meters and whose façade was graced with more than four hundred sandstone figures. This massive three-wing building was crowned with a high dome and connected to equally imposing outbuildings by two curved colonnades. Its interiors were sumptuous. There were four ceremonial halls in the middle of the structure: two on the ground floor and two on the floor above. Behind the vestibule on the back side was the Grotto Room, a cool place to relax on hot summer days. Its walls were decorated with shells, minerals, and fossils.

One of the most beautiful rooms in the palace was the theater. Its rows were arranged in semicircles, like in an ancient amphitheater. A royal loggia—a mainstay in every other court theater—was not to be found in this room consecrated to the Muses. Frederick insisted on always taking in the performances amid his invited guests, from whom he had no desire to separate himself as a theatergoer. His seat was in the third row of the orchestra. The plays, operas, and oratorios performed in the intimate atmosphere of this new royal theater were supposed to provide the audience not only with the customary pleasure but also with new knowledge about the place of man in the universe. This intention was symbolized by an Enlightenment sun, carved in stucco on the ceiling right above the magnificent chandelier.

The new palatial building in Potsdam was known as the Neues Palais (New Palace). Its intentionally exaggerated proportions were meant to demonstrate to contemporaries that the vitality of the Brandenburg-Prussian state remained unbroken after the enervating Seven Years' War. It therefore became a grandiose expression of ostentation. Frederick himself knew this. He rarely spent time in the New Palace, and he referred to it as a fanfaronade, an instance of braggadocio. Yet he could also provide sober justification for the building of this monstrosity. After years of war in which local manufactories and craftsmen were idle, the planning and construction of the New Palace provided them with work.

Frederick also intervened much more directly in the economy of his state. Now that the war was over, he encouraged the opening of production facilities for cotton, cloth, and velvet, expanded existing sugar refineries, and ordered by royal privilege the creation of the Compagnie zum Herrings-Fang. Based in Emden on the North Sea, this Herring Fishing Company was to enter into competition with the Dutch, Danish, and Swedish fishing fleets. Unlike in the Dutch Republic, in Great Britain, and in the American cities of Philadelphia, Boston, and New York, where a class of merchants engaged in free trade had established itself, in Brandenburg-Prussia the king was still a devoted practitioner of mercantilism. That is, he and his government oversaw the careful planning and coordination of all economic activity in the country. When private companies that produced indispensable or prestigious goods failed to perform adequately, he did not shy away from nationalizing them and running them himself.

A prominent example of this kind of state-controlled economic policy was Frederick's takeover of the Berlin porcelain factory run by the energetic businessman Johann Ernst Gotzkowsky. Frederick acquired the business in 1763 and renamed it the Königliche Porzellan-Manufaktur (Royal Porcelain Manufactory). From then on, the king had great influence over the choice of designs and the way the porcelain was painted. Frederick also issued a "Royal Prussian edict on the illegal importation" of "goods produced in manufactories and factories" in "the Electorate of Saxony and its incorporated lands," especially "all Saxon porcelain, both authentic and inauthentic." The main point of the edict was to keep popular Meissen porcelain out of the Prussian market, thus encouraging Prussians to buy the goods made in the Berlin manufactory. Similar importation bans were issued for other sectors of the economy; they were typical of the state control of all Prussian trade.

Farming and animal husbandry were also under the king's purview. Like his father before him, he had swamps and moors drained to create a great deal of new cultivable land. For example, in the immediate wake of the Peace of Hubertusburg, a vast swampland in the Netze District was surveyed. It was a boggy, sporadically settled landscape that was flooded on many days of the year, located between Landsberg (now Gorzów, Poland) and Driesen (now Drezdenko, Poland) in the Neumark region of Prussia on the Polish border. Under the direction of Franz Balthasar Schönberg von Brenckenhoff, administrator of the royal estates in Pomerania and Neumark, a network of dykes and trenches was constructed that over time drained the swamp and created inhabitable, arable land. The majority of the people Frederick invited to settle the area were Saxons and German-speaking immigrants from Poland. Soon enough, many more than 2,000 new arrivals had settled the area around Driesen in thirty-eight colonies. Their names, such as Brenckenhoffswalde, Schönberg, Franzthal, and Friedrichshorst, recalled either the director of the drainage project or the king himself, to whom the settlements owed their foundation.

The agrarian policy Frederick pursued after the Seven Years' War quickly bore the desired fruit. Three years after peace had been enshrined in Hubertusburg and Paris, Benjamin Franklin toured Germany and a few parts of Brandenburg-Prussia as a diplomatic agent for the colony of Pennsylvania. What he saw amazed him: The land was not as devastated by the last war as one might have expected, and the fields were all well planted. And in a letter to the colonial legislature of Pennsylvania, Franklin conjectured that "the king of Prussia" seemed at the moment more "intent on repairing the damages of the last war than projecting new ones. So that we may reasonably expect a tranquility of some duration."

One of the gravest ills wrought by the Seven Years' War that Frederick now sought to cure was the broken health of many soldiers who had sacrificed their bodies in the fight to maintain the Brandenburg-Prussian state. The king promised compensation to every decrepit and mutilated war veteran who could no longer fend for himself. He started a fund from which small pensions were paid monthly to the needy. In addition, a retirement home was opened in Berlin that could accommodate and care for up to 600 disabled veterans. Finally, to all those disabled veterans who were still able to perform nonmanual labor more or less independently, he gave suitable jobs at customs offices and other state agencies.

As much as the king conscientiously cared for disabled war veterans, his main focus after the Peace of Hubertusburg was to encourage as many of his able-bodied subjects as possible to devote themselves to autonomous industriousness. Fully in the spirit of the Enlightenment, he wanted the residents of Brandenburg-Prussia to learn to mobilize their own intellectual talents and abilities. They were to be enabled to make prudent decisions that would let them consistently pursue their daily lives and professional duties according to the dictates of reason and in the service of the common good. First, Frederick attempted to improve educational opportunities for children and teenagers. His father, Frederick William I, had made school attendance mandatory back in 1717, but the educational institutions in rural Brandenburg were still in a terrible state. A large number of the children living in the countryside could not regularly attend classes. Therefore, on August 12, 1763, Frederick issued new guidelines for rural schools. They were to be "adhered to uniformly in all lands belonging to His Royal Majesty, the King of Prussia."

The guidelines not only stipulated regular school attendance for the children of farmers and agricultural laborers, but they also prescribed a precise schedule and curriculum. Only after thorough training and examination in pedagogical institutes, such as had been created in model fashion at the University of Halle, could teachers find permanent and adequately paid positions at country schools. Moreover, school visitations were carried out, mostly by supervisors from the clergy. After only a few short years, a slow but steady improvement was seen in the Brandenburg-Prussian educational system.

There were limits, however, to Frederick's formidable efforts to impart a basic level of knowledge to people from lower social strata and thus help them shed the shackles of superstition and ignorance. The king certainly wanted to promote enlightened thought and behavior on an individual level, but only in a manner defined and controlled by him. When people pursued paths of Enlightenment education that were too independent and idiosyncratic—and overtly tried to improve the state of those Prussian subjects who were blatantly disadvantaged by the law—the king could react in an extremely illiberal and pedantic way. In such cases, he proceeded with an unyielding, authoritarian, and cold severity that rattled even his closest friends and philosophical companions. No resident of Berlin experienced this as painfully as the Jewish scholar Moses Mendelssohn.

It was precisely twenty years before the Peace of Hubertusburg when Mendelssohn, only fourteen, walked barefoot to Berlin from his home city of Dessau in the hope of pursuing his religious studies with the city's leading rabbi, David Fränkel. When he arrived at Hallesches Tor—the only city gate at which Jews were allowed to enter—and was asked why he had come to Berlin, he answered simply, "To learn." And Mendelssohn learned so well and so much that he was soon one of Berlin's foremost minds. During the day, he worked as a bookkeeper in a factory belonging to the Jewish silk dealer Isaak Bernhard. In his hours of leisure, he not only devoted himself to the Talmud but also gave himself thorough training in modern philosophy through a program of self-directed, independent reading. His favorite thinker by far was John Locke. In 1758, Mendelssohn began publishing a weekly magazine in Hebrew entitled *Qohelet Musar* (Preacher of Morality), which was inspired by Addison's *Spectator*. In its pages, he encouraged other Jewish students of the Talmud to acquire secular knowledge as well, urging that through an enhanced education they could improve their station in life.

Under Frederick's comparatively tolerant government, Jews were better off in many respects in Berlin than in most other German lands. For example, Jews in Frankfurt am Main were only allowed to live on one narrow alley in a self-contained ghetto. At the end of the Seven Years' War, they submitted a petition to the Frankfurt City Council to be allowed to leave the alley on Sunday afternoons. It was brusquely rejected, the Lutheran city fathers considering the very fact that the Jews had made such a request to be "evidence of the boundless arrogance of this people, which makes every effort to gain equality with the Christian population at every opportunity." In a remarkable contrast, the more than

2,000 members of the Jewish community in Berlin were permitted to live with the rest of the capital's 120,000 inhabitants in any part of the city they chose.

A large synagogue was built in Berlin in 1714, on Heidereutergasse in the middle of the Marienviertel neighborhood. It was much more splendid than all other Jewish places of worship in Germany, most of which were found in the private homes of pious members of the congregation. Nevertheless, Prussian Jews had to live within strict limitations. Most of them did not have a secure right to reside in the territory. They could stay only as long as they were vouched for by so-called *Schutzjuden* (protected Jews), who were given special status by the king and who only made up 10 percent of the total Jewish population of Berlin. Furthermore, in order to get all manner of public documents, such as marriage certificates, marriage dispensations, and wedding licenses for their children, Jews had to pay special taxes to the state from which Christians of all confessions were exempted.

Especially vexatious was a decree issued by Frederick the Great stipulating that every Jew who wanted to get married was required to purchase a large order of porcelain from the new Royal Porcelain Manufactory. Mendelssohn, too, had to buy twenty porcelain monkeys at Frederick's behest when he decided to marry Fromet Gugenheim of Hamburg toward the end of the Seven Years' War. To secure his place in the city, he now also stopped by the king's cabinet in the hope of acquiring a permanent residency permit for himself and his young wife.

The Marquis d'Argens, one of Frederick's philosophical companions, was a denizen of Sanssouci Palace at the time. When he heard to his great astonishment that Mendelssohn, whom he knew, still did not have a permanent residency permit, he asked around in his circle of friends if this was indeed true. One acquaintance told him that the king only tolerated Mendelssohn because he worked for the rich silk dealer Bernhard. If Bernhard were to fire him and Mendelssohn were to find no other "protected Jew" to hire him, the police would force him to leave the city the very same day.

Only when the Marquis interceded personally for Mendelssohn did the scholar receive from Frederick the privilege of protected status in October 1763. Perhaps it was the French litterateur's wit that convinced the king. D'Argens had sent Frederick the following noble-minded and mordantly ironic overture: "A bad Catholic philosopher asks a bad Protestant philosopher to give protected status to a bad Jewish philosopher. There is not enough religion involved here for the request not to be considered rightful."

Despite repeated pleas, Frederick refused to extend the privilege to Mendelssohn's children—which is precisely what the philosopher had asked him to do in the most humble manner, hoping that "Your Royal Majesty will most graciously deign to grant me and my descendants the highest protection." And although the Jewish scholar—who was not a bad philosopher but rather quite a good one—won first prize from the Berlin Academy of Sciences for his *On Evidence in the Metaphysical Sciences*, Frederick raised an immediate and unmistakable objection when Mendelssohn was then elected a full member of the academy. Did the Prussian king harbor resentment against Jews per se? Mendelssohn had little interest in pursuing this uncomfortable question. In a letter to his Jewish friend Naftali Herz Homberg, who had applied in vain for a position with the emperor as a repetiteur, Mendelssohn commented, "As you know, I have suffered a similar fate. The Academy elected me a member, but His Majesty the King did not approve the choice. Why not? I am as ignorant of that as you are of why the Emperor does not want you as his repetiteur."

Why the king stayed aloof from the gifted Jewish philosopher Mendelssohn was a mystery. But Frederick's behavior did make one thing perfectly clear: When the decisions of institutions that were supposed to be free and independent did not suit him, he did not hesitate to override their authority. That is what he did in the case of judicial verdicts of which he did not approve. And that is what he did now when he ignored the vote of the Berlin Academy of Sciences. By taking such action, he contravened the will of the very society that, more than any other institution in Brandenburg-Prussia, was supposed to contribute to expanding the reach of the Enlightenment.

Frederick also singlehandedly decided what taxes his subjects would pay. The Seven Years' War had gobbled up enormous sums of money despite the financial support from Great Britain. As a result, very soon after peace had been declared, Frederick was keen to refill the state treasury as quickly as possible by means of new customs duties and excise taxes. On April 14, 1766, Frederick ordered excise rates for beer, brandy, wine, liquor, coffee, and butchered meat to be steeply increased. The same year, he issued an edict creating the Adminstration générale des accises et des péages (General Administration of Excise Duties and Tolls), a tax office often simply called the Regie (which could be translated as "Directorate"). Modeled on a similar French tax office and headed by Marc Antoine Andre de la Haye de Launay, a French expert on the subject summoned to Prussia for this purpose, it was responsible for collecting all indirect taxes.

Apart from the taxation overseen by the Regie, Brandenburg-Prussia's regular tax revenue came primarily from the countryside in the form of the so-called Contribution, levied on propertied farmers as a land tax and on propertyless rural residents as a head and business tax. Frederick adopted this tax system from his father, but he made sure to spread the burden as fairly as possible by having agricultural land constantly reassessed, in part on the basis of soil quality. In a second *Politisches Testament* (*Political Testament*) dating to 1768, he elaborated a forceful justification of this tax policy, although he had to admit that the assessment and collection of taxes was always very difficult, as it was rarely possible to undertake such a complicated procedure with the required precision.

He also reiterated his understanding of his role as king in this *Political Testament*. As usual, he portrayed himself as an enlightened, absolute sovereign. He emphasized that, in a political commonwealth, "nothing big and useful can ever happen" if "the prince does not himself rule." For "only inside a single head can a plan be hatched" that "leads government policy, the military, and financial administration all to the same end." "Everything" only comes together "when the prince wills it." It was therefore essential to Frederick that his "successors imprint this principle in their mind," so that the Prussian state remain "immutable" in its felicity.

The king spoke optimistically of his "successors" in the plural, although his heir Frederick William—the son of his deceased brother Augustus William—had not yet produced a son. Nor could he, as his beautiful and headstrong wife, Elisabeth of Brunswick-Wolfenbüttel, was not a pleasure to him but rather preferred to amuse herself with the handsome young officers of the Potsdam Guard. When Frederick was informed about the princess's moral conduct, he pressed his nephew to get a divorce, which he did on April 18, 1769. On July 14 of the same year, Frederick William wed Princess Frederica Louisa of Hesse-Darmstadt, only seventeen years old, in the chapel of Charlottenburg Palace. To Frederick's deep satisfaction, on August 3, 1770, this future queen of Prussia bore a son; he was named Frederick William like his father. Now the continued existence of the Kingdom of Prussia and the Hohenzollern dynasty was secure beyond Frederick's death.

Perhaps it was the prospect of a long future for the Prussian state, which had sprung from a singular act of will by his grandfather Frederick I, that moved the king to turn his thoughts to political philosophy again. In 1770, he fully explored the Prussian variety of the social contract that Hobbes had recommended back in the seventeenth century as the most promising means of preserving civil peace and promoting light in the world. Hobbes taught that a sustainable social contract could be either democratic or monarchical in character. From its first days, Prussia had opted for the way of monarchy, which Leibniz had also favored. And since Frederick had followed this track and achieved incredible success on it, he saw less reason than ever to doubt the Prussian path to enlightened government.

In his philosophical *Essay on Self-Love, Considered as a Principle of Morality*, which he had read out at the Berlin Academy of Sciences in early 1770, Frederick emphasized that people always and only obey the driving force of "self-love" or "self-interest." For "in general, man is born more to a life of the senses than to one ruled by reason." On the other hand, this insight should not fool us into adopting the false assumption that one may always oppose the orders of a monarch when they run counter to one's own subjective interests. Anyone who thinks that way "sins, by using faulty reasoning." The consequence of such a fallacy must necessarily be "civil war." In order to live in a society with one another in peace, people must instead realize that they only act as "good citizens" when they follow the will of the absolute sovereign. In a just consideration of the nature of things, it was very much in the subjects' highest interest to obey their king at all times and in all places. Only the "unjust man" would break "the social covenant" and thus destroy "the laws under whose protection he lives" in Prussia.

The secret to Prussia's success was clearly that Frederick's political philosophy met with widespread approval among the people whose first servant he tried to be. Indeed, there was no palpable opposition to the king's political ideal in the lands that he ruled. On the contrary, the vast majority of Brandenburg-Prussia's inhabitants were attached to their monarch in silent and grateful subservience. The Seven Years' War seemed actually to have promoted sincere Prussian patriotism. Like their king, even in hindsight they considered the war to have been inevitable. And in terms of domestic policy, many of Frederick's subjects indeed saw him as a devoted, enlightened sovereign who cared about the sciences and education. It is therefore no surprise that the people regarded their Old Fritz with deferential admiration when he passed them by on his rides around Berlin and Potsdam, wearing a plain blue coat cinched with a frayed sash and a tricorn hat adorned with white feathers. There can be no doubt that, seven years after the signing of the Peace of Hubertusburg, Frederick found himself at the height of his reputation and power.

With the end of the Seven Years' War, the British Empire had also achieved a new high point in its international standing. It now stretched from Canada to the Central American Mosquito Coast of Nicaragua, from the Caribbean to West Africa, and from Madras in southern India to Bengal. What is more, as Washington wrote to a distant relative living in England, the British were the only remaining European masters "of this great continent," now that they had defeated the French. They had already settled one-third of its area, and its quietude thus seemed secured for a long time to come without interruption. As he put it, "We live in a state of peaceful tranquility." Washington wrote at greater length in another letter to the same relative, in which he explained the particular causes, beyond the general political situation, that contributed to the great peace of mind he enjoyed at Mount Vernon. "I am now, I believe, fixed at this seat with an agreeable consort for life and hope to find more happiness in retirement than I ever experienced amidst a wide and bustling world."

The retired colonel spoke of domestic pleasures in many other letters of this period as well. They consisted primarily in renovating the stately main building of Mount Vernon, which he now owned rather than leased. After the death of his sister-in-law Anne on March 14, 1761, the entire property had passed to him. He added a story to the house and small wings to each side. The former surveyor had all of the renovations done on the basis of his own drawings; the idea was to create a harmonious balance of built architecture and natural landscape. One English traveler who visited Mount Vernon after the end to hostilities in North America observed in a letter to its proud owner, "The house is most beautifully situated upon a very high hill on the banks of the Potomac, and commands a noble prospect of water, of cliffs, of woods and plantations."

Washington's domestic bliss was now also augmented by the constant presence of the two children Martha had brought into their marriage. He and his wife could not have children of their own, most likely because he was infertile. He therefore cared all the more devotedly for John and Martha Parke Custis, who were five and three years old, respectively, when he married their mother. It is quite possible that he was even more solicitous of their welfare than their deceased father could have been. For Washington believed that adopted children had to be handled with much greater prudence by a stepfather than by their "natural parent," since experience had shown that "a *faux pas* committed by [their guardian]," even "when the intention may be strictly laudable," would weigh very heavily on his conscience.

Washington's part in caring for Martha's children, whom he called Jacky and Patsy, consisted mainly in spoiling them and giving them copious gifts. Like the offspring of a European prince, they were given their own African servants. Furthermore, Washington insisted that they have fine clothing that was sent from England to Virginia especially for them. When Jacky was seven years old, his stepfather gave him a hat with silver trim. The six-year-old Patsy received a coat of fashionable silk. Both children were provided with fine writing paper, and from an early age each possessed their own little Bible along with a small Book of Common Prayer.

There was also no shortage of high-quality toys from which they could pick and choose at will. These included a wooden cuckoo that cooed like a real bird, a carved wooden parrot that spun on a stick, books for children, an aviary, and a small play store. Patsy also had her own wax doll that she dressed in all manner of pretty little clothes. Jacky received a whole arsenal of toy soldiers, perhaps with an eye to his having a more successful military career than the one Washington had so reluctantly abandoned. The pride of his collection was a cavalry soldier that his stepfather had ordered from London. The small, mounted figure, which galloped across the wooden floors of Mount Vernon in Jacky's hand, was a rider from a European army that Washington admired above all others: It was a dragoon from the Ansbach-Bayreuth Regiment, the elite Prussian cavalry unit upon which Frederick the Great had heaped honors upon honors.

Nor did Washington spare any cost for the children's education. At the request of his wife, he summoned to Mount Vernon a tutor named Walter Magowan, who took up residence in a room there and taught Jacky and Patsy reading, writing, and arithmetic. Every good book that Magowan considered indispensable to a thorough, modern education was made available to the siblings. When Jacky made so much progress in Latin that he was able to read longer passages in context, his stepfather assembled a full library of the best Latin literature for him. Since many of the books were not published in America, they had to be ordered at great cost from England. As a precaution, Washington always ordered two copies of each book. That way, if one got lost or damaged, a second one was always available.

Wishing to be a well-informed gentleman of the Enlightenment, Washington also placed a high premium on his own continuing literary and scientific education at Mount Vernon. His personal book collection grew quickly and steadily until it reached several hundred volumes. In one of his extravagant orders from the London merchant Cary & Company, he requested more than

400 bookplates. With a keen sense of aesthetics, tidiness, and order, he was in the habit of meticulously marking every book as his personal property with one of these beautiful, artfully designed labels. An unmistakably large portion of his carefully kept library was composed of works on the British constitution and the history of English parliamentarianism. He avidly read these titles. Information from books was the essential basis upon which, in a second stage of learning, knowledge gained from experience always had to be built. Constant practice in writing was also important to him. Besides penning personal messages and official letters, he therefore constantly took notes about his everyday activities.

In one of his ledger-like diaries, to which he gave the jejune title "Where & How My Time Is Spent," he carefully listed the various leisure activities in which he continued to engage even after getting married. According to this diary, he often visited neighboring planters to play cards or go foxhunting with them. Being a passionate dancer, he attended boisterous balls. In a letter to Sally Fairfax, he compared the quick rhythms of dance steps to the skillful movements of soldiers in close combat, declaring dancing to be the "gentler conflict." In addition, he often went to the theater when on visits to Williamsburg or Alexandria. Once, he went to a traveling zoo, observing the tigers and lions with keen curiosity. He was also a regular spectator at cockfights, a popular Virginia pastime.

The animals most dear to his heart, however, and which he passionately bred, raised, and cared for at Mount Vernon, were horses and dogs, his most faithful hunting companions. He meticulously detailed in his diary which mares were covered by which of his noble stallions. There was one mare, he noted with amusement, that had been covered several times and that had been regularly paired with one of his younger horses. She had developed such an attraction for the stallion that it required a very high degree of effort for Washington to keep them apart. He also paid very close attention to the mating habits of his hunting dogs, in order to discover which of the newborn puppies could best be trained to be a good tracker or retriever like its parents.

Naturally, Washington also kept stock animals at Mount Vernon. In particular, he raised a considerable number of pigs. Their meat, turned into hams and sausages, provided a large portion of the food eaten by his family and workers, and it was also sold in great quantity at local markets. Washington produced upwards of 6,000 pounds of pork in the first year after the end of the Seven Years' War. His farm likewise contained large numbers of cows and sheep, chickens and turkeys, ducks and geese. And since his huge estate was located on the bank of the Potomac, Washington also dipped into the fish reserves of the broad river and the Chesapeake Bay, sending out fishing boats to catch herring. While still on board the boat, the crew packed the herring in brine in order to preserve the fish for a longer period of time.

However, Washington's most significant agricultural product in the first years after his marriage to Martha Custis was tobacco. Like most farmers and planters in Virginia, the master of Mount Vernon devoted a large portion of the fields on his lands to it. Tobacco had been raised in large quantity ever since the early days of the colony, and it was still Virginia's most important export. It sold very well on European markets from Scandinavia to Naples and from Great Britain to Russia, as it was desired by princes, townspeople, and farmers alike. Looking casually at the river from the window of his house, Washington could watch as his goods were loaded at Alexandria onto larger ships, their sails billowing in the wind, and transported down the Potomac and into the Chesapeake Bay, from which they would then glide across the Atlantic Ocean to the Old World.

It vexed Washington, however, that he realized much less revenue from the sale of tobacco than he expected to. As of late, good profits were hard to come by with this traditional Virginia export good, as tobacco, even of high quality, had become a mass product. The Spanish in particular, who raised excellent tobacco in ever-greater quantities in their Central American and Caribbean colonies, were a serious competitor to the North American colonists on the European market. This situation was not affected in the least by the regular letters of complaint that Washington wrote to his London trade partner Robert Cary, who not only sent him European luxury goods and other wares but also sold his tobacco on commission.

On September 20, 1765, the concerned Virginia planter complained in a letter to London that his balance sheet was very much in the red, and this situation had only arisen because "the sales [of tobacco] are pitifully low" and "meet with such unprofitable returns." The perennially low prices for Virginia tobacco instilled in Washington a fear of slipping into debt—and worse still, a kind of debt not quickly paid off but rather one that was permanent and increased annually. As he had written the previous year, this prospect was "irksome," especially for a "free mind" who never wanted to fall into any kind of dependency. Therefore, Washington decided to drastically reduce the amount of tobacco he planted, focusing instead on other crops that would be sold primarily not in Europe but on the domestic American market.

In order to determine which varieties of grain would thrive best on his plantations and which types of soil were best suited to quick growth, Washington performed a series of lengthy experiments whose results he punctiliously recorded in his diaries. After completing these practical studies, in which he also tested the viability of hemp, flax, and legumes, Washington concluded that in the future he would plant mostly wheat and maize. By 1765, he had stopped producing almost any tobacco. Instead, he harvested nearly 7,000 bushels of wheat and almost 10,000 bushels of maize. He now also expanded the tiny mill located on his estate so that the increased yield of grain could be ground immediately after being harvested. The flour he produced on his own farm was not only a good source of revenue, but, being used to bake bread in his own bakehouse, it also increased his self-sufficiency. He now made and saved more money than ever before.

The produce from his fruit trees, especially the apples that grew in large numbers on the grounds and in the gardens at Mount Vernon, was turned into cider, an alcoholic refreshment that was especially popular in the hot Virginia summer. As keen as Washington was to increase his plantations' utility, he was equally passionate about the beauty of the gardens that he artfully embellished with carefully planted flower borders. In this endeavor he was guided by the advice of the noted English garden designer Batty Langley, whose definitive *New Principles of Gardening*, first published in 1728, he ordered from Cary & Company right after his wedding. The book's subtitle highlights the complexity of the garden design to which Washington so enthusiastically aspired, encompassing "the laying out and planting" of "parterres, groves, wildernesses, labyrinths, avenues, parks, etc."

In order to realize his highly ambitious plans for creating an aesthetic park—and naturally to pursue Mount Vernon's agricultural production as well—Washington now needed many helping hands. In 1765, there were seventy-eight African slaves working on his Potomac plantation. Many of them had children, and they were likewise taught to perform all manner of duties. The master had some of his slaves trained as expert cabinetmakers and carpenters. In this way, he was able to have all necessary repairs made to his buildings and stables.

The structures where the slaves slept never lay farther than a half-hour walk from where they worked. They labored under the direction of overseers, who also had the job of monitoring the slaves after work and at night in order to check their irrepressible yearning for freedom. Despite extensive precautionary measures, individual slaves still managed to escape from the plantations every now and again. They were then always sought with a certain tenacity, but not always successfully. Washington even posted high rewards for the return of escaped slaves whom he wanted to put back to work. In such cases, he always provided very precise personal descriptions to aid in tracking them down. Once, when four slaves had run off together, he had handbills circulated around Mount Vernon and farther afield in which he emphasized in puzzlement that his Africans, who had only been brought to America a few years prior—and thus frequently spoke "very broken and unintelligible English"—had not been treated poorly by himself or his overseers. "They went off" even though they had not suffered "the least angry word or abuse." Was Washington, despite his own instinctive revulsion toward every form of dependency, truly unable to understand that it was the mere deprivation of freedom—and attendant loss of all independent autonomy—that had driven these people to escape?

As a member of the House of Burgesses in 1765, at any rate, he insisted very forcefully on the liberties that were such a core part of the identity of Virginia and the other American colonies. At the first session of the General Assembly in that year, he received, blushing and bowing, the express thanks of the body's other members for his faithful service to the king and colony—and for his courageous and steadfast behavior since the initial encroachments and hostilities of the French and the Indians. Since first entering the House of Burgesses, he had sat on a committee for military affairs, dealing primarily with the concerns of war veterans. Now, in late June 1765, he took up the fight against a law that threatened to place a permanent wedge between the colonies and the mother country.

Since the end of the Seven Years' War, which had been costly in part due to the years of subsidies paid to Frederick the Great, England had been faced with a mountainous debt of 137 million pounds. Under the leadership of the new prime minister, George Grenville, in early 1765 the British government decided to take measures to balance its overdrawn budget. One was to place a tax on the American colonists. Property taxes in England had already been doubled during the war. Thus, an additional tax on British subjects in North America seemed appropriate to the prime minister, especially considering that they had profited most from the end of French colonial rule in the Ohio Valley and Canada.

The tax proposal that Grenville submitted to the king's cabinet foresaw placing a fee-based stamp or seal on every paper product and deck of cards sold in the British colonies in North America. One of the supporters of this stamp tax was Secretary of the Treasury Thomas Whatley. In his view, since the American colonies were part of the British dominion, they should discharge their duty in this way along with all the rest. After thorough debate, both houses of Parliament approved the Stamp Act by a wide majority on March 22, 1765.

In the American colonies, the tax bill met with incomprehension. From Massachusetts to Pennsylvania to Virginia, most colonists were convinced that only their own legislatures could determine what taxes they paid—certainly not the British Parliament in Westminster, where they did not even have their own representatives. To make it clear they had no intention of ever accepting a tax that they had not imposed on themselves through their own elected representatives, the colonists penned numerous protest resolutions that were sent to the British government that same summer, shortly after the Stamp Act had been announced.

There were other forms of protest as well. In London newspapers, American colonists insisted in May 1765 that they were obviously willing to contribute to the necessary measures to pay off the debt, but they could not countenance the renunciation of a fundamental English liberty—namely, the privilege of demonstrating their loyalty by granting money of their own accord whenever the monarch felt obliged to ask for it. In New England, militant patriotic clubs formed everywhere, sometimes taking the shape of rabid mobs to intimidate tax collectors by ransacking their homes. In the fall, American merchants and politicians widened the spectrum of the protest, calling for a targeted boycott of British goods.

On September 20, 1765, Washington wrote a detailed letter to his chief London merchant, Robert Cary, in which he elaborately justified the American point of view. As he explained to the English merchant with whom he had been corresponding extensively for years, "The Stamp Act, imposed on the colonies by the Parliament of Great Britain," had dominated conversation for months because the Americans "look upon this unconstitutional method of taxation as a direful attack upon their liberties." It was therefore understandable that they "loudly exclaim against the violation," in part to clearly label it as such. He was also certain that the Americans, on account of their clear sense of liberty and justice, would find it "morally impossible" to conform to the British Parliament's will on the tax issue.

"What may be the result of this . . . ill-judged measure," Washington continued, "I will not undertake to determine." No doubt, however, "the

advantages accruing to the Mother Country will fall far short of the expectations of the Ministry," since the boycott now being introduced as a reaction to
it would do more damage to the English than to the Americans. For the economy of England, Washington argued, was hugely dependent on exports to
America. In contrast, the Americans were capable of dispensing with the
"luxuries" that they had been in the habit of ordering from Great Britain. As
for "necessities of life," they could "be procured (for the most part) within
ourselves." Washington knew what he was talking about, as even before the
boycott, economic considerations had forced him to change his own individual trade policy accordingly at Mount Vernon.

This clear and unambiguous stance paid off for him personally. His work as
a planter was attended by growing success, and as a politician he enjoyed
immense popularity. In 1765, he decided to give up his seat from Winchester
in the House of Burgesses and run instead as a representative of his home
precinct of Fairfax County. He was rewarded with reelection by an overwhelming majority. When he participated in the legislature's debates, which could be
quite heated, he spoke calmly and judiciously. One of Washington's fellow
burgesses admired him for always comporting himself as a modest but reasonable man, one who spoke little and possessed a cool control of his body. When
he rose to speak, he was as composed as a man at prayer. Another member of
the legislature observed that Washington never spoke for longer than ten minutes, and only when it was necessary to decide a contentious point. Furthermore, Washington dealt solely with the big issues, as he knew that the smaller
ones took care of themselves.

One contentious point of politics that for months did not resolve itself was
the Stamp Act. The American boycott was well conducted and made an impression on the British Parliament. In February 1766, it declared itself willing
to call twenty-six merchants and politicians from England and North America
as expert witnesses to offer testimony to the House of Commons on how they
thought the Stamp Act crisis could best be ended. Only then did the situation
change. One of the Americans who answered the call was the Pennsylvania
colonial agent Benjamin Franklin; he was interviewed for four hours. Like
Washington, Franklin considered the Stamp Act to be "unconstitutional and
unjust," because the Americans "could not be taxed in a parliament" in which
they "were not represented." At best, the Americans could be compelled by
military force to pay the tax against their will; but even such brutal measures
would have an uncertain outcome. As Franklin solemnly declared in the name

of all Americans, "No power, how great soever, can force men to change their opinions."

Franklin's words and the testimony of other Americans who spoke before the British Parliament had the desired effect. On March 18, 1766, exactly one year after the Stamp Act had been passed, both houses of Parliament concurred in revoking the contentious law. In both England and the North American colonies, the repeal of the Stamp Act was celebrated as a return to a peaceful and amicable coexistence. Church bells tolled in London the day the act was repealed. Two months later, when the happy news reached America, the colonists received it with similar euphoria. In Philadelphia, the whole city was solemnly illuminated by thousands of candles on May 21. Washington was relieved and believed that those who had facilitated the repeal of the law were entitled to the gratitude of all well-meaning friends of Great Britain and her colonies. Indeed, one could only feel great joy upon hearing the news that much confusion and chaos had been avoided thanks to their efforts.

Only one year later, however, it turned out that the majority in Parliament that had voted to repeal the Stamp Act was a fleeting coalition. By May 1767, the new Chancellor of the Exchequer, Charles Townshend, gave a rousing speech—which earned for the inebriated speaker the nickname "Champagne Charlie"—convincing Parliament that the country's abiding financial difficulties made a tax on the Americans absolutely necessary. He proposed imposing import duties on glass, porcelain, paper, lead, paint, and tea in order to raise 40,000 pounds annually for the treasury. This met with immediate approval from most members of Parliament. On June 29, 1767, the first of the Townshend Acts was passed.

Most American colonists reacted to the Townshend Duties as vehemently as they had to the stamp tax. Again, violence erupted, and again, influential merchants agreed to the nonimportation of English goods. In early 1768, John Dickinson, a Philadelphia lawyer, appealed to his fellow Americans to remain steadfast in their protest. "If you *once* admit," he wrote in an influential pamphlet, "that Great Britain may lay duties upon her exportations to us, for the purpose of levying money on us only," then in the future it must only "lay those duties on the articles which she prohibits us to manufacture—and the tragedy of American liberty is finished."

The British government reacted to the massive American protests by establishing an entirely new Customs Board for the North American Colonies. Lord Hillsborough, a brawny, uncompromising politician, was named the first

Colonial Secretary. The very first actions he took in his new post indicated that he was willing to resort to military force if necessary to resolve the conflict over taxation with the American colonies. For example, on June 8, 1768, he ordered several regiments of regular British troops to Boston simply because he had received reports that there had been rambunctious celebrations in the Massachusetts capital on the second anniversary of the repeal of the Stamp Act.

The American colonists refused to be intimidated by this demonstration of military power, and they remained true to their trusty campaign of boycotting British goods. Washington had bought Dickinson's pamphlet *Letters from a Farmer in Pennsylvania* and was convinced by its arguments. He, too, believed the boycott to be the best means of bringing the British government to its senses. On April 5, 1769, he wrote a letter to his wealthy and astute neighbor George Mason, who regularly devoted himself to the study of constitutional history at his Gunston Hall estate, located close to Belvoir. There the gentleman of Mount Vernon explained his view of the current situation.

"At a time when our lordly masters in Great Britain will be satisfied with nothing less than the deprivation of American freedom," Washington wrote, "it seems highly necessary that something should be done to avert the stroke and to maintain the liberty which we have derived from our ancestors." Therefore, an attempt had to be made to have the British government's "attention to our rights and privileges . . . awakened . . . by starving their trade and manufactures"—that is, by a concerted boycott in all the colonies. The longer he considered such a plan, the more passionately it recommended itself. For the "scheme" seemed to him "a good one" for effecting resistance if it could "be carried pretty generally into execution."

In Washington's view, however, such a plan would only be legal if the individual colonial legislatures issued their approval. For in a parliamentary system, the general will of the people could only be reliably expressed by this legitimizing process. Just as no absolute monarch or foreign parliament was allowed to impose its own will on a people, the chaotic and uncoordinated actions of individual rabblerousers could not be thought to represent the will of an entire population. The people's elected representatives always had to vote about the concerns affecting the entire country in order to then express in their majority decision the binding general will of all citizens. For that reason, "when the Court and Assembly . . . meet together in Williamsburg" in May, he would make sure a "uniform plan" was supported by a "concerted" action of the legislature. And indeed, on May 18, 1769, he successfully recommended to the representatives assembled in Williamsburg that the whole colony of

Virginia be called upon to boycott a long list of manufactures from Great Britain.

The boycott was put into action rather smoothly in July, and not only in Virginia but in all the other colonies as well. In the view of most colonists, all they had to do was wait for the British government to give in a second time. If the boycott should fail, however, Washington secretly considered there to be one "last resource" of resistance. So far, he had only dared to mention it confidentially in his April 5 letter to Mason. If the British government should remain unyielding or resort to further military retaliation, then "no man should scruple or hesitate a moment to use arms in defense of so valuable a blessing" as freedom.

The events of the following months would show that Washington had good reason to express this proviso. In the late summer of 1769, the British Colonial Secretary Lord Hillsborough signaled that he intended to repeal at least some of the Townshend Duties. Yet these considerations were still extremely vague in early 1770. Furthermore, the Americans would only have been satisfied with the repeal of all the new taxes. Then, in early March, there was an attack by British soldiers on American civilians, leading to the escalation feared by Washington.

On March 5, 1770, a group of colonists clashed with British soldiers on the snowy streets of Boston. The soldiers threatened the Americans with their bayonets, at which point a crowd that had gathered around the two groups began hurling snowballs at the regulars. The commanding officer ordered his men to fire. Five citizens of Boston died in the attack. In the following days, the inhabitants of all the American colonies were furious when they read the news of the tragic shots and the travesty they unleashed, now known as the Boston Massacre. The conflict that had been brewing for five years between the British citizens of America and the governmental and military authorities back in England had produced its first casualties. The burial of the first four victims of the massacre turned into one of the largest public assemblies ever known in North America. It became a rallying point for a new form of American resistance in which Washington now took a leading role.

9

Freedom and Servitude
(1770–1785)

AT THE same time as freedom-loving Americans were reading the earth-shattering news that their loud insistence on legislative self-government had been answered by fatal shots from royal soldiers, Frederick the Great was mesmerized by violent civil unrest in the east of Europe. In the spring of 1770, government troops in Poland were also engaged in bitter fighting with rebels protesting the recent infringement of their traditional liberties. The armed uprising in this venerable eastern European kingdom was the work of a group of nobles who called themselves Konfederacja barska (the Bar Confederation), after a meeting at the fortress of Bar in the Ukrainian part of Poland (and now part of Ukraine) where two years prior they had formed a military alliance. These Polish nobles sought to defend the independence of the Polish state from the Russian Empire, which, with increasing ruthlessness, treated it as a protectorate.

Large units of the Russian army had been deployed in Poland to fight the Prussian king during the Seven Years' War. When the war ended, they never left. The new empress, Catherine II, who had succeeded her husband, Peter III (after overthrowing him and having him killed by the brother of her lover Grigory Orlov), then had 14,000 more Russian soldiers stationed near Warsaw. The idea was to use military pressure to influence future Polish politics. The Elector of Saxony and King of Poland Augustus III died shortly after the Peace of Hubertusburg, giving Catherine a free hand to meddle in the election of his successor. She used her power to push for her preferred candidate, Stanisław Poniatowski, a Polish nobleman and former ambassador in Saint Petersburg who had preceded Orlov as her lover for many years. With Poniatowski's election as King Stanislaus II Augustus, Poland definitively became a vassal state of Russia.

In order to check Russia's influence in eastern Europe, in early 1770, the French Minister of Foreign Affairs Étienne-François de Choiseul began sending monthly subsidies of 100,000 livres to the more than 10,000 fighters of the Bar Confederation. He also provided them with a military adviser in the person of the secret agent and skilled lieutenant colonel Charles-François Dumouriez. Meanwhile, the Prussian king remained entirely passive. He decried Choiseul as an arsonist of Europe whose actions thoughtlessly risked the happy outcome of the peace treaties of Hubertusburg and Paris. Unlike the French foreign minister, Frederick considered it an utterly hopeless enterprise to try to shake off Russia's dominance over Poland and the eastern part of the continent. Therefore, he had no intention of needlessly rousing the Russian empress against him, especially since, to his great relief, she had reconfirmed the pact Peter III had made with Prussia at the end of the Seven Years' War expressly as a defensive alliance.

In consequence, Frederick gave no thought to how he could rush to the aid of the Polish rebels. On the contrary, he meditated on how he and his state of Prussia could best defend themselves from possible Russian incursions in the future. While the two powers may have been allies, Frederick continued to see the gigantic tsardom as an eerie, utterly unpredictable political entity. His deep-seated fears of Russia had preoccupied him for a long time; even before the Seven Years' War, he had given extremely haunting voice to them in a few intimate poems.

In one of them, he wrote that the endless Asian landmass of Siberia gave birth to "a swarm of barbarians" that set out ever more often to make war in the west. In addition, "the cold ice" of northern European Russia incessantly produced "thousands of bold murderers" who rivaled the Asian Russians in their "sinister fervor." Thus, even on the banks of the Don and on the Baltic Sea, the harsh climate that prevailed everywhere in Russia created a people of "savage boldness" that, "spurred on by a demon," unabashedly cast its greedy gaze on the territories of the civilized nations of Europe. At home, these hostile Russians bent their backs brutishly in harsh slavery before an empress who ruled as "a political tyrant." How different was the situation in Prussia, a state that Frederick described in the same poem as a happy commonwealth with virtuous, law-abiding, and hardworking citizens. This well-ordered Prussian state was governed by a king who, in his description, acted not like a despot but rather as "a mild and good monarch."

With this Russia—which he described in such bleak words so full of prejudice and bigotry—the Prussian king wanted to avoid military conflict if he could. He felt vindicated in this stance when the Ottoman Empire, having joined France in the fight against Russia and its occupation of Poland, suffered a series of humiliating defeats at the hands of Russian units both on land and at sea in the course of 1770. On July 5, two Russian squadrons even destroyed the Ottoman fleet while it lay at anchor north of Çeşme Bay in western Turkey. However, the Turks did manage to tie up critical forces of the Russian army for quite some time, allowing the Bar Confederation to continue its fight for liberty against the Russians and their puppet Stanislaus II Augustus for much longer than Frederick had anticipated. On October 13, 1770, the confederation of Polish nobles declared the king installed by Catherine II deposed, although they could not back it up with corresponding action in Warsaw.

In October 1770, the Prussian king sent his brother Henry to Saint Petersburg to find out what Russia had in store for embattled Poland beyond quelling the rebellion. Henry pricked up his ears when, at a soirée to which the empress had invited him, she mentioned that Austria had occupied Spisz, a Polish exclave south of the border region of Galicia, in the summer of 1769. This small land was surrounded by Austrian territory and had been taken by the Habsburgs to prevent the chaos reigning in Poland from spilling over the border into their own dominion. Since Spisz had now been under Austrian control for two years, Catherine II asked the Prussian prince with a laugh why the two of them should not also take some territory. Sparked by this candid proposal, a very lively debate ensued about the possible partition of Polish territory among Russia, Prussia, and Austria. In addition to Henry and Catherine, the participants in the discussion included the Russian war minister Count Zakhar Chernyshev and the Prussian envoy Count Viktor von Solms-Sonnenwalde.

On January 23, 1771, one day after his fifty-ninth birthday, Frederick received a letter from his brother in which Henry gave a detailed report of his recent conversation with Catherine II. The king had himself long dreamed of taking possession of the section of Poland located between Farther Pomerania and East Prussia, thus creating a land bridge to connect the two Prussian provinces. He had informed Solms, his envoy in Saint Petersburg, about this idea back in 1769. If Catherine were truly sincere in her offer, then he could now go about fulfilling his dream. Frederick also believed that a continuous Prussian territory from East Prussia to Farther Pomerania would provide better defensive capabilities against any future Russian attacks. Observing the situation from this point of view, the annexation of a part of the Kingdom of Poland to the Prussian dominion now even seemed imperative—a defensive measure necessary to protect his country against its outsize neighbor Russia. Just like when he invaded Silesia in 1740 and occupied Saxony in 1756, considerations of self-defense melded with his bald desire for territorial expansion to form a complete thought. But what would Austria say about the idea?

In April 1771, Frederick presented his plan to the Austrian envoy in Berlin Gottfried van Swieten, suggesting that Russia, Prussia, and Austria divide up the Kingdom of Poland between them. In his opinion, the venerable elected monarchy had descended into anarchy, and partition would restore it to order. In May, van Swieten let him know that Austria would only agree to carving up Poland in this manner if, in return, Frederick indicated his willingness to give Silesia back to Maria Theresa. To the mind of the Prussian king, this suggestion was nothing short of insanity, but he reined in his displeasure at the indecent proposal. First, he wanted to see if and how the Austrian government would approach Russia about the plan to partition Poland. Sure enough, Chancellor Kaunitz invited the Russian envoy, Prince Golitsyn, to discuss the question in Vienna that fall. After the extensive interview, Frederick knew that the Russian empress had not been joking when she talked to Prince Henry about the possible division of Poland among its three neighbors.

On February 4, 1772, van Swieten then reiterated Austria's apparently generous offer to the Prussian king, whereby he could take a large section of Poland in exchange for giving up Silesia. This time, Frederick rejected the offer immediately and stridently. At least, that is what van Swieten wrote to Chancellor Kaunitz the next day. Supposedly, Frederick screamed at him, "You take whichever part you please, but not at my expense!" According to Frederick's own letter to his envoy Solms, he had answered van Swieten thusly: "Gout has rotted my feet, not my brains."

The Austrians were now faced with a difficult dilemma. On the one hand, they could stand by and do nothing while Prussia and Russia carved up Polish territory as they saw fit. On the other, Vienna could take part in the apparently inevitable partition, annexing the largest possible amount of land for itself. On February 28, van Swieten notified the Prussian king of his government's decision: Austria would forget about Silesia, but it would nonetheless participate actively in the partition of Poland. Catherine II was informed of the plan in March, and then Russia, Austria, and Prussia set to work with astonishing speed. The three states agreed that Austria would get all of Galicia and Lodomeria, Russia a territory of similar size north and south of the city of Vitebsk, and Prussia a land bridge between Farther Pomerania and East Prussia. From his new territory, Frederick created the provinces of Ermland (now Warmia,

Poland), Kulmerland (now Chełmno Land, Poland), the Netze District, and West Prussia. In the regions annexed, only the cities of Danzig (now Gdansk, Poland) and Thorn (now Toruń, Poland) remained independent of Prussia.

By October 1772, Russian, Austrian, and Prussian troops had fully occupied the territories claimed by their governments. They met with no significant Polish resistance. Even the Bar Confederation gave up its cause for lost and disbanded. The Polish legislative body, the Sejm, was coerced into issuing a decree officially renouncing its claim to the annexed territories. After the fact, Austria, Prussia, and Russia went to great pains to legitimize their more than questionable actions in law. Naturally, many Poles complained bitterly. Ignacy Twardowski, the vaivode, or governor, of Kalisz, observed the partition of his country in disbelief. "We are finished," he commented in resignation. "Those cut off by the partition, once free, will become slaves. The thought brings tears to my eyes, for in large measure, I, too, will succumb to this fate under the Prussian yoke."

In the rest of Europe, reactions to the Polish partition varied. For the most part, Great Britain remained silent about the actions taken by its longtime ally Frederick. France, which had initially supported the Bar Confederation in its fight against the Russian occupation, felt betrayed that its ally Austria had participated in the predatory partition of Poland. Yet it knew a fait accompli when it saw one; a realistic appraisal of the situation revealed there was nothing to be done. For her part, Maria Theresa had not been easily persuaded by Kaunitz and her son Joseph II, who, since the death of her husband in 1765, had ruled as Holy Roman Emperor. She did not hide the fact that she suffered terrible pangs of conscience, even though Austria had just gained a large, attractive territory and more than two million new subjects thanks to its annexation of Galicia and Lodomeria. She feared that the betrayal of Poland meant the end of good faith in Europe forever. Yet she was not strong enough to govern affairs in Austria on her own, and so for better or worse she had to let Kaunitz and her son have their way—although not without her deepest sorrow: "Nothing in the world causes me more pain than the loss of our good reputation."

In contrast, Frederick the Great felt no sorrow at having brought West Prussia, Ermland, Kulmerland, and the greater Netze District under the dominion of the Prussian Crown. Thanks to this expansion, more than half his territory now lay outside the borders of the Holy Roman Empire and thus under his sole royal authority. Furthermore, he did not see himself at all as a tyrant or an enslaver—as Vaivode Twardowski had characterized him—but rather as a liberator able to provide his new subjects with a better life. Indeed, in the fall of 1772 he announced a reform of the justice system in the lands formerly possessed by the Polish Crown and now taken by the king of Prussia. As part of this reform, he abolished slavery as well as serfdom for farmers in his newly acquired lands. He also issued an edict ordering benighted rural areas to be brought up to a standard of living conforming to Enlightenment principles.

One year later, while Frederick was instituting the judiciary reform of the newly acquired province of West Prussia and finishing the first large-scale surveying of the farmland there, a London periodical named *The Public Advertiser* published a brand-new "Edict by the King of Prussia" on September 22, 1773. It left readers gaping incredulously. As was plain to see from the newspaper, the edict had been issued in "Dantzick" (i.e., Danzig) on September 5. Had the Prussian king, unnoticed by the world, now also taken this Baltic Sea port and added it to West Prussia despite the fact that it was still under Polish dominion? Even stranger were the tone and the content of the edict, in which Frederick demanded that the inhabitants of Great Britain promptly pay taxes to him.

To substantiate this shocking claim, the Prussian king marshaled bewildering arguments. For one, the first Germanic nomads who had settled in Great Britain were subjects of his ancestors. Therefore, he must still be regarded as the true master of all Britons. Consequently, Great Britain was a Prussian colony. Furthermore, he had successfully defended Great Britain's "colonies against the power of France" in the Seven Years' War "and thereby enabled them to make conquests from the said power in America." For this invaluable service, he should now at least be given "adequate compensation" in the form of customs duties. For these reasons, he demanded from that moment forward "that all ships or vessels bound from Great Britain to any other part of the world" first "touch at our port of Königsberg," where they would "be unladen, searched, and charged with the said duties."

In reality, the newspaper article was the work of Benjamin Franklin, the Americans' agent in London. It was meant as a parody of British tax policy toward the American colonies. For the Americans considered Britain's unyielding and authoritarian stance on the tax question to be as outrageous as Frederick's actions in Poland. Of course, many readers of the ostensible royal edict, initially believing it to be authentic, only burst out "with an abundance of laughing" upon coming to the end. The reason for their gullibility, Franklin surmised, was the "the king of Prussia's *character*": Everyone believed him capable of such temerity.

The British government continued to adhere stubbornly to its plans to tax the Americans. Most of the Townshend Duties had been lifted in the previous two years, but on principle Parliament insisted on retaining the duty on tea, as a symbol of its right to tax the American colonies as it saw fit. Many regiments of British regulars were also still stationed in America, on the ready to be deployed against the colonists. Since 1771, the latter had kept the memory of the Boston Massacre alive by holding public memorial ceremonies every year on March 5.

In the summer of 1773, Parliament passed a new law allowing the East India Company to sell tea in the American colonies for less than the market price. The idea was to encourage the Americans to buy this tea (instead of that of competitors) and thus to implicitly sanction the hated tax. This only added fuel to the fire of the colonists' discontent. Toward the end of the year, American resistance to obstinate British tax policy took on a new dimension when three ships belonging to the East India Company docked in Boston Harbor in November and December. An assembly of citizens demanded that the tea be sent back to England immediately and decided to use all means necessary to prevent its unloading. Governor Thomas Hutchinson, however, refused to allow the fully loaded ships to leave the harbor. The result was the Boston Tea Party, a three-hour raid on December 16 in which more than thirty Boston citizens, dressed as Indians, boarded the ships and threw 342 chests of tea overboard. An amount of tea worth 9,000 pounds sterling dissolved in the saltwater of Boston Harbor.

The very next day, John Adams, one of the most influential politicians and lawyers in Boston, described this "most magnificent . . . destruction of the tea" as an "epocha"—that is, an epochal event—that would have "so important consequences, and so lasting." Exactly how the Crown would choose to retaliate for "so bold, so daring, so firm, intrepid and inflexible" a deed was unclear to Adams. Many possibilities were conceivable. "Will they punish us? How? By quartering troops upon us? By annulling our charter? By laying on more duties? By restraining our trade?"

Answers were given to these pressing questions between March and June 1774, when Parliament drafted and passed four laws in succession that would soon be known in the American press only as the Intolerable Acts. They called for Boston Harbor to be closed to trade until the destroyed tea was paid for. Furthermore, town meetings could only be held with the permission of the governor. Moreover, agents of the Crown could now be brought to trial in England instead of in the colonies. Finally, soldiers were allowed to be quartered in private homes in all the colonies. In addition, eleven more regiments of British regulars were redeployed to Boston to ensure peace and order there—by force if necessary.

Since these legal and military measures not only punished the insubordinate residents of Massachusetts but also made all the other colonies in America suffer for the offenses committed in Boston, a wider resistance movement began to take shape in the colonial legislatures in May 1774. When the Virginia House of Burgesses met on May 4 in Williamsburg to debate the closure of Boston Harbor, George Washington joined the ranks of those critical of the British government. He voted for a resolution calling upon the residents of Virginia to observe a day of common fasting and prayer as a symbol of protest against the sanctions. On May 26, Lord Dunmore, the governor of Virginia, dissolved the legislative session in order to stifle the sentiment of opposition growing there. Washington then joined a group of representatives in a local tavern who held the view that only a congress of all the colonies had a chance of getting the British government to see reason.

Washington expressed his immeasurable anger and disappointment at the hardened position of the Crown and Parliament in a letter to his longtime friend and neighbor George William Fairfax, who had moved to England with his wife, Sally, the year before. On June 10, 1774, Washington reported from the capital of Williamsburg that the House of Burgesses would meet again on August 1, even without being formally called to session by the governor if necessary, to discuss what "vigorous measures" needed to be adopted all over America in order to defend their traditional rights. The British "ministry may rely on it that Americans will never be taxed without their own consent." Furthermore, "the cause of Boston"—that is, "the despotic measures" taken by the British government to close the harbor—"now is and ever will be considered as the cause of America."

At this point in his letter, Washington emphasized that he did not uncritically "approve their conduct in destroying the tea" in Boston in December 1773. On the other hand, the wanton demolition of a shipload of tea was in no way sufficient grounds to use "every piece of art and despotism to fix the shackles of slavery upon us." In two further letters, sent to George William's brother Bryan Fairfax on July 4 and 20, Washington reiterated his position forcefully. It was, he wrote, unbearable for him to see the British government trying to "[reduce] us to the most abject state of slavery that ever was designed for mankind." Was it not "as clear as the sun in its meridian brightness," he therefore asked, "that there was a regular, systematic plan formed to fix the right and practice of taxation" on the colonists?

The reasons the Americans were defending themselves so vehemently, Washington pointed out, was not that they considered paying a tax on tea to be particularly "burdensome." Rather, the only reason they opposed the policy of the British government so passionately was that they did not want to "be deprived of this essential and valuable part of our constitution"—namely, to decide for themselves about how they would be taxed. The American colonists were indebted to the values of enlightened government elucidated by John Locke. They rejected "a system of tyranny" and desired instead a "free government." And it was especially galling that the government of the mother country, which since 1689 had itself professed parliamentarianism, was now dead set on enslaving free Americans. Fairfax could assume, Washington assured him, that this deep feeling of outrage "filled the breast of every American."

Twelve days after Washington wrote this second letter to Bryan Fairfax, the House of Burgesses met in Williamsburg and chose from its ranks seven Virginia delegates to the large Continental Congress that Washington had mentioned in his letter to George Fairfax. It was to assemble in Philadelphia, the seat of Pennsylvania government, whose central location and economic and cultural significance had earned for it the status of a pan-American capital. Peyton Randolph, the Speaker of the Virginia colonial legislature, received the most votes, with 104. But Washington, who was one of the colony's most famous and reliable politicians, was given an almost equally large vote of confidence: Ninety-eight representatives cast a ballot for him, making him the third-highest vote-getter of all the candidates.

With so much faith placed in him, Washington traveled to Philadelphia. From September 4 to October 27, 1774, he participated at the sessions of the Congress with great vigilance and a profound sense of responsibility. As in the Virginia House of Burgesses, he only spoke at the Continental Congress when the debates of the fifty-six delegates—whose number also included John Adams—dealt with the most important issues to be voted on. Under the presidency of Peyton Randolph (who had been chosen by the assembled delegates as their leader), the Congress condemned the coercive measures of the Intolerable Acts as incommensurate with the British constitution and called for a ban on the importation of all British goods.

At the suggestion of the Congress, committees were formed in all the American cities to ensure the effective policing of the comprehensive trade embargo and boycott. Toward the end of its deliberations in Philadelphia, the Continental Congress then issued an ominous statement to the effect that if the British government resorted again to military force, it could expect the

Americans to answer with arms as well. Before adjourning the Congress on October 26, the delegates agreed that a Second Continental Congress should begin meeting no later than May 1775. In this way, it would be ready to react accordingly if a more serious conflict arose.

Over the winter, militias were formed in all the American colonies to prepare for a possible attack from the British army. In Virginia, five voluntary companies of militiamen immediately chose as their commander in chief the man who had so commendably led the Virginia militia at the start of the Seven Years' War: Washington. The gentleman of Mount Vernon, who had not commanded a military unit in seventeen years, felt honored that after so much time he still enjoyed the reputation of being the best and most experienced officer that his colony had to offer. At the same time, he had no desire to fight the well-trained and well-supplied British army. On February 25, he admitted in a letter to the Pennsylvania land speculator John Connolly that he hoped "the ministry would willingly change their ground, from a conviction that forcible measures will be inadequate to the end designed."

Elections were held for the Second Continental Congress in the week between March 20 and 27. The results showed that Washington's star had risen even higher in the preceding five months. This time, he received 106 of 108 votes. Only Peyton Randolph, the former and presumptive next president of the Congress, received more. One of the newly elected Virginia delegates was Thomas Jefferson, a young lawyer only thirty-two years of age. All of the Virginia delegates to the assembly in Philadelphia prepared assiduously for their upcoming parliamentary role. On April 27, however, only one week before their planned departure for Pennsylvania, a message arrived that made it clear to everyone that the dreaded military conflict with the mother country had already begun.

Eight days earlier in Massachusetts, bloody skirmishes had erupted between the British army and New England militiamen in the western Boston suburb of Cambridge and in the nearby cities of Lexington and Concord. The British units stationed in Boston were unwilling to stand by and do nothing as the newly formed New England militias around the city supplied themselves with guns and ammunition. In secret, 700 British soldiers set off for Concord to destroy the arms stored in the magazine there. However, the British plan was exposed, leaving 500 American militiamen enough time to take up positions before the regulars arrived. In the early-morning hours of April 19, 1775, militiamen in Lexington began firing on the British, who retreated in surprise. Applying constant fire, the Americans managed to drive the British back to Boston. In the following days, more and more militiamen flocked to the city, where they trapped and besieged the British units stationed there.

A few weeks later, Washington justified the actions of the New England militiamen in a letter to George William Fairfax. As the British troops advanced, he argued, the New Englanders had no choice but to attack them in order to defend their "private property"—that is, the guns and ammunition stored in the magazine. Nor had it been unlawful to stock a magazine near Boston. Indeed, "self-preservation obliged the inhabitants to establish" it. Naturally, it was unfortunate "that a brother's sword has been sheathed in a brother's breast, and that the once happy and peaceful plains of America are either to be drenched with blood or inhabited by slaves. Sad alternative!" And yet, "can a virtuous man hesitate in his choice?" No one should have any doubt but that "the Americans will fight for their liberties and property."

When Washington set off from Mount Vernon in a coach-and-four on May 4 to attend the Second Continental Congress in Philadelphia, he brought his old Virginia uniform with him as a sign of his willingness to fight. He was joined on the road by numerous Virginians. Upon his arrival in Philadelphia, he was accompanied by 500 riders playing spirited martial music on fifes and drums. The burly Washington was the only delegate to the assembly who participated as a uniformed officer. When, on June 15, the Congress selected a commander in chief for the united militias of the American colonies, it was no surprise to anyone that their choice was Washington. The delegates unanimously agreed that no man but Washington could lead the Americans with so much dignity, resolve, and experience in the fight against the British. Washington himself was not so convinced, although by wearing his uniform he had implicitly proposed himself for high military office.

The next day, Washington gave a short speech to the assembled delegates in which he accepted the rank of "General and Commander in Chief of the American Forces." He humbly admitted that, while "truly sensible of the high honor done me in this appointment," he feared that he might not be "equal" to the task. Indeed, it was now his duty to prepare a voluntary army of raw recruits to take the field against the best army in the world—the same one that had achieved internationally famous victories against the French in the Seven Years' War. He was concerned that his "ability and military experience" might be insufficient to justify "the extensive and important trust" placed in him. Nevertheless, "as the Congress desire it," he would "exert every power I possess in their service and for the support of the glorious cause" of America.

Washington's concern about the difficulty of the military task ahead of him was outweighed by the pride he felt when considering the revolutionary manner in which his new office had been bestowed upon him. No prince or despot had selected him as general. Nor had he usurped supreme power over the army of the combined troops of North America. He had been chosen commander in chief of the Continental Army by a vote of the legislative representatives of the American people. From that moment forward, he was borne aloft by the "unanimous voice of the colonies," as he would later write to his brother-in-law Burwell Bassett.

That also meant that everything he now did and ordered had to be explained and justified to the Continental Congress in regular reports, since the Americans' highest civilian authority was superior to the highest military command of the colonies. This hierarchy of political and military decision-making was heartily embraced by Washington, who had been a convinced proponent of Locke's parliamentary theory since his youth. Not even in light of the precarious military situation in which the colonies now found themselves did he seek unlimited authority. At no point did he entertain the notion that a general without parliamentary oversight could act with greater power and strength than a commander who was required to constantly coordinate with representatives of the people. Furthermore, he was secure in the knowledge that his view coincided with that of his fellow Americans. As he wrote in a letter to the newly formed Provincial Congress of New York on June 26, "When we assumed the soldier, we did not lay aside the citizen." Accordingly, even as a general, no title seemed more honorable to him than that of free American citizen.

Shortly after taking up headquarters in Cambridge in July 1775, he wrote a letter to Thomas Gage, the British military governor of Massachusetts. There he explained to his adversary in no uncertain terms that he, as an American general, enjoyed a much more honorable military authority than even the highest officer in the regular British army. Even Gage himself, an English aristocrat, was only a servant of the British Crown named by the king, whereas Washington achieved his high "rank" thanks to the "uncorrupted choice of a brave and free people." Not the grace of a sovereign but the free vote of a free citizenry was "the purest source and original fountain of all power." Both the civil administration and the military hierarchy of the American colonies—which were now referred to as the United Colonies of North-America—were thus morally and constitutionally far superior to the corresponding governmental and decision-making authorities of the British.

Gage and the 10,000 British soldiers trapped in Boston may have refused to recognize Washington's moral integrity and superiority, but they had to admit that the siege tactics employed by the Virginian had given him a clear military advantage. The 16,000 soldiers of the Continental Army, whose funding had been approved by the Continental Congress in June, kept the British regiments tied up in Boston far into the autumn, denying them the possibility of escaping by land and thus cutting them off from the outside world. For the Americans, this was a major success.

In a proclamation issued in London on August 23, King George III declared all the American colonies to be in a state of rebellion. As the Americans learned of this in early October, they had to brace themselves for the imminent arrival of many more regiments of British regulars on North American shores. Franklin, who was elected a Pennsylvania delegate to the Continental Congress upon his return from England in the spring of 1775, was tasked with traveling from Philadelphia to Cambridge to receive a personal report from Washington about the state of the Continental Army. When the two men met at Washington's headquarters in October, the general informed Franklin that his men could only withstand a protracted war if the Congress increased the size of the army to at least 20,000 soldiers. He and Franklin agreed that the Congress also had to begin searching for friends of America on the other side of the Atlantic. Accordingly, on November 29, the Congress set up a secret committee for foreign affairs that made contact with Achard de Bonvouloir, the French king's agent in Philadelphia.

Before any such friendship could bear fruit, the Americans managed to eject the British regiments from Boston on their own power in 1776. After a siege lasting nearly one year, the British were loath to abide any longer in the Massachusetts capital. Boarding their ships, they escaped by the only avenue open to them, sailing out of Boston Harbor and to far-off Halifax in Canada. The cheers of the Americans were loud. Washington thanked the intervention of providence. He believed with religious fervor that divinely ordained fate had granted the besiegers victory over their foes on account of the just cause that they championed. "With the greatest of pleasure," he thus informed John Hancock—who had taken over the presidency of the Continental Congress after the death of Peyton Randolph—that "the Ministerial Army evacuated the town of Boston, and that the forces of the United Colonies are now in actual possession thereof."

Hancock, in turn, thanked Washington for his victory. At the head of a hastily assembled voluntary army, he had defeated a British force "commanded by the most experienced generals" with only a "band of husbandmen." In May, Hancock invited Washington to Philadelphia to discuss with him and the Congress what military strategy the Americans should now pursue. In light of the new regiments expected from England, Washington, Hancock, and the other delegates agreed that the Continental Army should now be moved from the liberated city of Boston to New York.

In June, while Washington and his army took up a position on Manhattan Island to prepare for the arrival of the British fleet, the congressional delegates in Philadelphia discussed the political consequences of the armed conflict with the mother country that had now lasted for over a year. Many were influenced by the ideas of Thomas Paine, an Enlightenment thinker and printer who in 1774 had immigrated from England to Pennsylvania. In his 1776 pamphlet *Common Sense*, he called for the Americans to sever their ties with "the remains of monarchical tyranny in the person of the king." Since then, more and more congressional delegates had become convinced that the colonies currently at war with England should form a new, independent union of states.

By the summer of 1776, Paine's pamphlet had been read by nearly one million people in the colonies—quite a feat, considering that the total population was only three million. He taught the Americans that "*it is wholly owing to the constitution of the people, and not to the constitution of the government*, that the crown is not as oppressive in England as in Turkey." Those who found it difficult to bid farewell to the highly esteemed British constitution should undertake "to examine the component parts of the English constitution." They would then find that it was only "the new republican materials" of the constitution that guaranteed the much-vaunted "freedom of England." As a result, the contributions of the king and the deputies of the aristocracy were no longer necessary in government affairs. Only "representatives" elected by the citizens, whose mandate ought to be continually renewed by "having elections often," could govern in the interest of the people. Therefore, "nothing can settle our affairs so expeditiously"—thus Paine concluded his call for the establishment of a democratic republic in America—"as an open and determined declaration for independence."

In part as a result of the great influence Paine's arguments had on the American colonies, the faction in support of declaring independence gained the upper hand in the Congress. In early June, the Virginia delegate Thomas Jefferson was tasked with sketching out a first draft of such a declaration. Three weeks later, on June 28, the entire Congress reviewed his work. A few changes were made to Jefferson's text, and then it was signed by the delegates on July 4,

1776. On that day in Philadelphia, William Penn's "city of brotherly love," the colonies already united in their war with Great Britain became the fully independent, sovereign "United States of America." This new name of the fledgling nation—the first territorial republican state founded on the principle of popular sovereignty in the modern age—appeared boldly at the head of the Declaration of Independence. On July 9, Washington read the document aloud to his assembled army in New York.

Jefferson's text resonated with Washington in nearly every aspect, especially the passages touching on natural rights and the religious basis of the republic. The Declaration of Independence claimed

> that all men are created equal, that they are endowed by their creator with certain unalienable rights, that among these are life, liberty, and the pursuit of happiness. That to secure these rights, governments are instituted among men, deriving their just powers from the consent of the governed. That whenever any form of government becomes destructive of these ends, it is the right of the people to alter or abolish it, and to institute new government, laying its foundation on such principles and organizing its powers in such form, as to them shall seem most likely to effect their safety and happiness.

These words signified more than just the birth of a true political union of the individual American states, of the kind that Franklin and many other American politicians had yearned for since the Albany Congress of 1754. Their scope was much broader. The foundation of the first democratic republic of the modern age was supposed to be a shining example to the rest of the human race, a source of guidance to other states and nations. More powerfully than any other document of the eighteenth century, the American Declaration of Independence proclaims the ideals of freedom, equality, and popular sovereignty to be the common goal of all humankind.

In 1733, Voltaire had claimed in his *Philosophical Letters* that Philadelphia was the place where, since 1701, the golden age of reason, freedom, and tolerance had in all probability existed. Now, in 1776, there seemed to be no doubt that the light of this city shone out into the world brighter than ever before. The Declaration of Independence issued by the Congress in Philadelphia was a clear signal to all human beings that the political realization of Locke's parliamentary version of enlightened government had entered a new dimension of epochal importance.

Riding high on the earth-shattering moment, Jefferson knew perfectly well that the universal human rights he proclaimed must be guaranteed to Black people as well. Indeed, there was a passage in his first draft of the Declaration that severely criticized the slave trade. Yet it was removed from the document under pressure from the southern delegates in the Congress. Unlike Vermont, New Hampshire, Massachusetts, Pennsylvania, and Rhode Island, which gradually abolished slavery in the state constitutions they adopted in the wake of July 4, 1776, the overwhelmingly agrarian states in the south could not imagine—even if just for economic reasons—doing without the unpaid agricultural labor of enslaved Blacks. Of the 460,000 slaves living in the territory of the United States in the summer of 1776, only 6,000 of them were in Pennsylvania, whereas there were more than 100,000 in the state of Virginia.

Even the most enlightened white Americans, however, harbored deep prejudices about Black people that were only slowly overcome. Franklin, who owned enslaved Africans as house servants until the 1760s, became a vehement critic of slavery. However, in a letter to his English friend John Waring, he admitted that the evolution of his thinking had been a long time coming. Contrary to his older views, he had now "conceived a higher opinion of the natural capacities of the black race than I had ever before entertained," and he did not even want to try to "justify all my prejudices nor to account for them." Just how rare Franklin's position was for his time, in which even educated white people considered Black people to be intellectually inferior, is illustrated by a statement of the Prussian Enlightenment philosopher Immanuel Kant. In his *Observations on the Feeling of the Beautiful and Sublime*, which he published in 1764 and did not revise after 1776, he announced, "The Negroes of Africa have by nature no feeling that rises above the trifling." Supposedly, "among the hundreds of thousands of blacks who are transported elsewhere from their countries, although many of them have even been set free, still not a single one was ever found who presented anything great in art or science or any other praiseworthy quality, even though among the whites some continually rise aloft from the lowest rabble, and through superior gifts earn respect in the world."

For the Prussian philosopher Kant, "the difference between these two races of man" was "as great in regard to mental capacities as in color."

As for the American commander in chief George Washington, his stance toward Black people was ambiguous. Consider his relationship to Phillis Wheatley. She had been brought as a slave from Senegal to Boston and had fought in the Revolution on the American side against the British. When she wrote a poem for "His Excellency George Washington" glorifying the Continental Army, he thanked her with moving words in a personal letter and acknowledged her "great poetical talents." Yet at the same time, the slaves who performed indispensable labor for him at Mount Vernon—and whom he thought he treated irreproachably—he did not set free. On the other hand, when a council of war decided to "reject slaves and by a great majority to reject Negroes altogether" as soldiers in the Continental Army, his was one of the few voices opposed to the latter idea. Not only did he accept free Black people into his army of revolutionaries, but he also had his decision legitimized legislatively by a vote in Congress. From that moment forward, in some units Black and white soldiers fought side by side for American independence.

In the case of this decision, a lack of soldiers probably played a role. Washington had no choice but to accept every available man into his army if he was going to effectively oppose the British. This emerged clearly in late July 1776, when a massive British fleet of over 400 ships reached American shores in New York. More than 30,000 soldiers—most of whom were mercenaries provided to the British government by indebted territorial princes in Germany (especially the prince of Hesse-Kassel)—took up positions a few miles south of New York on Staten Island and Long Island. North America had never witnessed such a gigantic deployment of troops.

The British and Hessian soldiers attacked Washington's army on August 27 at Brooklyn, where the Americans had dug in to defend New York. For three days, the attackers tenaciously advanced bit by bit, inflicting heavy casualties on the defenders. Nearly 1,000 Americans lost their lives in the bloody Battle of Long Island before Washington, with a heavy heart, decided to surrender New York in order to at least save the majority of his army. In the dark of night on August 29, he retreated from Brooklyn across the East River to Manhattan. After further intense skirmishes, by mid-September he was forced to march his army to Harlem and then lead it across the Hudson River to New Jersey. Ultimately, the cautious general was forced to abandon the field there as well, taking his troops over to Pennsylvania in December. In great peril, he then had to conceive a new strategy for defending the American cause.

Worried by the permanent retreat of the Continental Army, the Congress sent Franklin as chief representative of the United States to Paris on October 29. Highly esteemed in Europe as a scientist and politician, his mission was to convince the French to support the Americans in their fight against Great Britain. Of course, many months could pass before the French sent money and weapons. Until then, the Americans had to do everything in their own power

FIGURE 9.1. Cool decisiveness: Washington crossing the Delaware.
Painting by Emanuel Gottlieb Leutze, 1851 (akg-images).

to hold the field if they did not want to so swiftly lose the independence that
they had just declared.

In this exceedingly precarious situation, Washington decided to stage a
surprise attack on the city of Trenton, New Jersey, located on the Delaware
River, where three regiments of Hessians totaling 1,400 men were in winter
quarters. On December 25, he took 2,400 soldiers of the Continental Army to
the ferry landing, where at night they crossed over the icy water to Trenton. A
heavy snowstorm had blown through a few hours earlier, lulling the Hessians
into a feeling of false security. None of them anticipated an American attack
on this freezing cold Christmas Day. For that reason, the usual sentries were
not posted.

When Washington arrived with his soldiers at Trenton in the early-morning
hours of December 26, the city lay defenseless before him. He ordered his
soldiers to attack immediately. The Hessians, startled and still hungover from
their Christmas festivities, could not answer the fire of the American artillery.
Washington took more than 900 German mercenaries prisoner and captured
over 1,000 weapons along with the corresponding gunpowder. It was a god-
send to the battered Continental Army. Then the Americans left Trenton as
quickly as they had come and headed for Philadelphia, where Washington had
the prisoners paraded through the city in triumph. The effect was to raise the

morale of the congressional delegates, especially since Washington, in a letter to John Hancock dated December 27, congratulated not himself but "you"— that is, the president of the Congress and the American people he represented—"upon the success of an enterprise which I had formed against a detachment of the enemy lying in Trenton."

On January 3, 1777, Washington pulled off another spectacular coup, attacking Princeton, New Jersey, with 7,000 soldiers. Shortly before, 6,000 British troops had set off for Trenton to help the Hessian regiments fooled by the Americans. That left only 1,400 British soldiers in Princeton; they put up as little resistance to the overwhelming American force as the Hessians in Trenton had. Once again, Washington quickly withdrew from the conquered city. This tactic of swift advances followed by hasty retreats became a mainstay of Washington's strategy throughout 1777. He could not hope to decisively defeat the British army in that manner, but his quick troop movements did demonstrate to his opponent that he had no intention of ever surrendering.

In addition, Washington achieved something truly significant with his two psychologically meaningful victories at Trenton and Princeton: He immediately boosted the morale of his debilitated Continental Army. More than 8,000 enthusiastic new recruits voluntarily joined up in the following months. Even when the British took Philadelphia in the fall of 1777 and the Congress was forced to flee to York in the Pennsylvania interior, the Americans took courage from Washington's undisputed qualities as a military leader. His soldiers protected the American Congress while it was on the run, making him the guardian angel of the most important parliamentary experiment in the Age of Enlightenment. By 1777 at the latest, the name of Washington was known throughout the world. In Goethe's words, he now became a shining and twinkling star "in the firmament of politics and war" in Europe as well.

Not everyone in Europe who expressed an opinion about the democratic and republican General Washington was immediately able to get his name right. Frederick the Great was one of those who needed a little time to get used to it. In his political correspondence in the period following the American Declaration of Independence, the Prussian king initially called the new American hero "Walsington" and then "Wasincton." Only in the second half of 1777, by which point he had become increasingly fascinated by the military abilities of the American commander in chief, did he master the correct spelling of his name.

Frederick observed the events of the American Revolution with a strict and distanced neutrality toward both sides in the conflict. In October 1776, he

confidentially informed his lord chamberlain, Gebhard Werner von der Schulenburg, that the Americans' fight for liberty would "not last long, for the
English will soon have quashed the colonies." Nevertheless, he wanted to wait
and see how the fortunes of the war played out. When the Americans retreated
from New York, he felt justified in his opinion. In a letter to Joachim Karl von
Maltzahn, the Prussian envoy in London, Frederick wrote on January 20, 1777,
that "it was not surprising in the least that the regular British soldiers had carried the day against the provincial American troops." Frederick clearly thought
Washington's army was truly weak.

However, when the first news of Washington's surprise successes in Trenton
and Princeton reached the king, he changed his mind. Suddenly, his letters
contained enthusiastic comments about Washington's brilliant victories. It
seemed as if he were now secretly rooting for the scrappy revolutionaries. No
doubt, he still perceived the general as "the chief of upstart rebels." Yet in a
letter to the French mathematician Jean-Baptiste le Rond d'Alembert, he lamented that "those poor Americans" had to suffer at the hands of the power-
hungry British. In a letter to Bernard Wilhelm von der Goltz, the Prussian
ambassador in Paris, he praised Washington's military tactics to the skies: The
shrewd American general consistently opted to withdraw, but so far not one
American retreat in the face of the enemy had been decisive.

The Americans achieved another unexpected victory in the autumnal forests of Saratoga (near Albany), where they were joined by Colonel Tadeusz
Kościuszko. The Polish military engineer had left his native land after the partition to fight for the cause of universal human freedom. At that point, the Prussian king began following General Washington's every move. In November 1777, Frederick wrote to his brother Henry, instructing him to carefully
"observe" all Washington's troop movements and then report back to him on
them in detail. From Washington more than nearly any other general, he believed they could "learn about this great art of war, about which one could
never learn enough." Still, Frederick was unwilling to forge an alliance with the
Americans despite requests to do so from American envoys in Europe. No
matter how much sympathy he felt for Washington, the new political commonwealth "of Philadelphia" was simply too foreign to him. After all, as Frederick wrote to Voltaire, it was essentially the English Enlightenment
philosopher Locke, so highly esteemed by the Americans, who "gave the laws"
to that polity.

As the year 1778 was dawning, one mighty European state did make an
alliance with the American rebels. The new French foreign minister, Charles

Gravier de Vergennes, relented to Franklin's constant entreaties, and, after the Battle of Saratoga, he was able to convince Louis XVI to formally recognize the independence of the United States of America in December 1777. On January 8, 1778, Vergennes informed the Americans that the king was ready to agree to an alliance. On January 28, the French government promised the United States an annual aid package of six million livres. On February 6, a comprehensive Franco-American treaty of alliance was signed in Paris that opened the door to French military intervention in the American War of Independence.

In endorsing the Franco-American alliance, the king of France doubtless saw an enticing opportunity to do long-term damage to his archrival Great Britain. Yet there were also people in France who very deliberately took up the cause of the democratic and republican version of enlightened government. One of them was Voltaire. On April 29—with only seven months to live, and well aware that death was coming—he went to the Paris Academy of Sciences to meet Franklin, the representative of the American revolutionaries. As the two men stood opposite one another, the crowd around them cried out for them to embrace in the French manner. And indeed, the two Enlightenment thinkers took one another in their arms and kissed each other on both cheeks in the presence of the deeply touched academicians. It was Voltaire's final blessing for the parliamentarianism, personified by Franklin, that he had praised as the political model of the future since the publication of the *Philosophical Letters* almost half a century earlier.

Frederick the Great mourned the death of his philosophical teacher in an obituary read out at the Berlin Academy of Sciences at the end of the year. Unlike Voltaire, however, he did not become a partisan of the Americans. On the other hand, in the spring of 1778 Washington did receive significant support from a senior Prussian officer who had learned the art of war while serving at Frederick's headquarters in the Seven Years' War: Friedrich Wilhelm von Steuben, born in Magdeburg and himself the son of a Prussian major. After leaving the Prussian army, Steuben had served as court chamberlain to the prince of Hohenzollern-Hechingen. He ultimately burned with such zeal for the American cause of freedom that he sought out Franklin in Paris and requested to be appointed as a high-ranking officer in the Continental Army.

Thanks to Franklin's intercession, Steuben ended up at Washington's headquarters in Valley Forge, west of Philadelphia. On May 5, 1778, he was named inspector general of the American troops. From then on, Steuben was

FIGURE 9.2. Prussian officer in the Continental Army: Friedrich Wilhelm von
Steuben (1730–1794). Painting by Charles Willson Peale, 1782 (akg-images).

responsible for improving the organization and training of the Continental
Army. Despite drawing many freedom fighters from Europe in addition to
Steuben—including the Marquis de Lafayette, a major general from France,
and Casimir Pulaski, the erstwhile leader of the Bar Confederation—the
Americans were still far from being as well drilled and battle ready as their
British opponents.

Having served under Frederick the Great in one of the most disciplined
armies in the world, Steuben performed his duties in America with flying col-
ors. However, in a letter to his old friend Friedrich Wilhelm von Gaudy, who
was stationed as a Prussian officer in Wesel, he indicated that it was no easy
task to instill discipline in the democratically minded American troops. Their
spirit simply could not be compared to that of the Prussians. In Prussia, an

officer told "his soldier, 'Do this!' and it was done," Steuben wrote. "But I was forced to explain, 'You must do this or that for such-and-such a reason,' and only then did he do it."

In the very same month that his former staff officer Steuben was named inspector general of the Continental Army by Washington in America, Frederick the Great once again observed unsettling Austrian troop movements. Maximilian III Joseph, elector of Bavaria and the last of his Wittelsbach line, had died in December 1777. Upon his death, Bavaria was supposed to pass to the Elector Palatine Charles Theodore. At the request of Austria, in early 1778 Charles Theodore declared himself willing to give Lower Bavaria and the Upper Palatinate to the Habsburgs in exchange for a section of the Austrian Netherlands. This plan to trade large portions of territory within the Holy Roman Empire was anathema to many German princes. The most vehement opponent of the proposed exchange was Frederick. When Austrian troops marched into Lower Bavaria, the Upper Palatinate, Bohemia, and Moravia, Frederick mobilized his own forces. In April, he recruited an army in Silesia, and in May he waited for an opportune moment to once again attack the Austrians.

His brother Henry, who remained in Berlin, believed that this time a conflict with Austria could easily be avoided by diplomatic means. On May 17, he received an important Prussian ally from Weimar at his palace on the Spree. The noble guest from Thuringia was Duke Charles Augustus, and he was equally wary of being drawn into a superfluous war by any hasty reaction on Frederick's part to Austrian provocation. The duke was accompanied by Goethe, who had joined the court in Weimar almost two years earlier. With his keen sensitivity to atmospherics, he immediately perceived that the absent Frederick was not nearly as popular among the people and officers of Berlin as he had been a decade previously.

Goethe himself, who had once burned so enthusiastically for Frederick, had lost sympathy for the Prussian king during his student days in Leipzig in the late 1760s when he discovered how Prussian troops had ravaged Saxony in the Seven Years' War. In light of the stories he heard from his Saxon friends, "I felt the unbounded reverence which I had devoted to this remarkable prince . . . gradually cooling away." In contrast, since the early 1770s, he had warmed to the Americans. For a while, he even seriously considered immigrating to America. Now, as a minister in the service of Weimar, he noted how even Frederick's "own doggish rabble," as Goethe referred to the Prussian people, felt the urge to grumblingly "disparage" him. Apparently, the autocratic rule of

"Old Fritz," now sixty-six years of age, made him seem antiquated and obsolete in their eyes. The times had changed dramatically in the wake of the American Revolution.

Indeed, not even Frederick's martial ability was in demand. As his brother Prince Henry had hoped, the conflict over the Bavarian succession was resolved diplomatically in 1779. On May 13, an Austro-Prussian treaty was signed in the Austrian city of Teschen (now Cieszyn, Poland). According to its terms, the Habsburgs received the Innviertel region, stretching from Passau to the northern border of Salzburg. In return, Elector Palatine Charles Theodore's claim to the Electorate of Bavaria was respected.

Frederick may not have been able to shine as a general in 1779, but in the fall of that year he did cause quite a stir by interceding in a court case that became a cause célèbre. A miller named Christian Arnold living in Pommerzig (now Pomorsko, Poland) in the Neumark region had taken a hereditary lease on a watermill from Count Schmettau. Later on, fish ponds were created upstream from the mill, causing less water to flow in the mill race than before. Feeling he had been harmed by the infrastructure project, the miller stopped paying his lease. In the ensuing trial between Arnold and Count Schmettau, the provincial court found against the miller and ordered the mill to be auctioned off. The Kammergericht (literally "chamber court") in Berlin, the highest judicial body in Prussia, upheld the verdict. At that point, the miller petitioned the Prussian king, who then decided to review the case, believing that the judges had been partial to their fellow nobles on account of their shared status.

After a careful consideration of the facts, Frederick personally interrogated the Kammergericht judges on December 11, 1779, refusing to hear any of their objections. According to later testimony from Justice Ransleben, the monarch verbally abused them. When the one-sided questioning was over, the Kammergericht judges were even taken to the city jail. The judgment they had rendered in the "Miller Arnold" case, as it became known, was unilaterally annulled by the enraged king. In addition, he sentenced the judges to one year in prison and ordered them to pay damages to the miller. Frederick explained his handling of the case precisely to his minister of justice, Karl Abraham von Zedlitz: In his lands, he wanted justice to be rendered swiftly to each and every person, whether noble or lowborn, and to be administered impartially without distinction of rank and reputation, "since all people are equal before the law." And he added, "Be assured that I give greater credence to an honest officer with honor in his bones than to all lawyers and rights."

In the "Miller Arnold" case, Frederick benevolently championed the cause of a seemingly weak, disadvantaged party. Once again, however, he also arbitrarily disregarded a verdict rendered by the highest judges in his country. This was a lasting shock to the colleagues of the imprisoned justices. In response, on April 14, 1780, the king ordered the longtime Silesian Minister of Justice Johann Heinrich von Carmer to develop a plan for a more just legal system in Prussia. The latter used this call for reform as an opportunity to lay the foundation for a modern, liberal system of justice. Collaborating closely with Carl Gottlieb Svarez, Carmer now pursued the goal of safeguarding civic freedoms against the despotic dicta of the king by enshrining them in a brand-new law code. An initial blueprint for reforming procedural law appeared in 1781 as the first book of the *Corpus Juris Fridericianum*. The practical work of judicial reform, however, would take more than a decade to set in motion.

While Carmer and Svarez sought assiduously to improve Prussian civil liberties in their offices in Berlin, on a battlefield in Virginia the Americans struck the decisive blow that ensured their freedom to govern themselves. With the help of the French, who had finally sent numerous warships and soldiers to America, they trapped 8,000 British troops under the command of General Charles Cornwallis in the Virginia port city of Yorktown. Two French squadrons, including thirty-four warships and 3,000 soldiers, appeared off the coast of Yorktown on August 30, 1781, blockading the harbor of the city on the Chesapeake Bay.

Washington, who had originally planned a forced march with the Continental Army to the city of New York, turned the planned attack into a feint and then hastened back to Virginia in September with 2,000 American and 5,000 French soldiers. He gathered reinforcements en route, ultimately besieging Yorktown by land with an army of 11,000 American and 9,000 French troops. One of the most important French officers with Washington was the Marquis de Lafayette. On October 18, 1781, Cornwallis recognized the hopelessness of his situation. Agreeing to the surrender of the British forces, he yielded the city to the Americans.

As the news of Washington's capture of the city of Yorktown reached the British capital of London, the general dismay at the utterly unexpected defeat of General Cornwallis led to an about-face in Parliament. The House of Commons now refused to continue the costly war against the Americans any longer. On February 27, 1782, it voted to end all offensive military operations on the far side of the Atlantic. Frustrated by Washington's rigidity, Lord North stepped down as prime minister. The new government, led by Lord

Rockingham and Lord Shelburne, urged the immediate opening of peace talks with the Americans. On April 15, the British negotiator Richard Oswald met with Franklin in Paris to discover on what conditions it might be possible to make peace with the seceded colonies. These negotiations proceeded so smoothly that a preliminary version of a formal Anglo-American peace treaty was signed on November 30, 1782, at the Grand Hotel Muscovite in Paris. As the opening sentence of the treaty's first article emphasized, the United States of America was now recognized by Great Britain as a country of "free, sovereign, and independent states."

It was proof that a polity like the United States, which had taken a decidedly democratic and republican branch of the path to enlightened government, was not destined to lapse into chaos even when invaded by war at home as long as the majority of its inhabitants were of the same mind. As Hobbes had predicted in the seventeenth century, a liberal democracy could indeed rely on parliamentary processes to create a sustainable social consensus—one whose strength was not inferior to the general will imposed from above by a sovereign over a subject people. Especially proud of this fact was the commander in chief of the freedom-loving Americans.

For that reason, General Washington was outraged when, not long after the victory at Yorktown, an American officer named Lewis Nicola seriously proposed that he now seek the title of king of the United States. "No occurrence in the course of the war," the commander in chief answered him, "has given me more painful sensations" than to have such sentiments expressed by an officer in his army. Nicola's view was to be regarded "with abhorrence and reprehend[ed] with severity." It was not worthy of a citizen of a democratic republic.

To illustrate the fact that an elected legislature sufficed to govern the United States and that it had no need of a general endowed with royal authority in order to face the future with confidence, the famous Virginian resigned his commission in the Continental Army after the cessation of hostilities in 1783. At the same time, he refused to take on any further public office. He saw his future in Virginia, where he hoped to retire to a tranquil and peaceful life at Mount Vernon with his wife, Martha, whom he had only had with him in the foregoing years while in winter quarters. When it became known in Europe that the heroic American general, at the height of his military power, had steadfastly refused to even consider assuming the mantle of royalty, King George III was deeply impressed, calling Washington "the greatest man in the world."

Washington's voluntary decision not to pursue power or public office made it especially clear that the smooth functioning of democratic self-government in the United States was not dependent on individuals who considered themselves and their charisma to be indispensable. It also made an impression on many politically minded residents of Berlin. There was even a discussion group whose members were quite sympathetic to the republican and democratic ideal of the United States of America. The so-called Mittwochsgesellschaft (Wednesday Society), a group of "friends of the Enlightenment" and social reformers, began meeting weekly in 1783. Its members included the Prussian finance minister Karl August von Struensee, the journalists Friedrich Nicolai and Johann Erich Biester, and the jurist Svarez. The philosopher Moses Mendelssohn was an honorary member. In the wake of the Anglo-American peace treaty, he opined that the task of reordering society might "be achieved in practice more felicitously" in America than anywhere else.

The Wednesday Society published a popular periodical, edited by Biester, called the *Berlinische Monatsschrift* (Berlin Monthly). The April 1783 issue contained a downright revolutionary ode to America's freshly won freedom. Both the tone and the content of the hymnic verse are worthy of attention. The poem begins with an invocation:

> You are free! (Proclaim it victoriously,
> delighted song!) Free, America is free!

For Great Britain is "tired, bent, and covered in shame," and it has had to give up its despotic tyranny over its North American colonies for good. "The noble fight for freedom and fatherland" has been "gloriously fought"; the fruit of the War of Independence was a republic in which "equal citizens" determined their own political fate. The United States could be a model to other nations now, so that "whoever wanted to be free can be"—even in Prussia. Rebelliously, the ode intoned,

> And you, Europe, hold your head high!
> The shining day will come when your chains too break
> When you are noble and free, when your princes
> Are scorned and the people rule a flourishing state.

The fact that such verses could be printed in Prussia without the objection of censors is testament to Frederick's astonishing magnanimity—and to his

FIGURE 9.3. Teapot featuring a portrait of Frederick the Great. Made in
England ca. 1757 (i.e., during the Seven Years' War). Artist unknown, based
on a painting (1737) by Georg Wenzeslaus von Knobelsdorff
(Huis Doorn, Netherlands).

unbroken self-confidence. He was now just as certain as ever that as king he
was unrivaled in his lands. And he was convinced that the United States would
soon lose the fascination it clearly held for many citizens of European polities.
Even after their successful prosecution of the Revolutionary War, he did not
think the Americans capable of establishing an enduring democratic republic.
To the British envoy in Berlin, he averred that the American union could not
last long in its current form, as no republican government had ever abided in
a territory that was not small. He thought it risible that the United States could
have a future as a democratic republic—as absurd as the notion of establishing
a democracy in the area between Riga and Brest (i.e., the unpartitioned heart-
land of what remained of the Kingdom of Poland).

However, this skepticism did not stop Frederick from writing to American
diplomats in Europe and carefully plumbing the possibility of concluding a
treaty of amity and commerce with the United States. As long as the United

FIGURE 9.4. King of Prussia (Montgomery County, Pennsylvania).
© Jürgen Overhoff.

States existed, the Prussian king desired—more than all other European rulers—to profit thoroughly from trade with the young nation. For two whole years, Friedrich Wilhelm von Thulemeyer, the Prussian envoy in The Hague, negotiated with the American ambassador John Adams, hammering out the tiniest details of an eventual Prussian-American treaty.

FIGURE 9.5. The American town of King of Prussia sprang up around
a tavern named after Frederick the Great in the eighteenth century.
The tavern still exists today. © Jürgen Overhoff.

Frederick was primarily interested in providing his subjects with cheap
Virginia tobacco, rice, and indigo, as he informed Adams in the summer of
1784. In exchange, he wanted above all to sell Westphalian hardware, Silesian
linen, and Berlin porcelain to the citizens of the new republic. He and Adams
agreed that the Kingdom of Prussia and the United States must guarantee
complete freedom of speech and religion to the people of their respective enlightened nations. The final version of the treaty was ratified by Frederick in
Berlin on September 24, 1785. Its first article declared the indissoluble, steadfast, and sincere friendship and peace between the two powers. In letters to
Lafayette and Rochambeau, Washington called the agreement with the king
of Prussia the "most liberal treaty ever concluded by independent powers,"
heralding "a new era in negotiation" and promising "happy consequences."

Now that the two nations had become friends, idiosyncratic gestures of
mutual sympathy were made by the humble denizens of both: Locales outside

FIGURE 9.6. Philadelphia in Brandenburg
(outside Berlin, Germany). © Jürgen Overhoff.

Philadelphia and Berlin spontaneously changed their names. A tavern a few miles northwest of Philadelphia frequently patronized by Washington and his officers was redubbed "King of Prussia." A town sprang up around the inn in the following years, and to this day it is still known by that name. Around the same time, residents of Hammelstall, a village located southeast of Berlin near Storkow, gave their hamlet the more sonorous appellation of Philadelphia. This village also still exists, living on as a witness to a time when even the people of Frederick's enlightened Prussia began to think of the United States as the land of their dreams.

10

Endings and New Beginnings (1785–1801)

THE DETAILED Treaty of Amity and Commerce with the fledgling United States was not the only alliance the increasingly frail King Frederick entered into in what was now his seventy-fourth year. In parallel with the negotiations with the Americans, the Prussian monarch also held talks with the rulers of various midsize and smaller German principalities. Threatened by a renewed Austrian hunger for expansion, they desperately sought to win Frederick as an ally to protect them from the House of Habsburg. His archrival, Empress Maria Theresa, had died on November 29, 1780, at the age of sixty-three. Shortly thereafter, her son and sole heir, Emperor Joseph II, renewed his offer to Prince-Elector Charles Theodore to exchange part of Bavaria for a section of the Austrian Netherlands. Once again, Charles Theodore was open to the idea. However, a prudent group of petty rulers—Duke Charles Augustus of Saxe-Weimar, Margrave Charles Frederick of Baden, Duke Charles II August of Zweibrücken, and Prince Leopold III (also known as Prince Franz) of Anhalt-Dessau—fiercely opposed the plan. Accordingly, they appealed to the aged Prussian king to reprise the role he had played in the conflict over the Bavarian succession, namely, as the guarantor of the order that had reigned in the Holy Roman Empire since the Peace of Hubertusburg.

Initially, Frederick took a dim view of the idea. With one foot already in the grave, as he believed, he was in an extremely grumpy mood. Forced to double down on prudence and activity, he constantly contemplated the plans that Joseph, whom he cursed and damned, hatched with each passing day. Now that he had been asked for assistance by the imperial princes, he felt he was condemned to enjoy no peace until the earth covered his bones. Despite sensing that death was near, he agreed to provide assistance. With the help of his capable diplomats, he assembled a Fürstenbund (League of Princes) against Austria that even included Saxony and Hanover. On October 18, 1785, the group was also joined by Frederick Charles von Erthal, archbishop-elector of Mainz and archchancellor of the Holy Roman Empire. At that point, Joseph II had to abandon any and all hope of a territorial exchange within the boundaries of the Empire.

The following winter, it was then Frederick who had to give up a secretly nourished yearning: His deplorable state of health refused to improve. The painful bouts of gout that had plagued him for several years were now more protracted and often entailed episodes of paralysis that could last for days. Severe asthma made it agonizingly difficult for him to breathe, and a steadily worsening case of dropsy caused his legs to swell menacingly. The suffering monarch sarcastically compared himself to "a soul carrying around a cadaver." But Old Fritz did not let himself go entirely. Although he spent most of every day sitting in an armchair in a very unclean infirmary in the Potsdam City Palace, he nevertheless lived by the spirited words, "The cadaver must trot on!"

Accordingly, he continued to receive foreign dignitaries. One such visitor was George Washington's former officer Lafayette, the hero of the War of Independence for whom the king felt an especial sympathy. In two letters to Washington and Benjamin Franklin written in February 1786, Lafayette reported on the aged monarch's state of health. Frederick had "the most beautiful eyes I ever saw," which could both radiate an intense "fire" and express a boundless "mildness." On the other hand, he had the "appearance of an old, broken, dirty corporal, covered all over with Spanish snuff, with his head almost leaning on one shoulder, and fingers quite distorted by the gout." Yet even in his decrepitude, Frederick the Great was full of "endearing charms." Nevertheless, no one should be so mesmerized by the impression he made as to forget "what a tyrannic, hardhearted, and selfish man he is."

It was especially disappointing that the Prussian king harbored utterly false impressions of the potential and durability of American freedom. Despite his reputation as an enlightened ruler, Lafayette lamented, the king of Prussia did not understand in the least how the self-government of the United States actually worked—even though he did express great admiration for the military virtues the Americans had displayed during the War of Independence. Unlike his brother Prince Henry, who was known as a genuine admirer of the novel, modern social order of the United States, Frederick the Great still doubted that a truly democratic republic, with its liberal constitution, would be able to last long. The king of Prussia, Lafayette concluded harshly, was in this respect

FIGURE 10.1. Washington's French aide: the Marquis de
Lafayette (1757–1834). Painting by Joseph Boze, 1790.

deluded by evil habit and prejudice. However, perhaps Frederick was too sick
to any longer be capable of forming a sober, balanced, and just opinion. Indeed, "The king of Prussia is about leaving the stage and cannot last long—the
last accounts from Potsdam are very bad."

Right after Lafayette left Potsdam, the Prussian king's health declined so
rapidly that his life's end seemed near. With the arrival of spring, however, he
recovered again. On April 17, after a sprawling tour through the small villages
and hamlets of Havelland, he even had himself taken to his summer residence
of Sanssouci. He lived utterly alone there now. He countenanced neither

courtiers nor aides in his presence. He did not even post guards for his own protection. Visits from his brother Henry and his heir Frederick William were forbidden. Only his faithful servant Schöning stayed with him, helping him with his daily business and seeing to his meals.

In June, the unbearable pain and harshest symptoms of gout and dropsy returned with a vengeance. Frederick decided to seek advice on how best to relieve his suffering from one of the leading physicians of the day, Johann Georg Zimmerman of Hanover. When Zimmerman arrived in Potsdam, he found the king in a pitiful state. As the doctor later reported, Frederick's face "was not only very pale and thin but also of the pale-yellow pallor that is a sign of the worst constitution of the bodily fluids and the tissues and in such conditions is of the gravest consequence." In addition, his legs were "as terribly swollen as legs can be, all the way up to his loins."

The only suggestion the doctor could make to improve the terrible symptoms in this case was for Frederick to follow a strict diet. Yet the king, who feared detracting even further from the meager quality of life he currently enjoyed, refused to take the advice. Recognizing that there was no cure for what ailed his patient, Zimmerman left without having provided him with any relief. The doctor described his departure from Sanssouci on July 11 in moving words: "Now the king doffed his hat with indescribable dignity, grace, and kindness, nodded his head, and said, 'Farewell, good sir, my dear Mr. Zimmermann. Do not forget the fine old man you saw here!'" Then he sent him on his way with the observation that his patients in Hanover certainly had greater need of him.

On the morning of August 16, the king's speech could barely be understood. Severe bouts of coughing alternated with fits of paralysis and spasms lasting minutes. A high fever set in. The physician Christian Gottlieb Selle hurried from Berlin to Sanssouci, where he stayed with Frederick deep into the night. At two o'clock in the morning, the king, sitting in an armchair and supported by Schöning, fell into another terrible fit of coughing. Then he sighed, "We are over the mountain. Now it will be better." A short time later, he died. Selle, who kept close watch as Frederick the Great breathed his last, recalled later,

> The king's death was like his life. He remained fearless and stoic to the end. Before the fever set in, the king believed he would recover. At least he thought he had more time, and in his feverish state he was too confused to notice the danger he was in. In addition, he had often suffered from this wheezy cough, so it did not disconcert him. He passed away calmly and

FIGURE 10.2. Frederick the Great's death mask.
Cast in bronze by Johann Eckstein, 1786 (bpk).

gently, and his natural facial expression, his calm, earnest look, indicated even in his casket that he had departed this world without troubled or agonizing thoughts, even though he was still conscious a few minutes before death.

One hour after the death of Frederick the Great, upon the order of his successor, King Frederick William II, a death mask was made of the departed ruler. Then the body was dressed in an old blue silk cloak and laid out on a simple cot in the concert hall of Sanssouci. At eight in the evening, he was taken to the Potsdam City Palace, where four officers kept the deathwatch.

In the capitals of Potsdam and Berlin, there was little mourning for the death of the king who had ruled Prussia for nearly five decades and left his iron mark enduringly upon it. Many of his subjects, citizens, and courtiers breathed a sigh of relief when they heard that their autocratic ruler, once so exceedingly beloved, had died in Sanssouci. This relative apathy and indifference largely stemmed from the fact that the political philosophy of enlightened absolutism championed by Frederick the Great had come to be regarded as increasingly antiquated since the American Declaration of Independence.

The French Enlightenment thinker Honoré Gabriel Riqueti, Count of Mirabeau, had visited Frederick a few months before the latter's death. Although a fervent supporter of parliamentarianism, he admired the king as an individual. Traveling through Prussia now, he had occasion to note in a letter of August 17 to the abbé de Périgord the strange atmosphere that had settled over the Havel and the Spree in the wake of the king's passing. "It is deathly quiet," Mirabeau wrote, "but no one is in mourning. People are dazed but not sorrowful. There is no face that does not reveal a measure of relief, of hope. There is no lamenting, no sighing, no words of praise! Is this the outcome of so many victorious battles, of so much glory? Is this the end of a reign that lasted nearly half a century and that was so full of great deeds? All the world was hoping it would end—all the world rejoices!"

The will of the departed monarch, which only a few days before had been respected absolutely, was now widely flouted. Symbolic of this change, Frederick William II chose to bury his uncle in a manner that the latter had explicitly rejected. Instead of being entombed on the terrace of Sanssouci Palace as stipulated in his last will and testament, Frederick was laid to rest in the Garrison Church in Potsdam right next to his father's marble sarcophagus.

The day his uncle died, Frederick William II personally went to view the moldy underground crypt his predecessor had built on the outermost terrace of Sanssouci in 1744—long before the new summer palace in Potsdam was finished—to see whether he could comply with his burial wishes. What he found repulsed him. Countless caskets had already been interred in the hollowed-out terrace, containing the remains of Frederick the Great's favorite dogs: no fewer than eleven Italian greyhounds, their names inscribed on sandstone plaques covering the crypt. The new king decided to have the burial performed in a different setting. Frederick's life journey had ended, Prussia was ready for a fresh start, and Frederick William II wished to use his uncle's funeral as a stage on which to make this new beginning visible and palpable.

Instead of an unadorned grave under an open sky that recalled the decay in store for all plants, animals, and human beings, the new Prussian ruler had the departed monarch buried in the solemn interior of a church in which a Christian congregation assembled week after week to confess its hopeful belief in the bodily resurrection of all the faithful. Frederick was not laid to rest in a manner that radically contradicted the customary funeral ceremonies of European royal dynasties but rather in accordance with the practices of the House of Hohenzollern. And part and parcel to the Prussian, Hohenzollern tradition was that the will of the living king was the highest authority in the absolutist, monarchical state. In that sense, Frederick William II's conscious decision to flout the last wishes of his predecessor adhered fully with the Prussian logic of rule.

After a funeral procession with full military honors, the obsequies were performed on September 9 in the Garrison Church in Potsdam, where the casket was placed under a monopteros, a symbol of immortality. The funeral service was held under the head of an Old Testament verse from the first book of Chronicles in which the prophet Nathan says to King David, "I have made thee a name like the name of the great men that are in the earth." Obviously, this Bible verse was meant to be understood as an allusion to the honorary title Frederick had been given during his lifetime, when he was known throughout the world as "the Great."

Around the globe, the death of the great ruler caused quite a sensation. In no time at all, the news spread to all directions and even reached Goethe, who had arrived in Italy only a few weeks before. Just like the citizens of Potsdam and Berlin, he acknowledged the announcement that Frederick the Great had departed this life with a simple groan: "Finally." Even Goethe, who had once revered the deceased monarch so unreservedly, now shared the disillusioned opinion of many of his German countrymen—namely, that "the great king whose glory filled the world" had outlived himself by many years. For 1776 had changed everything.

In the United States as well, the end of the Frederician Age was acknowledged with an astonishing aloofness and detachment, despite the fact that Frederick the Great had played such an important role in the French defeat in North America during the Seven Years' War. In addition, the year before his death he had participated wholeheartedly in drafting the final version of the Prussian-American Treaty of Amity and Commerce. But now Washington, who had once ordered a stately bust of the king he admired so much from the London merchant Cary & Company, wrote a candid brief to the Marquis de Lafayette in which he vilified the Prussian monarch as a despot.

The victorious general of the American Revolution admitted that no one of their era could outmatch Frederick the Great as a soldier or a statesman, since the Prussian king had truly achieved extraordinary things as a military commander and a ruler. It was therefore all the more "to be lamented, however, that great characters are not without a blot." Despite concluding a treaty with the United States, he had developed no deeper understanding of the American system of democratic republicanism. More than that, he was an absolute monarch and inhibited parliamentary participation in his own lands. As a king, he "tyrannize[d] over millions."

Washington penned these harsh words in the library and study of his Mount Vernon estate, where he had devoted himself to agriculture and animal husbandry for the past three years. The intention he had announced after the Revolutionary War—to renounce all public office and withdraw to the life of a private citizen—had not been mere empty words. He had remained true to it just like the legendary Roman consul Lucius Quinctius Cincinnatus, who in the fifth century BC had been named dictator by the Roman Senate and tasked with saving his fellow citizens from attacks by the neighboring Aequi, Sabine, and Volsci peoples. Having completed his military duties as dictator and preserved Roman freedom, he immediately returned to his fields, beating his sword into a plowshare. In model fashion, Cincinnatus had resisted the temptation to retain the dictatorial power entrusted to him in war and wield it as a usurper in peacetime. Ever since, the Roman general and statesman had gone down as one of the most righteous, law-abiding, and selfless freedom fighters in world history.

Cincinnatus therefore served as an inspiration for several former American officers who, likewise having left the Continental Army after 1783 to return to their farms, formed a fraternal organization in memory of their fight for the freedom of the United States. They called it the Society of the Cincinnati. As their president they chose Washington, who in their eyes seemed to be the veritable reincarnation of Cincinnatus. According to the organization's bylaws, membership could only be passed on to a current member's first-born son— and only by virtue of heredity, without requiring any further merit or contribution on the part of the male descendant. On this account, the fraternity was accused of clandestinely seeking to create a new aristocracy in the United States, and Washington continually had to defend it on this point.

One apology for the society's bylaws was contained in a letter to the Virginia statesman and jurist James Madison dated December 16, 1786. At the time the Society of the Cincinnati was founded, Washington wrote, "not a member of it conceived that it would give birth to those jealousies or be chargeable with those dangers (real or imaginary) with which the minds of many, and some of respectable characters, were filled." In contrast, he argued, the Society of the Cincinnati was an utterly honorable association whose prime directive was to provide financial assistance to the destitute widows and children of those who had fallen in the fight for America's freedom. He categorically rejected any and all claims that he was a closeted aristocrat or was betraying the "republican principles" of the United States. Instead, he avowed the virtues of the Roman Cincinnatus, which were perfectly compatible with republicanism and had therefore been the justified inspiration for the society's name.

Most of Washington's fellow citizens accepted his explanation and believed that he would defend the republican principles of the United States without hesitation, even if the fledgling confederation found itself in the gravest danger. The French sculptor Jean-Antoine Houdon, who came to America in 1785 just to make a life mask of Washington, finished a bust of the heroic planter wearing a toga and tunic in 1786, thus deliberately portraying him as an American Cincinnatus. This classicizing depiction earned Washington's unreserved approval, although he preferred to be immortalized wearing the uniform of a general. For that reason, Houdon—whom Jefferson, in a letter to Washington, had praised as "the first statuary [i.e., foremost sculptor] in the world" before the artist's departure from Paris—made numerous additional bronze busts and marble statues of the victor of Yorktown, most of them showing the great American hero dressed as the commander in chief of the Continental Army.

Many painters now also made the pilgrimage to Mount Vernon in order to do color portraits of Washington in oil. They, too, preferred to depict the triumphant general for posterity wearing his elegant blue-and-yellow officer's uniform with gold epaulettes. The most popular portraitists of the day, including such prestigious artists as Charles Willson Peale and Robert Edge Pine, competed in the attempt to project onto canvas as realistic a depiction as possible of the great soldier. Washington displayed great patience during the sittings, which could often last for hours. "I am so hackneyed to the touches of the painter's pencil," he boasted, "that I am *now* altogether at their beck, and sit like patience on a monument whilst they are delineating the lines of my face." During the first such sittings, he had been as "impatient . . . as a colt is of the saddle," but now "no dray moves more readily to the thill than I do to the painter's chair."

All the masterful works of the sculptors, drawers, and painters that turned Washington into an icon of virtue and righteousness could easily have been seen as the culmination of a remarkable civic career: The son of a Virginia

FIGURE 10.3. Washington dressed as a Roman. Terra cotta bust (on a marble base) by Jean-Antoine Houdon, 1786 (akg/Erich Lessing).

farmer, who lost his father at a young age and had to earn his daily bread as a surveyor, succeeded by his own power in becoming the world-famous defender of the United States of America, the highest and most widely revered protector of an utterly new kind of democratic republic and civil society. Like his portraitists, Washington himself, now fifty-four years old, believed he had reached the pinnacle of his breathtaking life's pursuit. Greater fame than he now enjoyed was unthinkable. And yet, soon enough Washington was destined to reach new heights.

What concerned Washington and his fellow citizens most in 1786 was the state of crisis into which the fledgling nation had unexpectedly slipped in the space of a few months. Ten years after the founding of the country, it emerged that the independent United States, which conceived of itself as a loose confederation of sovereign entities, all too seldom was able to make far-reaching decisions that abidingly satisfied all its member states. All significant proposals in Congress had to be approved by at least nine of the thirteen founding states, but this quorum was rarely achieved due to their oft-conflicting interests. As a result, the American government was unable to act effectively on a vast number of political issues.

On September 11 of that year, delegations from New York, New Jersey, Pennsylvania, Delaware, and Virginia met in Annapolis to discuss essential questions of American transportation and commerce. At the suggestion of delegates James Madison and Alexander Hamilton, the participants at the poorly attended Annapolis Convention called for a new national convention to assemble in Philadelphia. It would not only deal with issues of commerce but would also subject the very system of American government to thorough review. As Madison and Hamilton explained, the highest goal of this convention, which was to be inaugurated in May 1787, was to overhaul the governmental frame of the United States so that it could in the future better meet the needs of a federal union.

While elections for the Constitutional Convention in Philadelphia were being prepared with the approval and support of Congress, the political crisis intensified. In western Massachusetts, 2,000 indebted farmers had rebelled, putting up armed resistance to tax increases and to the forced auctions imposed on those who could not pay. The leader was the veteran Daniel Shays, who had fought in the glorious Battle of Saratoga. He now threatened to maraud through the state of Massachusetts until the tax policies that displeased him were decisively changed.

Washington "lamented and deprecated" Shays' Rebellion in no uncertain terms. If the Massachusetts authorities did not respond with commensurate military vigor to Shays and his lawless men, the United States would "exhibit a melancholy proof . . . that mankind left to themselves are unfit for their own government." This is exactly "what our transatlantic foe have predicted." In light of the turmoil and unrest undermining America, he wrote, "I am mortified beyond expression whenever I view the clouds which have spread over the brightest morn that ever dawned upon any country." Was the sunlight of enlightened government that had shone so brightly and broadly over America since the beginning of the century still strong enough to break through—and perhaps even dispel completely—the dark clouds of anarchic rebellion and imminent constitutional chaos?

Many residents of the United States were unsettled by the malfunctioning of the government under the direction of its leading politicians, and faith in the success of the bold republican experiment was fragile. An illustration of this came in late 1786, when Frederick the Great's younger brother Prince Henry received an explosive letter from America, sent by Friedrich Wilhelm von Steuben. The former drillmaster of the Continental Army indicated that, due to the constitutional crisis in the United States, serious efforts were being made to replace the democratic, republican frame of government with a more practical system based on the English model. The Prussian prince was known to sympathize with the country. Might he be willing under the right circumstances, Steuben circumspectly asked, choosing his words carefully, to assume the office of king of the United States of America?

When the letter reached Prince Henry in April 1787, he answered immediately. First, he emphasized that he would only be willing to be considered for the position of king of the United States if France, as the Americans' chief ally, supported such a plan. After formulating this precondition, he acknowledged candidly that in his eyes the English constitution indeed seemed to be the most perfect of all systems, as it ensured a good balance between the sovereign and his subjects. On the other hand, he was skeptical of the desire to undo the democratic, republican system that had been established in the United States after the brilliant American victory in the War of Independence. Reverting to the pre-1776 state of affairs was, in his view, fundamentally unrealistic. In the wake of the American Revolution, the course of history could not be turned back. In his view, no one could seriously harbor the intention of altering the basic structure of the government of the United States of America.

Despite his distance from the situation, the Prussian prince put his finger directly on the pulse of the leading American politicians. When the Constitutional Convention opened in May 1787 to discuss a reform of the American government, it quickly emerged that the overwhelming majority of the fifty-five delegates sent to Philadelphia had no intention of undermining the democratic, republican regime of the United States, to say nothing of augmenting it with monarchical elements. The revolutionaries of 1776 were unwilling to carelessly risk the mission and the legacy of the Declaration of Independence. Although his withdrawal from politics had been intended as permanent, after much hesitation—and only in light of the grave emergency facing the

country—Washington declared himself willing to act as president of the Constitutional Convention. In the spring of 1787, he succinctly distilled the domi-
nant sentiment in the United States. "I am fully of the opinion," he wrote to
the Virginia delegate James Madison, "that those who lean to monarchical
government" had not sufficiently "consulted the public mind."

On the other hand, Washington and the other members of the convention
understood that the federal government was still too weak with respect to the
vast powers of the individual states, and that it had to be considerably strengthened in order to make the American union truly functional. After intense debates, the contingent led by Madison in favor of a powerful federal government won out. They convincingly argued that a national government that was
elected by the entirety of the American people, and that had to be regularly
reelected, would ultimately always respect the interests of the individual states.
Thus, the delegates created the new office of an elected head of state. Following
the tried-and-true model of the office of governor in the individual states, the
power was vested in a single executive. The new, democratically elected chief
of state would be given the title of "President of the United States."

In order to not weaken the principle of popular sovereignty that had reigned
in America since 1776, the new president was to be chosen not by the state
legislatures but rather by directly elected electors. The president had a rela-
tively wide spectrum of powers, including the role of commander in chief and
a legislative veto, but his term was limited to only four years. If he desired to
continue governing after his term was up, he had to be reelected to the office
by secret ballot. With this decision, the delegates to the Constitutional Convention in Philadelphia made history. The office of a popularly elected chief
executive of a democratic republic was a novelty in world history. However, it
was not yet clear who would fill the office first, giving it a definite shape and
establishing precedent for its future functioning.

There was one man among the delegates who stood out as the only American statesman to have had a hand in formulating and signing all of the founding documents of the United States, including the Declaration of Independence
of 1776, the Franco-American alliance of 1778, the Anglo-American Treaty of
Paris of 1783, and now also the new Constitution of 1787: Benjamin Franklin.
In addition, the famous scientist had served as president of Pennsylvania for
a few years, thereby gathering valuable experience in the governance of a
democratic republic. His reputation was so great and his authority so respected
that he had managed in the convention's concluding session to convince most

of the remaining uncommitted delegates of the necessity of accepting the text of the freshly framed constitution and sealing it with their signature.

In a long, moving, and humorous speech on September 17, 1787, Franklin acknowledged "that there are several parts of this Constitution which I do not at present approve." Nevertheless, he strongly urged the delegates to give it their assent, as it by and large furnished a reliable basis for the peaceful and fruitful coexistence of all American citizens. In addition, he doubted "whether any other Convention we can obtain may be able to make a better Constitution. For, when you assemble a number of men to have the advantage of their joint wisdom, you inevitably assemble with those men all their prejudices, their passions, their errors of opinion, their local interests, and their selfish views." Therefore, all the delegates had to be willing to make certain compromises, unless they were as convinced of their own infallibility "as a certain French lady, who, in a dispute with her sister, said, 'I don't know how it happens, sister, but I meet with nobody but myself that's always in the right.'" Accordingly, he vehemently hoped "that for our own sakes, as a part of the people, and for the sake of posterity, we shall act heartily and unanimously in recommending this Constitution." Franklin's rhetorically masterful speech convinced nearly all the members of the convention, such that ultimately only three delegates voted against adopting the new American constitution.

One by one, the supporters of the new governmental framework took up the quill and applied their signatures to the document. As the ink was drying, Franklin called the attention of the assembly to the relief of a sun that was carved into the curved back of the chair in which Washington had sat while presiding over the convention. Many artists, Franklin said, had great difficulty making a sufficiently clear distinction in their paintings or drawings between a setting sun and the rising sun of the Enlightenment. In the course of the preceding months, he, too, had wondered more than once whether the sun on Washington's chair was meant to be rising or setting. However, now that the new constitution had been approved by the overwhelming majority of the delegates, he was sure "that it is a rising and not a setting sun," and that it promised a bright future to the United States and thus to the whole world.

Yet despite his incomparable charisma, Franklin was ultimately not the right man to stand for the newly created office of president. At eighty-one years of age and afflicted with gout, he was simply too old and too sick to perform its duties for four years with the necessary bodily strength and mental focus. He himself knew this all too well, which is why he had pointed out the rising sun on Washington's chair, thereby craftily identifying the resplendent hero of the Revolutionary War as the man who would lead the United States safely into the future. Pierce Butler, a delegate from the state of South Carolina, admitted that "many of the members" of the convention in Philadelphia "cast their eyes towards General Washington as president and shaped their ideas of the powers to be given to a president by their opinions of his virtue."

Before a president could be elected, however, the new constitution had to be ratified by a two-thirds majority of the individual states. Washington campaigned actively for adoption of the Constitution, both publicly and in his private correspondence. As he wrote in September 1787, it was his ardent "wish" that the ratification process be crowned with success in order to avert the "anarchy" that threatened to engulf the United States. In addition, the new constitution was much more than just a stopgap. Above all, however, he emphasized that the office of president was not a danger to democracy. For, as he wrote to his relative Bushrod Washington, "the power of the Constitution will always be with the people. It is entrusted for certain defined purposes and for a certain limited period to representatives of their own choosing; and whenever it is exercised contrary to their interests, or not according to their wishes, their servants can, and undoubtedly will be, recalled."

Clearly, most of the inhabitants of the individual states shared Washington's assessment. This was in part owing to widely read newspaper articles written by Alexander Hamilton and James Madison, later collected as the famous *Federalist Papers*, that popularized and elaborated convincing arguments for adopting the Constitution. In December 1787, Delaware, Pennsylvania, New Jersey, and Georgia ratified it. By April 26, 1788, Connecticut, Massachusetts, and Maryland had also given their stamp of approval.

As a majority slowly but surely began to support adopting the Constitution, Washington signaled in a letter to Lafayette, dated April 28, that he was preoccupied by "the probability of my election to the presidency." Of course, he would much prefer retirement at Mount Vernon, "living and dying an honest man on my own farm." By early August, the Constitution had been ratified by South Carolina, New Hampshire, his home state of Virginia, and then even the most populous state, New York. At that point, Washington knew that he would soon be asked if he would accept the office of the presidency were he to be elected.

The closer this time came, the more he demurred. On October 3, 1788, he informed Hamilton that he would "rejoice" if the electors, "by giving their votes in favor of some other person" when they met in February, "would save me from the dreaded dilemma of being forced to accept or refuse." Should he win the election, he would only assume the office of president with "diffidence and reluctance," although he would certainly do everything "in my power to promote the public weal." Ideally, however, he would like "to pass an unclouded evening, after the stormy day of life, in the bosom of domestic tranquility" at Mount Vernon. For the first president of the United States would enter into wholly unknown terrain.

Who but an individual that Americans considered especially doughty and trustworthy could be the first to explore the undiscovered country of the American presidency? When the ballots that the electors had cast on February 4, 1789, were officially presented to the newly elected Congress in New York City on April 6, it emerged that thirty-four votes had been cast for John Adams, one of the original Boston revolutionaries and an experienced diplomat, who many of his fellow countrymen thought would make a strong and able president. Yet this impressive result only elevated the ambitious Adams to the vice presidency. The first president of the United States was George Washington, for whom sixty-nine electors had cast their vote.

The very same day, Charles Thomson, the secretary of the Congress, set off from New York to Mount Vernon to deliver the news to Washington of his overwhelming electoral victory. Eight days later, on April 14, at around one o'clock under the Virginia midday sun, Washington learned from Thomson that he had won the presidential election with a large majority over John Adams. Washington was overwhelmed by the faith his countrymen had placed in him, and he accepted the post immediately. That same afternoon, he composed a letter of appreciation and acknowledgment to Thomson in which he confessed, "I have been accustomed to pay so much respect to the opinion of my fellow-citizens that the knowledge of their having given their unanimous suffrage in my favor scarcely leaves me the alternative for an option." Washington simply had to accede to the results of the election: "I cannot, I believe, give a greater evidence of my sensibility of the honor which they have done me than by accepting the appointment."

In his diary, however, Washington struck a different, much less joyful, and indeed brooding tone. He now knew for certain that he would not be allowed to enjoy a long, tranquil retirement as the planter of Mount Vernon. On April 16, he noted, "About ten o'clock I bade adieu to Mount Vernon, to private life, and to domestic felicity." He then added, "and with a mind oppressed with more anxious and painful sensations than I have words to express, set out for New York." He was doubtless endowed "with the best dispositions to render service to my country in obedience to its call." At the same time, he felt "less hope of answering its expectations." Nevertheless, he rose to the challenge courageously and conscientiously.

In Manhattan, the heart of New York City where the votes of the electors had been counted, Washington delivered his programmatic inaugural oration on April 30, 1789. Once again, many of its passages sounded much more self-confident than his recent diary entries. First, the new president thanked "that Almighty Being who rules over the universe" for the unfailing support it had given the Americans in founding their trailblazing democratic republic. Indeed, "every step by which [the American people] have advanced to the character of an independent nation seems to have been distinguished by some token of providential agency." Therefore, humility before God's gracious guidance demanded that America forever preserve "the sacred fire of liberty" and "the republican model of government." All citizens were called upon to never allow their love for a truly "free government" to be extinguished, and thus to earn "the respect of the world" by their praiseworthy example.

Washington now received messages of greeting from every stratum of American society and all manner of religious and political organizations across the United States. The president used this correspondence as an opportunity to highlight his view that the unlimited freedom of religion and speech was the root of all American liberty. In May 1789, for example, he assured the United Baptist Churches of Virginia that he would never have signed the Constitution of 1787 if he had thought it "might possibly endanger the religious rights of any ecclesiastical society." The following year, he responded in similar terms to a letter of congratulations from the Hebrew Congregation in Newport, Rhode Island. "May the children of the stock of Abraham who dwell in this land continue to merit and enjoy the good will of the other inhabitants," he wrote. Every citizen of the United States "shall sit in safety under his own vine and fig tree, and there shall be none to make him afraid." In the same vein, he concluded, "May the father of all mercies . . . make us all in our several vocations useful here, and in his own due time and way everlastingly happy."

Being such a clear supporter of the right to the free exercise of religion, Washington also supported the Bill of Rights that, at Madison's urging, was passed by Congress on September 25, 1789, as an important addendum to the Constitution. Its very first amendment guaranteed that "Congress shall make no law respecting an establishment of religion or prohibiting the free exercise thereof." In addition, it prohibited Congress from "abridging the freedom of speech, or of the press; or the right of the people peaceably to assemble, and to petition the Government for a redress of grievances." These freedoms were guaranteed to all American citizens in the First Amendment to the Constitution as fundamental rights.

The main emphasis of Washington's term in his new office was thus to play the part of the dutifully watchful father of his country, delivering emotional speeches bordering on the sentimental and crafting solemn statements about the American people's political achievements and privileges. In the first year of his administration, he surrounded himself with an unusually capable cabinet to whom he gave a high degree of independence in the execution of their offices. Furthermore, he included Vice President Adams in the daily business of government. This freed him up to maintain his priorities as president beyond the day of his inauguration. The most prominent members of his cabinet were Alexander Hamilton, named secretary of the treasury, and Jefferson, who was made secretary of state. All cabinet officials were directly responsible to the president and served at his pleasure.

In the fall of 1789, Washington learned that sensational events had occurred in Europe in July that demonstrated how much the American Revolution had come to inspire political developments on the other side of the Atlantic. As Washington noted on October 13, a revolution had been "effected in France" that guaranteed the inhabitants of that country the same civic freedoms and rights that had long been standard in America. This development seemed to Washington to be "of so wonderful a nature that the mind can hardly realize the fact." Soon enough, the president hoped, "that nation will be the most powerful and happy in Europe."

Washington was especially pleased that his former officer and protégé Lafayette had played a leading role in the revolutionary uprising. On July 14, 1789, he was elected vice president of the newly created National Assembly. That same day, French citizens in Paris had stormed the Bastille, the detested bastion of arbitrary, absolutist despotism (and the very same massive prison where Voltaire had once served his sentence). Lafayette was also named commander in chief of the newly formed French National Guard. After the storming of the Bastille, he took the key to the defunct prison into his possession. At his urging, on August 26 the National Assembly read out a Declaration of the Rights of Man and of the Citizen, modeled on the American Bill of Rights. That same month, the National Assembly stripped the nobility and the clergy of all their privileges. Within the space of a few hours, a political and social order lasting nearly 1,000 years was laid to rest. French society was no longer divided into the clergy, the nobility, and the third estate of all other subjects; rather, all people were now equal. It was the end of the ancien régime.

Washington approved of the changes taking place in France, but the sheer speed at which they proceeded unnerved him. He wondered whether "the revolution is of too great magnitude to be effected in so short a space." The king and the nobility would probably "foment divisions" to undermine the radical innovations that were remaking the country. Nonetheless, when, in March 1790, Lafayette sent the key to the Bastille to Washington, the man he considered to be the father of freedom, the American president gladly received it as a "token of victory gained by liberty over despotism." When Benjamin Franklin died in April, Washington inherited his applewood cane. "If it were a scepter," Franklin had written in his will, then "he has merited it, and would become it." Washington now possessed two unusual insignia of democratic republicanism unrivaled throughout the world. First, Franklin's cane symbolized that the American president was buttressed by his knowledge of American history—a history that Franklin had decisively shaped and inhabited—and would continue to faithfully investigate the unexplored territory of the new American government. Second, the key to the Bastille illustrated that the American ideal of freedom reverberated throughout the rest of the world and would one day burst the door of every bastion of tyranny.

Starting in the fall of 1790, Washington devoted increasing attention to planning the new American capital that was to be built on the Potomac River, not far from Mount Vernon. Congress had just relocated from New York back to its old abode in Philadelphia, and Washington had moved his office into a simple red-brick building there. But in July, a law had been passed that provided for the construction of a new American capital. It was to be established as a federal city located in an independent district yet to be created, and it was to be called the District of Columbia (DC for short) after Columbia, the poetic name for America. There, on neutral soil not belonging to any state, Congress and the rest of the government of the United States were to take up permanent residence in the year 1800.

In honor of the first American president, only a few months after the law had been passed, the new federal city was officially named the City of Washington, DC. It was thus logical that its namesake would make all the major decisions about its planning and the architects who would design its buildings. Washington also personally chose the precise location (between Rock Creek and Goose Creek) of the city on the Potomac, which was to be laid out as a

FIGURE 10.4. Red-brick simplicity: George Washington's presidential office in Philadelphia (partial reconstruction, 2010). © Jürgen Overhoff.

perfect square. His preferred architect was the French-born artist and scientist Pierre L'Enfant, who had served as a major in the American Revolution. L'Enfant's plan for the city, inspired by the pathways at the French palace of Versailles, called for laying out a grid pattern of streets crisscrossed diagonally by broad avenues. The magnificent Capitol Building, or "Congress House," was later designed by William Thornton. Its mighty dome was reminiscent of the Pantheon in Rome. The "President's House" was the work of the Irish-born architect James Hoban. His design was inspired by the city palace of the Earl of Kildare, one of the most imposing aristocratic residences in the Irish capital of Dublin. In this manner, the city of Washington, DC, arose first on the drafting table under the watchful eye of the president. It shone with the luster of old European nobility and elegance—highly unusual in the American context.

Starting in 1790, Washington also oversaw the signing of numerous treaties with Native American tribes that had been pushed ever farther into the interior of North America by white Americans, either due to land purchases or through the unregulated settlement of traditional hunting grounds. Since the days of the Seven Years' War, Washington had known how important a friendly relationship with the indigenous inhabitants of the land was for the undisturbed development of the American states. He therefore put a premium on treating the Indians fairly. Between the Appalachians and the Mississippi, he sought to prevent illegal, private encroachment on Native American lands under all circumstances and for all time. For a stretch of several weeks in 1790, Washington received the chiefs of various tribes in Philadelphia, entertaining them with sumptuous banquets just like European dignitaries. In a letter to the chiefs of the Seneca Nation written in late December 1790, the president explained his Indian policy in great detail. He planned to use all of his presidential power to guarantee "the security of the remainder of your lands." Indeed, "no state nor person can purchase your lands, unless at some public treaty held under the authority of the United States." Furthermore, "the general government will never consent to your being defrauded." On the contrary, "it will protect you in all your just rights." In answer to the Indians' question whether they were allowed to practice agriculture, as there had not been sufficient wild game for some time, Washington responded that "the United States will be happy" if the nomadic Indians settled down and started "tilling the ground" as sedentary farmers. In that way, "the fatherly care the United States intend to take of the Indians" would be much easier to provide.

At the same time, Washington impressed upon the Seneca chiefs that, although "the United States desire to be the friends of the Indians," he would never "suffer the depredations of the bad people [among them] to go unpunished." The nature of his threat was revealed in the fall of 1791, when he sent several military expeditions into the Ohio Valley to counter uprisings among the Wyandots, Shawnee, and Miami. These missions were not blessed with success, however. The allied Ohio Indians put up fierce resistance, defending themselves effectively against the American soldiers.

Starting in 1792, Washington was preoccupied by a bitter quarrel within his cabinet. In the two preceding years, a rift had opened between Hamilton and Jefferson that could no longer be repaired. Jefferson harbored suspicions that Hamilton secretly desired to transform the United States into a monarchy ruled by Washington. For his part, Hamilton feared that the secretary of state and author of the Declaration of Independence yearned for radical popular government on the model of revolutionary France, one that would over time destroy the American constitutional framework.

Washington admonished both Jefferson and Hamilton to focus on their common political goals. On August 26, he wrote to Hamilton that "differences in political opinion" may be "unavoidable" even between members of the same cabinet, but only "to a certain point." Ultimately, all the members of the government had "the same *general* objects in view." On October 18, he also rebuked Jefferson: "I regret—deeply regret—the difference in opinions which have arisen and divided you and another principal officer of the government." He "devoutly" wished that the fight between Jefferson and Hamilton could be settled "by mutual yieldings."

As president, Washington sought constantly to unite all parts of society. When necessary, however, he was not averse to using all the power at his disposal to acquit his office, albeit rather in the guise of the patriarch of an extended family. The American voters were so pleased with his performance at the close of his first term that they reelected him to the presidency, again with an overwhelming majority. Despite the authority with which he was invested after his second electoral victory, however, he was not able to reconcile his squabbling cabinet secretaries Hamilton and Jefferson. The latter's enthusiasm for the French Revolution continued to be the cause of their discord.

Shortly after his second inauguration on March 4, 1793, Washington learned that King Louis XVI of France had been executed on January 21 and that the government, under the direction of the former justice minister Georges Danton, had now instituted a Reign of Terror in which all actual or perceived enemies of the Revolution were threatened with the guillotine. At that point, Washington began to gradually distance himself from Jefferson. Back in 1791, he had proclaimed that as president he would never forget how, as a general in the War of Independence, his "country in the hour of distress received such liberal aid from the French." Yet he emphasized that appreciation for this historical event should not dissuade Americans from deeply lamenting "the disorders and incertitude of that nation." When revolutionary France declared war on Great Britain in the spring of 1793, Washington did not take the side of his former ally but rather declared the strict neutrality of the United States.

For Jefferson, who was pleased that France had adopted a republican constitution after executing its king, Washington's neutrality policy was tantamount to siding with Great Britain. And in his eyes, the British system of government was anachronistic. He condemned Washington's aloofness to the stormy developments in the French republic as a betrayal of the political ideals of 1776. On December 31, the American secretary of state submitted his resignation. Washington accepted it the following day, albeit not without "sincere regret."

Over the course of the year 1794, it emerged that Jefferson was not the only American who was increasingly displeased by Washington's administration.

All over the country, "democratic societies" appeared whose members desired to introduce the same egalitarian version of republican democracy to the United States that they believed they saw in France. Jefferson and the democratic societies received valuable support from the journalist Benjamin Franklin Bache, Franklin's grandson. Using the printing press he had inherited from his grandfather, he published a newspaper that criticized the president and his policies with a hitherto unknown asperity. In the current situation, as the first political parties were forming in the United States, Washington could no longer play the role of the nonpartisan father of his country. He had to take a position that was clear and unmistakable to the public. And he did just that.

In August 1794, over 6,000 farmers in western Pennsylvania rebelled against an excise tax on whiskey that had been imposed by Congress. They put up armed resistance to tax collectors and even erected a symbolic guillotine outside Pittsburgh as a means of expressing their sympathy with the revolutionaries in France. In response, the president personally led American troops to quell the Whiskey Rebellion. First of all, he viewed "this insurrection as the first *formidable* fruit of the democratic societies," which "under popular and fascinating guises" undertook "the most diabolical attempts to destroy the best fabric of human government and happiness that has ever been presented for the acceptance of mankind." Moreover, in his opinion, the political ideas of the self-professed democratic rebels served only to sow "anarchy and confusion." Therefore, he personally took command of 13,000 soldiers and led them into western Pennsylvania with Hamilton at his side. No shots were fired, however, as the rebels took flight and laid down their arms. When Hamilton marched into Pittsburgh, he relayed Washington's promise of amnesty to all rebels who were willing to return to the foundation of government provided by the Constitution.

Washington could only imagine life in a thriving democratic republic within the framework of the Constitution of 1787, and he was willing to defend it with arms if necessary. Therefore, he was clearly opposed to all radical democratic tendencies *à la française* inside the borders of the United States. In 1795, he signed a commercial treaty with Great Britain that had been negotiated by Chief Justice John Jay. The terms of the treaty contradicted the neutrality principle he had long maintained in international trade, to the detriment of France. Once again, Washington's domestic enemies went on the rampage. Benjamin Franklin Bache published the text of the treaty on July 1, accompanying it with bitter commentary. Four weeks later, Washington groused in a private letter to Hamilton that "the cry against the treaty is like that against a mad dog," but it would die down when "the fever" that had been stoked by journalists in certain elements of the population "is a little abated."

But calm did not settle over the American people. Although Washington continued to avoid direct intervention in the war between revolutionary France and Great Britain, many of his fellow countrymen remained resentful of the Jay Treaty. As the radical democratic press thundered on against his administration and even questioned his personal integrity, Washington, offended and demoralized, decided not to run for a third term in office. And he announced this decision publicly. In a "Farewell Address" edited by Hamilton and printed in all the newspapers in America in the fall of 1796, the sixty-four-year-old president elaborated to his fellow citizens the reasons for his withdrawal from political life. At the same time, he explained what path he believed the United States should take in the future.

As he informed his "friends and fellow citizens," he had decided that, when it came time again to select "a citizen to administer the executive government of the United States," he no longer wished to be "considered among the number of those out of whom a choice is to be made." For every exhausting day that passed in the handling of government affairs reminded him mercilessly of "the increasing weight of years" that diminished his strength. Due to his advanced age, he now thought it "necessary" to spend his remaining days not in the heat of mundane politics but in "the shade of retirement" at Mount Vernon. Ultimately, every citizen of the United States knew that an elected American president only served the people for a limited term in office. And he thanked his "beloved country for the many honors it has conferred upon me."

He also gave some important advice for the future. For the people of this free, democratic, and republican nation, it was absolutely essential "that the free constitution" of 1787, "which is the work of your hands, may be sacredly maintained." Of course, "the basis of our political system is the right of the people to make and to alter their constitutions of government." On the other hand, the maintenance of "the constitution which at any time exists," and which guarantees the ability to regularly change the makeup of the government through the legal procedure of regular elections by secret ballot, "is sacredly obligatory upon all."

Moreover, "the very idea of the power and the right of the people to establish government presupposes the duty of every individual to obey the established government." All attacks on this understanding of government and constitutionalism were "destructive" and "fatal" to a freedom-loving society. Populist political associations not legitimized by elections might arrogate to themselves the right to speak for the people as a whole and, on the basis of that claim, "usurp for themselves the reins of government" in a coup d'état. In so doing, however, they would destroy "the very engines which have lifted them to unjust dominion."

When Washington left the office in the spring of 1797, he was succeeded as president by John Adams. Having served Washington loyally as vice president, Adams beat his opponent Jefferson by a hair, relegating him to second place. This electoral victory was a source of personal satisfaction to Washington, since Adams had likewise distanced himself from revolutionary France while at the same time maintaining his predecessor's policy of neutrality. Only one time, in the summer of 1798, as the French fleet stepped up its attacks on American ships engaged in trade with the British, was Adams seriously tempted to intercede in the European war. As a precautionary measure in this dangerous situation, he named Washington lieutenant general and commander in chief of the American military. But the crisis faded before Washington had to actually lead troops in battle.

The only official duty that now remained to him was to regularly monitor the building projects in the new federal city named after him, which was easy enough considering Mount Vernon's proximity to the site. He was especially concerned to establish a university there of nationwide reach and significance. Time and again, he expressed his view that, in this age of free investigation and enlightened reason, it was necessary to found a university that would provide "the polish of erudition in the arts, sciences, and belle letters in their full breadth." Every new generation of citizens had to be prepared for the future with a good education directed to the exigencies of public and private life. Consequently, it was imperative to gather "the youth from *all parts* of the United States" at such a university, where they "would by degrees discover that there was not that cause for those jealousies and prejudices which one part of the union had imbibed against another part."

Washington was still in tolerably good health, the only exception being occasional unpleasantries related to the fact that he had lost all his teeth—a situation he could only partially conceal with a set of dentures. Still, he began to ruminate more and more often about the course of his life, and, sensing that he did not have long to live, he drew up his will. There he ordered that all the slaves he owned should be freed upon the death of his wife. In this way, he was able to ease his conscience somewhat with regard to the system of slavery, which was still fully legal in the southern states and which represented the most egregious contradiction of the American social and political order.

In his personal letters as well, he sought to take stock of his life. For example, he felt the need to once again describe in detail the deep affection he still felt for the object of his youthful desire, Sally Fairfax, who was now an aging widow living in England. None of the "so many important events" that had occurred in his life, "nor all of them together," he assured her in moving words, "have been able to eradicate from my mind the recollection of those happy moments—the happiest of my life—which I have enjoyed in your company." While contemplating "the remainder of my days (which cannot be many)," he felt compelled to confess all this to her again.

Of the letters that he received in his retirement at Mount Vernon, he especially enjoyed reading those from John Quincy Adams, who had been sent by his father, President John Adams, as ambassador to Berlin. While residing in the Prussian capital on the River Spree, John Quincy would extend the life of the commercial treaty that Frederick the Great had negotiated with the Americans, updating its terms to reflect the many ways in which the world had changed since 1785. Washington did not think it improper for a president to entrust such an important task and so dignified an office to his own son. On the contrary, although the master of Mount Vernon could not predict that John Quincy Adams would himself become president a quarter-century hence, he espied in the young man great political talent that deserved to be fostered. Shortly before his death, Washington even prophesied that Ambassador Adams would "prove himself to be the ablest of all our diplomatic corps."

When death ultimately did come for Washington toward the end of 1799, he had all of his personal affairs in order. The cause of death was acute laryngitis, which the ex-president contracted on December 12 while touring his lands on horseback for several hours in a heavy snowstorm. Two days later, the swelling in his throat, which the attending doctor was unable to reduce, cut off his breathing. In the presence of his manservant and his wife, who sat at the foot of his bed, he placed his finger on his wrist to feel the weakening of his own pulse. The last comprehensible words Washington spoke, emitted with difficulty, were, "'Tis well." Four days later, he was buried in the vicinity of the manor house in a crypt dug into a thickly wooded hillside.

After the loss of the heroic father of the nation, the United States of America was ready for a new beginning. The larger world, too, started steering a course into a new era in the year 1800. And so the question arose: As one of the leading representatives of the Age of Enlightenment, what would Washington's enduring legacy for posterity be? Would his achievements last beyond the eighteenth century? What of the Constitution of the United States? What of the American democratic republic and its attendant social order?

These questions also occupied Ambassador John Quincy Adams in Berlin. When he learned of Washington's death, he recorded an initial, spontaneous reaction on February 4, 1800: "The loss of such a man is a misfortune to mankind." But what did the diplomat mean by that? Did he not have sufficient confidence in the proper functioning of the democratic mechanisms of the United States, which were designed to operate independently of the charisma of important individuals—and which had come to be seen as models to imitate in many parts of Europe as well? Had not the first alternation in the office of president, the transfer of power to Adams's own upright father, been a successful test of the American Constitution? Could one still have doubts about the felicitous outcome of the republican experiment in the United States?

Yes, one could. John Quincy Adams considered Washington's Francophile opponents, who had now become his father's political enemies, to be strong enough in their evil passions to create difficulties for the United States. What such difficulties might look like had just been demonstrated by the anarchy and terror into which France had lapsed, after initially embarking in 1789 on such a hopeful journey as a democratic republic. The revolutionary general Napoleon Bonaparte had staged a coup d'état in November 1799, arrogating all power in France to himself. Under the title of "First Consul," he now exercised a veiled dictatorship. Napoleon's triumph provoked queasiness in Ambassador Adams. Did it not show clearly that all experiments in democratic republicanism were destined sooner or later to end in dictatorship—indeed in terrible dictatorships that made Frederick the Great's enlightened absolutism look like the most desirable of all forms of government? Shortly before his death, Frederick himself had predicted to Lafayette that the United States would deteriorate into chaos.

John Quincy Adams had been an admirer of the Prussian king in his earliest youth. At the age of fourteen, he had even bought a four-volume set of Frederick's complete poetic works at a bookstore with his own pocket money. Now, in 1800, he still extolled the outstanding role that the king had played for decades as the enlightened educator of his people. Since the beginning of his appointment as ambassador in Berlin, Adams had many times met with Frederick's brother Prince Henry for long conversations. He now realized in amazement that Frederick the Great—in contrast to the years immediately following his death in 1786—once again enjoyed a high reputation in Berlin. Upon ascending the throne, Frederick's successor Frederick William II had radically curtailed freedom of the press and religion in Prussia. As a result, many Berliners now looked back with yearning at the reign of Old Fritz, which they romanticized as a liberal age.

When the new king died in 1797 with the reputation of having been a *dicker Lüderjahn*, a big, fat, no-good voluptuary, he was followed on the throne by his equally authoritarian son Frederick William III. Not unexpectedly, Frederick the Great continued to be held in memory as a touchstone of good and just governance. Compared with the two most powerful European rulers of the day—the dictator Napoleon Bonaparte and the eccentric Russian autocrat Tsar Paul I—the great Prussian king seemed in hindsight like a wise and enlightened sovereign, a ruler dedicated to dutiful service to his people. In light of the chaos of the times, was Frederick's moderate style of rule not an important standard by which other European governments should orient themselves? Or was it rather the presidency of Washington, who had discredited Frederick's absolutism as a tyranny, that ought to serve as a prototypical model for modern governance in the nineteenth century? Which path of enlightened government—that of Frederick the Great, or that of George Washington—would ultimately lead the way to the future?

Only the future itself could give an answer to that question. But on April 14, 1801, a prominent resident of Berlin who had great respect for the legacies of both Frederick the Great and George Washington reached his own very personal decision, thus making it clear which of these two world-shaping heroes of the eighteenth century he believed represented the royal road to the future. When John Quincy Adams baptized his firstborn son in Berlin on that day in April, he named him for the hero that to his mind, upon due reflection—and despite all the criticism aimed at him in his lifetime—embodied the political future: George Washington.

Epilogue

A TIMELY COMPARISON

FREDERICK THE Great and George Washington reflected very different ideals of statesmanship. The Prussian king's political vision was trained on unquestioned authority to the strictest and most uncompromising monarchical rule. By no means did he subscribe to Montesquieu's important liberal principle of the separation of powers. Nevertheless, Frederick knew and accepted that states existed that were governed according to republican or even democratic principles, such as the thirteen cantons of the Swiss Confederation, the seven United Provinces of the Netherlands, and—the most recent newcomer among the nations in the rapidly developing eighteenth-century world—the United States of America. He took these striving political entities seriously as undeniable realities of the time. That is why he was willing to negotiate a treaty of amity and commerce with the United States in 1785. But he held that his own distinct, autocratic style of government was clearly superior to democracy, at least in the long run. George Washington, on the other hand, was a staunch critic of Frederick's harsh monarchical rule. He had come to believe during the course of his life—like the other American founders Benjamin Franklin, Thomas Jefferson, Alexander Hamilton, James Madison, and John Adams—that a democratic republic was the only viable option in the modern world, and that the United States of America, paying tribute to the rights of humankind, had come into being as an entirely new kind of political system, dedicated to the principle of checks and balances, shining forth as an example for all nations on earth.

Throughout his life, Frederick defended the Prussian version of enlightened monarchy, beginning in 1740 when he ascended the throne and published his *Anti-Machiavel*. When he returned to the topic for the last time in 1786, a few months before he died, it was with full knowledge of the remarkable developments across the Atlantic. The king knew about all the high hopes built upon the promising prospects of the United States of America. And yet, he prophesied the fall of the fledgling country. He did not give a precise date, but he predicted that decline, chaos, and ruin would befall this union of democratic republics sooner or later. From a detailed report by the British member of Parliament Sir John Stepney, we learn that Frederick "was persuaded that the American union could not long subsist under its present form." The great extent of the country would alone be a sufficient obstacle, since "a republican form of government had never been known to exist for any length of time where the territory was not limited and united." The Prussian king himself had confided to his brother Henry in a similar vein that the now independent American states were "not made to form a republic. Each of them has other interests and the land they occupy is far too extensive for it to form a government similar to that of Venice, Switzerland, or Holland." The United States of America, he concluded, would not survive for long.

Ironically, however, it was the once so powerful Kingdom of Prussia—founded by the monarch's grandfather Frederick I in 1701—that did not survive. In the course of the German Revolution of November 1918, the state of Prussia, which had formerly been described as the "Iron Kingdom," was first converted into a republican "Free State" (Freistaat Preußen) and then, soon after the Second World War, formally and permanently abolished on February 25, 1947. On that day, a decree signed by Lucius D. Clay, commander in chief of American forces in Europe and military governor of the U.S. zone in Germany, stated with devastating rigor, "The Prussian State which from early days has been a bearer of militarism and reaction in Germany has de facto ceased to exist." With this statement, the victorious American general expressed his conviction that the Prussian ideal of monarchical government—which for him (as for Washington) was almost equivalent to a dictatorial or tyrannical kind of rule—had poisoned the German political system and ravaged the world with the calamities of war. Fortunately, the United States, the standard-bearer of democracy around the globe since 1776, had won the day, and Prussia was shattered.

As a result, it is not difficult to see Frederick the Great as a ludicrously false prophet. Contrary to his expectations over 200 years earlier, the United States of America proved superior to Prussia when that former kingdom—like the whole of Germany—became an enemy and perverted the standards of politics during the rule of Adolf Hitler and the Nazi Party. After the Second World

War, Germany had to be reconstructed from scratch as a democracy and as a federal republic with the essential help of the United States—a process that met with steady success. In the second half of the twentieth century and during the first two decades of the twenty-first century, the renewed, rejuvenated, and chastened Germany became a leading power of the ever-growing, democratic, and federal European Union, a political entity that was awarded the Nobel Peace Prize in 2012. Accordingly, Germany and the European Union enjoyed the uncompromising support of the United States up through the administration of Barack Obama and then again with Joe Biden. It seemed as if George Washington's political heirs had finally made the world safe for democracy on both sides of the Atlantic. "The end of history," as the American political philosopher Francis Fukuyama had famously put it before the turn of the century, appeared to be within reach.

But history never comes to an end. Since the second decade of the twenty-first century, a surprisingly large number of authoritarian rulers have emerged across the world, generating an astonishing amount of support and launching massive counterattacks to liberalism and the system of checks and balances. This development has delivered a dramatic setback to democratic values on a global scale. The latest shifts in political perspectives provide ample evidence that the eighteenth-century antagonism between Frederick the Great and George Washington is not just a relic of transatlantic history without relevance for us today. Indeed, the study of the lives, the times, and the very different political styles of the great Prussian king and the first American president may still serve as a valuable and indispensable analysis of the competing alternatives of modern politics. The fight between authoritarianism and democracy is back on the political agenda of the transatlantic world. History teaches us that this conflict first began in the eighteenth century, and we should draw lessons from the past in order to resolve it.

Looking back, it is clear that President George Washington taught the most important lesson in this context. In his "Farewell Address" of September 19, 1796, he argued that all democracies remained vulnerable and could be challenged at any given time in the future by autocrats and unlawful usurpers of power. Especially in turbulent times in which societies were changing rapidly, he maintained, unsettling events might "gradually incline the minds of men to seek security and repose" and to entrust themselves to "the absolute power of an individual." The result? "Sooner or later the chief of some prevailing faction more able or more fortunate than his competitors turns this disposition to the purposes of his own elevation, on the ruins of public liberty." This is why he felt obliged to issue several warnings to posterity, forceful admonitions that still strike a chord with all the vigilant observers of the realm of politics of our day and age.

First of all, healthy democracies ought to be ready and always prepared to defend themselves wholeheartedly, if necessary, against any kind of "external danger" brought about by all those aggressive and warmongering "foreign nations" that were "particularly hostile to republican liberty." But it was not only the threat from abroad that remained a continuous danger. "In contemplating the causes which may disturb" a democracy, Washington referred to enemies at home who one day might try to subvert the Constitution, agitating "the community with ill-founded jealousies and false alarms," kindling "the animosity of one part against another," and intentionally provoking "riot & insurrection." People should never leave the possibility of "an extremity of this kind" entirely "out of sight." The most promising way to prevent such a horrible scenario in a democracy would be the sound teaching of "compliance with its laws" and "acquiescence in its measures" combined with the explanation of the "maxims of true liberty."

Obviously, Washington lived with the idea that one day in the distant future an autocratic government might be able to regain the sympathies of many—even in America—and he warned his countrymen, as well as all other friends of democracy, not to fall for political seducers. When he wrote his "Farewell Address," he knew that the United States had won the day, but he also realized that "governments of a monarchical cast"—governments in the autocratic style of Frederick the Great—might become attractive again. Washington was not a clairvoyant. His sense of what the future might hold was informed by the study of history books, including Edward Gibbon's *History of the Decline and Fall of the Roman Empire*, which first appeared in the year the United Colonies declared themselves independent and which remained an important part of Washington's large library thereafter. He therefore also knew that history never comes to an end, and he expected the eighteenth and the twenty-first centuries to have more in common than most people are willing to think. He was right. Reflecting upon the comparative biographies of Frederick the Great and George Washington is a strangely timely enterprise.

NOTES

Frontmatter Epigraph

Page

ix   *How to explain what's in people's heads, what they think? It's like with love: impossible to explain. But who would we be if we did not try?* Per Orlov Enquist, *Lewis Resa: Roman* (Stockholm: Norstedts Förlag, 2001), p. 547: "Hur förklarar man sinnena. Med sinnena är det som med kärleken. De är omöjliga attförklara. Men vilka vore vi om vi inte försökte."

Introduction to the English Edition

Page

xvii   *the indispensable man.* James Thomas Flexner, *Washington: The Indispensable Man* (Boston: Little, Brown and Company, 1974).

xvii   *founding brothers.* Joseph J. Ellis, *Founding Brothers: The Revolutionary Generation* (New York: Alfred A. Knopf, 2000).

xviii   *Atlantic history.* Bernard Bailyn, *Atlantic History: Concepts and Contours* (Cambridge, MA: Harvard University Press, 2005); Jack P. Greene and Philip D. Morgan, eds., *Atlantic History: A Critical Appraisal* (Oxford: Oxford University Press, 2008); Joseph C. Miller, *The Princeton Companion to Atlantic History* (Princeton, NJ: Princeton University Press, 2015).

xix   *the stance Frederick the Great adopted . . . if at all.* Friedrich Kapp, *Friedrich der Große und die Vereinigten Staaten von Amerika* (Leipzig: Quandt & Händel, 1871), p. 1: "Die Stellung Friedrichs des Großen . . . zu den Vereinigten Staaten ist in der bereits zu einer Bibliothek angewachsenen Literatur über den König nur beiläufig oder gar nicht erörtert."

xx   *America was conquered in Germany.* See Brendan Simms, "Pitt and Hanover," in *The Hanoverian Dimension in British History, 1714–1837*, ed. Brendan Simms and Torsten Riotte (Cambridge: Cambridge University Press, 2007), p. 31.

xxi   *the most liberal treaty which has ever been entered into between independent powers.* Letter from George Washington to the Comte de Rochambeau, 31 July 1786, in *The Papers of George Washington* (hereafter *PGW*), Confederation Series, vol. 4, pp. 179–181, Founders Online, National Archives, https://founders.archives.gov/documents/Washington/04-04-02-0171.

1. Parallel Lives

Page

1–2 *yield the palm to none . . . politician . . . discernment . . . increase my opinion . . . to be lamented . . . great characters . . . not without a blot . . . one man . . . tyrannize over millions . . . a shade . . . always.* Letter from George Washington to Lafayette, 10 May 1786, in *PGW*, Confederation Series, vol. 4, pp. 41–45, Founders Online, National Archives, https://founders.archives.gov/documents/Washington/04-04-02-0051.

9 *morning sun.* Karl Philipp Moritz, *Sechs deutsche Gedichte, dem Könige von Preussen gewidmet,* 2nd ed. (Berlin: Verlag Arnold Wever, 1781), p. 15: "Morgensonne."

9 *century of Frederick.* Immanuel Kant, "An Answer to the Question: What Is Enlightenment?," in *Practical Philosophy,* ed. and trans. Mary J. Gregor (Cambridge: Cambridge University Press, 1996), p. 21.

9 *firmament of politics and war.* Johann Wolfgang von Goethe, *The Autobiography of Goethe. Truth and Poetry: From My Own Life,* trans. John Oxenford, rev. ed. (London: George Bell and Sons, 1897), p. 618, https://www.gutenberg.org/files/52654/52654-h/52654-h.htm.

10 *a slight thing like a phrase . . . in each particular case.* Plutarch, *Life of Alexander,* in *Plutarch's Lives,* vol. 7, trans. Bernadotte Perrin (Cambridge, MA: Harvard University Press, 1919), p. 225.

2. A Rising Sun (1701)

Page

12 *There is a mighty light which spreads itself over the world . . . in greater proportion than ever.* Anthony Ashley Cooper, Earl of Shaftesbury, *The Life, Unpublished Letters, and Philosophical Regimen of Anthony, Earl of Shaftesbury,* ed. Benjamin Rand (London: Swan, Sonnenschein, & Co., 1900), p. 353.

12 *emerged . . . some degree of reputation in the world.* Benjamin Franklin, *The Autobiography,* in *Writings,* ed. J. A. Leo Lemay (New York: Library of America, 1987), pp. 1307–1469, at 1307.

12 *light . . . the nature of things . . . the conveniences or pleasures of life.* Benjamin Franklin, "A Proposal for Promoting Useful Knowledge," 14 May 1743, in *The Papers of Benjamin Franklin* (hereafter *PBF*), vol. 2, pp. 373–383, Founders Online, National Archives, https://founders.archives.gov/documents/Franklin/01-02-02-0092.

12 *new luster . . . by dark clouds.* Letter from Gottfried van Swieten to Anton Wenzel von Kaunitz-Rietberg, 16 February 1774, in Ernst Wangermann, *Aufklärung und staatsbürgerliche Erziehung. Gottfried van Swieten als Reformator des österreichischen Unterrichtswesens, 1781–1791* (Vienna: Verlag für Geschichte und Politik, 1978), p. 17: "Es ist endlich der Zeitpunkt gekommen, wo die Warheit aus den finsteren Wolken, worinn sie verhüllet ware, mit einem neuen Glanz hervortritt, und alle Rechte erhält."

12 *ray of light . . . more luminous . . . this very century . . . dark days.* Mary Wollstonecraft, *A Vindication of the Rights of Men, in a Letter to the Right Honourable Edmund Burke, Occasioned by His Reflections on the Revolution in France* (London: Joseph Johnson, 1790), pp. 19 ("ray of light"), 64 ("more luminous"), 89 ("this very century"), 19 ("dark days").

Also available at The Online Library of Liberty (without page numbers), https://oll
.libertyfund.org/titles/wollstonecraft-a-vindication-of-the-rights-of-men.

15   *in an age of enlightenment.* Kant, "Answer to the Question," p. 21 (8:40).

15   *decisive events.* Chodowiecki created a series of copperplate engravings for the 1792 edition of the *Goettinger Taschen Calender,* ed. Georg Christoph Lichtenberg (Göttingen:
Dieterich, 1791). The series was called "Sechs grosse Begebenheiten des vorletzten De-
cenniums" (Six Decisive Events of the Century's Penultimate Decade).

15   *no more generally intelligible, allegorical symbol . . . most fitting.* Georg Christoph Lichtenberg, "Kurze Erklärung der Monatskupfer," in Lichtenberg, *Goettinger Taschen Calender*
(Göttingen: Dieterich, 1791), pp. 211–213, at 213: "noch kein allgemeiner verständliches
allegorisches Zeichen. . . . Es wird auch wohl lange das schicklichste bleiben."

18   *So long as the sun rises, no fog can detract from it.* Ibid., p. 213: "Indessen wenn die Sonne
nur aufgeht, so schaden Nebel nicht."

18   *What indeed are men! A dwelling place for grim pains. . . .* Andreas Gryphius, "Human
Misery," in Scott Horton, "Two Poems by Andreas Gryphius," *Harper's Magazine,*
August 11, 2007.

18   *greatest philosopher not merely of our own but of any age.* Quentin Skinner, *Reason and Rhetoric in the Philosophy of Hobbes* (Cambridge: Cambridge University Press, 1996), p. 254.

19–20 *dominion of passions . . . into the clearest light.* Thomas Hobbes, *De Cive, or, The Citizen*
(New York: Appleton-Century-Crofts, 1949), pp. 114 (10.1), 12 (preface), 3–4 (dedication), Internet Archive, https://archive.org/details/deciveorcitizen00inhobb.

20   *the lord acquires . . . lord over themselves.* Ibid., p. 69 (5.12).

20   *monarchy . . . absolute . . . supreme power.* Ibid., pp. 87 (7.1), 93 (7.11), 77 (6.13).

20   *democracy . . . met together . . . by the major part.* Ibid., pp. 87 (7.1), 90 (7.5).

21   *kindled a great light.* Letter from Gottfried Wilhelm Leibniz to Thomas Hobbes, 13/23
July 1670, in Thomas Hobbes, *The Correspondence,* ed. Noel Malcolm, vol. 2, *1660–1679*
(Oxford: Clarendon Press, 1994), pp. 713–716 (Latin text of the letter), quotation at 714
(English translation on p. 717).

21   *for the Emperor to become a perpetual dictator or absolute monarch.* Gottfried Wilhelm
Leibniz, "Bedencken welchergestalt Securitas publica interna et externa (und status
praesens) im Reich (jetzigen Umbständen nach) auf festen fuß zu stellen," August 1670,
Pars I, in *Die Werke von Leibniz gemäß seinem handschriftlichen Nachlasse in der Königlichen Bibliothek zu Hannover,* ed. Onno Klopp, Reihe 1, *Historisch-politische und staatswissenschaftliche Schriften,* vol. 1 (Hanover: Klindworth, 1864), p. 198: "und [der Kaiser]
dadurch perpetuus dictator oder ein absoluter monarch werden würde."

23   *pillars.* The prince-electors are referred to as *columnae* (i.e., "columns" or "pillars" that
support and sustain the Empire) several times in the text of the Golden Bull—e.g., in
cap. 3 and 12. An English translation is available online in "The Golden Bull of the Emperor Charles IV 1356 A.D.," Avalon Project, Yale Law School, https://avalon.law.yale
.edu/medieval/golden.asp.

24   *with absolute power and without the previous limitations.* "Friede und Bündniss zwischen
Johann Casimir König von Polen und Kurfürst Friedrich Wilhelm von Brandenburg
unter Anerkennung Preussens als souverainen Herzogthums," in *Kurbrandenburgs
Staatsverträge von 1601 bis 1700. Nach den Originalen des Königl. Geh. Staats-Archivs,* ed.

Theodor von Moerner (Berlin: Reimer, 1867), p. 221 (§5): "mit der höchsten absoluten Gewalt, ohne jedwede vordem getragene Lasten."

25   *Since I possess everything pertaining to royal dignity....* Margrave Frederick III of Branden-burg, "Eigenhändige Antwort des Kurfürsten auf das Votum des Paul von Fuchs," in Albert Waddington, *L'Acquisition de la Couronne Royale de Prusse par les Hohenzollern* (Paris: Leroux, 1888), appendix, pp. 405–409, at 405: "Wan ich alles habe, was zu der königlichen Würde gehöret, auch noch mehr als andere Könige, warum sol ich dann auch nicht trachten, den Namen eines Königs zu erlangen?"

25   *Reputation of power is power.* Thomas Hobbes, *Leviathan*, ed. Richard Tuck (Cambridge: Cambridge University Press, 1991), p. 62 (chap. 10).

26   *independent king.* Margrave Frederick III of Brandenburg, "Eigenhändige Antwort des Kurfürsten auf das Votum des Paul von Fuchs," in Waddington, *L'Acquisition de la Cou-ronne Royale de Prusse*, p. 405: "independanter König."

26   *immediately honor, esteem, and recognize...* "Erneuerte geheime Defensiv-Alliance vom 16. November 1700 zwischen Kaiser Leopold und Kurfürst Friedrich III., in welcher dem Letztern die Annahme der Königl. Würde zugestanden wird (Der sogenannte 'Krontrac-tat')," in *Kurbrandenburgs Staatsverträge von 1601 bis 1700*, pp. 810–823, at 814: "soforth... in- und ausser Reichs vor einen König in Preußen ehren, würdigen und erkennen."

27   *Berlin, light of the world.* Johann Kayser, *Parnassus Clivensis oder Clevischer Musen-Berg und seine darauff gewachsene Poetische Früchte* (Cleves: Tobias Silberling, 1698; facsimile reprint, Cleves: Buchhandlung H. Fingerhut, 1980), p. 29: "Berolinum. Orbi lumen. / Quotidie accrescens, Berolinum lumen es Orbi / Inque Tuo Caelo sidera multa nitent" (Growing daily, Berlin, you are the light of the world / And in your sky shine many stars).

30   *Thus, in the beginning, all the world was America.* John Locke, *Two Treatises of Government*, in *The Works of John Locke*, new ed., 10 vols. (London: Printed for Thomas Tegg et al., 1823), vol. 5, p. 125 (2nd Treatise, chap. 5, sec. 49), https://www.yorku.ca/comninel /courses/3025pdf/Locke.pdf.

32   *settle a free, just, and industrious colony... good prosperity and security.* William Penn, *Some Account of the Province of Pennsylvania*, in *William Penn and the Founding of Pennsylvania: A Documentary History*, ed. Jean R. Soderlund (Philadelphia: University of Pennsylvania Press, 1983), pp. 58–66, at 62 (sec. 2, "The Constitutions," points 1, 3, 4).

33   *yearly chosen... at Philadelphia... in any of the King's plantations in America.* William Penn, "The Charter of Privileges," in *The Papers of William Penn*, vol. 4, *1701–1718*, ed. Richard S. Dunn and Mary Maples Dunn (Philadelphia: University of Pennsylvania Press, 1987), pp. 104–110, at 107. Also available at the Online Library of Liberty, where it is called the "Pennsylvania Charter of Liberties," https://oll.libertyfund.org/pages/1701 -pennsylvania-charter-of-liberties.

34   *year of our Lord one thousand seven hundred and one.* Penn, "Charter of Privileges," p. 110.

3. War and Peace (1702–1713)

Page

36   *the people... best for their safety and security.* Locke, *Two Treatises of Government*, p. 169 (2nd Treatise, chap. 13, sec. 149).

39   *on the behalf of.* William Penn, "Address to the Queen [Anne]," 3 June 1702, in *Papers of William Penn*, pp. 172–174, at 173.

39   *I know mine own heart to be entirely English.* "Queen Anne's Speech to Both Houses of Parliament," 11 March 1702, in Edward Gregg, *Queen Anne* (London: Routledge & Kegan Paul, 1980), pp. 151–153, at 151. Also available on British History Online, https://www .british-history.ac.uk/commons-hist-proceedings/vol3/pp197-203.

41   *discourage[d]... dissuade[d]... their wives... leaving their business.* Letter from Andrew Hamilton to William Penn, 19 September 1702, in Penn, *Papers of William Penn*, p. 186.

42   *As things are now, we lie under the greatest discouragements.* Letter from James Logan to William Penn, 14 July 1704, in Penn, *Papers of William Penn*, p. 289.

43   *by the last Charter of Privileges... and dissolve them as he should see cause.* Letter from the Pennsylvania Assembly to William Penn, 25 August 1704, in Penn, *Papers of William Penn*, p. 300.

45   *with his own eyes... give us this great and glorious victory.* Letter from Prince Eugene to Frederick I, 16 August 1704, as quoted (without attribution) in Werner Schmidt, *Friedrich I. Kurfürst von Brandenburg, König in Preußen* (Munich: Diederichs, 1996), p. 166: "mit Augen gesehen... mit einer unerschrockenen Standhaftigkeit wider den Feind gefochten... entfliehen und uns das Veld... diese so herrliche Victori überlassen müssen."

46   *answered to no one but God... justify his rule.* Letter from Frederick I to his wife, Queen Sophia Charlotte, 4 February 1702, in Ernst Berner, *Aus dem Briefwechsel König Friedrichs I. von Preußen und seiner Familie: Gelegentlich der zweihundertjährigen Jubelfeier des preußischen Königtums* (Berlin: Alexander Duncker, 1901), p. 23: "Denn ich bin keinem Rede und Antwort von meiner Regierung schuldig als Gott allein."

47   *utterly submitted my will to the will of God.* Ibid., p. 23: "Ich [habe] meinen willen gantz Gottes willen ergeben."

48   *He's a good screamer... and is nice and plump.* Letter from Frederick I to his wife, Queen Sophia Charlotte, 24 January 1712, in Berner, *Aus dem Briefwechsel König Friedrichs I. von Preußen*, p. 265: "Er schreiet braf und ist recht fett und frisch."

49   *that little Prince Fritz now has six teeth... is pulling through just fine.* Letter from Frederick I to his wife, Queen Sophia Charlotte, 30 August 1712, in Berner, *Aus dem Briefwechsel König Friedrichs I. von Preußen*, p. 330: "Dass der kleine Prinz Fritz nuhn mero 6 zehne hat.... Daran kann man auch die predestination sehen, dass alle seine Brüder haben daran sterben müßen, dieser aber bekömmt sie ohne mühe wie seine Schwester."

4. Fathers and Sons (1713–1732)

Page

53   *neither counsel nor hollow reasoning, but only obedience.* "Nachschrift zum Berichte des Sächsischen Gesandten Freiherrn von Manteuffel an den Generalfeldmarschall Grafen von Flemming," in *Acta Borussica: Denkmäler der Preußischen Staatsverwaltung im 18. Jahrhundert* (hereafter *Borussica*), vol. 1, p. 312: "Il a répondu qu'il ne demandait ni conseil ni raisonnement, mais de l'obéissance."

53   *drivel... achieve my purpose, firm up my sovereignty... as solidly as a block of bronze.* Frederick William I, "Kabinettsorder," 1717, in *Borussica*, vol. 2, p. 490: "Ich komme zu

meinem Zweck und stabiliere die Souveränität und setze die Krone fest wie einen rocher von bronce und lasse den Herren Junkers den Wind vom Landtag."

55   *a novelty in every sense.* "Bericht des Sächsischen Gesandten Freiherrn von Manteuffel," in *Borussica*, vol. 1, p. 737: "sehr neu in jedem Sinne."

56   *Rogue . . . buffoon . . . rascal . . . riffraff . . . scoundrel.* "Bericht des Sächsischen Gesandten Freiherrn von Manteuffel an den Generalfeldmarschall Grafen von Flemming," in *Borussica*, vol. 1, p. 319: "Schelm . . . Narr . . . Canaille . . . Schurke . . . Hundsfott."

56   *The king doesn't eat supper . . .* Montesquieu, *Mes Voyages*, ed. Jean Ehrard (Paris: Éditions Classiques Garnier, 2012), p. 441: "Le roy ne soupe point et s'enferme dans son cabinet avec quelques uns de ses officiers à fumer et boire de la bierre. . . . Il aime ses soldats les rosse tres bien et ensuite il les baise. . . . C'est une misere que d'etre sujet de ce prince."

58   *Where have you been, my son?* Written report (in French) by Ernst Christoph von Manteuffel, 25 February 1713, in *Borussica*, vol. 1, p. 310: "Où avez-vous été, mon fils?"

59   *Today I will make you crown prince again.* Report of the Mecklenburg resident Burmeister, 5 March 1713, as quoted in Carl Hinrichs, *Friedrich Wilhelm I. König in Preussen. Eine Biographie. Jugend und Aufstieg. Ergänzt durch: Der Regierungsantritt Friedrich Wilhelms I.* (Darmstadt: Wissenschaftliche Buchgesellschaft, 1968), p. 720: "Heute mache ich dich wieder zum Kronprinzen."

59   *to the military profession.* Personal instructions of King Frederick William I on the education of the crown prince, 13 August 1718, as quoted in Friedrich Cramer, *Zur Geschichte Friedrich Wilhelms I. und Friedrichs II. Könige von Preußen* (Hamburg: Hofmann und Campe, 1829), p. 11: "Wahre Liebe zum Soldatenstand."

59   *cradle lay amid the weapons of war . . . I was brought up in the thick of troubles . . .* Frederick the Great, "Epistle XX: To My Soul" (À mon esprit), in *Frederick the Great's Philosophical Writings* (hereafter *FGPW*), pp. 116–124, at 123.

60   *Seldom is a teacher chosen in the trenches.* As quoted in Ernst Bratuscheck, *Die Erziehung Friedrichs des Großen* (Berlin: Georg Reimer, 1885), p. 109, n. 23: "Es ist ein seltener Fall, daß man einen Präceptor in einem Laufgraben wählt."

61   *when suddenly my father entered the room . . . into the inner room.* Henri de Catt, *Frederick the Great: The Memoirs of His Reader, Henri de Catt (1758–1760)*, trans. F. S. Flint (London: Constable and Company, 1916), p. 59 (translation adapted).

61   *He took me by the hair . . . I will let you know what is what.* Ibid., p. 59.

61–62 *order . . . to parents, on pain of penalty . . . remedy . . . gross ignorance. Corpus Constitutionum Marchicarum*, Decree (*Verordnung*) No. 97, 28 September 1717, ordering parents to send their children to school and preachers to teach catechism, Preußische Rechtsquellen Digital / Corpus Constitutionum Marchicarum, https://web-archiv.staatsbibliothek -berlin.de/altedrucke.staatsbibliothek-berlin.de/Rechtsquellen/CCMT11/intro.html: "Verordnung, daß die Eltern ihre Kinder zur Schule, und die Prediger die Catechisationes halten sollen. Wir vernehmen mißfällig und wird verschiedentlich von denen Inspectoren und Predigern bey Uns geklaget, daß die Eltern, *absonderlich auf dem Lande*, in Schickung ihrer Kinder zur Schule sich sehr säumig erzeigen, und dadurch die arme Jugend in *grosse Unwissenheit . . .* aufwachsen laßen. Weshalb Wir *umb* diesem höchst verderblichen Uebel auff ein mahl *abzuhelffen* in Gnaden resolvieret . . . zu *verordnen . . .* daß hinkünfftig . . . *die Eltern bey nachdrücklicher Straffe gehalten seyn sollen Ihre Kinder . . . in die Schuel zuschicken*" (quoted words in italics).

62   *Frederick William, King in Prussia . . . capable expander of his realm . . . useful for raising crops and animals.* Plaque on the village church at Königshorst: "Friedrich Wilhelm König in Preußen . . . glücklicher Vermehrer Seines Reichs . . . diesen vormahligen grundlosen Morast und Auffenthalt wilder Thiere, durch große Mühe . . . des Menschen Nutzen urbahr . . . zum Acker-Bau und Vieh-Zucht nutzbar gemacht."

64   *Saracens and pagans . . . invade, search out, capture, vanquish, and subdue.* Nicholas V, "*Romanus Pontifex*," papal bull of 8 January 1455, as translated in *European Treaties Bearing on the History of the United States and Its Dependencies to 1648*, ed. Frances Gardiner Davenport (Washington, DC: Carnegie Institution of Washington, 1917), pp. 20–26 (original Latin text at 13–20). The English text of the bull is also available online at https://www.nativeweb.org/pages/legal/indig-romanus-pontifex.html.

66   *Here [in Pennsylvania] is liberty of conscience, which is right and reasonable; here ought to be likewise liberty of the body.* Quoted in Katharine Gerbner, "'We Are Against the Traffik of Men-Body': The Germantown Protest of 1688 and the Origins of American Abolitionism," *Pennsylvania History: A Journal of Mid-Atlantic Studies* 74:2 (Spring 2007): 149–172, at 168.

70   *grasp everything shown to him with the greatest of ease.* Johann Michael von Loen, "Der königlich Preußische Hof in Berlin, 1718," in *Gesammelte kleine Schriften*, vol. 1 (Frankfurt and Leipzig: Philipp Heinrich Huttern, 1750), pt. 3, pp. 22–39, at 27: "Er fasset, er lernet alles was man ihm vorlegt, mit der größten Leichtigkeit."

70   *the deepest affection for him.* Letter from Wilhelmine to Frederick, 13 May 1732, in Frederick the Great and Wilhelmine of Bayreuth, *Friedrich der Große und Wilhelmine von Baireuth*, vol. 1, *Jugendbriefe (1728–1740)*, ed. Gustav Berthold Volz (Leipzig: Koehler, 1924), p. 93: "versicherte Dich meiner lebhaftesten Zärtlichkeit."

70   *Then my sister [Wilhelmine], . . . seeing that I never sought to occupy myself . . .* Catt, *Frederick the Great*, pp. 129–130.

71   *When my governor Marshal Finck and my valet were sleeping . . .* Ibid., p. 130 (translation adapted).

72   *Frédéric le philosophe.* Letter from Frederick to Wilhelmine, 26 January 1728, in Frederick the Great and Wilhelmine of Bayreuth, *Friedrich der Große und Wilhelmine von Baireuth*, p. 65.

72   *I want to know what's going on in that tiny head of yours. . . . But they are scamps!* Quoted in Reinhold Koser, *Geschichte Friedrichs des Großen*, vol. 1 (Darmstadt: Wissentschaftliche Buchgesellschaft, 1963), p. 7: "Ich möchte wohl wissen, was in diesem kleinem Kopf vorgeht. Ich weiss, dass er nicht so denkt wie ich, und dass es Leute gibt, die ihm andere Gesinnungen beibringen und ihn veranlassen, alles zu tadeln; das sind aber Schufte."

72–73   *effeminate fellow . . . do nothing but follow his own mind.* Letter from Frederick William I to Frederick, September 1728, in *Œuvres de Frédéric le Grand* (hereafter *ŒFG*), vol. 27.3, p. 11: "Zum Andern weiss er wohl, dass ich keinen *effeminirten Kerl* leiden kann, der keine menschliche Inclination hat, der sich schämt, *nicht reiten noch schiessen kann*, und dabei mal-propre an seinem Leibe, *seine Haare wie ein Narr sich frisiret* . . . und er *Alles dazu nichts Lust hat, als seinem eigenen Kopf folgen*" (quoted words in italics).

73   *Il hait son père souverainement.* Letter from Konrad Alexander von Rothenbourg to the Court of Versailles, Summer 1726, as quoted in Koser, *Geschichte Friedrichs des Grossen*, p. 17.

74   *very sensitive soul.* As quoted in Koser, *Geschichte Friedrichs des Großen*, p. 11: "sehr stillen Wesens, bedachtsam."

74   *cheering up . . . to drive away my melancholy.* As quoted in ibid., p. 10: "habe ich selbst der Aufheiterung vonnöten, um meine Melancholie zu zerstreuen."

74   *While the others smoke . . . I entertain myself by cracking nuts.* As quoted in ibid., p. 25: "Meine Unterhaltung in der Tabagie ist, Nüsse aufzuknacken."

75   *Gentlemen, I've had enough of this stuff!* As quoted in ibid., p. 36: "Meine Herren, ich habe genug von dem Zeug!"

77   *plotting desertion.* Carl Hinrichs, *Der Kronprinzenprozeß. Friedrich und Katte* (Hamburg: Hanseatische Verlagsanstalt, 1936), p. 106: "zur Desertion complot machen."

77   *no deed had been done or actual escape attempted.* As quoted in ibid., p. 123: "zu keiner Tat und wirklichen Flucht gekommen."

77   *informed in good time.* As quoted in ibid., p. 114: "bei Zeiten zu verstehen gegeben."

78   *cause him to do some serious thinking.* As quoted in ibid., p. 123: "zum ernstlichen und gründlichen Nachdenken zu bringen."

79   *neither pretty nor ugly.* Letter from Frederick to Wilhelmine, 6 March 1732, in *ŒFG*, vol. 27.1, p. 4: "ni belle ni laide."

79   *the price to be paid.* Letter from Frederick to Grumbkow, 4 September 1732, in *ŒFG*, vol. 16, p. 61: "on m'a proposé ce mariage nolens volens, et que la liberté en était le prix."

5. Education and Leisure (1732–1740)

Page

80   *Name this child.* In 1732, the rite probably would have followed the text of the 1662 version of the Book of Common Prayer. An online version, specifically of "The Ministration of Publick Baptism of Infants," is available at http://justus.anglican.org/resources/bcp /1662/Orig_manuscript/baptism.htm.

82   *kindly nature.* This is the characterization of Augustine Washington in Douglas Southall Freeman, *George Washington: A Biography*, 7 vols. (New York: Scribner, 1948–1957), vol. 1, p. 33.

82–83 *Whether [he] liked it or not . . . the price to be paid. . . . Violence is ever at odds with love, and love cannot be won by force.* Letter from Frederick to Grumbkow, 4 September 1732, in *ŒFG*, vol. 16, p. 61: "on m'a proposé ce mariage nolens volens, et que la liberté en était le prix. . . . Vous m'avouerez pourtant que la force est une voie bien oppose à l'amour, et que j'amais l'amour ne se laisse forcer."

83   *pretty . . . fine features and a handsome face.* Wilhelmine of Bayreuth, *Memoiren der Markgräfin Wilhelmine von Bayreuth*, vol. 2, ed. Annette Kolb (Leipzig: Insel Verlag, 1910), p. 32: "Sie ist hübsch, hat einen blühenden Teint und feine Züge, so daß ihr Gesicht schön zu nennen ist."

83   *Marriage will make me independent. . . . Long live freedom!* Letter from Frederick to Grumbkow, 4 September 1732, in *ŒFG*, vol. 16, p. 61: "Le mariage rend majeur, et dès que je le suis, je suis le souverain dans ma maison. . . . Vive la liberté!"

83   *the Brunswick comedy.* Letter from Frederick to Grumbkow, 25 January 1733, in *ŒFG*, vol. 16, p. 85: "Enfin je jouerai la comédie de Brunswic."

86   *I have just come from drilling . . . live like a rich man in Berlin.* Letter from Frederick to Grumbkow, 21 April 1733, in *ŒFG*, vol. 16, p. 98: "Je viens de l'exercise, j'exerce, et j'exercerai. Voilà

tout ce que je puis dire de plus nouveau . . . et j'aime mieux exercer ici depuis le crepuscule du jour jusqu'au crepuscule de la nuit que de vivre en homme riche à Berlin."

86   *with reading and music.* Letter from Frederick to Grumbkow, 23 October 1732, in *ŒFG*, vol. 16, p. 75: "Je me divertis à lire ou à la musique."

86   *God knows . . . that I am as secluded at present as one can possibly be.* Ibid.: "Dieu sait que je suis si retiré à présent que l'on peut être."

90   *even the shadow of Prince Eugene instilled . . . awe.* As quoted in Koser, *Geschichte Friedrichs des Großen*, p. 96. "Noch der Schatten des Prinzen Eugen . . . Ehrfurcht einflößte"; "alle diese berühmten Schlachten vor ihr Auge . . . seine Tapferkeit, seine Kriegserfahrung, und seine Sieghaftigkeit."

90   *miraculous fire.* Koser, *Geschichte Friedrichs des Großen*, p. 95: "Dasselbe wunderkräftige Feuer, das . . . Eugen . . . zum Helden schuf."

91   *God . . . rules everything in the world . . . as determined by his holy will.* Letter from Frederick to his sister Wilhelmine, 2 September 1734, in *ŒFG*, vol. 27.1, p. 21: "Le bon Dieu, qui dirige tout dans le monde, et qui est le premier principe des événements qui arrivent, en disposra selon sa sagesse et selon que sa sainte volonté l'aura résolu."

91   *It's a miracle of the rarest kind.* Letter from Frederick to his sister Wilhelmine, 10 January 1735, in *ŒFG*, vol. 27.1, p. 30: "C'est un miracle aussi extrordinaire qu'il y en a eu."

91   *He improves when he feels like it . . . beastly nature.* Letter from Frederick to his sister Wilhelmine, June 1735, in *ŒFG*, vol. 27.1, pp. 30–31: "Il se porte bien dès qu'il en a l'envie, et se rend plus malade lorsqu'il le trouve à propos. J'y ai été trompé dans le commencement, mais à présent je m'aperçois du mystère. . . . Il a la nature d'un Turc."

92   *pleasure trip.* Letter from Frederick William I to Frederick, 6 September 1735, in *ŒFG*, vol. 27.3, p. 107: "eine Lustreise nach Preussen zu thun."

92   *taking a trip to Prussia . . . only slightly more alluring than going to Siberia, but not by much.* Letter from Frederick to his sister Wilhelmine, 8 September 1735, in *ŒFG*, vol. 27.1, p. 39: "Faire un voyage en Prusse; c'est un peu plus honnête qu'en Sibérie, mais pas de beaucoup."

93–94   *the vilest kind of man . . . in order to make me happy.* As quoted in Friedrich von Oppeln-Bronikowski and Gustav Berthold Volz, eds., *Gespräche Friedrichs des Großen* (Berlin: Reimer Hobbing, 1919), p. 21: "Ich müßte der niedrigste Mensch auf Erden sein, wenn ich sie nicht aufrichtig schätzen würde. Denn sie hat ein sanftes Gemüt und ist so gelehrig, wie sich nur denken läßt. Sie ist darüber hinaus bis zum äußersten gefällig, so daß sie mir alles an den Augen abliest, womit sie mir eine Freude zu machen glaubt."

94   *If I work as hard as those bucks that are in rut at the moment . . . nephews or great-nephews . . . successor.* As quoted in Gustav Mendelssohn-Bartoldy, ed., *Der König. Friedrich der Große in seinen Briefen und Erlassen* (Ebenhausen: Langewiesche-Brandt, 1932), p. 72: "Wenn ich dieselbe Bestimmung habe wie die Hirsche, die gegenwärtig in der Brunst sind, dann könnte jetzt in neun Monaten geschehen, was Sie mir wünschen. Ich weiß nicht, ob es ein Glück oder ein Unglück für unsere Neffen und Großneffen sein würde; die Königreiche finden immer Nachfolger."

95   *I've never known days as happy as these.* Letter from Frederick to Ulrich Friedrich von Suhm, 16 November 1736, in *ŒFG*, vol. 16, p. 326: "Je n'ai jamais passé de jours aussi heureux que ceux que j'ai été ici."

95   *regarded the destruction with a cheerful, serene expression . . . in that moment he retired to his room.* Jakob Friedrich von Bielfeld, as quoted in Gerhard Büchner and Georg Dittrich,

Rheinsberg und Sanssouci. Geselligkeit und Freundschaft (Leipzig: Georg Kummer, 1928), p. 35: "Mitten unter diesem Greuel der Verwüstung war der Prinz der einzige, der auf die Trümmer mit heiterem, ruhigen Auge herabsah; als sich aber der sichtbare Jubel zu einem vollständigen Tumult umgestaltete, zog er sich in sein Zimmer zurück. Die Prinzessin verschwand in demselben Augenblick."

96   *enlighten me.* Letter from Frederick to Ulrich Friedrich von Suhm, 1 January 1737, in *ŒFG*, vol. 16, p. 338: "la philosophie m'éclaire."

97   *treasures of the mind . . . an infinity of other knowledge. Letters of Voltaire and Frederick the Great* (hereafter *Letters*), pp. 19–20.

97–98   *loving the truth . . . bring back the golden age to his dominions. Letters*, p. 24.

98   *genius . . . Monsieur Locke . . . more solid and more methodical . . . that the origin of all our ideas is from the senses.* Voltaire, "Locke," in *Philosophical Letters*, trans. William F. Fleming, vol. 19 in *The Works of Voltaire: A Contemporary Version*, 21 vols. (New York: E. R. DuMont, 1901), Online Library of Liberty, https://oll.libertyfund.org/titles/fleming-the-works-of-voltaire-vol-xix-philosophical-letters.

99   *wise and wholesome laws . . . body of citizens without any distinctions.* Voltaire, "The Religion of the Quakers," in *Philosophical Letters*.

99   *William Penn might . . . boast of having brought down upon earth the Golden Age, which in all probability, never had any real existence but in his dominions.* Ibid.

100   *addicted to poetry.* Frederick the Great, "Epistle XX," 117.

100–   *watch-maker . . . the hand which marks the hours . . . He necessarily directs and governs men.*
101   *Letters*, pp. 98, 100.

101   *The famous Pesne is working on the ceiling painting . . . to make space for the dawn.* As quoted in Büchner and Dittrich, *Rheinberg und Sanssouci*, p. 35: "Der berühmte Pesne arbeitet am Plafond-Gemälde, das den Aufgang der Sonne vorstellt. Auf der einen Seite sieht man die Nacht, in dichte Schleier gehüllt, von ihren traurigen Vögeln . . . begleitet. Sie scheint sich zu entfernen, um der Morgenröte Platz zu machen."

101   *venturing to take the side of humanity.* In the second paragraph of Voltaire's twenty-fifth letter, on the thought of Blaise Pascal ("Sur les pensées de M. Pascal"), which was added later to the collection of twenty-four epistles that originally composed the *Philosophical Letters*: "J'ose prendre le parti de l'humanité." https://www.atramenta.net/lire/lettres-philosophiques/820/25#oeuvre_page.

101   *I venture to defend humanity against this monster, whose aim is to destroy it.* Frederick the Great, *Anti-Machiavel, or a Study of Machiavelli's "The Prince"* (hereafter *Anti-Machiavel*), p. 13 (foreword).

102   *all the arts and all the sciences. Anti-Machiavel*, p. 63 (chap. 21).

102   *competition among an infinity of wills.* Frederick the Great, *L'Antimachiavel*, in *Philosophische Schriften—Œuvres philosophiques*, vol. 6, ed. Anne Baillot and Brunhilde Wehinger (Berlin: Akademie Verlag, 2007), 45–260, at p. 54 (chap. 2): "Dans une république, il faut le concours d'une infinité de volontés." This passage is absent from the edition of the *Anti-Machiavel* that appears in *FGPW*.

102   *the ruler of a country . . . through the election of the people who hold power. Anti-Machiavel*, pp. 15–16 (chap. 2).

102   *through succession . . . hereditary kingdoms are the easiest to govern.* Ibid., pp. 15–16 (chaps. 1–2).

102   *first servant . . . all their separate interests into a single common interest.* Ibid., p. 15 (chap. 1).

102   *if his will and his power truly manifested his benevolence.* Frederick the Great, *L'Antimachiavel,* p. 108 (chap. 9): "puisque sa volonté et sa puissance rendent sa bonté efficace." This passage is absent from the edition of the *Anti-Machiavel* that appears in *FGPW.*

102   *see with their own eyes . . . all affairs touching on government policy. Anti-Machiavel,* p. 65 (chap. 22). The phrases "all decrees, all laws, all edicts" and "all affairs touching on government" are absent from the edition of the *Anti-Machiavel* that appears in *FGPW.* They are included in Frederick the Great, *L'Antimachiavel,* p. 214: "toutes les ordonnances, toutes les lois, tous les édits émanent d'eux, et ils remplissent . . . en gros tout ce qui peut avoir relation avec la politique."

103   *to be fearful of his people. Anti-Machiavel,* p. 50 (chap. 17).

103   *the founder of a sect . . . many sects . . . fanaticism.* Ibid., p. 24 (ch. 6).

104   *Containing the freshest Advices, Foreign and Domestick.* An example is available on the Colonial Williamsburg website: *Virginia Gazette,* January 18–25, 1739, https://research .colonialwilliamsburg.org/DigitalLibrary/va-gazettes/VGSinglePage.cfm?issueIDNo =40.P.05.

105   *for our doctors are commonly so exorbitant in their fees . . . cheapest and easiest ways of getting well again. Every Man His Own Doctor: or, The Poor Planter's Physician* (Williamsburg, VA: William Parks, 1734), pp. 4, 6, Evans Early American Imprint Collection, University of Michigan, https://quod.lib.umich.edu/e/evans/N03178.0001.001/.

106   *my inclinations are strongly bent to arms.* Letter from George Washington to William Fitzhugh, 15 November 1754, in *PGW,* Colonial Series, vol. 1, pp. 225–227, Founders Online, National Archives, https://founders.archives.gov/documents/Washington/02-01 -02-0114.

6. Glory and Ordeal (1740–1754)

Page

107   *Goodbye, Berlin. I am going to Potsdam to die.* Koser, *Geschichte Friedrichs des Großen,* p. 179: "Leb wohl Berlin, in Potsdam will ich sterben."

107   *beloved hounds . . . I am done hunting in this world, and my oldest son is no lover of hunting, nor will he ever become one.* Ibid., p. 179: "schönen Parforcehunde . . . weil ich in dieser Welt ausgejagt habe und mein ältester Sohn doch kein Liebhaber der Jagd ist noch jemals werden wird."

107   *what I want you to do with my body when the Almighty takes me to himself in the great beyond. Friedrich der Grosse. Ausstellung des Geheimen Staatsarchivs Preußischer Kulturbesitz anlässlich des 200. Todestages König Friedrichs II. von Preußen* (hereafter *Ausstellung*), p. 56: "Wie ich will, daß Ihr es mit meinem Leibe halten sollet, wenn der Allerhöchste mich aus dieser zeitlichen Welt wird zu sich nehmen."

108   *He promised that he will maintain the army, and I am sure he will keep his word. I know now that he loves the troops.* Koser, *Geschichte Friedrichs des Großen,* p. 179: "Er hat mir versprochen, dass er die Armee beibehalten wird, und ich bin sicher, dass er mir sein Wort halten wird. Ich weiß, dass er die Truppen liebt."

108   *whirlwind. Letters*, p. 135.

108   *singular thought . . . serve my fellow citizens.* Letter from Frederick to Voltaire, 23 March 1740, in *ŒFG*, vol. 22, pp. 404–405: "Ce qui me console est l'unique pensée de servir mes concitoyens."

108   *to make all of our subjects happy . . . to make no distinction.* Royal decree, 1 June 1740, printed in *Berlinische Privilegirte Zeitung*, no. 77 (1740), in *Ausstellung*, p. 62: "Unsere gröste Sorge wird dahin gerichtet seyn, das Wohl des Lands zu befördern, und einen jeden unserer Unterthanen glücklich zu machen . . . keinen Unterschied setzen."

109   *All religions must be tolerated . . . everyone should find their own bliss.* Comment in Frederick's hand in the margin of a report on Catholic proselytism, 22 June 1740, in *Ausstellung*, p. 64: "Die Religionen müssen alle Tolleriret werden . . . den hier mus ein jeder nach Seiner Faßon Selich werden."

109   *all religions are equal and good as long as those who profess them are honest people . . . Turks.* Frederick's opinion on a Catholic man's application for citizenship in Frankfurt an der Oder, 15 June 1740, in *Ausstellung*, p. 64: "Alle Religionen Seindt gleich und Guht, wan nuhr die leüte, so sie profesiren Erliche leüte seindt, und wen Türken und Heiden Kähmen und Wollten das Landt Pöpliren, so wollen wier sie Mosqueen und Kirchen bauen."

109   *that gazettes, if they are to be interesting, must not be censored.* Letter from Minister Podewils to Minister Thulemeier, 5 June 1740, in *Ausstellung*, p. 63: "daß Gazetten wenn sie intereßant seyn sollten nicht geniret werden müsten."

109   *My fortune has changed, dear friend. I await you impatiently. Do not make me wait too long.* Letter from Frederick to Duhan de Jandun, 3 June 1740, in *ŒFG*, vol. 17, p. 315: "Mon sort a changé, mon cher. Je vous attends avec impatience; ne me faites pas languir."

111   *seen this Voltaire whom I had been so eager to meet . . . Madame du Châtelet is lucky to have him.* Letter from Frederick to Jordan, 24 September 1740, in *ŒFG*, vol. 17, pp. 76–77: "J'ai vu ce Voltaire, que j'étais si curieux de connaître; . . . Son esprit travaille son cesse; chaque goutte d'encre est un trait d'esprit partant de sa plume . . . et je n'ai pu que l'admirer et me taire. La du Châtelet et bien heureuse de l'avoir."

111   *one of the most amiable men in the world . . . a sovereign with an army of a hundred thousand men.* Letter from Voltaire to Cideville, 18 October 1740, in Voltaire, *Œuvres complètes de Voltaire*, vol. 35, *Correspondance 3 (1738–1740)* (Paris: Garnier, 1880), p. 534 (letter 1367), Wikisource, https://fr.wikisource.org/wiki/Correspondance_de_Voltaire/1740/Lettre_1367: "C'est là que je vis un des plus aimables hommes du monde, un homme qui serait le charme de la société, qu'on rechercherait partout, s'il n'était pas roi; un philosophe sans austérité, rempli de douceur, de complaisance, d'agréments, ne se souvenant plus qu'il est roi dès qu'il est avec ses amis, et l'oubliant si parfaitement qu'il me le faisait presque oublier aussi, et qu'il me fallait un effort de mémoire pour me souvenir que je voyais assis sur le pied de mon lit un souverain qui avait une armée de cent mille hommes."

111   *The Emperor is dead. His death alters all my pacific ideas. Letters*, pp. 142–143.

111   *it will be rather a matter of cannon-powder, soldiers, and trenches than of actresses, of balls and stages. Letters*, p. 143.

111   *plate of mushrooms changed the destiny of Europe.* Voltaire, *Memoirs of the Life of Monsieur de Voltaire*, trans. Andrew Brown (London: Hesperus, 2007), p. 47.

112   *If the Emperor dies in the next few days, what upheavals the world will know! Everyone would want a portion of his realm, and we would see as many factions arise as sovereigns.* Letter from Frederick to Grumbkow, 24 March 1737, in Frederick the Great, *Briefe Friedrichs des Großen*, vol. 2, ed. Max Hein (Berlin: Reimar Hobbing, 1914), p. 97: "Stürbe der Kaiser an einem der vier nächsten Tage, welche Umwälzungen würde die Welt dann nicht erleben! Jeder möchte an seinem Erbe teilhaben, und man sähe ebensoviel Parteien wie Herrscher."

112–   *there are precautionary wars, which princes are wise to undertake . . . rather than waiting until*
113   *matters become desperate. Anti-Machiavel*, p. 79 (chap. 26).

113   *the nature of the government seems to demand that all regiments be directed by me alone.* Letter from Frederick to Leopold I of Anhalt-Dessau, 11 December 1740, in Frederick the Great, *Politische Correspondenz Friedrichs des Großen* (hereafter *Correspondenz*), vol. 1, p. 136: "inmassen es die Natur und Art der Regierung zu erfordern scheinet, dass alle Regimenter Mir allein angewiesen sind und bleiben."

114   *a great folly . . . a folly too difficult to banish when once we dote on it. Letters*, p. 146.

114   *love[d] . . . war . . . on account of the glory.* Letter from Frederick to Jordan, 24 February 1741, in *ŒFG*, vol. 17, p. 97: "J'aime la guerre pour la gloire."

115   *beautiful and peaceful beech trees.* Letter from Frederick to Jordan, May 1740, in *ŒFG*, vol. 17, p. 237: "Ces beaux et paisibles hêtres de Remusberg."

116   *to lose everything and have the Prussian name buried with me.* Letter from Frederick to Podewils, 27 April 1745, in *Correspondenz*, vol. 4, p. 134: "J'ai passé le Rubicon, et ou je veux soutenir ma puissance ou je veux que tout périsse et que jusqu'au nom prussien soit enseveli avec moi."

117   *Who would have thought . . . that providence would choose a poet to upset the political order of Europe and turn the calculations of its kings on their head?* Letter from Frederick to Jordan, May 1742, in *ŒFG*, vol. 17, p. 237: "Qui aurait dit que la Providence eût choisi un poëte pour bouleverser le système de l'Europe et changer en entier les combinaisons politiques des rois qui y gouvernent?"

117–   *Any man who makes up his mind to pull out a decayed tooth will give battle when he wishes*
118   *to end a war . . . At such a time, to shed blood is to spare it. Letters*, p. 163.

119   *as big as they want or are able to make it.* Frederick's "Potsdamer Patent" on building a Roman Catholic church in Berlin, 22 November 1746, in *Ausstellung*, p. 120: "So groß, als sie solche immer haben wollen oder können, mit einem oder mehreren Thürmen, groß und kleinen Glocken."

120   *You are my sole heir.* Letter from Frederick to his brother Augustus William, 9 April 1741, in *Friedrich der Große*, ed. Otto Bardong (Darmstadt: Wissenschaftliche Buchgesellschaft, 1982), p. 96: "Du bist mein alleiniger Erbe."

121   *ignorant and stupid, and does not know what is at stake in the decisions it makes.* Letter to General Bredow, "On Reputation," in Frederick the Great, *Werke des Philosophen von Sanssouci—Œuvres du Philosophe de Sans-Souci*, ed. Jürgen Overhoff and Vanessa de Senarclens, Potsdamer Ausgabe, vol. 7 (Berlin: Akademie Verlag, 2012), p. 254: "Que les troisquarts du monde ignorant et stupide / Ne sait pas dans ses choix quell motif le decide."

121   *who began the quarrel . . . who won, with weapon in hand, a province and six battles . . . your Majesty writes beautiful verses, but you laugh at the world. Letters*, p. 188.

124   *common sailor . . . any considerable preferment . . . liberty of the subject . . . like a Negro, or rather, like a dog.* Letter from Joseph Ball to Mary Washington, 19 May 1747, in Marion Harland, *The Story of Mary Washington* (New York: Houghton, Mifflin & Co., 1893), pp. 79–80.

125   *Nothing remarkable happened.* George Washington, "A Journal of My Journey over the Mountains" (hereafter "Journey"), March 1747/1748, e.g., entries of March 12 and March 18.

125– *We had some liquor with us of which we gave them part, it elevating their spirits . . . drumming*
126   *all the while the others is* [sic] *dancing.* "Journey," March 1747/1748, entry of March 23.

126   *men, women, and children . . . they would never speak English but when spoken to they speak all Dutch . . . as ignorant a set of people as the Indians.* "Journey," April 1748, entry of April 4.

126   *richness of the land . . . sugar trees . . . wild turkeys.* "Journey," March 1747/1748, entries of March 13 ("richness of the land," "sugar trees") and March 29 ("wild turkeys").

126   *every[one] was his own cook . . . tent.* "Journey," April 1748, entry of April 8.

126   *the open air . . . the worst road that ever was trod by man or beast.* "Journey," March 1747/1748, entries of March 15 ("open air") and March 21 ("worst road").

127   *her charms . . . her amiable beauties.* Letter from George Washington to Sarah Cary Fairfax, 12 September 1758, in *PGW*, Colonial Series, vol. 6, pp. 10–13, Founders Online, National Archives, https://founders.archives.gov/documents/Washington/02-06-02-0013.

128   *down to or below the bent of the knee.* George Washington, *Writings*, ed. John Rhodehamel (New York: Library of America, 1997), p. 17.

128   *burying that chaste and troublesome passion in the grave of oblivion or eternal forgetfulness.* Letter from George Washington to Robin, 1749–1750, in *PGW*, Colonial Series, vol. 1, pp. 40–41, Founders Online, National Archives, https://founders.archives.gov/documents/Washington/02-01-02-0001-0007.

129   *prospect . . . by land . . . and by sea . . . pleasant.* George Washington, "Voyage to Barbados," 1751–1752, in *The Diaries of George Washington* (hereafter *DGW*), vol. 1, pp. 38–117, at 77, Founders Online, National Archives, https://founders.archives.gov/documents/Washington/01-01-02-0002-0005.

130   *strongly attacked.* Washington, "Voyage to Barbados," p. 82.

130   *hurry home to my grave.* Letter from Lawrence Washington to a friend, 6 April 1752, in *The Writings of George Washington*, vol. 2 (Boston: Russel, 1834), p. 423.

132   *the cold was so extreme severe that Mr. Gist got all his fingers and some of his toes froze* [sic] *. . . French Indians . . . not fifteen steps . . . into custody.* George Washington, "Journey to the French Commandant: Narrative," in *DGW*, vol. 1, pp. 130–161, Founders Online, National Archives, https://founders.archives.gov/documents/Washington/01-01-02-0003-0002.

133   *the rights of the king* [of France] *. . . to the lands situated along the Ohio are incontestable.* Letter from Legardeur de Saint-Pierre to Dinwiddie, 15 December 1753, in *Wilderness Chronicles of Northwestern Pennsylvania*, ed. Sylvester K. Stevens and Donald H. Kent (Harrisburg: Pennsylvania Historical and Museum Commission, 1941), p. 78.

7. Might and Right (1754–1762)

Page

136   *Fire!* DGW, vol. 1, p. 195 (entry of May 27, 1754).

136   *Thou art not yet dead, my father!... several hatchet blows.* Fred Anderson, *Crucible of War: The Seven Years' War and the Fate of Empire in British North America, 1754–1766* (New York: Alfred A. Knopf, 2000), p. 67.

137   *the extreme difficulty... governments and assemblies to agree in any speedy and effectual measures for our common defense and security... the destruction of the British interest, trade, and plantations in America.* Letter from Benjamin Franklin to Richard Partridge, 8 May 1754, in *PBF*, vol. 5, pp. 272–275, Founders Online, National Archives, https://founders.archives.gov/documents/Franklin/01-05-02-0085.

138   *president general... grand council to be chosen by the representatives of the people of the several colonies... remain in their present state.* Benjamin Franklin, "The Albany Plan of Union, 1754," in *PBF*, vol. 5, pp. 374–392, Founders Online, National Archives, https://founders.archives.gov/documents/Franklin/01-05-02-0104.

138   *the colonies so united would have been... would have been avoided.* Franklin, *Autobiography*, p. 1431.

139   *naked... without credit even for a hat.* Letter from George Washington to Robert Dinwiddie, 20 August 1754, in *PGW*, Colonial Series, vol. 1, pp. 189–192, Founders Online, National Archives, https://founders.archives.gov/documents/Washington/02-01-02-0089.

140   *impossible... savages... make an impression.* Franklin, *Autobiography*, p. 1437.

141   *the shocking scenes... the dead—the dying—the groans—lamentation—and cries... enough to pierce a heart of adamant.* George Washington, "Remarks, 1787–1788," in *PGW*, Confederation Series, vol. 5, pp. 515–526, Founders Online, National Archives, https://founders.archives.gov/documents/Washington/04-05-02-0463-0002.

142   *trembling in excitement... ecstasy of their senses... breathless and worn out... lovers' happy destiny.* Trans. Giles MacDonogh, in his blog post "Frederick the Great's Erotic Poetry," September 20, 2011, http://www.macdonogh.co.uk/blog_archive.htm. This poem was discovered by Vanessa de Senarclens in 2011 and first published in Frederick the Great, *An meinen Geist. Friedrich der Große in seiner Dichtung. Eine Anthologie*, ed. Jürgen Overhoff and Vanessa de Senarclens (Paderborn: Schöningh, 2011), pp. 80–82.

142–   *Nowhere in the world did people ever speak more freely of all the superstitions of men... and*
143   *never were these treated with more mockery and contempt... freedom of conscience and prick.* Voltaire, *Memoirs*, pp. 30–31 with note 34.

143   *to prevent the abuse of power, it is necessary that by the very disposition of things power should be a check to power.* Charles-Louis de Secondat, baron de Montesquieu, *The Spirit of the Laws*, trans. Thomas Nugent, bk. 11, chap. 4, https://en.wikisource.org/wiki/The_Spirit _of_Laws_(1758)/Volume_I.

143   *the king's power finds itself ceaselessly in conflict with that of Parliament... changes its laws endlessly, by Act of Parliament, as circumstances and events require.* Frederick the Great, *Dissertation on the Reasons for Establishing or Repealing Laws*, in *FGPW*, pp. 87–106, at 96.

144   *a frightful tyranny over his subjects.* Montesquieu, *Mes Voyages*, p. 449: "Le roy de Prusse exerce sur ses sujets une tirannie effroyable."

144 *the greatest madman who ever lived.* Letter from Montesquieu to his close friend Jean Barbot, 2 February 1742, in Charles-Louis de Secondat, baron de Montesquieu, *Correspondance de Montesquieu*, 2 vols., ed. François Gebelin and André Morize (Bordeaux: Imprimeries Gounouilhou, 1914), vol. 1, p. 365, Wikisource, https://fr.wikisource.org/w/index.php?title=Page:Montesquieu_-_Correspondance,_t._1,_éd._Gébelin,_1914.djvu/407&action=edit&redlink=1: "Nous sommes à présent, pour celles de Bohême, entre les mains du plus grand fou qui fût jamais."

144 *one squeezes the orange and then one throws away the peel . . . Will he never get tired of sending me his dirty linen to wash!* Voltaire, *Correspondence*, vol. 20, *August 1751–July 1752*, ed. Theodore Besterman (Geneva: Institut et Musée Voltaire, 1956), pp. 43, 390–391.

144 *your conduct deserves chains. Letters*, p. 233.

145 *angry . . . enchanted . . . live with you or without you. Letters*, p. 247.

146 *must be thwarted.* Address of Wenzel Anton von Kaunitz-Rietberg to Emperor Francis and Empress Maria Theresa, 27 June 1755, in "Denkschriften des Fürsten Wenzel Kaunitz-Rittberg," ed. Adolf Beer, *Archiv für Österreichische Geschichte* 48, no. 1 (1872): 1–162, at 21: "Die unabänderliche Staats-Maxime des Durchlauchtigsten Ertzhauses, dass bey allen Gelegenheiten und in allen Zeiten . . . fürzudenken seye . . . wie . . . die Gefahr vor diesem Feind verminderet, und derselbe, wann es möglich wäre, übern Hauffen geworffen werden könne."

146 *I have received the answer and it is worthless.* Letter from Frederick to Duke Ferdinand of Brunswick, 26 August 1756, in *Ausstellung*, p. 164: "Die Antwort ist gekommen und ist nichts wert."

146 *Since I now lack all security, both at present and in the future, arms are the only path left to me to foil the plans of my enemies.* Ibid., p. 164: "Da ich keine Sicherheit mehr habe, weder für die Gegenwart noch für die Zukunt, so bleibt mir nur der Weg der Waffen übrig, um die Anschläge meiner Feinde zu vereiteln."

148 *the war . . . began in America.* Letter from Frederick to his sister Wilhelmine, 21 September 1755, in *ŒFG*, vol. 27.1, p. 311: "La guerre . . . a commencé en Amérique."

148 *We have advice here, and it seems well attested . . . immediately entered Prague sword and hand . . . e'er you see this.* Letter from George Mercer to George Washington, 17 August 1757, in *PGW*, Colonial Series, vol. 4, pp. 370–375, Founders Online, National Archives, https://founders.archives.gov/documents/Washington/02-04-02-0242.

148 *powerful dispensations of Providence.* Letter from George Washington to John Augustine Washington, 18 July 1755, in *PGW*, Colonial Series, vol. 1, p. 343, Founders Online, National Archives, https://founders.archives.gov/documents/Washington/02-01-02-0169.

149 *Discipline . . . is the soul of an army. It makes small numbers formidable, procures success for the weak, and esteem to all.* George Washington, instructions to company captains, 29 July 1757, in *PGW*, Colonial Series, vol. 4, pp. 341–346, Founders Online, National Archives, https://founders.archives.gov/documents/Washington/02-04-02-0223.

150 *the coat blue, faced and cuffed with scarlet, and trimmed with silver.* George Washington, orders of 6 October 1755, in *PGW*, Colonial Series, vol. 2, pp. 75–77, Founders Online, National Archives, https://founders.archives.gov/documents/Washington/02-02-02-0070.

150 *vast extent of land we have lost since this time twelve-month.* Letter from George Washington to John Robinson, 9 November 1756, in *PGW*, Colonial Series, vol. 4, pp. 11–18,

Founders Online, National Archives, https://founders.archives.gov/documents /Washington/02-04-02-0002.

151   *As you seem so earnest to go . . . I now give you leave.* Letter from Robert Dinwiddie to George Washington, 2 February 1757, in *PGW*, Colonial Series, vol. 4, p. 107, Founders Online, National Archives, https://founders.archives.gov/documents/Washington/02 -04-02-0056.

151   *nipping in the bud our rising hopes . . . being Americans should deprive us of the benefits of British subjects, nor lessen our claim to that preferment.* Letter from George Washington to Robert Dinwiddie, 10 March 1757, in *PGW*, Colonial Series, vol. 4, pp. 112–115, Founders Online, National Archives, https://founders.archives.gov/documents/Washington/02 -04-02-0062.

152   *quitting my command . . . I now see no prospect of preferment in a military life.* Letter from George Washington to John Stanwix, 4 March 1758, in *PGW*, Colonial Series, vol. 5, pp. 100–103, Founders Online, National Archives, https://founders.archives.gov /documents/Washington/02-05-02-0073.

153   *force of her amiable beauties . . . the animating prospect of possessing Mrs. Custis . . . the recollection of a thousand tender passages . . . destiny . . . the strongest efforts of human nature . . . resist . . . to conceal.* Letter from George Washington to Sarah Cary Fairfax, 12 September 1758, in *PGW*, Colonial Series, vol. 6, pp. 10–13, Founders Online, National Archives, https://founders.archives.gov/documents/Washington/02-06-02-0013.

155   *with grief . . . must strive to forget.* Letter from George Washington to the officers of the Virginia Regiment, 10 January 1759, in *PGW*, Colonial Series, vol. 6, pp. 186–187, Founders Online, National Archives, https://founders.archives.gov/documents/Washington/02 -06-02-0152.

156   *The scale of fortune in America is turned greatly in our favor.* Letter from George Washington to Richard Washington, 20 September 1759, in *PGW*, Colonial Series, vol. 6, pp. 358– 359, Founders Online, National Archives, https://founders.archives.gov/documents /Washington/02-06-02-0190.

156   *a firm resolution to aid the victorious king of Prussia . . . surpassed all expectations.* Letter from George William Fairfax to George Washington, 6 December 1757, in *PGW*, Colonial Series, vol. 5, pp. 68–70, Founders Online, National Archives, https://founders .archives.gov/documents/Washington/02-05-02-0042.

156   *America was conquered in Germany.* See Simms, "Pitt and Hanover," p. 31.

157   *We are in pain here for the king of Prussia.* Letter from George Washington to Richard Washington, 10 August 1760, in *PGW*, Colonial Series, vol. 6, pp. 452–454, Founders Online, National Archives, https://founders.archives.gov/documents/Washington/02 -06-02-0260.

158   *All my brother ever wanted was to give battle. That was his entire art of war.* As reported in Herfried Münkler, "Krieg und Frieden bei Clausewitz, Engels und Carl Schmitt: Dialektik des Militarismus oder Hegung des Krieges," *Leviathan* 10, no. 1 (1982): 16–40, at 20: "Mein Bruder wollte immer bataillieren, das war seine ganze Kriegskunst."

160   *I proclaim to you the miracle of the House of Brandenburg . . . just when the enemy had crossed the Oder and could have waged a second battle and ended the war . . . marched away.* Letter from Frederick to his brother Henry, 1 September 1759, in Bardong, *Friedrich der Große,*

p. 405: "Ich verkündige Ihnen das Mirakel des Hauses Brandenburg. In der Zeit, als der Feind die Oder überschritten hatte und eine zweite Schlacht hätte wagen und den Krieg beenden können, ist er . . . abmarschiert."

160   *old good humor . . . flare up from time to time . . . without cheer, without fire, without imagination.* Letter from Federick to d'Argens, 28 May 1759, in *ŒFG*, vol. 19, pp. 82–83: "Quelques lueurs de mon ancienne bonne humeur reviennent de temps en temps; mais ce sont des étincelles qui s'évanouissent, faute d'un brasier qui les nourrisse . . . si vous me voyiez, vous ne reconnaîtriez plus les traces de ce que je fus autrefois. Vous verriez un vieillard grisonnant, privé de la moitié de ses dents, sans gaieté, sans feu, sans imagination."

160–   *Fritzian . . . rejoiced undisturbed in the Prussian victories, which were commonly announced*
161   *with great glee . . . the personal character of the great king.* Goethe, *Autobiography* p. 33.

161   *Heroine, him you cannot conquer . . . Please make peace apace!* Johann Wilhelm Ludwig Gleim, *Preussische Kriegslieder in den Feldzügen 1756 und 1757: Mit Melodien* (Berlin: Voß, 1758), p. 133, MDZ, https://www.digitale-sammlungen.de/de/view/bsb11251624?page =96,97: "Heldin, den bezwingst Du nicht! / Gott kann Wunder thun! / Schenk ihm Freundesangesicht, / Bitte Frieden nun!"

161   *copied the songs of triumph, and almost more willingly the lampoons directed against the other party, poor as the rhymes might be . . . enthusiasm of his worshippers . . . hatred of his enemies . . . image of Frederick.* Goethe, *Autobiography*, p. 55.

161   *Their large number has become their undoing . . . masters of time . . . missed many good opportunities.* Frederick the Great, "Réflexions sur la tactique et sur quelques parties de la guerre," 27 December 1758, in *ŒFG*, vol. 28, p. 183: "Mais leur puissance même leur a été nuisible; ils ont mis leur confiance les uns dans les autres, le général de l'Empire dans l'Autrichien, celui-là dans le Russe. . . . S'endormant aux flatteuses idées de leurs espérances et dans la sécurité de leurs succès futurs, ils ont regardé le temps comme à eux. Combien de moments favorables ont-ils laissés échapper!"

8. Autonomy and Independence (1763–1770)

Page

164   *madness of humanity . . . and all that just to see the rulers back in the old* status quo. Ernst Ahasverus Heinrich von Lehndorff, *Dreißig Jahre am Hofe Friedrichs des Großen. Tagebücher,* ed. Karl Eduard Schmidt-Lötzen (Gotha: Perthes, 1907), p. 451 (16 February 1763): "Wenn mann nur aber bedenkt, welche unzähligen Opfer dieser Krieg gefordert hat, wieviel Provinzen verwüstet, wieviel Familien ruiniert worden sind, und das alles, um die Herrscher in dem status quo ante zu sehen, so möchte man über den Wahnwitz der Menschheit laut aufschreien."

165   *the worth, the dignity, and the stubbornness.* Goethe, *Autobiography*, p. 238.

165   *Madame has gotten fatter.* Lehndorff, *Dreißig Jahre am Hofe Friedrichs des Großen*, p. 457: "Madame sind korpulenter geworden."

168   *Royal Prussian edict on the illegal importation . . . all Saxon porcelain, both authentic and inauthentic.* "Königlich Preußisches Edict, wegen verbothener Einfuhre, Erhandlung und

Debitirung aller innenbenanten Chur-Sächsischen und denenselben incorporirten Landen verfertigten Manufactur- und Fabriquen-Waaren, besonders auch alles Sächsischen-sowohl ächten, als unächten Porcelains" (Berlin: Decker, 1765), https://resolver.staats bibliothek-berlin.de/SBB0003455200000000.

169   *the king of Prussia . . . intent on repairing the damages of the last war than projecting new ones. So that we may reasonably expect a tranquility of some duration.* Letter from Benjamin Franklin to the Pennsylvania Assembly Committee of Correspondence, 10 June 1766, in *PBF,* vol. 13, p. 299.

169   *adhered to uniformly in all lands belonging to His Royal Majesty, the King of Prussia.* "Königlich-Preußisches General-Land-Schul-Reglement, wie solches in allen Landen Seiner Königlichen Majestät von Preussen durchgehends zu beobachten" (Berlin and Magdeburg: Hechtel, 1763), https://opendata.uni-halle.de/handle/1981185920/56624.

170   *To learn.* As reported in Jürgen Overhoff, *Vom Glück, lernen zu dürfen. Für eine zweckfreie Bildung* (Stuttgart: Cotta, 2009), p. 197: "Lernen."

170   *evidence of the boundless arrogance of this people, which makes every effort to gain equality with the Christian population at every opportunity.* Isidor Kracauer, *Die Geschichte der Judengasse in Frankfurt am Main* (Frankfurt am Main: J. Kauffmann, 1906), p. 418: "Beweis von dem grenzenlosen Hochmut dieses Volkes, und wie sie alle Mühe anwenden, um sich bei allen Gelegenheiten den christlichen Einwohnern gleich zu setzen."

171   *A bad Catholic philosopher asks a bad Protestant philosopher to give protected status to a bad Jewish philosopher. There is not enough religion involved here for the request not to be considered rightful.* Letter from the Marquis d'Argens to Frederick, 19 July 1763, in *ŒFG,* vol. 19, p. 433: "Un philosophe mauvais catholique supplie un philosophe mauvais prot-estant de donner le privilége à un philosophe mauvais juif. Il y a dans tout ceci trop peu de religion pour que la raison ne soit pas du côté de la demande."

172   *Your Royal Majesty will most graciously deign to grant me and my descendants the highest protection.* Letter from Moses Mendelssohn to Frederick the Great, April 1763, in Moses Mendelssohn, *Gesammelte Schriften. Jubiläumsausgabe,* vol. 12.1, *Briefwechsel 2.1 (1763–1770),* ed. Alexander Altmann (Stuttgart-Bad Cannstatt: Frommann-Holzboog, 1976), p. 8: "Ew. Königl. Majestät wollen allergnädigst geruhen, mir mit meinen Nachkommen Dero allerhöchsten Schutz . . . angedeihen zu lassen."

172   *As you know, I have suffered a similar fate. The Academy elected me a member . . .* Letter from Moses Mendelssohn to Herz Homberg, 20 November 1784, in Moses Mendels-sohn, *Gesammelte Schriften. Jubiläumsausgabe,* vol. 13, *Briefwechsel 3 (1781–1785),* ed. Alexander Altmann (Stuttgart-Bad Cannstatt: Frommann-Holzboog, 1977), p. 8: "Ich habe, wie Sie wissen, ein ähnliches Schicksal gehabt. Die Academie hat mich zum Mit-gliede gewählt, des Königs Majestät aber die Wahl nicht bestätigt. Warum? Das weiß ich eben so wenig, als Sie jetzt wissen, warum Sie der Kaiser nicht zum Correpetitor haben will."

173   *nothing big and useful can ever happen . . . the prince does not himself rule . . . successors imprint this principle in their mind . . . immutable.* Richard Dietrich, ed., *Die Politischen Testamente der Hohenzollern* (Cologne: Böhlau, 1986), p. 666: "Daß in einem Staat niemals etwas Großes und Nützliches geschehen kann, in dem der Fürst nicht selbst regiert, weil nur in einem einzigen Kopf ein Plan aufgestellt werden kann und die Politik, Heerwesen

und Finanzen alle zum gleichen Ziel geführt werden können. Wenn der Fürst etwas will, fügt sich alles ... daß meine Nachfolger sich diesen Grundsatz einprägen und ihn immer befolgen, damit das Glück des Staates unabänderlich sei und sein Bestand den der ältesten Monarchien übertreffen möge."

174   *self-love ... self-interest ... the laws under whose protection he lives.* Frederick the Great, *Essay on Self-Love, Considered as a Principle of Morality,* in *FGPW,* pp. 139–148, at 140 ("in general, man is born"), 141 ("self-love ... self-interest"), 143 ("civil war"), 144 ("unjust man ... the social covenant ... the laws ... sins, by using faulty reasoning").

175   *of this great continent ... We live in a state of peaceful tranquility.* Letter from George Washington to Richard Washington, 20 October 1761, in *PGW,* Colonial Series, vol. 7, pp. 80–81, Founders Online, National Archives, https://founders.archives.gov/documents /Washington/02-07-02-0050.

175   *I am now, I believe, fixed at this seat with an agreeable consort for life and hope to find more happiness in retirement than I ever experienced amidst a wide and bustling world.* Letter from George Washington to Richard Washington, 20 September 1759, in *PGW,* Colonial Series, vol. 6, pp. 358–359, Founders Online, National Archives, https://founders.archives .gov/documents/Washington/02-06-02-0190.

175   *The house is most beautifully situated upon a very high hill on the banks of the Potomac, and commands a noble prospect of water, of cliffs, of woods and plantations.* Andrew Burnaby, *Burnaby's Travels Through North America,* reprinted from the 3rd ed. of 1798, ed. Rufus Rockwell Wilson (New York: A. Wessels Company, 1904), p. 67.

175   *natural parent ... a faux pas committed by [their guardian] ... when the intention may be strictly laudable.* Letter from George Washington to Jonathan Boucher, 13 May 1770, in *PGW,* Colonial Series, vol. 8, pp. 333–335, Founders Online, National Archives, https:// founders.archives.gov/documents/Washington/02-08-02-0226.

177   *gentler conflict.* Letter from George Washington to Sarah Cary Fairfax, 12 September 1758, in *PGW,* Colonial Series, vol. 6, pp. 10–13, Founders Online, National Archives, https:// founders.archives.gov/documents/Washington/02-06-02-0013.

178   *the sales [of tobacco] are pitifully low ... meet with such unprofitable returns.* Letter from George Washington to Robert Cary & Company, 20 September 1765, in *PGW,* Colonial Series, vol. 7, pp. 398–402, Founders Online, National Archives, https://founders .archives.gov/documents/Washington/02-07-02-0252-0001.

178   *irksome ... free mind.* Letter from George Washington to Robert Cary & Company, 10 August 1764, in *PGW,* Colonial Series, vol. 7, pp. 323–326, Founders Online, National Archives, https://founders.archives.gov/documents/Washington/02-07-02-0200-0001.

180   *very broken and unintelligible English ... They went off ... the least angry word or abuse.* Advertisement for Runaway Slaves, 11 August 1761, in *PGW,* Colonial Series, vol. 7, pp. 65–68, Founders Online, National Archives, https://founders.archives.gov /documents/Washington/02-07-02-0038.

181–
182   *The Stamp Act, imposed on the colonies by the Parliament of Great Britain ... be procured (for the most part) within ourselves.* Letter from George Washington to Robert Cary & Company, 20 September 1765, in *PGW,* Colonial Series, vol. 7, pp. 398–402, Founders Online, National Archives, https://founders.archives.gov/documents/Washington/02 -07-02-0252-0001.

182– *unconstitutional and unjust . . . could not be taxed in a parliament . . . were not represented . . .*

183 *No power, how great soever, can force men to change their opinions.* The Examination of Doctor Franklin Before the Committee of the Whole of the House of Commons, 13 February 1766, in *PBF*, vol. 13, pp. 129–161, at 137, 158.

183 *If you once admit . . . that Great Britain may lay duties upon her exportations to us, for the purpose of levying money on us only . . . lay those duties on the articles which she prohibits us to manufacture—and the tragedy of American liberty is finished.* John Dickinson, *Letters from a Farmer in Pennsylvania to the Inhabitants of the British Colonies* (Philadelphia: J. Almon, 1774), letter 2, p. 23.

184 *At a time when our lordly masters in Great Britain will be satisfied with nothing less than the deprivation of American freedom . . . be carried pretty generally into execution.* Letter from George Washington to George Mason, 5 April 1769, in *PGW*, Colonial Series, vol. 8, pp. 177–181, Founders Online, National Archives, https://founders.archives.gov /documents/Washington/02-08-02-0132.

184– *when the Court and Assembly . . . meet together in Williamsburg . . . uniform plan . . .*

185 *concerted . . . last resource . . . no man should scruple or hesitate a moment to use arms in defense of so valuable a blessing.* Ibid.

9. Freedom and Servitude (1770–1785)

Page

187 *a swarm of barbarians . . . spurred on by a demon.* Frederick the Great, "La guerre présente," in *Werke des Philosophen von Sanssouci*, p. 62: "La Sibérie enfante essaim de barbares, / Les froids glaçon du Nord, mille fiers assassins; / . . . Quel démon excita votre farouche audace?"

187 *a political tyrant.* Frederick the Great, "Les troubles du Nord," in *Werke des Philosophen von Sanssouci*, p. 68: "un tyran politique."

187 *a mild and good monarch.* Frederick the Great, "La guerre présente," in *Werke des Philosophen von Sanssouci*, p. 60: "un tendre et bon monarque."

189 *You take whichever part you please, but not at my expense!* As quoted in *Correspondenz*, vol. 31, p. 726: "Prenez votre part là où cela vous conviendra le mieux, mais que ce ne soit à mes dépens!"

189 *Gout has rotted my feet, not my brains.* *Correspondenz*, vol. 31, p. 730: "Je repartis que je n'avais la goutte que dans les pieds, et que ce serai tune proposition à me faire, si je l'avais dans la tête."

190 *We are finished . . . under the Prussian yoke.* Jerzy Lukowski, *The Partitions of Poland: 1772, 1793, 1795* (London: Routledge, 1999), p. 105.

190 *Nothing in the world causes me more pain than the loss of our good reputation.* Friedrich Walter, ed., *Maria Theresia. Briefe und Aktenstücke in Auswahl* (Darmstadt: Wissenschaftliche Buchgesellschaft, 1968), p. 306: "Nichts aus der Welt schmerzt mich mehr als der Verlust unseres guten Rufs."

191 *Edict by the King of Prussia . . . be unladen, searched, and charged with the said duties.* Benjamin Franklin, "An Edict by the King of Prussia," 22 September 1773, in *PBF*, vol. 20,

pp. 413–418, Founders Online, National Archives, https://founders.archives.gov/documents/Franklin/01-20-02-0223.

191   *with an abundance of laughing . . . the king of Prussia's* character. Letter from Benjamin Franklin to William Franklin, 6 October 1773, in *PBF*, vol. 20, pp. 436–439, Founders Online, National Archives, https://founders.archives.gov/documents/Franklin/01-20-02-0230.

192   *most magnificent . . . destruction of the tea . . . By restraining our trade?* John Adams, diary entry, 17 December 1773, in *Diary and Autobiography of John Adams*, vol. 2, *1771–1781*, ed. L. H. Butterfield, Adams Papers (Cambridge, MA: Harvard University Press, 1961), pp. 85–87, Founders Online, National Archives, https://founders.archives.gov/documents/Adams/01-02-02-0003-0008.

193   *vigorous measures . . . fix the shackles of slavery upon us.* Letter from George Washington to George William Fairfax, 10–15 June 1774, in *PGW*, Colonial Series, vol. 10, pp. 94–101, Founders Online, National Archives, https://founders.archives.gov/documents/Washington/02-10-02-0067.

193   *[reduce] us to the most abject state of slavery that ever was designed for mankind.* Letter from George Washington to Bryan Fairfax, 20 July 1774, in *PGW*, Colonial Series, vol. 10, pp. 128–131, Founders Online, National Archives, https://founders.archives.gov/documents/Washington/02-10-02-0081.

193   *as clear as the sun in its meridian brightness . . . the right and practice of taxation.* Letter from George Washington to Bryan Fairfax, 4 July 1774, in *PGW*, Colonial Series, vol. 10, pp. 109–110, Founders Online, National Archives, https://founders.archives.gov/documents/Washington/02-10-02-0075.

194   *burdensome . . . filled the breast of every American.* Letter from George Washington to Bryan Fairfax, 20 July 1774, in *PGW*, Colonial Series, vol. 10, pp. 128–131, Founders Online, National Archives, https://founders.archives.gov/documents/Washington/02-10-02-0081.

195   *the ministry would willingly change their ground, from a conviction that forcible measures will be inadequate to the end designed.* Letter from George Washington to John Connolly, 25 February 1775, in *PGW*, Colonial Series, vol. 10, pp. 273–274, Founders Online, National Archives, https://founders.archives.gov/documents/Washington/02-10-02-0207.

196   *private property . . . the Americans will fight for their liberties and property.* Letter from George Washington to George William Fairfax, 31 May 1775, in *PGW*, Colonial Series, vol. 10, pp. 367–368, Founders Online, National Archives, https://founders.archives.gov/documents/Washington/02-10-02-0281.

196   *General and Commander in Chief of the American Forces . . . the support of the glorious cause.* George Washington, Address to the Continental Congress, 16 June 1775, in *PGW*, Revolutionary War Series, vol. 1, pp. 1–3, Founders Online, National Archives, https://founders.archives.gov/documents/Washington/03-01-02-0001.

197   *unanimous voice of the colonies.* Letter from George Washington to Burwell Bassett, 19 June 1775, in *PGW*, Revolutionary War Series, vol. 1, pp. 12–14, Founders Online, National Archives, https://founders.archives.gov/documents/Washington/03-01-02-0006.

197   *When we assumed the soldier, we did not lay aside the citizen.* George Washington, Address to the New York Provincial Congress, 26 June 1775, in *PGW*, Revolutionary War Series,

vol. 1, pp. 41–42, Founders Online, National Archives, https://founders.archives.gov /documents/Washington/03-01-02-0019.

197   *rank ... uncorrupted choice of a brave and free people ... the purest source and original fountain of all power.* Letter from George Washington to Lieutenant General Thomas Gage, 19 August 1775, in *PGW*, Revolutionary War Series, vol. 1, pp. 326–328, Founders Online, National Archives, https://founders.archives.gov/documents/Washington/03-01-02 -0227.

198   *With the greatest of pleasure ... are now in actual possession thereof.* Letter from George Washington to John Hancock, 19 March 1776, in *PGW*, Revolutionary War Series, vol. 3, pp. 489–491, Founders Online, National Archives, https://founders.archives.gov /documents/Washington/03-03-02-0363.

198–   *commanded by the most experienced generals ... band of husbandmen.* Letter from John
199   Hancock to George Washington, 2 April 1776, in *PGW*, Revolutionary War Series, vol. 4, pp. 16–17, Founders Online, National Archives, https://founders.archives.gov /documents/Washington/03-04-02-0016.

199   *the remains of monarchical tyranny in the person of the king.* Thomas Paine, *Common Sense*, in *The Writings of Thomas Paine*, ed. Moncure Daniel Conway, vol. 1 (New York: G. P. Putnam's Sons, 1894), Online Library of Liberty, https://oll.libertyfund.org/pages/1776 -paine-common-sense-pamphlet.

199   *it is wholly owing to the constitution of the people ... as an open and determined declaration for independence.* Paine, *Common Sense* (italics in original).

200   *that all men are created equal ... their safety and happiness.* Declaration of Independence, National Archives, America's Founding Documents, https://www.archives.gov /founding-docs/declaration-transcript.

201   *conceived a higher opinion of the natural capacities ... justify all my prejudices nor to account for them.* Letter from Benjamin Franklin to John Waring, 17 December 1763, in *PBF*, vol. 10, pp. 395–396, Founders Online, National Archives, https://founders.archives.gov /documents/Franklin/01-10-02-0214.

201   *The Negroes of Africa have by nature no feeling that rises above the trifling ... as great in regard to mental capacities as in color.* Immanuel Kant, *Observations on the Feeling of the Beautiful and Sublime*, trans. John T. Goldthwait (Berkeley: University of California Press, 1960), pp. 110–111.

202   *His Excellency George Washington.* Letter from Phillis Wheatley to George Washington, 26 October 1775, in *PGW*, Revolutionary War Series, vol. 2, p. 242, Founders Online, National Archives, https://founders.archives.gov/documents/Washington/03-02-02 -0222-0001.

202   *great poetical talents.* Letter from George Washington to Phillis Wheatley, 28 February 1776, in *PGW*, Revolutionary War Series, vol. 3, p. 387, Founders Online, National Archives, https://founders.archives.gov/documents/Washington/03-03-02-0281.

202   *reject slaves and by a great majority to reject Negroes altogether.* Council of War, 8 October 1775, in *PGW*, Revolutionary War Series, vol. 2, pp. 123–128, Founders Online, National Archives, https://founders.archives.gov/documents/Washington/03-02-02-0115.

204   *you ... upon the success of an enterprise which I had formed against a detachment of the enemy lying in Trenton.* Letter from George Washington to John Hancock, 27 December 1776,

in *PGW*, Revolutionary War Series, vol. 7, pp. 455–461, Founders Online, National Archives, https://founders.archives.gov/documents/Washington/03-07-02-0355.

204 *in the firmament of politics and war.* Goethe, *Autobiography*, p. 618.

205 *not last long, for the English will soon have quashed the colonies. Correspondenz*, vol. 38, p. 383: "Cela ne durera pas, parceque les Anglais ont battu les colonies."

205 *it was not surprising in the least that the regular British soldiers had carried the day against the provincial American troops. Correspondenz*, vol. 39, p. 27: "Il n'est nullement surprenant que des troupes réglées aient des succès contre des provinciales."

205 *the chief of upstart rebels.* Frederick the Great, *De ce qui c'est passé de plus important en Europe depuis l'année 1774 jusque à l'année 1778*, in *ŒFG*, vol. 6, p. 130: "Le général Washington, . . . le chef des rebels."

205 *those poor Americans.* Letter from Frederick to Jean-Baptiste le Rond d'Alembert, 23 June 1777, in *ŒFG*, vol. 25, p. 87: "On continuera donc de faire la guerre à ces pauvres Américains."

205 *observe . . . learn about this great art of war, about which one could never learn enough.* Letter from Frederick to his brother Henry, 3 November 1777, in *ŒFG*, vol. 26, p. 457: "observons . . . Washington, pour apprendre . . . ce grand art de la guerre dont on ne trouve jamais le bout."

205 *of Philadelphia . . . gave the laws.* Letter from Frederick to Voltaire, 30 October 1770, in *ŒFG*, vol. 23, p. 195: "Je préférerais bien la colonie . . . , dont Voltaire est le législateur, à celle . . . de Philadelphia, auxquels Locke donna des lois."

207– *his soldier, "Do this!" . . . and only then did he do it.* Letter from Friedrich Wilhelm von
208 Steuben to Friedrich Wilhelm von Gaudy, 1787, in Max Jähns, *Geschichte der Kriegswissenschaften vornehmlich in Deutschland* (Munich and Leipzig: Oldenbourg, 1891), p. 2605: "Ihrem Soldaten sage Sie z.B.: Mache das! Und er macht's. Dem meinigen mußte ich dagegen zuerst sagen: Dies und das ist der Grund, warum Du dieses oder jenes machen sollst, und dann erst machte er's."

208 *I felt the unbounded reverence which I had devoted to this remarkable prince . . . gradually cooling away.* Goethe, *Autobiography*, p. 252.

208 *own doggish rabble . . . disparage . . . Old Fritz.* Letter from Goethe to Johann Heinrich Merck, 5 August 1778, in Johann Wolfgang von Goethe, *Briefe (Hamburger Ausgabe)*, vol. 1, ed. Karl Robert Mandelkow (Munich: Beck, 1976), p. 253: "und dem alten Fritz bin ich recht nah worden . . . und habe über den großen Menschen seine eigenen Lumpenhunde räsonniren hören."

209 *since all people are equal before the law . . . with honor in his bones than to all lawyers and rights. Borussica*, vol. 16.2, p. 585: "indem vor Justiz alle Leute gleich sind . . . Ihr könnet nur gewiss sein, dass ich einem ehrlichen Officier, der Ehre im Leib hat, mehr glaube, als ale Advocaten und Rechte."

211 *free, sovereign, and independent states.* Definitive Treaty of Peace Between the United States and Great Britain, 3 September 1783, in *PBF*, vol. 40, pp. 566–575, Founders Online, National Archives, https://founders.archives.gov/documents/Franklin/01-40-02-0356.

211 *No occurrence in the course of the war . . . has given me more painful sensations . . . with abhorrence and reprehend[ed] with severity.* Letter from George Washington to Lewis Nicola, 22 May 1782, in Washington, *Writings* (1997), pp. 468–469.

211   *the greatest man in the world.* Joseph Farington, *The Farington Diary*, ed. James Greig, 8
       vols. (London: Hutchinson & Co., 1923–1928), vol. 1, p. 278, https://archive.org/details
       /faringtondiary01fariuoft/page/278/mode/2up?view=theater.

212   *be achieved in practice more felicitously.* Moses Mendelssohn, *Jerusalem oder über religiöse*
       Macht und Judentum, ed. David Martyn (Bielefeld: Aisthesis, 2001), pt. 1, p. 32: "glückli-
       cher praktisch beygelegt."

212   *You are free (Proclaim it victoriously . . . Are scorned and the people rule a flourishing state.* "Die
       Freiheit Amerikas. Ode," *Berlinische Monatsschrift,* April 1783, pp. 386–391, https://ds.ub
       .uni-bielefeld.de/viewer/image/2239816_001/389/LOG_0048/: "Frei bist du, (sag's
       in höherem Siegeston, / Entzücktes Lied), frei, frei nun, Amerika, / Erschöpft, gebeugt,
       bedeckt mit Schande / . . . gleiche Bürger . . . / Und du, Europa, hebe das Haupt empor!
       / Einst glänzt auch dir der Tag, da die Kette bricht, / Du, Edle, frei wirst; deine Fürsten
       / Scheuchst, und Ein glüklicher Volkstaat grünest. / . . . Frei ist, wer's sein will."

215–   *most liberal treaty ever concluded by independent powers . . . a new era in negotiation . . .*
216   *happy consequences.* Letter from George Washington to Lafayette, 15 August 1786, in
       PGW, Confederation Series, vol. 4, pp. 214–216, Founders Online, National Archives,
       https://founders.archives.gov/documents/Washington/04-04-02-0200. Washington
       expressed similar sentiments about the agreement in a letter to Rochambeau, calling it
       "the most liberal treaty which has ever been entered into between independent powers."
       Letter from Washington to Rochambeau, 31 July 1786, in *PGW,* Confederation Series,
       vol. 4, pp. 179–181, Founders Online, National Archives, https://founders.archives.gov
       /documents/Washington/04-04-02-0171.

10. Endings and New Beginnings (1785–1801)

Page

219   *a soul carrying around a cadaver . . . The cadaver must trot on!* Letter from Frederick to his
       brother Henry, 27 September 1784, in *ŒFG,* vol. 26, p. 579: "un âme qui traîne un ca-
       davre . . . il faut que le cadavre trotte."

219   *the most beautiful eyes I ever saw . . . what a tyrannic, hardhearted, and selfish man he is.*
       Letter from Lafayette to George Washington, 6 February 1786, in *PGW,* Confederation
       Series, vol. 3, pp. 538–547, Founders Online, National Archives, https://founders.archives
       .gov/documents/Washington/04-03-02-0461.

220   *The king of Prussia is about leaving the stage and cannot last long—the last accounts from*
       Potsdam are very bad. Ibid.

221   *was not only very pale and thin . . . all the way up to his loins.* Johann Georg Zimmermann,
       Über Friedrich den Großen und meine Unterredungen mit ihm kurz vor seinem Tode
       (Leipzig: in der Weidmannischen Buchhandlung, 1788), p. 21: "war nicht nur sehr blass
       und mager, sondern zumal von der weissgelben Blässe, welche nicht nur die übelste
       Beschaffenheit der Säfte, sondern auch der festen Teile anzeigt und unter solchen Um-
       ständen von der übelsten Bedeutung ist . . . Auch die Hände fand ich äußerst entfärbt,
       mager und dürr, den Leib sehr stark und die Beine bis ganz oben an die Lenden so
       fürchterlich geschwollen, als nur irgend Beine geschwollen sein können."

221   *Now the king doffed his hat . . . "Do not forget the old man you saw here!"* Ibid., p. 27: "Nun nahm der König seinen Hut mit unbeschreiblicher Würde, Huld und Freundlichkeit ab, neigte sein Haupt und sprach: Adieu, mein guter, mein lieber Herr Zimmermann. Vergessen Sie den guten alten Mann nicht, den Sie hier gesehen haben!"

221   *We are over the mountain. Now it will be better.* As related in Johannes Kunisch, *Friedrich der Große. Der König und seine Zeit* (Munich: C. H. Beck, 2004), p. 529: "La montagne est passée, nous irons mieux."

221   *The king's death was like his life. He remained fearless and stoic to the end . . . was still conscious a few minutes before death.* Christian Gottlieb Selle, *Krankheitsgeschichte des Höchstseeligen Königs von Preußen Friedrichs des Zweyten Majestät* (Berlin: August Mylius, 1786), p. 26: "Der Tod des Königs war wie sein Leben. Furchtlos und gleichmütig blieb er bis zum letzten Zuge seines Odems. Vor dem Fieber glaubte sich der König in der Besserung, wenigstens hatte er sein Ziel noch einige Zeit hinaus gerückt, und im Fieber war ihm der Kopf zu eingenommen, als dass er seine Todesgefahr hätte bemerken können. Auch hatte er zu oft von diesem mit Röcheln verbundenen Husten gelitten, als dass er ihn hätte befremden sollen.—Er verschied also ruhig und sanft, und seine ganz unverstellten Gesichtszüge, sein ruhiger, ernster Blick zeigten noch im Sarge, dass er mit keinem besorgten und quälenden Gedanken aus der Welt gegangen war, ob er gleich noch einige Minute vor dem Tode Bewusstsein hatte."

223   *It is deathly quiet . . . but no one is in mourning . . . all the world rejoices!* Letter from Mirabeau to the Abbé de Périgord, 17 August 1786, as reported in Gustav Berthold Volz, ed., *Friedrich der Große im Spiegel seiner Zeit*, vol. 3, *Geistesleben, Alter und Tod* (Berlin: Reimar Hobbing, 1926), p. 255: "Es herrscht Totenstille, aber keine Trauer; man zeigt sich benommen ohne Kummer. Man sieht in kein Gesicht, das nicht den Ausdruck von Erleichterung, von Hoffnung trüge. Kein Bedauern wird laut, man hört keinen Seufzer, kein lobendes Wort! Ist das das Resultat so vieler gewonnener Schlachten, so großen Ruhms? Ist das das Ende einer beinahe ein halbes Jahrhundert währenden Regierung, die so reich war an glanzvollen Taten? Alle Welt wünschte das Ende herbei—alle Welt beglückwünschte sich!"

224   *I have made thee a name like the name of the great men that are in the earth.* 1 Chron. 17:8.

224   *Finally . . . the great king whose glory filled the world.* Johann Wolfgang von Goethe, *Italienische Reise*, in *Werke (Hamburger Ausgabe)*, vol. 11, ed. Erich Trunz (Munich: Beck, 1981), p. 162 (19 January 1787): "So hat denn der große König, dessen Ruhm die Welt erfüllte . . . endlich auch das Zeitliche gesegnet."

225   *to be lamented, however, that great characters are not without a blot . . . tyrannize[d] over millions.* Letter from George Washington to Lafayette, 10 May 1786, in *PGW*, Confederation Series, vol. 4, pp. 41–45, Founders Online, National Archives, https://founders .archives.gov/documents/Washington/04-04-02-0051.

225–   *not a member of it conceived that it would give birth . . . republican principles.* Letter from
226   George Washington to James Madison, 16 December 1786, in *PGW*, Confederation Series, vol. 4, pp. 457–459, Founders Online, National Archives, https://founders.archives .gov/documents/Washington/04-04-02-0395.

226   *the first statuary [i.e., foremost sculptor] in the world.* Letter from Thomas Jefferson to George Washington, 10 December 1784, in Thomas Jefferson, *The Papers of Thomas Jefferson*, vol. 7, *2 March 1784–25 February 1785*, ed. Julian P. Boyd (Princeton, NJ: Princeton

University Press, 1953), pp. 566–567, Founders Online, National Archives, https://
founders.archives.gov/documents/Jefferson/01-07-02-0407.

226   *I am so hackneyed to the touches of the painter's pencil . . . no dray moves more readily to the
thill than I do to the painter's chair.* Letter from George Washington to Francis Hopkinson,
16 May 1785, in *PGW*, Confederation Series, vol. 2, pp. 561–562, Founders Online, National Archives, https://founders.archives.gov/documents/Washington/04-02-02
-0411.

228   *lamented and deprecated . . . exhibit a melancholy proof . . . that ever dawned upon any country.* Letter from George Washington to Henry Lee Jr., 31 October 1786, in *PGW*, Confederation Series, vol. 4, pp. 318–320, Founders Online, National Archives, https://founders
.archives.gov/documents/Washington/04-04-02-0286.

230   *I am fully of the opinion . . . that those who lean to monarchical government . . . consulted the
public mind.* Letter from George Washington to James Madison, 31 March 1787, in *PGW*,
Confederation Series, vol. 5, pp. 114–117, Founders Online, National Archives, https://
founders.archives.gov/documents/Washington/04-05-02-0111.

231   *There are several parts of this Constitution which I do not at present approve . . . unanimously
in recommending this Constitution.* James Madison, *Debates in the Federal Convention of
1787 by James Madison, a Member*, ed. Gordon Lloyd (Ashland, OH: Ashbrook Center,
2014), 546–552, 564.

231   *that it is a rising and not a setting sun.* Ibid., p. 86.

232   *many of the members . . . cast their eyes towards General Washington as president and shaped their
ideas of the powers to be given to a president by their opinions of his virtue.* Letter from Pierce
Butler to Weedon Butler, 5 May 1788, in Max Farrand, *The Records of the Federal Convention
of 1787*, rev. ed., 4 vols. (New Haven, CT: Yale University Press, 1966), vol. 3, p. 302.

232   *wish . . . anarchy.* Letter from George Washington to Benjamin Harrison, 24 September 1787, in *PGW*, Confederation Series, vol. 5, pp. 339–340, Founders Online, National
Archives, https://founders.archives.gov/documents/Washington/04-05-02-0316.

232   *the power of the Constitution will always be with the people . . . their servants can, and undoubtedly will be, recalled.* Letter from George Washington to Bushrod Washington, 9 November 1787, in *PGW*, Confederation Series, vol. 5, pp. 420–425, Founders Online, National
Archives, https://founders.archives.gov/documents/Washington/04-05-02-0388.

232   *the probability of my election to the presidency . . . living and dying an honest man on my own
farm.* Letter from George Washington to Lafayette, 28 April–1 May 1788, in *PGW*, Confederation Series, vol. 6, pp. 242–246, Founders Online, National Archives, https://
founders.archives.gov/documents/Washington/04-06-02-0211.

232–   *rejoice . . . by giving their votes in favor of some other person . . . after the stormy day of life, in
233   the bosom of domestic tranquility.* Letter from George Washington to Alexander Hamilton, 3
October 1788, in *PGW*, Presidential Series, vol. 1, pp. 31–33, Founders Online, National
Archives, https://founders.archives.gov/documents/Washington/05-01-02-0020.

233   *I have been accustomed to pay so much respect to the opinion . . . they have done me than by
accepting the appointment.* Address to Charles Thomson, 14 April 1789, in *PGW*, Presidential Series, vol. 2, pp. 56–57, following the version of the letter contained in Washington's letter book, Founders Online, National Archives, https://founders.archives.gov
/documents/Washington/05-02-02-0057.

233– *About ten o'clock I bade adieu to Mount Vernon, to private life, and to domestic felicity . . . less*
234 *hope of answering its expectations.* DGW, vol. 5, pp. 445–447 (entry of 16 April 1789), Founders Online, National Archives, https://founders.archives.gov/documents /Washington/01-05-02-0005-0001-0001.

234 *that Almighty Being who rules over the universe . . . free government . . . the respect of the world.* "First Inaugural Address," final version, 30 April 1789, in *PGW*, Presidential Series, vol. 2, pp. 173–177, Founders Online, National Archives, https://founders.archives.gov /documents/Washington/05-02-02-0130-0003.

234 *might possibly endanger the religious rights of any ecclesiastical society.* Letter from George Washington to the United Baptist Churches of Virginia, May 1789, in *PGW*, Presidential Series, vol. 2, pp. 423–425, Founders Online, National Archives, https://founders .archives.gov/documents/Washington/05-02-02-0309.

234 *May the children of the stock of Abraham who dwell in this land . . . and in his own due time and way everlastingly happy.* Letter from George Washington to the Hebrew Congregation in Newport, Rhode Island, 18 August 1790, in *PGW*, Presidential Series, vol. 6, pp. 284–286, Founders Online, National Archives, https://founders.archives.gov /documents/Washington/05-06-02-0135.

235 *effected in France . . . of so wonderful a nature that the mind can hardly realize the fact . . . that nation will be the most powerful and happy in Europe.* Letter from George Washington to Gouverneur Morris, 13 October 1789, in *PGW*, Presidential Series, vol. 4, pp. 176–179, Founders Online, National Archives, https://founders.archives.gov/documents /Washington/05-04-02-0125.

236 *the revolution is of too great magnitude to be effected in so short a space . . . foment divisions.* Letter from George Washington to Gouverneur Morris, 13 October 1789, in *PGW*, Presidential Series, vol. 4, pp. 176–179, Founders Online, National Archives, https://founders .archives.gov/documents/Washington/05-04-02-0125.

236 *token of victory gained by liberty over despotism.* Letter from George Washington to Lafayette, 11 August 1790, in *PGW*, Presidential Series, vol. 6, pp. 233–235, Founders Online, National Archives, https://founders.archives.gov/documents/Washington/05-06-02-0112.

236 *If it were a scepter . . . he has merited it, and would become it.* Letter from Henry Hill to George Washington, 7 May 1790, in *PGW*, Presidential Series, vol. 5, pp. 388–390, Founders Online, National Archives, https://founders.archives.gov/documents /Washington/05-05-02-0248.

238 *the security of the remainder of your lands . . . no state nor person can purchase your lands . . . suffer the depredations of the bad people [among them] to go unpunished.* Letter from George Washington to the Seneca Chiefs, 29 December 1790, in *PGW*, Presidential Series, vol. 7, pp. 146–150, Founders Online, National Archives, https://founders.archives .gov/documents/Washington/05-07-02-0080.

238– *differences in political opinion . . . unavoidable . . . to a certain point . . . the same* general *objects*
239 *in view.* Letter from George Washington to Alexander Hamilton, 26 August 1792, in *PGW*, Presidential Series, vol. 11, pp. 38–40, Founders Online, National Archives, https://founders.archives.gov/documents/Washington/05-11-02-0015.

239 *I regret—deeply regret—the difference in opinions . . . devoutly . . . by mutual yieldings.* Letter from George Washington to Thomas Jefferson, 18 October 1792, in *PGW*, Presidential

Series, vol. 11, pp. 238–239, Founders Online, National Archives, https://founders
.archives.gov/documents/Washington/05-11-02-0126.

239   *country in the hour of distress received such liberal aid from the French . . . the disorders and
incertitude of that nation.* Letter from George Washington to Lafayette, 28 July 1791, in
PGW, Presidential Series, vol. 8, pp. 377–381, Founders Online, National Archives,
https://founders.archives.gov/documents/Washington/05-08-02-0260.

239   *sincere regret.* Letter from George Washington to Thomas Jefferson, 1 January 1794, in
PGW, Presidential Series, vol. 15, p. 1, Founders Online, National Archives, https://
founders.archives.gov/documents/Washington/05-15-02-0001.

240   *this insurrection as the first formidable fruit of the democratic societies . . . that has ever been
presented for the acceptance of mankind.* Letter from George Washington to Henry Lee, 26
August 1794, in *PGW*, Presidential Series, vol. 16, pp. 600–605, Founders Online, National
Archives, https://founders.archives.gov/documents/Washington/05-16-02-0418.

240   *anarchy and confusion.* Letter from George Washington to Daniel Morgan, 8 October 1794, in *PGW*, Presidential Series, vol. 17, pp. 39–40, Founders Online, National
Archives, https://founders.archives.gov/documents/Washington/05-17-02-0024.

240–   *the cry against the treaty is like that against a mad dog . . . the fever . . . is a little abated.* Letter
241   from George Washington to Alexander Hamilton, 29 July 1795, in *PGW*, Presidential
Series, vol. 18, pp. 458–460, Founders Online, National Archives, https://founders
.archives.gov/documents/Washington/05-18-02-0311.

241–   *friends and fellow citizens . . . a citizen to administer the executive government of the United
242   States . . . the very engines which have lifted them to unjust dominion.* George Washington,
"Farewell Address," 19 September 1796, in *PGW*, Presidential Series, vol. 20, pp. 703–722,
Founders Online, National Archives, https://founders.archives.gov/documents
/Washington/05-20-02-0440-0002.

242   *the polish of erudition in the arts, sciences, and belle letters in their full breadth . . . would by
degrees discover that there was not that cause for those jealousies and prejudices which one
part of the union had imbibed against another part.* Letter from George Washington to
Alexander Hamilton, 1 September 1796, in Alexander Hamilton, *The Papers of Alexander
Hamilton*, vol. 20, *January 1796–March 1797*, ed. Harold C. Syrett (New York: Columbia
University Press, 1974), pp. 311–314, Founders Online, National Archives, https://
founders.archives.gov/documents/Hamilton/01-20-02-0199.

243   *so many important events . . . nor all of them together . . . the remainder of my days (which
cannot be many).* Letter from George Washington to Sarah Cary Fairfax, 16 May 1798, in
PGW, Retirement Series, vol. 2, pp. 272–275, Founders Online, National Archives,
https://founders.archives.gov/documents/Washington/06-02-02-0204.

243   *prove himself to be the ablest of all our diplomatic corps.* Letter from George Washington
to John Adams, 20 February 1797, in *PGW*, Presidential Series, vol. 21, pp. 720–721,
Founders Online, National Archives, https://founders.archives.gov/documents
/Washington/05-21-02-0325.

243   *'Tis well.* Peter R. Henriques, "The Final Struggle Between George Washington and the
Grim King: Washington's Attitude Towards Death and the Afterlife," in *George Washington Reconsidered*, ed. Don Higginbotham (Charlottesville: University Press of Virginia,
2001), pp. 250–271, at 270.

244   *The loss of such a man is a misfortune to mankind.* Letter from John Quincy Adams to Joseph Pitcairn, 4 February 1800, in John Quincy Adams, *Writings of John Quincy Adams,* ed. Worthington Chauncey Ford, 7 vols. (New York: Macmillan, 1913), vol. 2, p. 451.

Epilogue

Page

247   *was persuaded that the American union could not long subsist under its present form . . . where the territory was not limited and united.* Quoted in *Correspondenz,* vol. 47, p. 535.

247   *not made to form a republic. Each of them has other interests and the land they occupy is far too extensive for it to form a government similar to that of Venice, Switzerland, or Holland.* Letter from Frederick to his brother Henry, 3 November 1782, in *Correspondenz,* vol. 47, p. 576: "les possessions américaines qui vont devenir indépendantes ne sont pas faites pour former une République, chacune d'elles a d'autres intérêts et le terrain qu'elles occupent est beaucoup trop étendu pour qu'il forme un gouvernement pareil à celui de Venise, de Suisse ou de Hollande."

247   *Iron Kingdom.* See Christopher Clark, *Iron Kingdom: The Rise and Downfall of Prussia, 1600–1947* (London: Allen Lane, 2006).

247   *The Prussian State which from early days has been a bearer of militarism and reaction in Germany has de facto ceased to exist.* "Control Council Law No. 46 (25 February 1947) Abolition of Prussia," Wikisource, last updated February 6, 2022, https://en.wikisource .org/wiki/Control_Council_Law_No_46_(25_February_1947)_Abolition_of _Prussia.

248   *The end of history.* Francis Fukuyama, *The End of History and the Last Man* (New York: Free Press, 1992).

248–
249   *gradually incline the minds of men to seek security and repose . . . governments of a monarchical cast.* Washington, "Farewell Address."

WORKS CITED

Abbreviations

Anti-Machiavel = Frederick the Great. *Anti-Machiavel, or a Study of Machiavelli's "The Prince."* In *FGPW*, pp. 13–81.

Ausstellung = *Friedrich der Grosse. Ausstellung des Geheimen Staatsarchivs Preußischer Kulturbesitz anlässlich des 200. Todestages König Friedrichs II. von Preußen.* Edited by Friedrich Benninghoven, Helmut Börsch-Supan, and Iselin Gundermann. Berlin: Nicolaische Verlagsbuchhandlung, 1986.

Borussica = *Acta Borussica. Denkmäler der Preußischen Staatsverwaltung im 18. Jahrhundert.* 35 vols. Berlin: Parey, 1982–1936. The following volumes are cited in the present book:

Vol. 1: *Akten von 1701 bis Ende Juni 1714.* Edited by Gustav Schmoller and Otto Krauske. Berlin: Parey, 1894.

Vol. 2: *Akten vom Juli 1714 bis Ende 1717.* Edited by Gustav Schmoller, Otto Krauske, and Victor Loewe. Berlin: Parey, 1898.

Vol. 16.2: *Akten vom Januar 1778 bis zum August 1786.* Edited by Peter Baumgart and Gerd Heinrich. Berlin: Parey, 1982.

Correspondenz = Frederick the Great. *Politische Correspondenz Friedrichs des Großen.* Edited by Johann Gustav Droysen et al. 48 vols. to date. The following volumes are cited in the present book:

Vol. 1: Edited by Johann Gustav Droysen, Max Duncker, and Heinrich von Sybel. Berlin: Duncker, 1879.

Vol. 4: Edited by Johann Gustav Droysen, Max Duncker, and Heinrich von Sybel. Berlin: Duncker, 1880.

Vol. 31: Edited by Gustav Berthold Volz. Berlin: Hobbing, 1906.

Vol. 38: Edited by Gustav Berthold Volz. Berlin: Hobbing, 1925.

Vol. 39: Edited by Gustav Berthold Volz. Berlin: Hobbing, 1925.

Vol. 47: Edited by Peter Baumgart. Cologne: Böhlau, 2003.

DGW = *The Diaries of George Washington.* Also available at Founders Online, National Archives, https://founders.archives.gov/about/Washington. The following volumes are cited in the present book:

Vol. 1: *11 March 1748–13 November 1765.* Edited by Donald Jackson. Charlottesville: University Press of Virginia, 1976.

Vol. 5: *1 July 1786–31 December 1789.* Edited by Donald Jackson and Dorothy Twohig. Charlottesville: University Press of Virginia, 1979.

FGPW = Frederick the Great's Philosophical Writings. Edited by Avi Lifschitz. Translated by Angela Scholar. Princeton, NJ: Princeton University Press, 2021.

"Journey" = Washington, George. "A Journal of My Journey over the Mountains." In *DGW*, pp. 6–16 (March 1747/1748) and 16–23 (April 1748). All quotations from "Journey" are from Founders Online, National Archives, where the text is divided into two parts based on the month of the diary entries:

March 1747/1748: https://founders.archives.gov/documents/Washington/01-01-02-0001 -0002.

April 1748: https://founders.archives.gov/documents/Washington/01-01-02-0001-0003.

Letters = Letters of Voltaire and Frederick the Great. Translated by Richard Addington. London: George Routledge and Sons, 1927.

ŒFG = Œuvres de Frédéric le Grand. Edited by Johann D. E. Preuss. 30 vols. Berlin: Imprimerie royale (Decker), 1846–1856. The following volumes are cited in the present book:

Vol. 6: *Œuvres historiques 6.* Edited by Johann D. E. Preuss. Berlin: Decker, 1847.

Vol. 16: *Correspondance 1.* Edited by Johann D. E. Preuss. Berlin: Decker, 1850.

Vol. 17: *Correspondance 2.* Edited by Johann D. E. Preuss. Berlin: Decker, 1851.

Vol. 19: *Correspondance 4.* Edited by Johann D. E. Preuss. Berlin: Decker, 1852.

Vol. 22: *Correspondance 7.* Edited by Johann D. E. Preuss. Berlin: Decker, 1853.

Vol. 23: *Correspondance 8.* Edited by Johann D. E. Preuss. Berlin: Decker, 1853.

Vol. 25: *Correspondance 10.* Edited by Johann D. E. Preuss. Berlin: Decker, 1854.

Vol. 26: *Correspondance 11.* Edited by Johann D. E. Preuss. Berlin: Decker, 1855.

Vol. 27.1: *Correspondance 12.1.* Edited by Johann D. E. Preuss. Berlin: Decker, 1856.

Vol. 27.3: *Correspondance 12.3.* Edited by Johann D. E. Preuss. Berlin: Decker, 1856.

Vol. 28: *Œuvres militaires 1.* Edited by Johann D. E. Preuss. Berlin: Decker, 1856.

PBF = The Papers of Benjamin Franklin. 44 vols. to date. New Haven, CT: Yale University Press, 1959–. Volumes cited in the present book are listed here. All quotations from *PBF* are from Founders Online, National Archives, https://founders.archives.gov/about/ Franklin.

Vol. 2: *January 1, 1735, Through December 31, 1744.* Edited by Leonard W. Labaree. New Haven, CT: Yale University Press, 1961.

Vol. 5: *July 1, 1753, Through March 31, 1755.* Edited by Leonard W. Labaree. New Haven, CT: Yale University Press, 1962.

Vol. 10: *January 1, 1762, Through December 31, 1763.* Edited by Leonard W. Labaree. New Haven, CT: Yale University Press, 1959.

Vol. 13: *January 1, 1766, Through December 31, 1766.* Edited by Leonard W. Labaree. New Haven, CT: Yale University Press, 1969.

Vol. 20: *January 1, 1773, Through December 31, 1773.* Edited by William B. Willcox. New Haven, CT: Yale University Press, 1976.

Vol. 40: *May 16 Through September 15, 1783.* Edited by Ellen R. Cohn. New Haven, CT: Yale University Press, 2011.

PGW = The Papers of George Washington, published in five series. Volumes cited in the present book are listed here. All quotations from *PGW* are from Founders Online, National Archives, https://founders.archives.gov/about/Washington.

COLONIAL SERIES

Vol. 1: *7 July 1748–14 August 1755*. Edited by W. W. Abbot. Charlottseville: University Press of Virginia, 1983.

Vol. 2: *14 August 1755–15 April 1756*. Edited by W. W. Abbot. Charlottesville: University Press of Virginia, 1983.

Vol. 4: *9 November 1756–24 October 1757*. Edited by W. W. Abbot. Charlottesville: University Press of Virginia, 1984.

Vol. 5: *5 October 1757–3 September 1758*. Edited by W. W. Abbot. Charlottesville: University Press of Virginia, 1988.

Vol. 6: *4 September 1758–26 December 1760*. Edited by W. W. Abbot. Charlottesville: University Press of Virginia, 1988.

Vol. 7: *1 January 1761–15 June 1767*. Edited by W. W. Abbot and Dorothy Twohig. Charlottesville: University Press of Virginia, 1990.

Vol. 8: *24 June 1767–25 December 1771*. Edited by W. W. Abbot and Dorothy Twohig. Charlottesville: University Press of Virginia, 1993.

Vol. 10: *21 March 1774–15 June 1775*. Edited by W. W. Abbot and Dorothy Twohig. Charlottesville: University Press of Virginia, 1995.

REVOLUTIONARY WAR SERIES

Vol. 1: *16 June 1775–15 September 1775*. Edited by Philander D. Chase. Charlottesville: University Press of Virginia, 1985.

Vol. 2: *16 September 1775–31 December 1775*. Edited by Philander D. Chase. Charlottesville: University Press of Virginia, 1987.

Vol. 3: *1 January 1776–31 March 1776*. Edited by Philander D. Chase. Charlottesville: University Press of Virginia, 1988.

Vol. 4: *1 April 1776–15 June 1776*. Edited by Philander D. Chase. Charlottesville: University Press of Virginia, 1991.

Vol. 7: *21 October 1776–5 January 1777*. Edited by Philander D. Chase. Charlottesville: University Press of Virginia, 1997.

CONFEDERATION SERIES

Vol. 2: *18 July 1784–18 May 1784*. Edited by W. W. Abbot. Charlottesville: University Press of Virginia, 1992.

Vol. 3: *19 May 1785–31 March 1786*. Edited by W. W. Abbot. Charlottesville: University Press of Virginia, 1994.

Vol. 4: *2 April 1786–31 January 1787*. Edited by W. W. Abbot. Charlottesville: University Press of Virginia, 1995.

Vol. 5: *1 February 1787–31 December 1787*. Edited by W. W. Abbot. Charlottesville: University Press of Virginia, 1997.

Vol. 6: *1 January 1788–23 September 1788*. Edited by W. W. Abbot. Charlottesville: University Press of Virginia, 1997.

PRESIDENTIAL SERIES

Vol. 1: *24 September 1788–31 March 1789*. Edited by Dorothy Twohig. Charlottesville: University Press of Virginia, 1987.

Vol. 2: *1 April 1789–15 June 1789*. Edited by Dorothy Twohig. Charlottesville: University Press of Virginia, 1987.

Vol. 4: *8 September 1789–15 January 1790*. Edited by Dorothy Twohig. Charlottesville: University Press of Virginia, 1993.

Vol. 5: *16 January 1790–30 June 1790*. Edited by Dorothy Twohig, Mark A. Mastromarino, and Jack D. Warren. Charlottesville: University Press of Virginia, 1996.

Vol. 6: *1 July 1790–30 November 1790*. Edited by Mark A. Mastromarino. Charlottesville: University Press of Virginia, 1996.

Vol. 7: *1 December 1790–21 March 1791*. Edited by Jack D. Warren Jr. Charlottesville: University Press of Virginia, 1998.

Vol. 8: *22 March 1791–22 September 1791*. Edited by Mark A. Mastromarino. Charlottesville: University Press of Virginia, 1999.

Vol. 11: *16 August 1792–15 January 1793*. Edited by Christine Sternberg Patrick. Charlottesville: University Press of Virginia, 2002.

Vol. 15: *1 January–30 April 1794*. Edited by Christine Sternberg Patrick. Charlottesville: University Press of Virginia, 2009.

Vol. 16: *1 May–30 September 1794*. Edited by David R. Hoth and Carol S. Ebel. Charlottesville: University Press of Virginia, 2011.

Vol. 17: *1 October 1794–31 March 1795*. Edited by David R. Hoth and Carol S. Ebel. Charlottesville: University Press of Virginia, 2013.

Vol. 18: *1 April–30 September 1795*. Edited by Carol S. Ebel. Charlottesville: University Press of Virginia, 2015.

Vol. 20: *1 April–21 September 1796*. Edited by David R. Hoth and William M. Ferraro. Charlottesville: University Press of Virginia, 2019.

Vol. 21: *22 September 1796–3 March 1797*. Edited by Adrina Garbooshian-Huggins. Charlottesville: University Press of Virginia, 2020.

RETIREMENT SERIES

Vol. 2: *2 January 1798–15 September 1798*. Edited by W. W Abbot. Charlottesville: University Press of Virginia, 1998.

Other Works Cited

Adams, John. *Diary and Autobiography of John Adams*. Vol. 2, *1771–1781*. Edited by L. H. Butterfield. Adams Papers. Cambridge, MA: Harvard University Press, 1961.

Adams, John Quincy. *Writings of John Quincy Adams*. Edited by Worthington Chauncey Ford. 7 vols. New York: Macmillan, 1913.

Anderson, Fred. *Crucible of War: The Seven Years' War and the Fate of Empire in British North America, 1754–1766*. New York: Alfred A. Knopf, 2000.

Bailyn, Bernard. *Atlantic History: Concepts and Contours*. Cambridge, MA: Harvard University Press, 2005.

Bardong, Otto, ed. *Friedrich der Große*. Darmstadt: Wissenschaftliche Buchgesellschaft, 1982.

Beer, Adolf, ed. "Denkschriften des Fürsten Wenzel Kaunitz-Rittberg." *Archiv für Österreichische Geschichte* 48, no. 1 (1872): 1–162.

Berner, Ernst. *Aus dem Briefwechsel König Friedrichs I. von Preußen und seiner Familie: Gelegentlich der zweihundertjährigen Jubelfeier des preußischen Königtums*. Berlin: Alexander Duncker, 1901.

Blanning, Tim. *Frederick the Great: King of Prussia*. London: Allen Lane, 2015.

Bled, Jean-Paul. *Frédéric le Grand*. Paris: Fayard, 2004.

Bratuscheck, Ernst. *Die Erziehung Friedrichs des Großen*. Berlin: Georg Reimer, 1885.

Büchner, Gerhard, and Georg Dittrich. *Rheinsberg und Sanssouci. Geselligkeit und Freundschaft*. Leipzig: Georg Kummer, 1928.

Burnaby, Andrew. *Burnaby's Travels Through North America*. Reprinted from the 3rd ed. of 1798. Edited by Rufus Rockwell Wilson. New York: A. Wessels Company, 1904.

Carlyle, Thomas. *History of Friedrich II of Prussia, Called Frederick the Great*. 8 vols. London: Chapman and Hall, 1897–1898.

Catt, Henri de. *Frederick the Great, The Memoirs of His Reader, Henri de Catt (1758–1760)*. Translated by F. S. Flint. London: Constable and Company, 1916.

Clark, Christopher. *Iron Kingdom: The Rise and Downfall of Prussia, 1600–1947*. London: Allen Lane, 2006.

"Control Council Law No. 46 (25 February 1947) Abolition of Prussia." Wikisource. Last updated February 6, 2022. https://en.wikisource.org/wiki/Control_Council_Law_No_46 _(25_February_1947)_Abolition_of_Prussia.

Corpus Constitutionum Marchicarum. Preußische Rechtsquellen Digital / Corpus Constitutionum Marchicarum, November 25, 2002. https://web-archiv.staatsbibliothek-berlin.de /altedrucke.staatsbibliothek-berlin.de/Rechtsquellen/quellen.html.

Cramer, Friedrich. *Zur Geschichte Friedrich Wilhelms I. und Friedrichs II. Könige von Preußen*. Hamburg: Hofmann und Campe, 1829.

Declaration of Independence. National Archives, America's Founding Documents. https://www .archives.gov/founding-docs/declaration-transcript.

Definitive Treaty of Peace Between the United States and Great Britain. 3 September 1783. In *PBF*, vol. 40, pp. 566–575. Founders Online, National Archives. https://founders.archives .gov/documents/Franklin/01-40-02-0356.

Dickinson, John. *Letters from a Farmer in Pennsylvania to the Inhabitants of the British Colonies*. Philadelphia: J. Almon, 1774.

"Die Freiheit Amerikas: Ode." *Berlinische Monatsschrift*, April 1783, 386–391. https://ds.ub.uni -bielefeld.de/viewer/image/2239816_001/389/LOG_0048/.

Dietrich, Richard, ed. *Die Politischen Testamente der Hohenzollern*. Cologne: Böhlau, 1986.

Ellis, Joseph J. *Founding Brothers: The Revolutionary Generation*. New York: Alfred A. Knopf, 2000.

Enquist, Per Olov. *Lewis Resa: Roman*. Stockholm: Norstedts Förlag, 2001.

Every Man His Own Doctor: or, The Poor Planter's Physician. Williamsburg, VA: William Parks, 1734. Evans Early American Imprint Collection, University of Michigan. https://quod.lib .umich.edu/e/evans/N03178.0001.001/.

Farington, Joseph. *The Farington Diary*. Edited by James Greig. 8 vols. London: Hutchinson & Co., 1923–1928. https://archive.org/details/faringtondiary01fariuoft.

Farrand, Max. *The Records of the Federal Convention of 1787*. Rev. ed. 4 vols. New Haven, CT: Yale University Press, 1966.

Flexner, James Thomas. *Washington: The Indispensable Man*. Boston: Little, Brown and Company, 1974.

Franklin, Benjamin. "The Albany Plan of Union, 1754." In *PBF*, vol. 5, pp. 374–392. Founders Online, National Archives. https://founders.archives.gov/documents/Franklin/01-05-02-0104.

———. *The Autobiography.* In *Writings,* edited by J. A. Leo Lemay, pp. 1307–1469. New York: Library of America, 1987.

———. "An Edict by the King of Prussia." 22 September 1773. In *PBF,* vol. 20, pp. 413–418. Founders Online, National Archives. https://founders.archives.gov/documents/Franklin /01-20-02-0223.

———. "A Proposal for Promoting Useful Knowledge." 14 May 1743. In *PBF,* vol. 2, pp. 373–383. Founders Online, National Archives. https://founders.archives.gov/documents/Franklin /01-02-02-0092.

Frederick the Great. *An meinen Geist. Friedrich der Große in seiner Dichtung. Eine Anthologie.* Edited by Jürgen Overhoff and Vanessa de Senarclens. Paderborn: Schöningh, 2011.

———. *Briefe Friedrichs des Großen.* Vol. 2. Edited by Max Hein. Berlin: Reimar Hobbing, 1914.

———. *Dissertation on the Reasons for Establishing or Repealing Laws.* In *FGPW,* pp. 87–106.

———. "Epistle XX: To My Soul" (À mon esprit). In *FGPW,* pp. 116–124.

———. *Essay on Self-Love, Considered as a Principle of Morality.* In *FGPW,* pp. 139–148.

———. *L'Antimachiavel.* In *Philosophische Schriften—Œuvres philosophiques,* vol. 6, edited by Anne Baillot and Brunhilde Wehinger, pp. 45–260. Berlin: Akademie Verlag, 2007.

———. *Werke des Philosophen von Sanssouci—Œuvres du Philosophe de Sans-Souci.* Potsdamer Ausgabe, vol. 7. Edited by Jürgen Overhoff and Vanessa de Senarclens. Berlin: Akademie Verlag, 2012.

Frederick the Great and Wilhelmine of Bayreuth. *Friedrich der Große und Wilhelmine von Baireuth.* Vol. 1, *Jugendbriefe (1728–1740).* Edited by Gustav Berthold Volz. Leipzig: Koehler, 1924.

Freeman, Douglas Southall. *George Washington: A Biography.* 7 vols. New York: Scribner, 1948–1957.

Fukuyama, Francis. *The End of History and the Last Man.* New York: Free Press, 1992.

Gaxotte, Pierre. *Frédéric II.* Paris: Fayard, 1938.

Gerbner, Katharine. "'We Are Against the Traffik of Men-Body': The Germantown Protest of 1688 and the Origins of American Abolitionism." *Pennsylvania History: A Journal of Mid-Atlantic Studies* 74, no. 2 (Spring 2007): 149–172.

Gleim, Johann Wilhelm Ludwig. *Preussische Kriegslieder in den Feldzügen 1756 und 1757: Mit Melodien.* Berlin: Voß, 1758. Also available online at MDZ, https://www.digitale-sammlungen .de/de/view/bsb11251624.

Goethe, Johann Wolfgang von. *The Autobiography of Goethe: Truth and Poetry: From My Own Life.* Translated by John Oxenford. Rev. ed. London: George Bell and Sons, 1897. https:// www.gutenberg.org/files/52654/52654-h/52654-h.htm.

———. *Briefe (Hamburger Ausgabe).* Vol. 1. Edited by Karl Robert Mandelkow. Munich: Beck, 1976.

———. *Italienische Reise.* In *Werke (Hamburger Ausgabe),* vol. 11, edited by Erich Trunz. Munich: Beck, 1981.

Goettinger Taschen Calender. Edited by Georg Christoph Lichtenberg. Göttingen: Dieterich, 1791.

"The Golden Bull of the Emperor Charles IV 1356 A.D." Avalon Project, Yale Law School. https://avalon.law.yale.edu/medieval/golden.asp.

Greene, Jack P., and Philip D. Morgan, eds. *Atlantic History: A Critical Appraisal*. Oxford: Oxford University Press, 2008.

Gregg, Edward. *Queen Anne*. London: Routledge & Kegan Paul, 1980.

Gryphius, Andreas. "Human Misery." In Scott Horton, "Two Poems by Andreas Gryphius." *Harper's Magazine*, August 11, 2007.

Hamilton, Alexander. *The Papers of Alexander Hamilton*. Vol. 20, *January 1796–March 1797*. Edited by Harold C. Syrett. New York: Columbia University Press, 1974. Founders Online, National Archives. https://founders.archives.gov/about/Hamilton.

Harland, Marion. *The Story of Mary Washington*. New York: Houghton, Mifflin & Co., 1893.

Henriques, Peter R. "The Final Struggle Between George Washington and the Grim King: Washington's Attitude Towards Death and the Afterlife." In *George Washington Reconsidered*, edited by Don Higginbotham, pp. 250–271. Charlottesville: University Press of Virginia, 2001.

Hinrichs, Carl. *Der Kronprinzenprozeß. Friedrich und Katte*. Hamburg: Hanseatische Verlagsanstalt, 1936.

———. *Friedrich Wilhelm I. König in Preussen. Eine Biographie. Jugend und Aufstieg. Ergänzt durch: Der Regierungsantritt Friedrich Wilhelms I.* Darmstadt: Wissenschaftliche Buchgesellschaft, 1968.

Hobbes, Thomas. *The Correspondence*. Edited by Noel Malcolm. Vol. 2, *1660–1679*. Oxford: Clarendon Press, 1994.

———. *De Cive, or, The Citizen*. New York: Appleton-Century-Crofts, 1949. Internet Archive. https://archive.org/details/deciveorcitizen00inhobb.

———. *Leviathan*. Edited by Richard Tuck. Cambridge: Cambridge University Press, 1991.

Jähns, Max. *Geschichte der Kriegswissenschaften vornehmlich in Deutschland*. Munich and Leipzig: Oldenbourg, 1891.

Jefferson, Thomas. *The Papers of Thomas Jefferson*. Vol. 7, *2 March 1784–25 February 1785*. Edited by Julian P. Boyd. Princeton, NJ: Princeton University Press, 1953. Founders Online, National Archives. https://founders.archives.gov/about/Jefferson.

Kant, Immanuel. "An Answer to the Question: What Is Enlightenment?" In *Practical Philosophy*, edited and translated by Mary J. Gregor, pp. 11–22. Cambridge: Cambridge University Press, 1996.

———. *Observations on the Feeling of the Beautiful and Sublime*. Translated by John T. Goldthwait. Berkeley: University of California Press, 1960.

Kapp, Friedrich. *Friedrich der Große und die Vereinigten Staaten von Amerika*. Leipzig: Quandt & Händel, 1871.

Kayser, Johann. *Parnassus Clivensis oder Clevischer Musen-Berg und seine darauff gewachsene Poetische Früchte*. Cleves: Tobias Silberling, 1698. Facsimile reprint, Cleves: Buchhandlung H. Fingerhut, 1980.

"Königlich Preußisches Edict, wegen verbothener Einfuhre, Erhandlung und Debitirung aller innenbenanten Chur-Sächsischen und denenselben incorporirten Landen verfertigten Manufactur- und Fabriquen-Waaren, besonders auch alles Sächsischen- sowohl ächten, als unächten Porcelains." Berlin: Decker, 1765. https://digital.staatsbibliothek-berlin.de/werkansicht/?PPN=PPN1838759492.

"Königlich-Preußisches General-Land-Schul-Reglement, wie solches in allen Landen Seiner Königlichen Majestät von Preussen durchgehends zu beobachten." Berlin and Magdeburg: Hechtel, 1763. https://opendata.uni-halle.de/handle/1981185920/56624.

Koser, Reinhold. *Geschichte Friedrichs des Großen*. 4 vols. Darmstadt: Wissentschaftliche Buchgesellschaft, 1963.

Kracauer, Isidor. *Die Geschichte der Judengasse in Frankfurt am Main*. Frankfurt am Main: J. Kauffmann, 1906.

Kunisch, Johannes. *Friedrich der Große. Der König und seine Zeit*. Munich: C. H. Beck, 2004.

———. Review of *Frédéric le Grand: Œuvres du Philosophe de Sans-Souci*, vol. 7, edited by Vanessa de Senarclens and Jürgen Overhoff. *Historische Zeitschrift* 298, no. 1 (2014): 213.

Kurbrandenburgs Staatsverträge von 1601 bis 1700. Nach den Originalen des Königl. Geh. Staats-Archivs. Edited by Theodor von Moerner. Berlin: Reimer, 1867.

Langley, Batty. *New Principles of Gardening, or, The Laying Out and Planting Parterres, Groves, Wildernesses, Labyrinths, Avenues, Parks, etc.* London: Printed for A. Bettesworth and J. Batley, 1728.

Lehndorff, Ernst Ahasverus Heinrich von. *Dreißig Jahre am Hofe Friedrichs des Großen. Tagebücher*. Edited by Karl Eduard Schmidt-Lötzen. Gotha: Perthes, 1907.

Leibniz, Gottfried Wilhelm. "Bedencken welchergestalt Securitas publica interna et externa (und status praesens) im Reich (jetzigen Umbständen nach) auf festen fuß zu stellen." August 1670, Pars I. In *Die Werke von Leibniz gemäß seinem handschriftlichen Nachlasse in der Königlichen Bibliothek zu Hannover*, edited by Onno Klopp, Reihe 1, *Historisch-politische und staatswissenschaftliche Schriften*, vol. 1, pp. 193–257. Hanover: Klindworth, 1864, pp. 193–257.

Lichtenberg, Georg Christoph. "Kurze Erklärung der Monatskupfer." In *Goettinger Taschen Calender*, edited by Georg Christoph Lichtenberg, pp. 211–213. Dieterich, 1791.

Locke, John. *Two Treatises of Government*. Vol. 5 in *The Works of John Locke*, new ed. London: Printed for Thomas Tegg et al., 1823. https://www.yorku.ca/comninel/courses/3025pdf/Locke.pdf.

Loen, Johann Michael von. "Der königlich Preußische Hof in Berlin, 1718." In *Gesammelte kleine Schriften*, vol. 1, pt. 3, pp. 22–39. Frankfurt: Philipp Heinrich Huttern, 1750.

Luh, Jürgen. *Der Große. Friedrich II. von Preussen*. Munich: Siedler, 2011.

Lukowski, Jerzy. *The Partitions of Poland: 1772, 1793, 1795*. London: Routledge, 1999.

MacDonogh, Giles. "Frederick the Great's Erotic Poetry." Blog post, September 20, 2011. http://www.macdonogh.co.uk/blog_archive.htm.

Madison, James. *Debates in the Federal Convention of 1787 by James Madison, a Member*. Edited by Gordon Lloyd. Ashland, OH: Ashbrook Center, 2014.

Mendelssohn, Moses. *Gesammelte Schriften. Jubiläumsausgabe*. Vol. 12.1, *Briefwechsel 2.1 (1763–1770)*. Edited by Alexander Altmann. Stuttgart-Bad Cannstatt: Frommann-Holzboog, 1976.

———. *Gesammelte Schriften: Jubiläumsausgabe*. Vol. 13, *Briefwechsel 3 (1781–1785)*. Edited by Alexander Altmann. Stuttgart-Bad Cannstatt: Frommann-Holzboog, 1977.

———. *Jerusalem oder über religiöse Macht und Judentum*. Edited by David Martyn. Bielefeld: Aisthesis, 2001.

Mendelssohn-Bartoldy, Gustav, ed. *Der König. Friedrich der Große in seinen Briefen und Erlassen*. Ebenhausen: Langewiesche-Brandt, 1932.

Miller, Joseph C. *The Princeton Companion to Atlantic History*. Princeton, NJ: Princeton University Press, 2015.

Montesquieu, Charles-Louis de Secondat, baron de. *Correspondance de Montesquieu*. Edited by François Gebelin and André Morize. 2 vols. Bordeaux: Imprimeries Gounouilhou, 1914.

Wikisource. https://fr.wikisource.org/wiki/Livre:Montesquieu_-_Correspondance,_t._1, _éd._Gébelin,_1914.djvu.

———. *Mes Voyages*. Edited by Jean Ehrard. Paris: Éditions Classiques Garnier, 2012.

———. *The Spirit of the Laws*. Translated by Thomas Nugent. 3rd ed. London: Printed for J. Nourse and P. Vaillant in the Strand, 1758. https://en.wikisource.org/wiki/The_Spirit_of _Laws_(1758)/Volume_I.

Moritz, Karl Philipp. *Sechs deutsche Gedichte, dem Könige von Preussen gewidmet*. 2nd ed. Berlin: Verlag Arnold Wever, 1781.

Münkler, Herfried. "Krieg und Frieden bei Clausewitz, Engels und Carl Schmitt: Dialektik des Militarismus oder Hegung des Krieges." *Leviathan* 10, no. 1 (1982): 16–40.

Nicholas V. "*Romanus Pontifex*." Papal bull of 8 January 1455. In *European Treaties Bearing on the History of the United States and Its Dependencies to 1648*, edited by Frances Gardiner Davenport, pp. 13–26. Washington, DC: Carnegie Institution of Washington, 1917. https://www .nativeweb.org/pages/legal/indig-romanus-pontifex.html.

Oppeln-Bronikowski, Friedrich von, and Gustav Berthold Volz, eds. *Gespräche Friedrichs des Großen*. Berlin: Reimer Hobbing, 1919.

Overhoff, Jürgen. *Vom Glück, lernen zu dürfen. Für eine zweckfreie Bildung*. Stuttgart: Klett-Cotta, 2009.

Paine, Thomas. *Common Sense*. In *The Writings of Thomas Paine*, edited by Moncure Daniel Conway, vol. 1. New York: G. P. Putnam's Sons, 1894. Online Library of Liberty. https://oll .libertyfund.org/pages/1776-paine-common-sense-pamphlet.

Penn, William. "Address to the Queen [Anne]." 3 June 1702. In *The Papers of William Penn*, vol. 4, *1701–1718*, edited by Richard S. Dunn and Mary Maples Dunn, pp. 172–174. Philadelphia: University of Pennsylvania Press, 1987.

———. "The Charter of Privileges." In *The Papers of William Penn*, vol. 4, *1701–1718*, edited by Richard S. Dunn and Mary Maples Dunn, pp. 104–110. Philadelphia: University of Pennsylvania Press, 1987. Also available at the Online Library of Liberty (where it is called the "Pennsylvania Charter of Liberties"), https://oll.libertyfund.org/pages/1701-pennsylvania -charter-of-liberties.

———. *The Papers of William Penn*. Vol. 4, *1701–1718*. Edited by Richard S. Dunn and Mary Maples Dunn. Philadelphia: University of Pennsylvania Press, 1987.

———. *Some Account of the Province of Pennsylvania*. In *William Penn and the Founding of Pennsylvania: A Documentary History*, edited by Jean R. Soderlund, pp. 58–66. Philadelphia: University of Pennsylvania Press, 1983.

Plutarch. *Life of Alexander*. In *Plutarch's Lives*, vol. 7, translated by Bernadotte Perrin. Cambridge, MA: Harvard University Press, 1919.

Reyburn, Susan, and Zach Klitzman, eds. *The Two Georges: Parallel Lives in an Age of Revolution*. Chapel Hill: University of North Carolina Press, 2025.

Saur, Christoph. *Das Leben und Heroische Thaten Des Königs von Preussen, Friederichs des III [i.e., II]. Von seiner Geburth an, bis zu Ende des 1760sten Jahrs*. Germantown, PA: Saur, 1761.

Schmidt, Werner. *Friedrich I. Kurfürst von Brandenburg, König in Preußen*. Munich: Diederichs, 1996.

Selle, Christian Gottlieb. *Krankheitsgeschichte des Höchstseeligen Königs von Preußen Friedrichs des Zweyten Majestät*. Berlin: August Mylius, 1786.

Sethe, Paul. *Morgenröte der Gegenwart. Von Friedrich dem Großen bis George Washington*. Stuttgart: Deutsche Verlagsanstalt, 1963.

Shaftesbury, Anthony Ashley Cooper, Third Earl of. *The Life, Unpublished Letters, and Philosophical Regimen of Anthony, Earl of Shaftesbury*. Edited by Benjamin Rand. London: Swan, Sonnenschein, & Co., 1900.

Simms, Brendan. "Pitt and Hanover." In *The Hanoverian Dimension in British History, 1714–1837*, edited by Brendan Simms and Torsten Riotte, pp. 28–57. Cambridge: Cambridge University Press, 2007.

Skinner, Quentin. *Reason and Rhetoric in the Philosophy of Hobbes*. Cambridge: Cambridge University Press, 1996.

Stevens, Sylvester K., and Donald H. Kent, eds. *Wilderness Chronicles of Northwestern Pennsylvania*. Harrisburg: Pennsylvania Historical and Museum Commission, 1941.

Unruh, Fritz von. *Duell an der Havel*. Berlin: Krüger & Co., 1954.

Voltaire. *Correspondence*. Vol. 20, *August 1751–July 1752*. Edited by Theodore Besterman. Geneva: Institut et Musée Voltaire, 1956.

———. *Memoirs of the Life of Monsieur de Voltaire*. Translated by Andrew Brown. London: Hesperus, 2007.

———. *Œuvres complètes de Voltaire*. Vol. 35, *Correspondance 3 (1738–1740)*. Paris: Garnier, 1880.

———. *Philosophical Letters*. Translated by William F. Fleming. Vol. 19 in *The Works of Voltaire: A Contemporary Version*. New York: E. R. DuMont, 1901. Online Library of Liberty. https://oll.libertyfund.org/titles/fleming-the-works-of-voltaire-vol-xix-philosophical-letters.

———. "Sur les pensées de M. Pascal." https://www.atramenta.net/lire/lettres-philosophiques/820/25#oeuvre_page.

Volz, Gustav Berthold, ed. *Friedrich der Große im Spiegel seiner Zeit*. Vol. 3, *Geistesleben, Alter und Tod*. Berlin: Reimar Hobbing, 1926.

Waddington, Albert. *L'Acquisition de la Couronne Royale de Prusse par les Hohenzollern*. Paris: Leroux, 1888.

Walter, Friedrich, ed. *Maria Theresia. Briefe und Aktenstücke in Auswahl*. Darmstadt: Wissenschaftliche Buchgesellschaft, 1968.

Wangermann, Ernst. *Aufklärung und staatsbürgerliche Erziehung. Gottfried van Swieten als Reformator des österreichischen Unterrichtswesens, 1781–1791*. Vienna: Verlag für Geschichte und Politik, 1978.

Washington, George. "Farewell Address." 19 September 1796. In *PGW*, Presidential Series, vol. 20, pp. 703–722. Founders Online, National Archives. https://founders.archives.gov/documents/Washington/05-20-02-0440-0002.

———. "First Inaugural Address." Final version, 30 April 1789. In *PGW*, Presidential Series, vol. 2, pp. 173–177. Founders Online, National Archives. https://founders.archives.gov/documents/Washington/05-02-02-0130-0003.

———. "Journey to the French Commandant: Narrative." October 1753–January 1754. In *DGW*, vol. 1, pp. 130–161. Founders Online, National Archives. https://founders.archives.gov/documents/Washington/01-01-02-0003-0002.

———. "Voyage to Barbados." 1751–1752. In *DGW*, vol. 1, pp. 38–117. Founders Online, National Archives. https://founders.archives.gov/documents/Washington/01-01-02-0002-0005.

———. *Writings*. Edited by John Rhodehamel. New York: Library of America, 1997.

————. *The Writings of George Washington.* Vol. 2. Boston: Russel, 1834.

Wilhelmine of Bayreuth. *Memoiren der Markgräfin Wilhelmine von Bayreuth.* Vol. 2. Edited by Annette Kolb. Leipzig: Insel Verlag, 1910.

Wollstonecraft, Mary. *A Vindication of the Rights of Men, in a Letter to the Right Honourable Edmund Burke, Occasioned by His Reflections on the Revolution in France.* London: Joseph Johnson, 1790. Online Library of Liberty. https://oll.libertyfund.org/titles/wollstonecraft-a -vindication-of-the-rights-of-men.

Zimmermann, Johann Georg. *Über Friedrich den Großen und meine Unterredungen mit ihm kurz vor seinem Tode.* Leipzig: in der Weidmannischen Buchhandlung, 1788.

BIBLIOGRAPHICAL ESSAY

IN THE composition of this book, I have occasionally consulted and quoted from unpublished manuscripts that I found while doing research in the Geheimes Staatsarchiv Preußischer Kulturbesitz in Berlin and the American Philosophical Society in Philadelphia. They include long-lost poems by Frederick the Great and letters from George Washington's friend Lafayette about his stay in Prussia. The vast majority of this book, however, is based on a thorough examination of the carefully edited collected works of George Washington and Frederick the Great.

The definitive version of the Prussian king's writings is still Johann David Erdmann Preuss's critical edition of his complete works, *Œuvres de Frédéric le Grand*, in 30 volumes (vols. 1–7: *Œuvres historiques*; vols. 8–9: *Œuvres philosophiques*; vols. 10–15: *Œuvres poétiques*; vols. 16–27: *Correspondance*; vols. 28–30: *Œuvres militaires*). The volumes of this edition appeared between 1846 and 1856 from the Imprimerie royale (R. Decker) in Berlin. The most important edition of Frederick's works in German translation is *Die Werke Friedrichs des Großen*, ed. Gustav Berthold Volz, 10 vols. (Berlin: Reimar Hobbing, 1912–1914). The texts of these standard editions by Preuss and Volz can also be viewed on a website maintained by the Trier University Library, friedrich.uni-trier.de.

Another important collection of primary sources is *Die Politische Correspondenz Friedrichs des Großen*, ed. Johann Gustav Droysen, Max Duncker, Reinhold Koser, Gustav Berthold Volz, et al., 46 vols. (Berlin/Leipzig: A. Duncker et al., 1879–1939). It documents written communications from 1740 to March 1782. The series was revived in the current millennium, with volume 47 (April 1782–December 1782) appearing in 2003 (Cologne: Böhlau) and volume 48 (January 1783–June 1783) in 2015 (Berlin: Duncker & Humblot), both edited by Frank Althoff. Volume 49 (July 1783–March 1784) is currently in preparation. A French-German dual-language edition of Frederick the Great's writings is also in progress, edited by Günther Lottes et al. and published as the Potsdamer Ausgabe / Édition de Potsdam. It is projected to include 12 volumes, of which volume 6, *Philosophische Schriften* (Berlin: Akademie Verlag, 2007), and volume 7, *Œuvres du Philosophe de Sans-Souci* (Berlin: Akademie Verlag, 2012), have appeared so far.

Important editions of the Prussian king's letters include *Briefwechsel Friedrichs des Großen mit Grumbkow und Maupertuis (1731–1759)*, ed. Reinhold Koser (Leipzig: S. Hirzel, 1898); *Briefwechsel Friedrichs des Großen mit Voltaire*, ed. Reinhold Koser and Hans Droysen, 3 vols. (Leipzig: S. Hirzel, 1908–1911; facsimile reprint, Osnabrück: Otto Zeller, 1965); and *Briefe Friedrichs des Großen*, ed. Max Hein, trans. Friedrich von Oppeln-Bronikowski and Eberhard König, 2 vols. (Berlin: Reimar Hobbing, 1914; facsimile reprint: Braunschweig: Archiv Verlag, 1999). Another highly valuable edition of primary sources is Henri de Catt, *Unterhaltungen mit Friedrich dem Großen. Memoiren und Tagebücher von Heinrich de Catt*, ed. Reinhold Koser (Leipzig: S. Hirzel, 1884), also available in English translation: *Frederick the Great, The Memoirs of His Reader, Henri de Catt (1758–1760)*, trans. F. S. Flint (London: Constable and Company, 1916). A significant portion of Frederick's correspondence with Voltaire is translated into English in *Letters of Voltaire and Frederick the Great*, trans. Richard Addington (London: George Routledge and Sons, 1927).

Recent, reliable, and affordable collections of letters, writings, and poems by Frederick the Great include *Voltaire—Friedrich der Große: Briefwechsel*, ed. and trans. Hans Pleschinski (Munich: Hanser, 2004); *Friedrich der Große: Ausgewählte Schriften*, ed. Ulrike-Christine Sander (Frankfurt am Main: Fischer, 2011); the French-German edition *An meinen Geist. Friedrich der Große in seiner Dichtung: Eine Anthologie*, ed. Jürgen Overhoff and Vanessa de Senarclens (Paderborn: Ferdinand Schöningh, 2011); and the French-German edition *Friedrich der Große (Potsamer Ausgabe) / Frédéric le Grand (Edition du Potsdam)*, vol. 7, *Werke des Philosophen von Sanssouci / Œuvres du Philosophe de Sans-Souci*, ed. Jürgen Overhoff and Vanessa de Senarclens (Berlin: Akademie Verlag, 2012).

For a long time, the most important edition of George Washington's works was *The Writings of George Washington from the Original Manuscript Sources, 1745–1799*, 39 vols., ed. John C. Fitzpatrick (Washington, DC: U.S. Government Printing Office, 1931–1944). Unfortunately, it included no letters written *to* Washington. In the 1970s, the University of Virginia began preparing a comprehensive modern standard edition of *The Papers of George Washington* (Charlottesville: University Press of Virginia, 1983–), which has appeared in five series since 1983: Colonial Series, 10 vols. (1983–1995); Revolutionary War

Series, 30 vols. to date (1985–); Confederation Series, 6 vols. (1992–1997); Presidential Series, 21 vols. to date (1987–); and Retirement Series, 4 vols. (1998–1999).

Other essential sources for the study of Washington's life include *The Diaries of George Washington*, 6 vols., ed. Donald Jackson and Dorothy Twohig (Charlottesville: University Press of Virginia, 1976–1979); and *The Journal of the Proceedings of the President, 1793–1797*, ed. Dorothy Twohig (Charlottesville: University Press of Virginia, 1981). A good, compact selection of Washington's chief writings is provided by the single-volume *George Washington: Writings*, ed. John Rhodehamel (New York: Library of America, 1997). *The Papers of George Washington*, *The Diaries of George Washington*, and *The Journal of the Proceedings of the President, 1793–1797* are largely available in digital format on the Founders Online website of the National Archives: https://founders.archives.gov/about/Washington.

Until the present volume, no attempt had been made to trace the lives of Frederick the Great and George Washington from a comparative perspective. Nevertheless, the following two titles do contain a few passages discussing the potential fruitfulness of such an undertaking: Friedrich Kapp, *Friedrich der Große und die Vereinigten Staaten von Amerika* (Leipzig: Quandt & Händel, 1871); and Paul Sethe, *Morgenröte der Gegenwart. Von Friedrich dem Großen bis Washington. Bilder und Texte* (Stuttgart: Deutsche Verlagsanstalt, 1963).

There have been other interesting attempts to explore Frederick's life through the lens of comparative biography, all of them pairing him with one or two other figures of the European Enlightenment, including with his brother Prince Henry: Christian Graf von Krockow, *Die preußischen Brüder. Prinz Heinrich und Friedrich der Große. Ein Doppelportrait* (Stuttgart: dtv, 1996); with the Holy Roman Empress Maria Theresa and Catherine the Great of Russia: Dieter Wunderlich, *Vernetzte Karrieren: Friedrich der Große, Maria Theresia, Katharina die Große* (Regensburg: Friedrich Pustet, 2000); with his wife, Elisabeth Christine: Paul Noack, *Elisabeth Christine und Friedrich der Große. Ein Frauenleben in Preußen* (Stuttgart: Klett-Cotta, 2001); and with Maria Theresa alone: Klaus Günzel, *Der König und die Kaiserin. Friedrich II. und Maria Theresia* (Düsseldorf: Droste, 2005), and Sven Externbrink, *Friedrich der Große, Maria Theresia und das alte Reich. Deutschlandbild und Diplomatie Frankreichs im Siebenjährigen Krieg* (Berlin: Akademie Verlag, 2006).

Washington's life has also been traced at various times within a comparative framework, albeit only in the American context: Stuart Leibiger, *Founding Friendship: George Washington, James Madison, and the Creation of the American*

Republic (Charlottesville: University Press of Virginia, 1999); James R. Gaines, *For Liberty and Glory: Washington, Lafayette, and Their Revolutions* (New York: W. W. Norton, 2007); Dave R. Palmer, *George Washington and Benedict Arnold: A Tale of Two Patriots* (Washington, DC: Regnery History, 2006); and most recently Susan Reyburn and Zach Klitzman, eds., *The Two Georges: Parallel Lives in an Age of Revolution* (Chapel Hill: University of North Carolina Press, 2025).

The classic biographical monument to Frederick the Great is Reinhold Koser's four-volume *Geschichte Friedrichs des Großen*, originally published in 1925 and available in a reprint of the 6th and 7th editions (Darmstadt: Wissenschaftliche Buchgesellschaft, 1963). It is the benchmark to which all later studies of the Prussian king's life must aspire. The most reliable and also the most original biographies that have appeared since Koser's include Theodor Schieder, *Friedrich der Große. Ein Königtum der Widersprüche* (Frankfurt: Propyläen, 1983); Karl Otmar von Aretin, *Friedrich der Große. Größe und Grenzen des Preußenkönigs* (Freiburg: Herder, 1985); and Gerd Heinrich, *Friedrich II. von Preußen. Leistung und Leben eines großen Königs* (Berlin: Duncker & Humblot, 2009). The standard modern biography is now Johannes Kunisch, *Friedrich der Große. Der König und seine Zeit* (Munich: C. H. Beck, 2004). Two studies stand out in particular for their stylistic brilliance and penetrating observations: Sebastian Haffner, *Preußen ohne Legende* (Hamburg: Gruner und Jahr, 1978); and Christian Graf von Krockow, *Friedrich der Große—Ein Lebensbild* (Bergisch-Gladbach: Gustav Lübbe, 1987).

The best biographies from the French perspective are Pierre Gaxotte, *Frédéric II* (Paris: Fayard, 1938), translated into English by R. A. Bell as *Frederick the Great* (New Haven, CT: Yale University Press, 1942); and Jean-Paul Bled, *Frédéric le Grand* (Paris: Fayard, 2004). From the British perspective, the most illuminating insights have been provided by Christopher Duffy, *Frederick the Great: A Military Life* (London: Routledge and Kegan Paul, 1985); Tim Blanning, "Frederick the Great and Enlightened Absolutism," in *Enlightened Absolutism: Reform and Reformers in Later Eighteenth-Century Europe*, ed. H. M. Scott (Houndsmills, UK: Macmillan, 1990), pp. 265–288; David Fraser, *Frederick the Great: King of Prussia* (London: Allen Lane, 2000); Christopher Clark, *Iron Kingdom: The Rise and Downfall of Prussia, 1600–1947* (London: Allen Lane, 2006); and Tim Blanning, *Frederick the Great: King of Prussia* (New York: Allen Lane, 2015).

Insightful books have also been written about discrete phases of Frederick's life and specific aspects of his character and significance. The most detailed study of his youth and education is Ernst Bratuschek, *Die Erziehung Friedrichs des Großen* (Berlin: Georg Reimer, 1885). The most thorough treatment of the crown prince's escape attempt and the subsequent trial of him and his co-conspirator Katte is Carl Hinrichs, *Der Kronprinzenprozeß. Friedrich und Katte* (Hamburg: Hanseatische Verlagsanstalt, 1936). Haunting studies of the traumatic experiences suffered by Frederick during his imprisonment in Küstrin include Ernst Lürßen, "Reinszenierung eines massiven Traumas. Leitmotive im Leben Friedrichs des Großen," in *"Die klugen Sinne pflegend." Psychoanalytische und kulturkritische Beiträge—Hermann Beland zu Ehren,* ed. Jutta Gutwinski-Jeggle and Johann Michael Rotmann (Tübingen: edition diskord, 1993), pp. 414–431; and Ernst Lewy, "Die Verwandlung Friedrichs des Großen. Eine psychoanalytische Untersuchung," *Psyche* 49 (1995), pp. 727–804. Frederick's early and sometimes odd affinity for animals is discussed in Jürgen Overhoff, "Of Dogs and Horses: Frederick the Great and His Dearest Animals," in *Human-Animal Interactions in the Eighteenth Century: From Pests and Predators to Pets, Poems and Philosophy,* ed. Stefanie Stockhorst et al. (Leiden: Brill, 2022), pp. 26–42.

Rheinsberg Palace, where Frederick moved after his wedding, is described with deep sensitivity by Christian Graf von Krockow, *Rheinsberg—Ein preußischer Traum* (Leipzig: E. A. Seemann, 1992). Humorous, ironic, and intellectually stimulating observations about the construction of Sanssouci Palace are provided by Heinz Dieter Kittsteiner, *Das Komma von SANS,SOUCI. Ein Forschungsbericht mit Fußnoten* (Heidelberg: Manutius, 2001). Frederick as a poet is the subject of Eduard Spranger, *Der Philosoph von Sanssouci,* 2nd ed. (Heidelberg: Quelle & Meyer, 1962). Frederick's relationship to the Enlightenment is explored in Martin Fontius, ed., *Frederick II. und die europäische Aufklärung* (Berlin: Duncker & Humblot, 1999). The judicial reform undertaken at Frederick's behest is examined by Peter Weber, "'Was jetzt eben zu sagen oder noch zu verschweigen sei, müßt ihr selbst überlegen.' Publizistische Strategien der preußischen Justizreform, 1780–1794," in *Appell an das Publikum. Die öffentliche Debatte in der deutschen Aufklärung, 1687–1796,* ed. Ursula Goldenbaum (Berlin: Akademie Verlag, 2004), vol. 2, pp. 729–812.

There are two standard biographies of Washington: Douglas Southall Freeman, *George Washington: A Biography,* 7 vols., with vol. 7 by John A. Carroll and Mary W. Ashworth (New York: Scribner, 1948–1957); and James Thomas Flexner, *George Washington,* 4 vols. (Boston: Little, Brown and Co., 1965–1972). In the decades following the publication of these older portraits, very important details were added to them by other essential Washington biographies that benefited from more recent research: Marcus Cunliffe, *George Washington: Man and Monument* (Boston: Little, Brown and Co., 1958); Noemie Emery, *Washington: A Biography* (New York: Putnam, 1976); Edmund S. Morgan, *The Genius of George Washington* (New York: W. W. Norton, 1980); Barry Schwarz, *George Washington: The Making of an American Symbol* (New York: Free Press, 1987); and John E. Ferling, *The First of Men: A Life of George Washington* (Knoxville: University of Tennessee Press, 1988).

Around the turn of the twenty-first century, two books appeared that subjected many details of the first American president's life to a thorough revision: Richard Brookhiser, *Founding Father: Rediscovering George Washington* (New York: Free Press, 1996); and Don Higginbotham, ed., *George Washington Reconsidered* (Charlottesville: University Press of Virginia, 2001). In the wake of these two books, two further studies of Washington's life appeared from the pens of stylistically brilliant, Pulitzer Prize–winning authors that offered both original insights and great reading pleasure: Joseph J. Ellis, *His Excellency: George Washington* (New York: Random House, 2004); and Ron Chernow, *Washington: A Life* (New York: Penguin, 2010).

From the German perspective, there are a few brief treatments worthy of mention, each devoted to specific aspects of Washington's presidency: Volker Depkat, "Die Erfindung der republikanischen Präsidentschaft im Zeichen des Geschichtsbruchs: George Washington und die Ausformung eines demokratischen Herrscherbildes," *Zeitschrift für Geschichtswissenschaft* 56 (2008): 729–742; Ronald D. Gerste, *Duell ums Weiße Haus: Amerikanische Präsidentschaftswahlen von George Washington bis 2008* (Paderborn: Ferdinand Schöning, 2008); and Jürgen Heideking, "George Washington, 1789–1797. Schöpfer der amerikanischen Präsidentschaft," in *Die amerikanischen Präsidenten. 44 historische Portraits von George Washington bis Barack Obama*, 5th ed., ed. Christoph Mauch (Munich: C. H. Beck, 2009), pp. 49–64.

Numerous studies have also been devoted to discrete periods of Washington's life and specific aspects of his personality and significance. Especially informative about his youth are Bernhard Knollenberg, *George Washington: The Virginia Period, 1732–1775* (Durham, NC: Duke University Press, 1964); and Paul Longmore, *The Invention of George Washington* (Berkeley: University of California Press, 1988). His early military experience in the Seven Years' War and his role as a model commanding officer are powerfully portrayed in Fred Anderson, *Crucible of War: The Seven Years' War and the Fate of Empire in British North America* (New York: Alfred A. Knopf, 2000); Don Higginbotham, *George Washington and the American Military Tradition* (Athens: University of

Georgia Press, 1985); and David Hackett Fischer, *Washington's Crossing* (Oxford: Oxford University Press, 2004).

Judicious consideration of Washington's life at Mount Vernon is given in Robert F. Dalzell Jr. and Lee Baldwin Dalzell, *George Washington's Mount Vernon: At Home in Revolutionary America* (Oxford: Oxford University Press, 1998). His private life is explored in Giles Unger, *The Unexpected George Washington: His Private Life* (Hoboken, NJ: Wiley, 2006). A critical review of his role as a slaveholder in Virginia and Philadelphia is provided by Fritz Hirschfeld, *George Washington and Slavery: A Documentary Portrayal* (Columbia: University of Missouri Press, 1997); Henry Wiencek, *An Imperfect God: George Washington, His Slaves, and the Creation of America* (New York: Farrar, Straus and Giroux, 2003); and Erica Armstrong Dunbar, *Never Caught: The Washingtons' Relentless Pursuit of Their Runaway Slave, Ona Judge* (New York: Simon & Schuster, 2017). The extent to which Washington can be considered an Enlightenment figure despite his participation in slavery is explored in Garry Wills, *Cincinnatus: George Washington and the Enlightenment* (Garden City, NY: Doubleday, 1984). The relationship between George Washington and the Indian tribes that bordered the emerging American republic is the subject of Colin G. Galloway, *The Indian World of George Washington: The First President, the First Americans, and the Birth of the Nation* (Oxford: Oxford University Press, 2018).

Washington's deist outlook and his promotion of religious tolerance are the subject of the following studies: Fritz Hirschfeld, *George Washington and the Jews* (Newark: University of Delaware Press, 2005); David L. Holmes, *The Faiths of the Founding Fathers* (Oxford: Oxford University Press, 2006); and Mary V. Thompson, *"In the Hands of a Good Providence": Religion in the Life of George Washington* (Charlottesville: University Press of Virginia, 2008).

Washington's massive political talent, his significance as president of the Constitutional Convention of 1787, and his conduct as the first American president are highlighted in the following books: Forrest McDonald, *The Presidency of George Washington* (Lawrence: University Press of Kansas, 1974); Glenn A. Phelps, *George Washington and American Constitutionalism* (Lawrence: University Press of Kansas, 1993); and John E. Ferling, *The Ascent of George Washington: The Hidden Political Genius of an American Icon* (New York: Bloomsbury, 2009).

Washington's critical aloofness to the French Revolution is treated by Louis Martin Sears, *George Washington and the French Revolution* (Detroit: Wayne State University Press, 1960); and James R. Gaines, *For Liberty and Glory:*

Washington, Lafayette, and Their Revolutions (New York: W. W. Norton, 2007). The Indian wars ordered by Washington during the period of the French Revolution and his attitude toward the Native Americans are analyzed in Wiley Sword, *President Washington's Indian War: The Struggle for the Old Northwest, 1790–1795* (Norman: University of Oklahoma Press, 1985).

The most informative studies of Washington's death, his posthumous reputation, and his enduring political legacy are Richard Norton Smith, *Patriarch: George Washington and the New American Nation* (Boston: Houghton Mifflin, 1993); Patrick J. Garrity, *A Sacred Union of Citizens: George Washington's Farewell Address and the National Character* (Lanham, MD: Rowman & Littlefield, 1996); and Peter R. Henriques, *The Death of George Washington: He Died as He Lived* (Mount Vernon, VA: Mount Vernon Ladies' Association, 2000).

Last but not least, a few bibliographical references are in order regarding the methodological foundations of the present volume and the narrative and heuristic approaches that have informed it. The possibilities and limitations of comparative biography are still best fathomed from a reading of Plutarch's *Parallel Lives*. One standard, easily accessible, and complete—albeit somewhat dated—version in English is the Loeb Classical Library edition: *Plutarch's Lives*, trans. Bernadotte Perrin, 11 vols. (Cambridge, MA: Harvard University Press, 1914–1926).

The influence of the writings of the English philosopher Thomas Hobbes on the discourse of the two main paths of enlightened government is demonstrated by Jürgen Overhoff, *Hobbes's Theory of the Will: Ideological Reasons and Historical Circumstances* (Lanham, MD: Rowman & Littlefield, 2000); and Richard Tuck, "Hobbes and Democracy," in *Rethinking the Foundations of Modern Political Thought*, ed. James Tully and Annabel Brett (Cambridge: Cambridge University Press, 2006), pp. 171–190.

Finally, the methodology of Quentin Skinner was an important inspiration for interpreting Frederick the Great and George Washington as participants in the discourse about enlightened government initiated by Hobbes. That methodology has been illuminated most thoroughly by James Tully, ed., *Meaning and Context: Quentin Skinner and His Critics* (Cambridge: Cambridge University Press, 1988); and in the brief summary by Eckhart Hellmuth and Martin Schmidt, "John G. A. Pocock, Quentin Skinner," in *Klassiker der Geschichtswissenschaft*, ed. Lutz Raphael, vol. 2, *Von Fernan Braudel bis Natalie Z. Davis* (Munich: C. H. Beck, 2006), pp. 261–279.

INDEX

Notes: Throughout the index, George Washington is referred to as "GW" and Frederick the Great is referred to as "FG." Page numbers in *italics* indicate figures.

A NOTE ON THE TYPE

This book has been composed in Arno, an Old-style serif typeface in the
classic Venetian tradition, designed by Robert Slimbach at Adobe.